RESEARCH METHODS

Francis C. Dane

Mercer University

Brooks/Cole
Publishing Company
Pacific Grove, California

For Jackie Fussell (my mom),
and Linda Dane (my life),
and Dedicated to the Memory of Norm Schultz

Brooks/Cole Publishing Company
A Division of Wadsworth, Inc.

Library of Congress Cataloging in Publication Data
Dane, Francis C.
     Research methods / Francis C. Dane.
          p.   cm.
     Includes bibliographical references and index.
     ISBN 0-534-09864-9
     1. Social science—Research—Methodology.   I. Title.
H62.D225   1990
300'.72—dc20   89-17438
                                                          CIP

Sponsoring Editor: *Philip L. Curson*
Editorial Assistant: *Heather L. Riedl*
Production Editor: *Timothy A. Phillips*
Manuscript Editor: *Alan R. Titche*
Permissions Editor: *Carline Haga*
Interior and Cover Design: *Flora Pomeroy*
Art Coordinator: *Lisa Torri*
Interior Illustration: *Lotus Art*
Typesetting: *BookMasters*
Cover Printing: *Phoenix Color Corporation*
Printing and Binding: *Arcata Graphics/Fairfield*

PREFACE

To the Student

Welcome to the world of research. Having taught this course many times, I know that some of you are taking this course because it is required and not because you have an undying intrinsic interest in research methodology. I also know that many of you do have an intrinsic interest in research. Whether you are the former or latter kind of student, I have written this text with you foremost in mind.

For those of you who are not overly thrilled about having to take this course, I have tried to present the material with a style designed to pique your interest. I thoroughly enjoy research and the methods used to produce it, and I have tried to convey that enjoyment in this text; I admit to a straightforward attempt to get you to enjoy it as well. For those of you who are thrilled about this course, welcome to the family. You are going to learn how to do well what you have wanted to do for some time.

Trying to convey my enjoyment of research is not the only aspect of this book that is designed to make your studying more effective. The running glossary is one example. Definitions appear in the text the first time a new term is introduced, so you don't have to interrupt reading to find the term in the back of the book. Just in case you can't remember a definition and can't remember where in the text the running glossary definition is, there is also an end glossary.

Throughout the text, statistical concepts and procedures are paired with the research methods for which they are appropriate. Those of you who have had a statistics course will find that this provides a handy review; those of you who have not had a course in statistics will find this to be a helpful introduction. You won't become proficient at statistics from the material in this text, but you will learn how statistics and methodology are part of the same process.

Finally, the front of the last page in this book is blank, and the back contains the address for Brooks/Cole. I would appreciate any comments, good or bad, you have about this book. Simply tear out the page, write your comments, fold the page so that the address is on the outside, and drop it in the mail. (The publisher pays for the postage.) Compliments are always delightful, but complaints are the source of improvement. If you don't like something, let me know; I'll try to change it in the next edition. In the meantime, I hope you enjoy your sojourn into research. It really is exciting.

To the Instructor

Research Methods is a primary text for the first course in research design and methodology. You and I both know there is no single, best way to teach such a course—except, of course, the way each of us does it. I have structured the order of presentation in the way I find most effective when I teach the course. The organization flows from an overview of what research is all about in the first chapter, to specific instruction about and examples of writing a research article in the last chapter. The major sections include The Nature of Research, Design, and Resource Chapters.

I also know you have your own presentation order, which may be different from mine. For this reason, the chapters within each section are fairly independent. You should encounter little difficulty using the chapters in whatever order you prefer. The major exception to this is the first chapter; it really should be read first.

A secondary purpose of this volume is its use as a reference after the student has completed the course. For this reason, the coverage is comprehensive, ranging from archival studies to experimental time-series designs. I have never been able to cover all of these topics in a single semester, and I wrote with the expectation that some chapters would receive slight, or no, coverage. Skipping entire chapters will not affect the readability of this text.

The first section, The Nature of Research, covers material students need to know before they can begin research (and perhaps even before they decide upon a research topic). It includes an overview of the research process, its logical and philosophical underpinnings, relevant ethics, and use of existing literature. It is designed to prepare novices to make the transition from an interesting topic to a researchable topic. At the end of this section, students should be able to answer the question "Why should someone else care about your research project?" and should be able to write a literature review in response to that question.

The second section, Design, covers specific research methods. Starting with experimental design, it includes the full range of behavioral science methods, including archival and survey methods. It also includes data organization strategies, a chapter on report writing, and a chapter about dealing with data that were not quite as expected. The order in which you cover these chapters, and whether or not you cover them, depends entirely on the particular approach you take in your course. If your students are not going to collect their own data, for example, then the data organization chapter can be skipped. It remains available, however, as reference material when the student does begin to collect data.

The last section, Resource Chapters, is most likely to be covered only if your students complete a research project. It includes chapters on measurement theory, statistical analyses, scaling, and other specialized topics. As its title implies, it is more of a resource than material to be covered sequentially as part of the course. Each chapter in this section is specifically organized and written to be independent. The order in which they are covered, or not covered, will have no effect on their utility.

As I've already explained in the students' preface, the back page is pre-addressed for your comments. I'm absolutely certain this book is not perfect, and your comments will help me to improve it. I trust you will enjoy using this book as much as I enjoyed writing it.

Acknowledgments

No one writes a book alone (it only seems that way at times). In addition to the many students, colleagues, and friends who have provided advice, assistance, and motivation, there are a number of people who deserve specific mention. They include C. Deborah Laughton, who first signed the book for Brooks/Cole, Phil Curson, who completed the editorial work begun by Deborah, and Timothy Phillips, the production editor who kept me on time (more or less) and on track (always). Without their expertise and willingness to work with the likes of me, you would not be reading this.

The rest of the Brooks/Cole production team also deserve specific mention. Flora Pomeroy was able to produce a design and cover that simultaneously exceeded "industry standards," added to the aesthetic appeal of the book, and coincided with my idiosyncratic tastes. Alan Titche, the copyeditor, very ably transformed some of my most convoluted drafts into readable English, and Linda Dane, the proofreader, was able to find errors the rest of us didn't know existed. Lotus Art, the graphic artists, showed me what can be done when computer mouse and software are placed in the hands of someone who knows what to with them.

Each of the reviewers put in an unknown numbers of hours providing commentary, clarification, and consistency to more drafts than I care to mention in writing. They include Jann Adams, Middle Tennessee State University, Murfreesboro, Tennessee; John Anson, Stephen F. Austin State University, Nacogdoches, Texas; James Blascovich, State University of New York at Buffalo; Stephen Davis, Emporia State University, Emporia, Kansas; Susan Dutch, Westfield State College, Westfield, Massachusetts; William Frederickson, Central State University, Edmond, Oklahoma; Robert Hamm, Virginia Commonwealth University, Richmond, Virginia; Rhoda Lindner, California State University at Long Beach; Henry Masters, Juniata College, Huntingdon, Pennsylvania; Ellen Susman, Metro State College, Denver, Colorado; John Uhlarik, Kansas State University at Manhattan. Their comments were most helpful.

I also want to mention the "best of the best," the students who suffered through using earlier drafts of the book as a textbook. They include Mike Copenhaver, John Lawson, Michelle Lyons, Merrie Jo Pitera, Chris Harkins, and several others whose names, but not influence, have faded into the oblivion of an imperfect memory. To all of the students who helped with the book: thanks, you may never know how helpful you were, and continue to be.

I also owe much of the knowledge conveyed in this book to those who taught me: Jackie Fussell, my mom, who first taught me the value of curiosity and the thrill of its satisfaction; Marshall Dermer, who first piqued my interest in psychological research and statistics; Jack Brehm, Michael Storms, and David Thissen, who helped focus and enhance my interest in research; Lawrence Wrightsman, whose mentoring showed me what it means to be professional and enabled me to find, define, and refine the pathways of my career; Claire Verduin, whose advice through the years, and particularly on my "Common and Uncommon Sense" book, transformed me from a writer into an author; and Norm Schultz, whose guidance and behavior as a "senior faculty member" and friend I will always remember.

Finally, I owe the greatest debt to Linda Dane (yes, the proofreader), whose companionship, love, trust, and confidence kept me writing and rewriting when I didn't want to, kept me "doing it right" when I wanted to settle for less, and keep me challenging myself to become better.

Frank Dane

CONTENTS

PART ONE
The Nature of Research 1

CHAPTER ONE: Introduction   **3**

Overview 3

Introduction 3

⚹ Goals of Research 5
    Exploration 5
    Description 6
    Prediction 7
    Explanation 7
    Action 8

Evaluation of Research 9
    The Who: Researchers, Participants, and Consumers
    of Research 10
Box 1.1 The Golden Fleece Awards 12
    The What: Research Topics and the Worldviews
    Behind Them 14
    The Where: Research Settings 16
    The When: The Time Frame of Research 16
    The Why: Additional Reasons for Research 17
    ⚹ The How: Research Methods 17

Summary 18

CHAPTER TWO: The Scientific Approach   **20**

Overview 20

Introduction 20

A Philosophy of Science   21
   When Is Something True?   22
   How Can We Tell Which Theory Is Better?   24
   How Can We Put What We Know Into Practice?   25
   Why Do We Do It the Way We Do?   26

Science and Nonscience Compared   27
   Observation   28
   Logical Analysis   29
   Research Reports   29
   Definitive Studies   30
   Determinism   31

Conducting Research   31
Box 2.1   Science Is . . . Science Is Not   32
   Choosing a Topic   32
   Operationalization   33

Summary   35

CHAPTER THREE: Research Ethics   **37**

Overview   37

Introduction   37
   A Question of Balance   38
   Learning From Experience   38

Ethical Issues Before the Project   38
   Voluntary Participation   39
   Informed Consent   40
Box 3.1   Informed Consent Form: Jury Decision Making   41
   Deception   42
   Physical Harm   44
   Psychological Harm   44
   Self-Determination   45

Ethical Issues During the Project   46
   Researcher's Identity   46
   Behavior Changes in Participants   46
   Considerate Treatment of Participants   48
   Retraction of Consent   48
   Debriefing of Participants   49
   Alleviating Harmful Aftereffects   50

Ethical Issues After the Project   50
   Anonymity of Participants   51
   Confidentiality   51
   Recompensing Control Groups   52
   Data Analyses   52
   Reporting Research Results   53

Formal Ethical Guidelines   55
  Legislation   55
Box 3.2   The Nuremburg Code   56
  ⚰ Codes of Ethics   58

Summary   58
Box 3.3   American Psychological Association Research with Human
  Participants   59

CHAPTER FOUR: Literature Review   **61**

Overview   61

Introduction   61
  Goals of a Literature Review   62

Deciding Which Information Is Relevant to Your Project   63
  Information Concerning Theory   63
  Information Concerning Methods   63
  Information Concerning Data Analysis   64

⚔ Finding Sources of Information   64
  Published Sources   64
  Key Topics   66
  Key Authors   67
  Key Studies   68
  Unpublished Studies   68
Box 4.1   A Summary of Citation Indexes   69

⚔ Organizing the Literature: Parting the Sea of References   69

Writing a Literature Review   70

Summary   71

PART TWO
Design   73

CHAPTER FIVE: Experimental Research   **75**

Overview   75

Introduction   75
  Causal Analysis in Experimental Research   76
  Demonstration Versus Demography   78

Alternative Explanations of Research Results   79
    History Effects   80
    Maturation Effects   80
    Testing Effects   81
    Instrumentation Effects   82
    Statistical Regression Effects   83
    Selection Effects   84
    Mortality Effects   85
    Participant Bias   86
    Experimenter Bias   87

Experimental Design   88
    The Basic Design   88
    The Basic Pretest Design   90
    The Solomon Four-Group Design   91
    Factorial Design   92
    Repeated Measures Design   96
    Participant Characteristics   99

Ethical Considerations in Experiments   99
    Random Assignment of Participants   100
    Manipulating Variables   100
    Blind Procedures   101
    Demonstration Versus Demography Again   101

Summary   102

CHAPTER SIX: Quasi-Experimental Research   104

Overview   104

Introduction   104

Time-Series Design   106
    Interrupted Time-Series Design   106
    Multiple Time-Series Design   109
    Regression-Discontinuity Design   109
    Nonequivalent Groups Basic Pretest Design   111
    Self-Selection   113
    Single-Participant Design   113

Summary   117

CHAPTER SEVEN: Survey Research   119

Overview   119

Introduction   119
    Survey Content   121

Survey Instruments   123
    Survey Topics   123
    Survey Instructions   124
    Survey Formats   125
    Arrangement of Survey Items   125
    Pretesting Survey Instruments   127

Administering Surveys   128
    Face-to-Face Interviews   128
    Telephone Interviews   131
    Mail Surveys   133
    Comparisons Among Administrative Methods   135
    Mixed-Method Surveys   135
Box 7.1   Face-to-Face, Telephone, and Mail Surveys
    Compared   136
Box 7.2   Checkpoints for Preparing a Survey Instrument   137

Data Analyses in Survey Research   138
    Description   138
    Association   140
    Elaboration   141

Summary   143

CHAPTER EIGHT: Field Research   146

Overview   146

Introduction   146

Validity of Field Research   148
    Internal Validity   148
    External Validity   149

Intrusion in Field Research   149
    Intrusion into Observations of Behaviors   149
    Intrusiveness of Settings   150
    Intrusiveness of Treatments   150

Systematic Observation in Field Research   151
    Selecting Events   151
    Recording Events   154
    Coding Events   155
    Interpreting Events   156
    Sources of Error   157
    Validity   158

Participant Observation   158
    Levels of Participation   158
    Selecting Settings   160
    Recording Observations   161

Coding Observations   163
Interpreting Observations   163

Numerical Data Analyses   164
Description   164
Correlation   164

Report Writing   165

Summary   166

CHAPTER NINE: Archival Research   **168**

Overview   168

Introduction   168

Content Analysis   169
"Who": The Source of Messages   170
"Says What": The Content of Messages   172
"To Whom": The Audience of Messages   172
"How": Communication Techniques in Messages   174
"With What Effect": The Effect of Messages   174
"Why": The Reasons for Communication   175
Methodological Issues in Content Analysis   175
Quantification in Content Analysis   178

Existing Data Analysis   180
Applications of Existing Data Analysis   181
Methodological Issues in Existing Data Analysis   185

Summary   186

CHAPTER TEN: Data Organization   **188**

Overview   188

Introduction   188

Data Storage Terminology   189

Data Storage Media   190
Computer Cards   191
Computer Disks   191
Magnetic Tapes   192

Data Coding   192
Numeric Representation   193
Codebooks   195
Coding Mechanisms   196

Data Cleaning   197
   Single-Field Analyses   197
   Multiple-Field Analyses   197
   Data Reduction   198

Summary   199

CHAPTER ELEVEN: Beyond Hypotheses   **201**

Overview   201

Introduction   201

Data Transformations   202
   Outliers   202
   Skewed Distributions   203
   Heterogeneous Variances   203
   Proportions   203
   Informal Guidelines   204

When Surprising Results Are Obtained   205
   Check Your Analyses for Errors   205
   Explore Reasons for the Results   206
   Return to Your Data   206
   Return to the Literature   207
   Develop a Curious Mind   207

Nonsignificant Versus Insignificant   207
   Horseshoes and Hand Grenades   207
   No Study Is Worthless   208

Summary   210

CHAPTER TWELVE: Writing a Research Report   211

Overview   211

Introduction   211

Research Report Organization   212

Writing Style   214
   Voice and Person   214
   Tense   214
   Avoiding Stereotypes   214
   Clarity   215

Introducing the Project   216
   Getting the Reader's Attention   216
   Reviewing the Literature   217

Describing the Method   219
      Describing Participants   219
      Describing Sampling   219
      Describing Apparatus or Materials   219
      Describing Procedure   220
      Describing Manipulations   221

Describing Your Results   221
      Describing Preliminary Results   221
      Describing Main Results   223

Describing the Conclusions   224

Writing Other Sections   226
      Summarizing the Report   226
      Identifying Your Sources   226
      Including Appendices   227

Having Your Research Report Reviewed   227

Summary   228

PART THREE
Resource Chapters   231

CHAPTER THIRTEEN: Conceptual Overview of Statistical Analyses   233

Overview   233

Introduction   233

Exploratory Research   234
      Appropriate Questions for Exploratory Research   234
      Appropriate Statistics for Exploratory Research   235

Descriptive Research   236
      Appropriate Questions for Descriptive Research   236
      Appropriate Statistics for Descriptive Research   237

Predictive Research   241
      Appropriate Questions for Predictive Research   242
      Prerequisites for Predictive Research   242
Box 13.1 Exploratory, Descriptive, and Predictive Research
      Questions   243
      Statistics for Predictive Research   243

Explanatory Research   245
    Appropriate Questions for Explanatory Research   245
    Appropriate Statistics for Explanatory Research   245

Summary   245

CHAPTER FOURTEEN: Measurement   **247**

Overview   247

Introduction   247
    Dimensionality   248

Measurement Levels   248
    Nominal Measurement   249
    Ordinal Measurement   250
    Interval Measurement   251
    Ratio Measurement   252

Reliability   252
Box 14.1   Summary of Measurement Levels   253
    Interrater Reliability   253
    Test-Retest Reliability   254
    Alternate Forms Reliability   254
    Split-Half Reliability   255
    Item-Total Reliability   256
Box 14.2   Summary of Reliability Procedures   257

Validity   257
    Face Validity   257
    Concurrent Validity   258
    Predictive Validity   258
    Construct Validity   259

Epistemic Correlation   260

Summary   261

CHAPTER FIFTEEN: Scaling   **263**

Overview   263

Introduction   263

Common Aspects of Scales   264
    Face Validity of Scale Items   264
    Instructions for Completing Scales   265
    Item Bias   265
    Formats for Scale Items   266

Thurstone Scales   268
    Item Generation in Thurstone Scales   269
    Item Analysis and Selection in Thurstone Scales   269
    Administration of Thurstone Scales   271
    Pros and Cons of Thurstone Scales   271

Likert Scales   272
    Item Analysis and Selection in Likert Scales   272
    Administration of Likert Scales   272
    Philosophies of Human Nature Scale   273

Guttman Scales   274
    Ideal Response Pattern in a Guttman Scale   274
    Item Generation in Guttman Scales   275
    Item Analysis in Guttman Scales   275
    Guttman Scaling to Study Riots and Political Participation   276
    Disadvantages of Guttman Scales   277

Semantic Differential Scales   277
    Item Generation in Semantic Differential Scales   278
    Administration of Semantic Differential Scales   278
    Semantic Differential Scaling to Study Officers of the
    Court   279

Q-sort Scales   280
    Administration of Q-sort Scales   280
    Use of Q-sort and Postcards to Examine Self-Concept   281
    Disadvantages of Q-sort Scales   282

Sociometric Scales   282
    Administration of Sociometric Scales   282
    Scoring of Sociometric Scales   283

Using Scales   285
    Multiple Scale Administration   285
    Using Existing Scales   286

Summary   286

CHAPTER SIXTEEN: Sampling   288

Overview   288

Introduction   288

Sampling Distributions   290
    The Population   291
    Random Selection   292
    Standard Error   292
    Confidence Intervals   294
    Sample Size   295

Probability Sampling 296
   Simple Random Sampling 297
   Systematic Random Sampling 298
   Stratified Random Sampling 299
   Cluster Sampling 300

Nonprobability Sampling 302
   Accidental Sampling 302
   Purposive Sampling 303
   Quota Sampling 303

Representative Samples 304

Summary 305

CHAPTER SEVENTEEN: Evaluation Research   307

Overview 307

Introduction 307
   Summative and Formative Evaluation 309
   Consumers of Evaluation Research 309

The Hartford Project: An Example of Evaluation
Research 310
   Operationalization 310
   Similarity to Basic Research 310
   The Problem 310
   The Program 311
   The Questions 312
   The Measures 312
   Ecosystem Measures 314
   The Results 314

The Controversy Over the Use of Experiments in Evaluation
Research 315
   Difficulties with Experiments in Evaluation Research 315
   Qualitative Information in Evaluation Research 316
   Innovation in Evaluation Research 316
   Ethics in Evaluation Research 317

Ethical Considerations in Evaluation Research 318
   Formulation and Negotiation 318
   Structure and Design 319
   Data Collection and Preparation 319
   Data Analysis and Interpretation 319
   Communication and Disclosure 320
   Use of Results 320

Summary 321

References 323

Glossary 331

Author Index 341

Subject Index 345

PART ONE

The Nature of
Research

CHAPTER ONE

Introduction

How can our intellectual life and institutions be arranged so as to expose our beliefs, conjectures, policies, positions, sources of ideas, traditions, and the like—whether or not they are justifiable—to maximum criticism, in order to counteract and eliminate as much intellectual error as possible?

—Bartley (1962, pp. 139–140)

Overview

This chapter is an introduction to research. Like most introductions, it is a broad overview of what's to come. Admittedly, it is also an attempt to pique your interest. You will learn what research is and what the goals of research are. You will also learn about a number of different research projects, projects that illustrate that no single research method is necessarily better than any other. Part of this new information includes a general framework for evaluating your own research as well as that of others. Finally, you will learn how the remainder of this book fits into the overall approach to learning about and conducting research.

Introduction

When I was in college, one of my favorite tunes was "Who'll Stop the Rain," written by John C. Fogarty and performed by Credence Clearwater Revival. For those of you who've not heard it, the rain is a metaphor for the confusions and mysteries of life. Somewhere behind all those rain clouds is the sun—the answers to the mysteries of life. Although everyone has been looking for the sun, the singer continues to wonder who'll stop the rain. My guess is that, right about now, you may be wondering the same thing about research, the course you are taking, and this book. What you need now is some sun, but all you see is rain.

Because you are majoring in psychology or a related science, I need not point out how important psychology has been, is, and will be in our lives. More important, however, is that knowing about research methods will help you to learn more about psychology and related topics, even if you never conduct a research project. The complex and rapidly changing character of our world does not allow us to be armchair theorists in our search for understanding. We use research to sort out the various theories and explanations we already have, as well as to point the way to more useful theories and explanations.

This book is about research—what it is, how to do it, how to evaluate it, how to tell people about it, and how to use it. It's about trying to find an answer to Bartley's question that began this chapter, and it's about stopping the rain. As you read further, you will come to realize that research is one of the means by which people avoid making intellectual errors; that is, research is a part of life, a particularly exciting part of life that involves trying to discover the whys and wherefores of the world in which we live. As you go through this book, you'll learn about research. You'll also have some fun and maybe, just maybe, you might even find the sun.

It's always best to begin at the beginning when attempting to learn about something, and for us that beginning is a definition of research. Unfortunately, it's not easy to arrive at a single definition of research. Just about everyone who has written about research has offered one or another definition. For example, Nachmias and Nachmias (1981) defined it as "the overall scheme of scientific activities in which scientists engage in order to produce new knowledge" (p. 22). Although research is conducted by scientists, it's also conducted by nonscientists. Of course, scientists and nonscientists tend to do research differently, a difference you will be learning about throughout this book, but that doesn't mean nonscientists necessarily do research poorly. Kerlinger (1973) doesn't restrict research to scientists in his definition—"systematic, controlled, empirical, and critical investigation of hypothetical propositions about the presumed relationships among natural phenomena" (p. 11)—but he added other restrictions. Research is not always systematic, and it's not always controlled. The more systematic and controlled research is, the better it is, but even poor research is still research.

I could go on citing other definitions, but that would only end up boring you to tears. When it comes down to what is important, the definition of research is rather simple. **Research** is *a critical process for asking and attempting to answer questions about the world.* Sometimes asking and attempting to answer questions involves a questionnaire, sometimes an interview, sometimes an experiment, and sometimes an entirely different method. But simple definitions can be misleading: there's more to research than its definition, or this would be the last page of the book.

Research as a critical process is one of the tools we use to achieve Bartley's state of maximum criticism. We do so not by pointing out only the negative qualities of something, but by examining all of its qualities—good, bad, or indifferent. The subject of our criticism is human behavior, something about which all of us already know a great deal. That knowledge, however, can sometimes get in our way. If, for example, we fail to critically examine some aspect of human behavior because "everyone knows that's true," then we have fallen short of the goal of research. Instead, researchers should be like a little child who continually asks why. Of course, we are more sophisticated than little children, but we need to turn to research to evaluate the answers we obtain to our questions. As critical questioners, we need not believe every answer we obtain. For that matter, research enables us to ascertain whether or not we've even asked the appropriate questions.

Goals of Research

The ultimate goals of research are to formulate questions and to find answers to those questions. Nestled within these goals are other goals toward which researchers strive. No one can ask all of the questions, and no one can find all of the answers to even a single question, so we need to find some way to limit what we attempt to do. The immediate goals of research—exploration, description, prediction, explanation, and action—provide us with a strategy for figuring out which questions to ask and which answers to seek.

Exploration

Exploratory research involves *an attempt to determine whether or not a phenomenon exists.* It is used to answer questions of the general form "Does X happen?" Exploratory research may be very simple, such as noting whether or not men or women are more likely to sit toward the front of a classroom. If one or the other gender does sit in front more often, then we may have discovered a social phenomenon that merits further investigation.

Exploratory research may also be very complex, and sometimes the object of exploratory research is the research process itself. For example, Durkheim's (1951) classic study of suicide statistics involved looking for patterns among a variety of different personal characteristics. Religious denomination was among them, and Durkheim found that Protestants were more likely to commit suicide than Catholics. He also found that people who lived in cities and who lived alone were more likely to commit suicide than were people who lived in rural areas or those who lived with a family. From such patterns, Durkheim concluded that **anomie,** *a lack of integration into a social network,* was one of the major factors leading to suicide. Many social scientists continued to use existing statistics to elaborate Durkheim's initial theory. Durkheim had explored suicide and had identified anomie as a major influence, and other researchers attempted to elaborate on his notions.

Jacobs (1967), however, noted that researchers were generally failing to consider another important source of information about suicide—the notes left behind by those who committed the act. His analysis of the content of such notes revealed that many people valued some degree of uncertainty in their lives. Believing that they knew what the future was going to be like—depressing—was extremely uncomfortable for them, and, presumably, such people preferred the uncertainty of death to the certainty that life would continue to become worse.

Jacobs's research does not replace Durkheim's monumental work, but it does add much to our understanding of suicide. Both researchers explored the same topic, and each arrived at a different answer: Durkheim's answer was anomie; Jacobs's answer was uncertainty. Just as Durkheim's initial exploration opened many new avenues for research, so does Jacobs's investigation. Neither researcher was testing a particular theory, although both researchers eventually arrived at a theoretical framework for their explorations. Neither researcher "discovered" suicide, but their explorations did uncover some new aspects of suicide.

Description

Descriptive research involves *examining a phenomenon to more fully define it or to differentiate it from other phenomena.* Assume, for example, that you have completed exploratory research in which you paid attention to where people sat in your classes, and you noticed that women are more likely than men to sit toward the front of the room. You may want to investigate this phenomenon further by defining exactly what is meant by the "front" of the room. You could partition the class into halves, quarters, and so on in order to determine the proportion of men and women in the ever-smaller "front" sections. Or you might visit different classrooms to determine the extent to which such behavior is related to the type of subject matter being taught, the size of the room, or some other characteristic.

This example may appear to be a bit innocuous, but meaningful research programs have been initiated with even less impressive beginnings. Munsterberg (1913), for example, began his inquiries into the consistency and accuracy of eyewitness testimony after wondering about his own perceptions following a burglary at his home. He wondered why he thought (and testified) that the burglars had broken through a basement window when they had actually forced open a door. Since he first questioned his own perceptions and began conducting systematic research on the topic, a number of researchers have investigated the accuracy of eyewitness accounts and have applied their results to courtrooms and other settings (Greenberg & Ruback, 1982; Parker, 1980; Wrightsman, 1987). Empirical attempts to more comprehensively describe the limits of eyewitness accuracy have been conducted from the time of Munsterberg's first musings to the present, and they are likely to continue well into the future. Indeed, even the most recent studies on eyewitnesses (Loftus, Loftus, & Messo, 1987) have some basis in the research Munsterberg conducted early in this century.

Perhaps the most extensive descriptive research is that conducted by the United States Bureau of the Census, the goal of which is to count and describe the characteristics of the entire U.S. population. The impact of this research is extensive. Billions of dollars in federal, state, and municipal aid shift with the changing population. Congressional districts appear and disappear, and hundreds of researchers rely on these data to assess the representativeness of their own research samples.

Descriptive research captures the flavor of an object, a person, or an event at the time the data are collected, but that flavor may change over time. The U.S. Bureau of the Census, for example, repeats its very costly research every ten years. Other research results may change even more rapidly. Research on unemployment is conducted monthly, and public opinion polls about certain issues may be conducted as often as daily. Research results are not "timeless" simply because change is one of the complexities inherent in our world. Thus, descriptive research can be used to examine change by comparing old results with new ones.

Prediction

Sometimes the goal of research is **prediction**—*identifying relationships that enable us to speculate about one thing by knowing about some other thing.* Although this may seem complicated, it really is not. We all conduct and use predictive research every day. We know, for example, about the relationship between the time of day and the probability of a certain business being open. And we understand the relationship between a thermometer reading and the necessity of a coat when going outside. Those who create college entrance examinations use research to predict performance in the first year of college or graduate school from the scores on such tests (Educational Testing Service, 1981). The importance of the latter type of research can be inferred from the number of truth-in-testing laws passed by various states in the United States.

Knowing someone's score on a college entrance examination enables us, as a result of predictive research, to speculate about their ability to complete the first year of college. Because some colleges and universities have more (or less) difficult curricula, admissions committees use the relationship between first-year performance and test scores to set minimum standards for accepting entering students. Of course, there are those who get very high scores on such examinations and flunk out in their first year, and those who get low scores and do very well. Such exceptions point out that predictive research enables us to speculate—to make informed guesses—but it does not lead us to absolute certainties.

Explanation

Explanatory research involves *examining a cause–effect relationship between two or more phenomena.* It is used to determine whether or not an explanation (a cause–effect relationship) is valid, or to determine which of two or more competing explanations is more valid. For example, Sales (1972) used explanatory research to test an explanation derived from Marx's claim that religion is the opium of the people. If religion is used to escape the reality of life, then one might expect that membership in religious organizations would increase during times of economic hardship, for people need escape more when things are bad than when they are good. Previous research, however, demonstrated no relationship at all between economic indicators and religious membership.

Sales, after reading that earlier research, noted that the researchers had not made distinctions among different kinds of religions. He attempted to make distinctions among religions by using the psychological concept of **authoritarianism,** which is characterized by *submission to authority figures, ethnocentrism, and preoccupation with strength or power* (Adorno, Frenkel-Brunswick, Levinson, & Sanford, 1950). Even though the concept was originally developed to describe people—a personality construct—Sales applied it to religions and created categories of authoritarian and nonauthoritarian religions.

Using various economic indicators and church membership records, Sales was able to demonstrate that membership increased in authoritarian religions, but decreased in nonauthoritarian religions, during times of economic hardship. Thus, the overall effect was no change in religious membership, which is just what previous researchers had found. Authoritarian religions are more likely to provide definite prescriptions for living, and such prescriptions are consistent with the notion of "opium" to which Marx was referring in his theory.

Sales's results do not prove that Marxist theory is correct, but Marxist theory can be offered as a possible explanation of Sales's results. As you will discover time and time again, it is not possible to prove that a theory is correct. However, Sales's use of psychological, sociological, and economic concepts was fruitful, and his research may provide us a better understanding of, and an interesting way to study, such phenomena as the increased popularity of the "Moral Majority" and similar organizations during difficult times (Hilton, 1981).

Action

Research can also be used to attempt to do something about a particular phenomenon. **Action research** refers to *research conducted to solve a social problem* (Lewin, 1946). Action research can involve any of the previously mentioned goals, but adds to such goals the requirement of finding a solution, of doing something. Becker and Seligman (1978) noted that many people continue to run their air conditioners in the evening even though the outside temperature is lower than the temperature inside their homes, for example. To address this problem, Becker and Seligman conducted an experiment to test potential solutions to this waste of energy. They created four different groups by providing some people with a chart showing them how much energy they were using, other people with a light that flashed whenever the outside temperature was lower than the inside temperature, yet other people with both chart and light, and still others with neither chart nor light.

They measured the amount of electricity used by each of the four groups and, using the group with neither chart nor light as the control group, discovered that the chart did not alter people's energy efficiency. The signaling device, with the chart or alone, did reduce electricity consumption by about 16%. Through their action research, they provided a solution to the problem of wasted electricity: a simple signaling device.

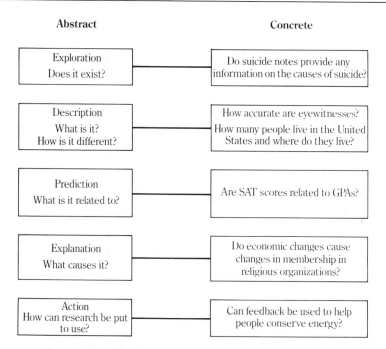

Figure 1.1 The five goals of research in terms of abstract and concrete questions

There are, of course, a variety of different theories that could be used to explain why the signaling device worked and the charts did not, but testing those theories was not of interest to Becker and Seligman. They did, however, rely on such theories to implement their study. They inferred from other research, for example, that feedback can be used to alter people's behavior, and so they selected two different forms of feedback—charts and flashing lights—as possible solutions to the problem. Action research, in general, is an extremely important aspect of science, for it is through action research that we are able to test applications of other research results. We might all want to make the world a better place, but the complexity of the world requires that we test proposed solutions to problems before applying them on a large scale.

By way of summary, Figure 1.1 depicts the five goals of research in both abstract and concrete terms.

Evaluation of Research

Before we apply research results, or even before we accept them as reasonable, we need to be able to know whether or not they are worthwhile. We need to evaluate research critically, which involves noting both positive and negative, the good and the bad. Critical evaluation also involves noting the indifferent—the things to which research is not related.

Research goals affect the methods used to conduct a research project, and they affect the ways in which we attempt to evaluate the research. It would not be appropriate to reject research because it did not meet goals it was not designed to meet. We can't, for example, devalue Becker and Seligman's research because it did not explain why flashing lights created more efficient use of energy; explaining why was not part of that project. We also cannot apply research results to goals different from the goals of the research. Sales's research, for example, explored the utility of suicide notes; it indicated that suicide notes provide useful information about suicide. However, we would be reaching well beyond the initial goals of the research if we used Sales's results to claim that people commit suicide only because they prefer the uncertainty of death to the certainty of depression.

For those of us who conduct formal research, the need for evaluation is obvious: we must be able to determine whether or not our research is worthwhile, if for no other reason than to prevent wasting our time. But even if we never conducted any research of our own, we would still need to know how to evaluate others' research. Whether or not we conduct research, we all use research to help us understand the world around us, and as consumers of research we must be able to determine which research is relevant and which is not. To construct a systematic framework for evaluating research, I have borrowed some familiar questions from journalism: who, what, where, when, how, and why.

The Who: Researchers, Participants, and Consumers of Research

The "who" of a research project involves three different questions: Who are the researchers, who are the participants in the project, and who are the consumers of the research? The answers, of course, vary from project to project, and all have something to do with how we evaluate the project.

Asking about the researchers involves more than simply discovering their names. What we really want to know is something about the characteristics of the researchers: their competence and their biases. We presume researchers to be competent until we learn otherwise. For example, I don't know anyone willing to place a great deal of faith in research conducted by Sir Cyril Burt in light of his fraudulent research on intelligence (Hearnshaw, 1979). Few things arouse the ire of researchers more than fraudulent research reports. Because research reports are the major source of information about research and because they serve as the basis for evaluating research, they must be as accurate as possible. Outright fraud is extremely rare, but even the most competent researchers are susceptible to biases.

Researchers' biases affect the direction of their research, just as our own biases affect the manner in which we evaluate our own and others' research. We would not be too surprised to learn, for example, that a longtime believer in extrasensory perception conducted a study that claimed to support its existence. We might be more likely to accept the same results, however, if the study was conducted by a known critic of extrasensory perception. There's no reason to believe that one or the other researcher is any better, but we tend to believe people more when they are presenting a position counter to their known beliefs (Dane, 1988b). Whether or not we agree with the biases of other researchers, we must be aware of them (and of our own biases as well) and be sensitive to their influence in the evaluation process.

Participants in a research project are also an important consideration in the evaluation of research. Suppose we were interested in studying how jurors arrived at their verdicts in criminal trials. It might not be particularly useful to study how college students decide on a verdict, simply because college students are not sufficiently similar to the majority of people who serve on juries (Ellison & Buckhout, 1981; Kerr & Bray, 1982; Simon, 1975). On the other hand, if we are using a trial setting simply as a means for investigating how people in general, not just jurors, make decisions, then it would be reasonable to ask students to decide about a portion of trial evidence. Students, while they may not be very much like jurors, certainly can be included among "people in general." Simply determining who the participants are is not sufficient; critical evaluation involves assessing the fit between the purpose of the research and the participants involved in it.

Sometimes, records about people, organizations, programs, or other objects are the participants in research. The data source in Jacobs's (1967) study was suicide notes, not the people who wrote them. We would not expect those writing such notes to have had an interest in the outcome of the research, but **self-presentation,** *concern for the impression one makes on others,* may be an important aspect of any research project. Participants, including those creating records that may be used for research, have a tendency to want to make themselves look good. Even people who write suicide notes expect someone to read them. Self-presentation is a problem because, when it occurs, what we observe is what the participants would like someone to believe is what they would do. To the extent that behavior motivated by self-presentation is different from behavior otherwise motivated, bias is introduced into the research results. Therefore, the extent to which self-presentation plays a role in a research project should always be assessed.

The intended consumers of research also play a role in our ability to evaluate a project. Researchers tend to write their reports for other researchers, as opposed to the general public. They often use jargon that they expect readers to understand. At this point, the phrase *a 2 × 2 factorial design* probably doesn't mean much to you, but it denotes a specific research design. This design entails a variety of assumptions, implications, and techniques, all of which would be very time-consuming—not to mention boring—to describe every time someone wrote about it. Readers' inability to understand jargon makes it difficult for them to evaluate research, which is one of the reasons why a glossary is included in this text.

On the other hand, too much jargon makes it difficult for anyone except another expert to understand the report. Thus misinterpretation of research procedures and conclusions likely contributed to Senator William Proxmire's creation of the "Golden Fleece Awards" (Baron, 1980; see also Box 1.1), although publicity and political considerations were likely motives as well. Sometimes, certain consumers of research may want to limit research. Shaver (1981; 1982), for example, noted that the Reagan administration's budget restrictions on social science research were politically motivated: Many of the budget cuts directly affected research designed to assess the impact of the administration's economic programs. Sensitivity to the consumers of research is a necessary part of the evaluation process, which includes noting the absence of research.

BOX 1.1   Golden Fleece Awards

The "Golden Fleece Award," the brainchild of Senator William Proxmire (Wisconsin), was, according to the senator, intended to publicize wastes of taxpayers' money by identifying research and other projects that were, again according to the senator, of little or no value. Reprinted below is one scientist's reaction to having received one of these awards.

A Note on Rude Awakenings: Some Effects of Being Fleeced

Robert A. Baron

Reprinted, with permission, from SASP Newsletter

©1980, SASP, Inc.

Several years ago, I was the recipient of one of Senator Proxmire's "Golden Fleece" awards. Many things happened to me as a result of receiving this dubious distinction, including all of the following:

• students in my classes cheered and applauded spontaneously when I entered the room (to them, at least, I was something of an instant folk hero);

• my neighbors banded together to subject me to merciless ribbing (most of it, fortunately, good-humored in spirit);

• I was deluged with calls from reporters and other media representatives who (bless them!) wanted to hear my side of the story;

• my mother-in-law called to say that she had just read about my supposed misdeeds in the *National Enquirer,* her comments left little doubt that she felt her worst fears about me had finally been confirmed;

• my mail box overflowed with an assortment of strange letters, ranging in scope from unabashed love notes to hate letters complete with warnings about mending my evil ways.

Needless to say, I remember all of these experiences vividly. This is hardly surprising, for all are rare occurrences in the tranquil life of a university professor. But what, in total, was the impact of these assorted events? How did they affect my career, my research activities, and my life as an individual? Looking back after the passage of several years, I can see that outwardly, at least, they produced little effect. I was already a tenured full professor with an actively functioning research program. Thus, the award had little impact on my career or scientific activities. It did, however, produce other effects—ones I now feel were of an important and lasting nature. Briefly, these were centered around shifts in my attitudes and perspectives about public support for science, the grounds on which scientific research may be criticized, and the problem of communication between scientists and the public.

Shifts in My Perceptions of Public Support for Science: Or, The Dangers of Taking Things for Granted

The first and perhaps most important effect of receiving the "Golden Fleece" that I wish to address involves development of a new perspective on public perceptions of the importance and value of science. As working scientists, we are usually to-

continued

tally immersed in a supportive, friendly environment. That is, virtually everyone we meet shares a basic assumption with us: science is important and valuable, and should be supported as strongly as possible. Our colleagues, students, and members of our university administration all share this view, and pay homage to the importance of basic scientific research. Further, our interactions are often restricted to an even more select group of persons—ones who share our specific research interests—and so assume that everything we do in our laboratories is of vital importance. One result of living in the cordial environment is obvious: *we often take the value of our work totally for granted.* In this context, the "Fleece" strikes like a bolt from the blue. How, one wonders, can anyone question the intrinsic merit of such work? Isn't its importance obvious to all? The answer is, of course, *no.* To persons who do not share our interests and scientific concerns, our research may appear trivial, banal, or even worse. Thus, one major effect of receiving the "Fleece" might be described as a rude awakening from complacency. Never again can a recipient such as myself view his or her research—or basic research in general—as resting on unquestioned and perhaps even unquestionable grounds. Rather, it becomes all too clear that the value of such activities must often be explicated and defended in a forceful manner.

A Broader Understanding of the Nature of Criticism: Or, Learning That All Critics Don't Play by the Same Rules

A second major impact of receiving the "Fleece" might be described as a basic lesson in the nature of criticism. As scientists, our training emphasizes the importance of careful, reasoned critiques. And in our professional careers, all of us experience a full measure of such feedback from our colleagues. Such criticism is usually based on careful logic, and is provided by individuals who are just as expert as ourselves in the topics under consideration. None of our experience, then, prepares us for the kind of criticism that accompanies the Senator's award. As I soon learned, the validity of a research program can be questioned on totally nonscientific grounds, such as its potential pay-off for society, or its practical importance in the eyes of specific individuals. Further, such criticism is often far from carefully reasoned and logical. Consider, if you will, my own experience in this respect.

The research for which I received the "Golden Fleece" was part of an ongoing project designed to examine the supposed "long, hot summer effect"—the suggestion that heat makes people irritable and so contributes to the occurrence of interpersonal aggression or even dangerous riots. For several years, we toiled in the confines of our laboratory, systematically varying ambient temperatures, and studying the impact of this factor on human behavior. Near the end of our project, after more than 95% of our funds (and effort) had been expended, we decided to venture outside the lab, in order to see if the findings we had uncovered would hold true in more natural settings. In order to gather preliminary evidence on this possibility, we conducted a simple (and admittedly humorous) study involving the observation of the reactions of drivers to brief delays in traffic on warm summer

continued

BOX 1.1   Golden Fleece Awards (*continued*)

days. Clearly, this was a very minor aspect of our research. Yet, it served as the basis for the Senator's entire critique. Further, his comments seemed to suggest that we had spent all of our time (and all of our funds) conducting such investigations. As you can well imagine, discovering that an entire, complex research project could be criticized in this fashion served as a second rude awakening. It brought home a very important fact: scientific work can be faulted on other than scientific grounds. And woe to the scientist who is unable or unwilling to respond adequately to such criticism!

Increased Awareness of the Need for Communicating With the Public: Or, The Communication Gap Strikes Again

A third major effect I experienced as a result of receiving the "Fleece" was a greatly heightened awareness of an important type of communication gap: one that often exists between scientists and the general public. As researchers, we are trained primarily to communicate with our colleagues—persons who share our expertise in a given area and can readily grasp the value and goals of our work. Usually, we direct little attention to the task of communicating such information to our friends and neighbors, let alone to the public in general. Receiving the "Fleece" awakened me to the fact that this can be a very dangerous state of affairs. Many of the persons who determine levels of support for scientific activities have been trained in nonscientific fields. Thus, it is crucial that we inform them clearly and succinctly about the goals we are trying to reach, and the reasons why our research is truly worthy of public support. After all, how can we expect them to be enthusiastic about our work in the absence of such information? This is especially true in a time of worsening economic conditions and tightening govern-

continued

The What: Research Topics and the Worldviews Behind Them

The "what" of research concerns both its topic and the theory on which the research is based. Theory includes the overall **worldview**—*the basic set of untestable assumptions underlying all theory and research.*

It should be obvious that different research topics require different methods. Attempting to interview people who have committed suicide is ridiculous, not to mention macabre. On the other hand, an interview or survey is entirely appropriate for a project investigating energy use. What may not be so obvious is that answering different questions about the same research topic may require different methods. If we are interested in *perceptions* about electricity use, interviews may be just the method to use; but if we are interested in *actual* electricity use, then we might do as Becker and Seligman (1978) did and read meters instead of asking people how much electricity they used.

The theory we used to derive our research questions also affects the manner in which we conduct the research. Sales (1972), for example, specifically tested Marxist theory, so he included economic conditions, one of the major components ment budgets. Thus, if we fail to accomplish this task—that is, if we fail in our attempts to close the communication gap—we may both invite and deserve the negative consequences that follow.

As this point I should hasten to add there is more at stake in this issue than simple self-interest. I firmly believe that as scientists, we have a direct responsibility to communicate clearly with our fellow citizens. Anything less than our best efforts in this regard is totally unacceptable.

Conclusion: Does the "Golden Fleece" Have a Potential Silver Lining?

To conclude: receiving the "Golden Fleece" resulted in a number of important shifts in my attitudes and perspectives about science and public support for it. In several respects, then, I feel that the entire episode was something of a "consciousness-raising" experience. And herein, I believe, lies the potential value for individual scientists such as myself, and for science in general. Through the "Golden Fleece" Senator Proxmire is, I feel, transmitting several important messages to the scientific community. Briefly, these may be summarized as follows: (1) don't take public support for science for granted; (2) be prepared for all kinds of criticism; and (3) close the communication gap currently existing between scientists and the public—or face the consequences. To the extent we heed these messages, science may actually reap important long-term benefits. It may improve its standing in the public eye, and also gain the ability to deal with criticism when this arises. I do not know if producing such benefits has been the Senator's purpose all along. But whether it has or not, I feel that his actions have served to awaken us from a state of collective complacency. In this respect, at least, we may all owe him a sincere vote of thanks!

of Marxist theory, as one of his research measures. If he had instead been interested in theories about psychological depression, he probably would have used a scale to measure depression and would have ignored economic indicators. Both economic conditions and depression may be related to membership in a religious organization, but whether one or the other (or perhaps neither) of these variables gets included in any particular research project is determined by the theory from which the research question is derived. The evaluation of research involves assessing whether or not what is included in a research project is appropriate to the theory on which it's based.

Beyond the level of theory, worldview also plays an important role in research. Kamin (1974) pointed out that researchers were willing to accept the notion that men and women did not differ in intelligence, and so they generally excluded from intelligence tests items that produced gender differences. These same researchers were not, however, so willing to accept the notion that racial and ethnic minorities were as intelligent as themselves. Thus, measures of intelligence do not exhibit a gender bias but do exhibit a number of racial and ethnic biases. Political beliefs may also affect the topics selected for research (Frank, 1981).

Worldviews also affect the way in which research results are interpreted. A current example is the debate between those favoring the creationist and evolutionist explanations of the origin of our planet and of the humans who inhabit it (Durant, 1985). The followers of each worldview base their conclusions (more or less) on the same data—the physical world. The creationists conclude that the world is about 10,000 years old and that it and humans result from divine intervention. They reject the scientific methods, and therefore the data, that are not consistent with their beliefs. Evolutionists conclude that the earth is billions of years old and that humans evolved from other species, and they reject untestable theistic evidence as valid sources of data. Evolutionists don't accept what is written in religious documents as scientific evidence, and creationists don't accept what is measured by the evolutionists as scientific data. Clearly, worldviews affect the conclusions as well as evaluations of research in this debate, just as worldviews affect evaluations of all research.

The Where: Research Settings

The "where" of research includes the physical and social environment in which research is conducted. Certain conditions are possible in one setting but not in another, and some settings do not allow certain types of research to be conducted at all. We cannot, for example, legally study jury deliberations in any systematic fashion by recording what occurs in the deliberation room, although some researchers were able to do so before it became illegal (Ellison & Buckhout, 1981; Simon, 1975). Similarly, we cannot ethically examine reactions to an emergency by shouting "Fire!" in a theater. On the other hand, we can study simulations of juries or of emergencies. Bringing trials or emergencies into a research laboratory may introduce an element of artificiality, but artificiality alone is not grounds for devaluing a research project. As with other evaluation questions, critical assessment of the relationship between the physical setting and the research goals is required.

The influence of the social environment may include very general aspects of the society in addition to cultural biases. Someone doing research in a country without a jury system—Japan, for example—might never decide to use a jury simulation to study group decision making. Indeed, the one attempt I made at cross-cultural research involved asking students in Japan to role-play jurors. The study was unsuccessful; the students refused to make any judgments, particularly guilt or innocence, about someone else's behavior. On the other hand, I learned a valuable lesson about the importance of the "where" of research.

The When: The Time Frame of Research

The time frame of a particular study may, of course, affect its utility, but it can also be the major purpose of the study.

Most of the time science operates on the basis of cumulative knowledge: each new bit of information adds to what is already known. The results of a particular study may be extremely valuable when first reported but may only bring a yawn after years of research on the topic. Demonstrating, for example, that social classes exist today in the United States might well bring a yawn and raise questions about why anyone is wasting time on such trivial research. On the other hand, a study that claims to demonstrate that social classes no longer exist in the United States would arouse considerable excitement and disagreement. Research should not occur in a vacuum, but should be placed in a context of the existing information about the research topic.

Changes in conditions over time may themselves be the focus of research, as is the case with research by developmental psychologists, among others. Similarly, the passage of time may have an impact on research. In a study involving deception, for example, the longer the study lasts the more likely it is that the deception is no longer feasible. If a study involves an interview, an extremely long interview may lead to fatigue or boredom, affecting the responses of the participants or the interviewer's ability to accurately record responses. Of course, the explanation is not time, per se, but changes in other conditions that occur with the passage of time. Nevertheless, the context of a research project and its length must be considered a part of a critical evaluation of the project.

The Why: Additional Reasons for Research

The main reasons for conducting research have already been discussed. These include exploration, description, prediction, explanation, and action. The possible motives that underlie these reasons are as varied as researchers themselves. I, for example, do it mainly because I am curious. I encounter something I don't understand fully, such as how juries make their decisions, and I spend my time doing research to satisfy my curiosity. When I publish the fruits of my curiosity, my research becomes available for critical evaluation. However, a different "why," contracts, may pose some problems for critical evaluation.

Contract research is conducted because someone hires a researcher specifically for the purpose of conducting the research. The Pepsi Taste Challenge is an example, although not necessarily a representative one. Research firms were hired to conduct the taste tests, but the results belonged to Pepsi. (I've often wondered whether or not the results would have been released had they not favored Pepsi, but I think I know the answer.) The primary consumers of contract research are those who pay the bills, and they have considerably greater influence than most researcher consumers. The consumer, rather than the contracted researcher, typically has control over the research process and almost always has control over the release of the results. In some cases, the exact methodology of the study may be kept secret, in which case it is impossible to evaluate the research critically.

The How: Research Methods

The goals of research affect its methods, and so we turn to some of those methods as a way to preview the remainder of this text. The design and procedures are likely to be the most critically evaluated aspects of a research project and so deserve the greatest amount of attention.

The "hows" of research begin with the manner in which you obtain an idea (Chapter 2) and end with the ways in which you write about the research results (Chapter 12). Nestled between these two activities are issues concerning ethics (Chapter 3), design of research projects (Chapters 5 through 9), data organization (Chapter 10), and interpretation of results (Chapter 11). In addition, this text contains a number of resource chapters that may or may not be relevant to your particular research project; scale construction (Chapter 15) and obtaining large, representative samples (Chapter 16) are just two topics addressed in the resource chapters.

Like most of life, research can be extremely boring if you only read about it. Although you may not be able to implement everything discussed in this text, you can think about applying your newly-gained knowledge of various topics as you encounter them. As you continue to read, think about what you might do with the information you are reading. Imagination cannot replace activity, but imagination is better than nothing. At some point, and I hope it's soon, you may be in a position to do some research. If you have thought about it ahead of time, you'll be better able to take advantage of the opportunity.

Summary

- Research can be defined in many ways. Most generally defined, research is a process through which questions are asked and answered systematically. As a form of criticism, research can include the question of whether or not we are asking the right question.

- The ultimate goal of research is to be able to answer the questions asked. Exploration, description, prediction, explanation, and action are different ways to ask the same question.

- Exploration involves attempting to determine whether or not a particular phenomenon exists. Description involves attempting to more carefully define a phenomenon, including distinguishing between it and other phenomena.

- Prediction involves examining the relationship between two things so that educated guesses can be made about one by knowing something about the other. Explanation also involves examining the relationship between two things, but it specifically attempts to determine whether or not one causes the other.

- Action involves using research to attempt to solve a social problem. Action research may involve any of the other goals of research but includes a specific application.

- Evaluating research involves the questions who, what, where, when, how, and why. Researchers, participants, and consumers of research may all affect the outcome of the research, as well as the manner in which the outcome is interpreted.

• The topic, theory, and worldview on which research is based are also involved in evaluating research critically, as are the physical setting of the research and the social climate in which it is conducted.

• Research results are not timeless, mainly because the world itself is dynamic. Changes in research results can themselves become the focus of research.

• Contract research often requires special consideration of the potential impact of those contracting the research. However, all research that becomes public should be subjected to equally stringent evaluation and criticism.

The Scientific Approach

It [science] is not perfect. It is only a tool. But it is by far the best tool we have, self-correcting, ongoing, applicable to everything. It has two rules. First: there are no sacred truths; all assumptions must be critically examined; arguments from authority are worthless. Second: whatever is inconsistent with the facts must be discarded or revised.

—Sagan (1980, p. 333)

Overview

This chapter describes the scientific approach as it applies to the theory and practice of research. You will learn why science, despite being the best approach to research, is not subject to proof from outside its own logical system. Scientific knowledge (and its growth as well) is a function of agreement, and you will learn how agreement is facilitated by the use of inductive reasoning. You will also learn about distinctions between scientific and nonscientific research, various misconceptions about science, and the importance of theory in the research process. Finally, you will learn how to use theory and other resources to initiate your own research project.

Introduction

Many people think of science as something done by intelligent-but-absent-minded people wearing white coats while surrounded by strange-looking equipment with blinking lights. Some may think of scientists as despoilers of a simple, nontechnical lifestyle. One of the goals of this chapter is to dispel these and other myths about science. Science is not something one does; rather, it is an approach toward doing things, and one of the most important things scientists do is research. Scientists certainly do not all wear white laboratory coats, nor do we all use strange equipment, with or without blinking lights. Some scientists may be extremely intelligent or absent-minded, but these qualities don't make a person a scientist; neither does adopting a scientific approach necessarily make someone intelligent or absent-minded.

We noted in Chapter 1 that everyone, not just scientists, does research. What distinguishes scientific from other kinds of research is not the activity itself, but the approach to the activity. Scientific research is, among other things, systematic. There are other guidelines about what is and what is not scientific research, as well as guidelines about what to do with scientific research once we have it. Scientists know what these guidelines are, agree about them, and attempt to adhere to them. Nonscientists either don't know them or don't consistently use them. It's not research that distinguishes scientists from nonscientists, it's the approach one takes toward research. **Science,** then, is *a systematic approach to the discovery of knowledge based on a set of rules that defines what is acceptable knowledge.* Just as there are rules to such things as tennis or international diplomacy, there are rules about science. And just like tennis or international diplomacy, not everyone necessarily operates according to the same set of rules.

A Philosophy of Science

Not long ago I was discussing religion with a friend. We disagreed about a lot of things, but we were calmly discussing the relative merits of our personal beliefs. At one point I asked my friend to explain why she believes what she does. She replied very simply, "I believe it because I know it's true." Then I asked how she knew it was true, and she said, "I know in my heart it's true." She could not explain why she believes what she believes, any more than I could explain why I believe what I do about religion. We both thought we were correct, but neither of us could logically prove we were correct in any absolute sense. At best, we could point out we were not alone in our beliefs. Of course, most people accept the notion that there is no absolute proof when the topic is religious beliefs. What many people do not understand is that the same is true about science.

Any set of rules that defines what is acceptable knowledge may be called a philosophy of science. Even among scientists, however, there is more than one accepted philosophy. This is partly because philosophy, like any other discipline, is growing, changing, and assessing new ideas and formulations in an attempt to improve upon what we know. Whatever their differences, however, all philosophies of science address the same four basic questions: (1) When is something true? (2) If we have more than one explanation, how can we tell which one is better? (3) How can we put what we know into practice? and (4) Why do we do it the way we do it?

In this chapter we'll concentrate on a particular philosophy of science called *nonjustificationism* (Weimer, 1979). The name of this viewpoint is derived from the notion that a scientific approach cannot be justified—proven valid—except through unproven assumptions; that is **nonjustificationism** is *a philosophy whose major premise is that we cannot logically prove that the way we go about doing research is correct in any absolute sense.*

When Is Something True?

This first question of any philosophy of science is usually called the question of **rational inference**—*the difficulty inherent in supporting any claim about the existence of a universal truth.* Just as when my friend and I were discussing religious beliefs there was more than one "truth," there is more than one solution to the problem of rational inference. Whatever we accept as our answer, our interim solution to the rational inference problem should be based on **facts**—*phenomena or characteristics available to anyone who knows how to observe them.* Recall Sagan's (1980) second rule of science: Whatever does not agree with the facts is wrong and must be changed or rejected completely. Although the statement is simple, deciding how to go about the process is a little more complex.

As behavioral scientists, for example, we are interested in understanding how people interact with each other at a variety of different levels. We want to understand as much about people and human phenomena as possible. No matter how many facts we have, however, we cannot understand them until we have a way to summarize those facts. Summarizing facts—making them comprehensible—is what theories are all about.

But anyone can make up a theory about human behavior. Given enough time, just about everyone in the world could articulate some sort of theory for any given phenomenon. Thus, we have the equivalent of a very large warehouse that is full of theories. This imaginary warehouse contains as many different theories about people as there are people in the world, multiplied by the number of different theories each of those people has for each of the various phenomena that make up human behavior. Clearly, we need to imagine a very large (and probably very disorganized) warehouse.

At a very simple level, all we have to do is compare each theory in the warehouse to the facts: if the theory doesn't fit the facts, we change it or throw it out of the warehouse. This process may sound good, but it just doesn't work that way. Theories are made up of **concepts**—*abstract words that represent concrete phenomena.* We can point to concrete examples of concepts, but the concepts themselves are abstract. Conflict, as a theoretical concept, is not the same thing as a family argument or a revolution. Family argument and revolution are, of course, concrete examples of conflict, but they are only examples and not complete definitions. No matter how compellingly practical a concept may be, it is only an approximation of reality, and any given concrete phenomenon is only an approximation of a concept (Wartofsky, 1968). Theories symbolize or represent the real world in which we live and behave, but the concepts within the theories are not the same thing as the real world. Because concepts are abstract and the facts we rely on to test them are concrete, deciding whether or not a theory fits the facts is rather difficult.

The difficulty arises because we must rely on inductive reasoning when fitting facts to a theory. **Inductive reasoning** is *a process of generalization; it involves applying specific information to a general situation or future events.* Let me illustrate with a story about a college instructor of mine who consistently arrived ten minutes late for class. About three weeks into the semester, I came to the conclusion that he would continue to do so, which meant I could sleep an extra ten minutes on those days and still arrive "on time" for class. This conclusion was a generalization, an inductive inference. Based on the instructor's specific behavior—arriving late during the first three weeks—I attributed to him a general or abstract quality—tardiness—and used that abstract concept to predict his behavior in the future. Unfortunately, it never occurred to me he would show up on time for the midterm exam, and I developed cramps trying to write fast enough to make up for the time I lost by arriving late. It was a rather painful way to learn that inductive reasoning does not necessarily lead to absolute truth.

Despite the inability of inductive reasoning to lead us to absolute truth, we must rely on it in any scientific approach to research. We simply cannot let all those theories pile up in the warehouse until all the facts are in, nor can we wait for all the facts before we begin to construct theories to put in the warehouse. Instead, we simply accept the notion that inductive reasoning is the best process of generalization we have until something better comes along.

Had I waited until after the midterm exam before attributing tardiness to my instructor, I could have saved myself some writing cramps (and perhaps gotten a better grade on the exam). But even then I could not have been sure that he would be on time for the final exam, nor could I be certain that he would not begin arriving on time after the midterm. Of course, I could have just arrived on time myself every day, but that would have meant missing out on hours of extra sleep. I weighed the alternatives and constructed my theory about his behavior. After he showed up late the first day after the midterm, I reverted back to sleeping an extra ten minutes, but I showed up on time for the final exam. I adjusted my initial theory to fit the new facts, but I didn't wait until I had all of the facts before constructing my new theory.

I have simplified the arguments involved in this issue, but the basic point of the rational inference problem is rather simple: inductive inferences cannot be proved true, but we need to use them to construct theories until we have evidence to the contrary. If we have enough contrary evidence, we can throw a theory out of our warehouse, but that doesn't mean that any of the theories remaining in the warehouse are true. We are left with no choice but to provide support for a theory by trying to show that alternative, competing theories are not true. If we make a prediction from a theory and test the prediction, and the prediction fits the facts, then we have *not* proved the theory to be true; instead, we have failed to prove that the theory is false. It is difficult to think in terms of double negatives—theory X is not not-true—but that is the logic forced on us by the rational inference problem. What this all means is that research that provides a test between two competing theories is better than research that tests only one theory.

How Can We Tell Which Theory Is Better?

The absence of absolute truth does not limit what we can learn in a scientific approach, but it does lead us down a particular path in our quests to learn about behavior and other real-world phenomena. We can, as I mentioned above, test between two different theories and decide which one is better. Testing between theories is like a grand tournament in which every theory is pitted against every other theory: The theory with the best win-loss record at the end of the tournament is the winner. Of course, that doesn't mean that the winning theory is true, only that it is the best theory we have until another, better theory is entered in the tournament. Like all tournaments, the tournament of scientific theories has some rules about which theories are entered and how many times a theory has to lose in order to be eliminated.

The rules of the grand tournament of science bring us to the problem called **criteria for growth**—*finding standards that can be used to decide that one explanation is better than another.* We all know, for example, that as an explanation of the apparent movement of the sun across the sky, current theories of astronomy are more accurate (but less poetic) than the myth about Helios, the sun god, waking every morning and driving his fiery chariot across the sky. We would scoff at anyone who seriously believed the Helios explanation, just as any ancient Greek would have scoffed at our current theories. How we came to decide astronomy is better than mythology involves our criteria for growth: paradigms and facts.

Theories, whether in or out of our imaginary warehouse, don't exist in a vacuum. Every theory is related to at least one other theory through shared concepts or propositions. Kuhn (1962) was the first to use the term *paradigm* to describe such groups of related theories. A **paradigm** is *a logical system that encompasses theories, concepts, models, procedures, and techniques.* The earth-centered solar system, for example, was once a paradigm in physics, just as instinct was once a paradigm in psychology (McDougall, 1908). At the time McDougall was theorizing about human behavior, the predominant explanations included some notion about instinctual processes; there was an instinct for survival, one for aggression, and so on. New observations about behavior were interpreted in terms of existing instincts, and if new observations didn't fit, then new instincts were invented to account for the observations.

During a period of time in which a particular paradigm is accepted, which Kuhn referred to as a period of normal science, research is directed toward solving problems related to matching current theories with observations. At such times research tends to be directed toward refining theories, toward trying to make them better. New research and the refinements of theories add to the strength of the paradigm, which in turn leads to the perception that the paradigm, including its associated theories and procedures, is the best way to explain what goes on in the world.

Eventually, however, problems with the paradigm emerge as more and more information cannot be fit into the existing theories. I say eventually because no matter how reasonable or useful a paradigm may be, it, too, is based on inductive reasoning and thus cannot be considered to be universal truth. When enough problems emerge and an alternative paradigm, complete with its own theories and procedures, arises that fits the observations better, then the old paradigm gives way to a new one during what Kuhn calls a scientific revolution. Thus Galileo started a scientific revolution with his notion of a sun-centered solar system, although it took years before the followers of the earth-centered paradigm accepted the new paradigm. Then the new paradigm becomes *the* paradigm and the field returns again to normal science.

Underlying all of normal and revolutionary science is reliance on facts. Observations are considered to be facts when people can point to concrete examples of the observation. Although it may seem tautological to require facts to be observable, that very requirement is one of the reasons why McDougall's instinct theories eventually gave way to modern explanations of behavior: there was no way to observe—to be able to point to concrete examples of—the processes by which instincts influence behavior. Today, of course, we have some evidence for instinctual processes as one of several possible explanations for some behaviors (see, for example, Snyder, 1987), but we do not use instinct as the primary explanatory concept for all behavior.

In addition to being observable, facts must also be objective. Within a scientific approach, **objectivity** *means that an observation can be replicated—that is, observed by more than one person under a variety of different conditions.* If I am the only researcher who can demonstrate a particular effect, it is not objective. If, however, several others note the same effect under different conditions, then we have an objective observation, a fact, that needs to be incorporated into existing theories.

Thus, during normal science, theories are compared on the basis of their fit into the existing paradigm as well as their ability to account for the existing facts. During revolutionary science, comparisons occur between old and new paradigms, but the basis for such comparisons remains the existing facts. Then, upon return to normal science, theories within the current paradigm are again evaluated in terms of their fit with the facts. It is important to note, however, that because a new paradigm may redefine what is an acceptable fact, the facts may change from time to time.

How Can We Put What We Know Into Practice?

By now you may be having some serious doubts about how a scientific approach can lead anywhere but to confusion. There are no absolute truths, and sometimes what were once considered to be facts are no longer considered to be so. We have arrived at the problem of **pragmatic action**—*determining how we should go about putting a scientific approach into practice.* Essentially, those who adopt a scientific approach must get together and decide how they are going to use that approach. The solution to the problem of pragmatic action—the answer to the question of how we put what we know into practice—lies in agreement.

Just as legal theorists assume that a decision made by 12 jurors is better than a decision made by one juror, scientists agree that evidence obtained by a number of different researchers is better than evidence obtained by one researcher; that is, objective data—repeatable observations—are agreed to be better than subjective data. The greater the number of researchers who produce the same research results, the more we consider those results to be facts to which we must fit our theories. A variety of reasonable arguments support this agreement about objectivity, but no one can prove, in any absolute sense, that the consensus is correct. As Sagan suggested, it's not perfect, but it is the best we've got.

One of the problems inherent in the use of objectivity is the variety of different research methods available to study human behavior (Watson, 1967). When researchers use different methods to study the same phenomena, they often come up with different observations. Consensus, then, must extend into agreement about which research methods are appropriate for which research questions, as well as agreement about whether or not a particular method was used properly. Essentially, that's what this book and the course you are taking is all about.

For example, in the early years of research about differences between men and women, one of the more common methods was to select a group of men and a group of women, have both groups do something such as solve math problems, and then compare the performances of the two groups. If the performances of the groups were different, then the researchers concluded that the results reflected basic differences between the two sexes. More recent research, however, clearly shows that such things as the context of the situation, self-presentation strategies, researchers' and participants' beliefs about whether or not the sexes ought to be different, and a variety of other factors can change the results obtained from such methods (Deaux & Major, 1987). Therefore, the potential influence of the factors must be considered before we conclude such differences reflect basic differences between men and women.

We now know that simply comparing a group of men to a group of women is not an effective way to examine gender differences. Then again, everyone "knew" back in the "old days" that such simple comparisons were the best way to study gender differences. Even though we rely on consensus for such purposes as fitting theories to facts and even for deciding what is a fact, we must keep in mind that a new consensus might emerge after we have obtained more information. Still, there can be no scientific approach without consensus.

Why Do We Do It the Way We Do?

Every time I discuss consensus as the basis for a scientific approach, I can hear my mother saying, "Would you jump off a cliff just because everyone else is doing it?" That was her response, for example, to my wanting to stay out late because my friends' parents allowed them to stay out late; I'm sure you've heard the same response when you have tried to use similar reasoning. What we have come to, then, is the problem of **intellectual honesty**—*the individual scientist's ability to* *justify the use of science itself.* If we can never prove that theories are true, if paradigms are only temporary, and if facts and methods for gathering them may change, then why would we ever accept a scientific approach as a valid way to learn anything?

Consider a simple survey of students' attitudes about current grading practices. In order to conduct that study, we must rely on a great deal of background information. We must accept research about students' reading levels when writing the questionnaire, accept research that suggests that a survey is a reasonable way to measure attitudes, accept research concerning the best way to format the questions on the survey, accept research about which statistics to use to analyze our data, and so on. All of that research comes from within a scientific approach, and we are using that information to add more facts to the same scientific approach. Where does it all end?

The solution to the intellectual honesty problem—the answer to why we do it the way we do—can again be found in Sagan's quote at the beginning of this chapter: it's "by far the best tool we have." We do it the way we do it because we have not found a better way. Very simply, we adopt a scientific approach because we have a certain amount of faith in it because it works; or, as my grandfather used to say, "If it ain't broke, don't fix it." Note, however, that the faith is placed in the approach itself, not in any particular theory that comes from the approach.

Recall the debate between evolutionists and creationists mentioned in Chapter 1. Theistic intervention (active causation by a god, not necessarily the existence of a god) serves as an explanation for creationists because they have faith in their approach. Similarly, evolution serves as an explanation for evolutionists because scientists have faith in their approach. Neither side will be able to convince the other because they don't have any common ground of agreement; they place their intellectual honesty on two entirely different points of view. If you refuse to place your faith in a scientific approach, no amount of argument on my part will convince you to do so. On the other hand, if you can accept the limitations of a scientific approach and still remain convinced it is the best tool we have for extending our knowledge about human behavior, then we can go on to discuss some of the differences between scientific and nonscientific approaches and we can begin to deal with the rules and guidelines of scientific research. But before moving on, see Figure 2.1 for a summary of our discussion of the philosophy of science.

Science and Nonscience Compared

I keep bringing up the notion that we all conduct research all of the time. We are all, in one way or another, gathering new information to increase our knowledge about our world. Such everyday research is not necessarily scientific, but it does provide us with a way to satisfy our curiosity. In addition to the points noted above, the differences between scientific and nonscientific research generally revolve around avoiding mistakes. Mistakes can occur when we make observations, when we interpret observations, or when we accept various misconceptions about what is included in a scientific approach toward research.

The Questions	Justificationist Approach to Science	Nonjustificationist Approach to Science
The rational inference problem: When is something true?	Facts ↓ One correct theory	Facts ↓ Many incorrect theories
Criteria for growth: How can we tell which theory is better?	Better fit with paradigm and Better fit with facts	Better fit with paradigm and Better fit with facts
Pragmatic action: How can we put what we know into practice?	Consensus ↓ Correct paradigm	Consensus ↓ Better, but not correct paradigm
Intellectual honesty: Why do we do science the way we do?	Science ↓ Absolute truth	Believe science is the best way to obtain knowledge

Figure 2.1   Justificationist and nonjustificationist approaches to the four basic questions inherent in any philosophy of science

Observation

Whenever we observe something, we make errors; period, no exceptions, ever. The errors come from selecting what to observe and interpreting what we observe, as well as from the act of observation itself. We cannot avoid error entirely, but we can attempt to reduce error to a minimum and be aware of error that we have not been able to eliminate.

For example, what we decide to observe creates a form of error because it prevents us from making other observations at the same time. This is an error of omission that results simply because we cannot be in two places at the same time. That doesn't mean that what we do observe is wrong or incorrect, but rather that it is incomplete. Essentially, we need to keep in mind that what we have been observing is not all that could be observed. For example, researchers before Jacobs's (1967) study on suicide notes had concentrated mainly on suicide statistics. Durkheim's (1951) original work had led them in that direction, and that approach was certainly adding to our understanding of suicide. But suicide statistics would never have given us the kind of information that Jacobs was able to obtain from his analysis of the contents of suicide notes. The error in this example involved looking in only one place, an error that Jacobs corrected with his study.

Of course, objectivity is another way to reduce, but not eliminate, the error inherent in observation. The more people who observe the same thing, under the same or different conditions, the more accurate the observation is. Different observers, different situations, different locations, and different definitions of what to observe all contribute to the objectivity of data, and all reduce observation error. Realizing that all observation contains some amount of error is an important part of a scientific approach to research, for it prevents anyone from saying, "Your results are wrong and mine are correct." If we accept the notion that everyone's data are a little bit wrong (contain some error), then we can concentrate on trying to figure out why our observations don't agree; that is, we can begin to refine our theories so that they more closely fit the existing facts.

Logical Analysis

The quality of observations is one distinction between scientific and nonscientific research, but it is far from being the only one. Once observations are made, we must interpret them and draw conclusions about them. We have already discussed the scientific reliance on inductive reasoning, so it should come as little surprise that induction plays an important role in data interpretation.

Suppose I look out my window and observe 90° displayed on the scale of a thermometer. I could, of course, reasonably conclude that the temperature outside my office is 90°, assuming I had reason to believe that my thermometer was accurate. Anyone else could also look out the same window and note the same reading, and they would probably come to the same conclusion. Inductive reasoning enters the interpretation process when we attempt to move our conclusions beyond the immediate area outside my window. Beyond my window is the remainder of the campus, the town, the county, the state, the country, and so on. How far beyond our immediate observations we can reasonably interpret those observations is both a matter of inductive reasoning and yet another distinction between scientific and nonscientific research.

Given our general knowledge about meteorology, we could reasonably conclude that the temperature around campus and town is about 90°. I would be reluctant to speculate about temperature across the state, as would most people. The same reluctance applies to interpreting data collected in a research project: how far we generalize our results beyond our research is limited by common sense and background information about our research topic. If college students participated in a study about jury decision-making processes, I would feel comfortable generalizing the results to actual jurors by claiming actual jurors may use the same decision-making *processes* that the students used. However, I would not feel comfortable claiming that actual jurors would make the same *decisions* that the students did. The way in which students and actual jurors go about making decisions may be the same, but the decisions produced by that same process may be quite different. Overgeneralization—drawing conclusions too far beyond the scope of immediate observations—brings scientific research into the realm of nonscientific research.

Research Reports

From time to time you may find yourself reading a research article in which it appears as though the researchers designed their study to test a theory, collected data, and supported the theory discussed in the introduction of the article. You should know, and the researchers should know, that logic does not enable us to support a theory. Yet, they write such phrases as "research supports the theory of . . . " or "the theory of X has received a great deal of empirical support." In such cases the language of scientific research appears to conflict with scientific philosophy.

Keep in mind that the reason that research cannot support a theory is that "support" for a theory comes not from finding results consistent with a theory, but from failing to find results that do not fit the theory. Remember the double negative logic of science: Failing to disconfirm a theory is the only empirical way to provide support for a theory. But support for a theory does not mean the same thing as proof that a theory is correct. It's a little too verbose to continually write "a number of researchers have attempted to disconfirm theory X and have failed to do so," and so we write "theory X has received empirical support."

Most research articles create the impression that the researchers knew, from the start, exactly how the major results of the study would come out. Instead, research is often conducted with extremely little certainty about how the results will turn out. The researchers are not trying to hide their inability to accurately predict the results; rather, they are succinctly providing a theoretical context for their results. No matter how unexpected the results of research may be, they cannot contribute to what we already know unless they can be placed into a theoretical context.

For example, when I was asked by a defense attorney to consult on the *voir dire* (often called "jury selection") process in a criminal trial, I took advantage of an opportunity to interview the jurors after the trial. What I noticed from these interviews was that jurors who seemed very different on the basis of such characteristics as age and socioeconomic status also ended up on opposite sides of the hung jury resulting from the trial (Whitman & Dane, 1980). If you read the publication that resulted from those interviews, it appears as though I had a very logical theoretical framework before I conducted the interviews and that I found support for the theory in the results of my study. Not so.

I did have an initial theoretical framework before conducting the research, but it was nowhere near as logically organized as it was presented in the article. It was more like a hunch based on what I knew about jury behavior and social psychology. However, a scientific approach to research does not involve telling everyone about hunches; it involves presenting research results that help evaluate theories. So, after interpreting the results, I wrote a very logical, organized, theoretical introduction to the article so that my presentation of the research results made sense in the context of the introduction.

Definitive Studies

Although any study may satisfy someone's curiosity about a particular issue, no study ever satisfies scientific interest in an issue. That is, there is no such thing as a **definitive study**—*a research project that completely answers a question.* Because human behavior is so complex, someone will always ask, "But what if . . . ?" Such questions point out the need for additional research. Proposing that a definitive study can exist produces premature closure of activity; as Yogi Berra is supposed to have said about a baseball game, "It ain't over 'til it's over." It is, of course, difficult to argue with such logic. Within a scientific approach to research, it's not over until it's no longer possible to ask "What if?"

Although definitive studies may not exist, there are highly influential studies that set an entire research program, or series of programs, in motion. These studies have a great deal of **heuristic value**—*they stimulate additional research activity.* Milgram's (1963) research on obedience is one example of a study with high heuristic value. It not only generated a great deal of controversy concerning research ethics (see Chapter 3); it also stimulated extensive research on compliance of individuals and groups. Munsterberg's (1913) studies of the accuracy of eyewitnesses' recollections, many of which were demonstrations conducted in the classroom, were also highly heuristic. Many examples of current research on eyewitnesses can be traced to one or another of his demonstrations.

Determinism

Perhaps the most misunderstood concept in a scientific approach to research is **determinism,** *the assumption that every event has at least one discoverable cause.* As defined here, determinism means nothing more than "events do not happen by themselves." We assume that there is always a causal agent and that the agent can be discovered through a scientific approach to research. If you think about it at all, you will realize that there could not be science without determinism. The purpose of psychology, for example, is to understand the causes of human behavior; if we did not assume that every human behavior had at least one cause, then there would be no point to trying to understand the causes of human behavior.

Many people, however, incorrectly mistake determinism for **predestination,** *the assumption that events are unalterable.* Clearly, the two are not similar assumptions. Indeed, there is some notion in determinism that once we are able to discover the cause of an event, we can alter the cause and thereby alter the event. There may, of course, be theories that include the assumption of predestination, and some of those theories may be tested through scientific research, but predestination is an aspect of a specific theory and not an assumption inherent in science.

Box 2.1 contains a summary of the differences between what is and what is not included in a scientific approach to research. Although there may be many other comparisons that could be drawn, you should have enough background in philosophy of science to begin putting it into practice. Therefore, we turn our attention to doing just that by choosing a research topic.

Conducting Research

The relationship between research and theory is an extremely strong one. Research results are always placed in the context of existing theory, and existing theory provides a framework for new ideas about what to research. There is no official starting point in this relationship, but I have chosen to begin discussing how to do research with choosing a topic.

BOX 2.1

Science Is:	Science Is Not:
A way to obtain new information	An activity per se
Described by a philosophy	Defined by only one philosophy
Generalizing from facts	A way to prove theories true
Grounded in paradigms	Blind acceptance of tradition
Based on consensus	Relying on personal authority
A matter of faith	Uncritical faith
Deterministic	Predestination
The best approach we have	Refusing to search for a better approach

Choosing a Topic

The first step in doing research is to choose a topic. There are no rules for this step, but there are some general guidelines. Sources for research topics are infinite, for anything may stimulate a research question. Indeed, anyone can come up with any number of research questions, but the trick is to develop a good question—one that can be answered. Recognizing and formulating a researchable question takes a little practice and requires some understanding of research methods, but one does not have to be an expert in research methodology to begin the process. Perhaps the most important suggestion that can be made about deciding upon a research question is to limit your questions to topics that are particularly interesting to you. I can think of no more boring task than conducting research on a topic in which I have no interest.

One excellent source for information about potential research topics is the textbook from an introductory course. Page through the text until you find a section on an interesting topic. Read the section and think about questions you would like to ask the author, or think about explanations other than those offered by the author; either will provide you with a starting point. The references in the text will enable you to gather more information about the topic and the research related to it. Another good source for research topics is a research journal. Scan the table of contents until you find a topic of particular interest. Read the article to find out what issues and questions are being addressed. Again, think about questions you would like to ask the author if you had the opportunity.

In addition to textbooks and journals, take the time to ask faculty members or graduate students about their own research programs. If one or more of their interests coincide with yours, you have yet another source of information; but don't ask him or her to do your work for you. Discovering the research interests of your faculty is always a good idea, for if you want to continue conducting research, you will probably need a faculty sponsor. Even if you are not tremendously interested in research, the information you gather might help you to choose an interesting course.

Once you have developed a question, regardless of its source, you have begun the research process. The next step is to become familiar with your topic. This point may seem too obvious to bother making, but more than a few researchers have begun collecting data only to discover that they were woefully unprepared to interpret those data. If your question concerns a formal theory, read about the theory and its related research; if your question does not come directly from a formal theory, reading about issues related to your question is likely to result in some familiarity with the applicable formal theory.

Operationalization

Once you have chosen a topic and become familiar with a theory related to it, the next step is to create **operational definitions**—*concrete representations of abstract theoretical concepts.* Heat is a theoretical concept, for example, and the number of units on a thermometer is one operational definition of it. Sales (1972) operationalized one component of Marxist theory, "opium" or the reduction of stress, in terms of membership in a religious denomination. The operational definition of a concept is not the same as the concept itself, but it does represent the concept. A score on an intelligence test, for example, is not the same thing as intelligence. Campbell (1969) coined the term **definitional operationism** to refer to *the failure to recognize the difference between a theoretical concept and its operational definition.* Leahy (1980) used the phrase "myth of operationism" to label the same problem. Theoretical concepts must have operational definitions before we can do any research related to the theory, and we need to maintain the distinction between a concept and its operationalization.

When you have an operational definition of a concept, it's called a **variable**— *a measurable entity that exhibits more than one level or value.* A thermometer reading is a variable, for it is measurable and it exhibits more than one level. Similarly, Sales's use of religious denomination is a variable; it's measurable and could be either authoritarian or nonauthoritarian. Other examples of variables include a score on an intelligence test, a rating of 1 to 10 on a scale of physical attractiveness, words related to depression in suicide notes, and the presence or absence of a gun in an eyewitness situation. Variables need not be numeric, but they must vary; there must be more than one level, at least the presence or absence of some quality.

Once you have operational definitions for your theoretical concepts, it's possible to form a **hypothesis**—*a statement that describes a relationship between variables*—to be tested in your research. A hypothesis is a concrete statement of an abstract relationship described in a theory. Sales tested the hypothesis that economic hardship and religious membership is related; worsening economic conditions should be accompanied by increased membership in authoritarian, but not in nonauthoritarian, religious denominations.

You may recognize the phrase "reverse psychology," the name used to describe the attempt to induce someone to behave in a manner that is contrary to suggestion. Brehm (1966) proposed reactance theory to explain this phenomenon. Briefly, **reactance** refers to *the proposition that whenever someone's perceived freedom is threatened, the person is motivated to reassert that freedom.* The salesperson who tells you that several other people are interested in the last remaining item, for example, may be trying to threaten your freedom to purchase the item in hopes of motivating you to reassert that freedom by purchasing it immediately. When a freedom is completely eliminated, reasserting that freedom involves increasing the attractiveness of something that represents the freedom. If you need a particular journal article for a paper and cannot find it, the importance of the article increases as you search for it. If you discover that it is permanently lost, you may even decide that it is no longer possible to complete the paper.

Mazis (1975) conducted a test of reactance theory by capitalizing on a serendipitous opportunity. The Dade County (Florida) authorities outlawed the sale, possession, or use of cleaning products containing phosphates. When the law was passed, some manufacturers were prepared and were immediately able to sell their brand-name products without phosphates. Other manufacturers were less well prepared, and it was several months before their brand names reappeared on the shelves *sans* phosphates. Mazis compared people who were able to continue using their favorite brand of laundry detergent to those whose favorite brand was unavailable for several months. According to his research hypothesis, people who could no longer use their favorite brand should exhibit an increase in its perceived value, whereas those who could continue to use their favorite brand should exhibit no change in its perceived value. The results supported the hypothesis: The temporary elimination of certain brand names was accompanied by an increase in their perceived value, and manufacturers unprepared for the new law actually benefited from it by an increase in customer loyalty to their products.

For any particular theory, the number of ways in which a concept may be operationalized is limited only by the imagination of the researcher. We cannot, however, evaluate variables solely on the basis of creativity. You probably would not want your instructor to creatively operationalize your knowledge of research methods in terms of your body temperature and award the highest grades to the most feverish students. This may be a creative approach, but it's not valid. **Validity,** in general, refers to *the extent to which a claim or conclusion is based on sound logic.* There are many specific kinds of validity in research, and we will eventually discuss all of them, but the relevant validity here is **construct validity,** *the accuracy with which a variable represents a theoretical concept.* Validity, including construct validity, is assessed through consensus.

If you agree with Sales's use of authoritarian versus nonauthoritarian religious denominations as a variable representing Marx's concept of "opium," then you consider it to be a valid variable. If you agree with the logic Mazis used to represent a threatened freedom with a banned laundry detergent, then Mazis's variable is valid. The consensus of science is not merely popularity—it is based on logic derived from the theory—but it is agreement. Sometimes, however, the popularity of a particular variable leads to its misuse as an operational definition. Deutsch (1980), for example, commented that extensive use of games, particularly the Prisoner's Dilemma, as an operationalization of conflict was "mindless—being done because a convenient experimental format was readily available" (p. 63). The mere existence of a valid operational definition is not sufficient reason to use it in your research; whatever variable you end up using in your research should be based on a logical analysis of the theory related to your research question.

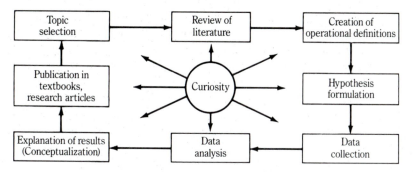

Figure 2.2 The cyclical nature of the practice of science

By the time you have an interesting research question, have found an applicable theory for your question, and have (at least temporarily) decided upon operational definitions and your research hypothesis, you have become intimately involved in the cyclical practice of science (see Figure 2.2). But before you proceed any further, it is time to consider the ethics of your proposed research. Research ethics, then, is the topic of the next chapter.

Summary

• Science is not an activity, but rather an approach to activities that share the goal of discovering knowledge. One of these activities is research.

• Like any approach, a scientific approach has limitations. These limitations include rational inference, criteria for growth, pragmatic action, and intellectual honesty.

• Rational inference limits the extent to which we can propose universal truths. Because we must rely on inductive reasoning for such proposals, we cannot prove their accuracy. Thus, we accept theories as temporarily true, while always assuming that another, better theory is likely to come along.

• Criteria for growth involves finding standards by which to judge the relative merits of explanations. Although such judgments are based on objective observations, we must be aware that the objectivity and relevance of observations are limited to the paradigm on which their relevance and objectivity are based.

• Pragmatic action revolves around methodological issues; it involves the practice of research. Consensus, based on sound reasoning, is the way we decide how best to practice research.

• Intellectual honesty refers to an individual's willingness to accept a scientific approach despite its limitations. Placing one's faith in the scientific approach, however, does not involve believing in one or another particular theory.

• It is axiomatic that all observations contain some degree of error. Objectivity—the extent to which more than one observer can make the same measurement—decreases measurement error but does not eliminate it.

• Although research reports are written so as to place research results in a theoretical context, it is often the case that the theoretical context was logically derived after the research was conducted.

• Despite the fact that a scientific approach includes the goal of comprehensively testing theories, there is no such thing as a definitive study. No study produces the final answer to a research question, in part because there is always the possibility that another theoretical context raises additional questions.

• One of the basic assumptions of a scientific approach to research is determinism—that every phenomenon has at least one discoverable cause. Although people often confuse determinism with predestination, the two concepts are entirely different. Predestination refers to the belief that events cannot be altered.

• Regardless of the point at which one begins a research project, the project is always related to one or another theory. Variables—logically derived, concrete representations of theoretical concepts—are used to form hypotheses; it is hypotheses that are directly tested in a research project.

• Construct validity refers to the extent to which a variable represents a theoretical concept. Consensus is necessary for validity, but it is possible to misuse a variable on which consensus has been achieved. Avoiding the belief that a variable is the same as the concept it represents prevents such misuse.

Research Ethics

Just as at the most primitive level, fear of the shaman's powers were matched by the claims he made, so our contemporary attitudes towards experiments of all kinds are focused on the question of power: How to attain it, how to limit it, how to hedge it about with sanctions so that it is beneficial, not detrimental to [all].

—Mead (1969, p. 369)

Overview

In this chapter you will learn about the ethical considerations of research. Ethical issues are illustrated here through discussions of controversial research projects and of the ways in which other researchers resolved ethical conflicts. You will also learn about relevant federal regulations and the code of ethical conduct published by the American Psychological Association.

Introduction

While collecting material for this chapter, I was continually reminded of Richard Nixon's infamous line, "But it would be wrong." This chapter is full of examples of controversial research practices, and the temptation to add "but it would be wrong" after each example is very strong. For most of the examples in this chapter, however, the phrase would seem as hollow and self-serving as it does in the transcripts of the White House Tapes. A few of the examples are ethically wrong, but most of them are not; then again, few of them qualify for the label "right." The nature of research ethics is such that the right/wrong dichotomy cannot easily be applied.

A Question of Balance

Behavioral scientists are strongly predisposed to ask and seek answers to questions about human behavior. Cook (1981) and others have also argued that more than being just predisposed, we are obligated to contribute to knowledge about phenomena. Indeed, Mindick (1982) cited the Talmud as one source of the argument that pursuit of knowledge is as great an obligation as are kindness and peace-keeping.

There are times when the practice of research produces conflict between the obligation to pursue knowledge and the obligation to be kind; we want to answer questions about people, and we want to treat people fairly. Such conflicts are the center of research ethics, and resolving them requires an **ethical balance;** *researchers must balance their obligations to promote intellectual freedom and contribute to knowledge with fair treatment of the very people to whom these obligations are owed and to whom the knowledge is to be distributed* (Erickson, 1967). The balancing act is rarely easy. As noted by Mead (1969), increases in knowledge often precipitate fear about how that knowledge will be used. As our knowledge about people grows, so too grow the number of ethical questions concerning the potential either to obtain more knowledge or to use the knowledge we have.

Learning From Experience

To illustrate the ethical balance required in research practice, ethical issues will be explored by discussing controversial studies. Some of the ethical conflicts were resolved by the researchers, although not necessarily to everyone's satisfaction. (Otherwise, the studies would not be controversial.) Other conflicts may have been overlooked by the researchers and recognized after the study was completed. Including these studies in this chapter is not meant to be an indictment of the researchers or their practices; instead, the intent is to provide examples of how others have dealt with conflicts. It is considerably easier on us to learn about research ethics from others' experiences instead of our own.

You may disagree with some of the points raised. I hope you do more than agree or disagree; I hope you think about the issues and discuss them with classmates and other people. Ethical balance affects us all, not only as producers and consumers of research, but as the people to whom other researchers owe their obligations.

Ethical Issues Before the Project

All of the ethical dilemmas to be discussed are related to research practice, but many of them should be resolved during the planning phase of the project. Ideally, the majority of the ethical balancing act ought to be completed before any data are collected. As with any other task, the more thorough the preparation, the more successful the outcome.

Voluntary Participation

The term **voluntary participation** refers to *the participants' rights to freely choose to subject themselves to the scrutiny inherent in research.* Anyone involved in research should be a willing participant. Sometimes, however, research practice may involve intentionally preventing people from knowing that research is being conducted. The ethical balance of voluntary participation includes two separate issues: coercion and awareness.

Coercion

The coercion issue is related to the phrase "freely choose" in the definition of voluntary participation. **Coercion** *includes using threats or force, as well as offering more incentive than what would reasonably be considered fair compensation.* It involves presenting participants an "offer they can't refuse." Incentives may be rewards, or they may be promises to prevent punishment. Sometimes coercion is rather clear, as when an administrator offers a prison inmate a "choice" between participation and solitary confinement, or when a researcher offers several hundreds of dollars to a prospective participant for a single day of participation.

At other times, coercion is not all that clear. Is it coercive, for example, to offer small amounts of money to someone who has very little money? If the prospective participant has very little money, even a small offer may limit his or her freedom of choice or ability to make a rational decision. The researcher must weigh the subjective value of the incentive (from the viewpoint of the prospective participant) against the researcher's subjective need to fulfill the obligation to pursue knowledge. That the researcher considers $5 an inconsequential amount of money is of little import; what is important is the value of $5 to the participant.

Awareness

Voluntary participation also includes awareness of being a part of a research project. Many projects, for example, involve **unobtrusive observation**—*observing others without their knowledge.* If the participant is unaware of his or her role in the project, voluntary participation is clearly not possible. Anastasi (1982) has noted that even the use of disguised items or subscales on measurement instruments may invalidate voluntary participation. Although the person is aware of completing a questionnaire, he or she may not know what is being measured by the questionnaire.

In some cases, however, the fact that people are aware that they are under observation will affect their responses in a variety of situations. Would you, for example, engage in some illicit activity if you knew your behaviors were being observed and recorded as part of a research project? This question was confronted by Humphreys (1975) in his attempt to describe the subculture known as tearoom trade—individuals who engage in brief, impersonal, homosexual encounters in public restrooms while otherwise maintaining a more traditional lifestyle. Humphreys became aware of this subculture through the pastoral counseling he conducted before becoming a graduate student in sociology. Describing and attempting to understand subcultures has long been a sociological tradition, but what made study of the tearoom trade subculture different was that the investigation was not likely to be completed through voluntary participation. Not only might the requirement of voluntary participation have made it impossible for Humphreys to collect his data, it might also have destroyed the participants' ability to maintain an otherwise traditional lifestyle.

Humphreys's problem involved how to study the tearoom trade subculture without altering it while simultaneously avoiding unethical treatment of the participants. His solution to this problem was to join the subculture without the knowledge of the other members. To do so, he adopted the role of "watchqueen," a lookout who warns the tearoom participants of the approach of someone unsympathetic to their activities. Humphreys was thereby able to study the subculture without interfering with the normal routines of its members; at the same time, his role as watchqueen did not cause the participants any concern or embarrassment, for they did not know they were part of a research project. Whether or not it is ethical to invade another's privacy in a public place, however, remains a matter of debate among those familiar with Humphreys's research.

To obtain descriptive information about the members of the subculture, Humphreys recorded a sample of car license numbers and obtained addresses through motor vehicle records. He later contacted these participants, ostensibly as a member of the survey team for an otherwise unrelated national health survey, and asked the participants to provide (voluntarily) demographic and attitudinal information. At no time, however, did Humphreys reveal that he was aware of the respondent's membership in the tearoom trade subculture.

It is not possible to present the full range of ethical issues Humphreys confronted in his research. I suggest you read the volume edited by Humphreys (1975), listed in the reference section. He believed that the sociological knowledge that could be obtained was sufficiently important to conduct the research and that the potential harm to the participants, such as exposure, was sufficient to require that he conduct the research without their awareness.

Lest you think that such dilemmas have no reality outside the academic setting, you should be aware that the resolution of ethical dilemmas can have implications beyond the practice of the research itself. Humphreys was arrested for loitering because he did not want to reveal why he was hanging around public restrooms. The chancellor of his university charged him with facilitation of felonies (the charges were dropped), attempted (unsuccessfully) to revoke his degree, and terminated both his teaching contract and his research grant. The chancellor also attempted (unsuccessfully) to have the National Institute of Mental Health delay awarding another grant to Humphreys's research advisor (Glazer, 1972).

Informed Consent

The principle of **informed consent** refers to *providing potential research participants with all of the information necessary to allow them to make a decision concerning their participation.* "Necessary" generally means any information that may

BOX 3.1 Informed Consent Form: Jury Decision Making

The purpose of this research is to determine the extent to which various factors may influence jurors' decisions in criminal trials. If the research produces useful information, it may be used by legislators, lawyers, and judges to improve the legal system. At the very least, it will provide important information about the ways in which people make decisions.

In this study, you will be asked to view a videotaped re-creation of a criminal trial and respond to a series of questions about the trial. You will be asked to role-play actual jurors, including a determination of whether you think the defendant in the trial is guilty or not guilty.

There will be no pain or discomfort involved in your participation. There is no risk to your safety. There is no direct benefit to your participation, but you may discover something about the way in which you make decisions. Also, if your instructor agrees, you may receive course credit for your participation.

The information obtained in this study will be used to prepare a research report. Any information obtained from you in connection with this study will be kept confidential and available only to the investigators. If the research report is published, your name will not be disclosed. In fact, your name will not appear on any of the data forms.

Your participation in this study is voluntary. If you decide to participate, you are free to withdraw your consent and to discontinue participation at any time.

The investigators will answer any additional questions that you may have regarding this study.

YOU ARE MAKING A DECISION WHETHER TO PARTICIPATE OR NOT TO PARTICIPATE. YOUR SIGNATURE INDICATES THAT YOU HAVE DECIDED TO PARTICIPATE HAVING READ THE INFORMATION PROVIDED ABOVE. YOU WILL BE GIVEN A COPY OF THIS CONSENT FORM TO KEEP.

_____   _____
Signature of Subject   Date

_____
Francis C. Dane, Ph.D.
Principal Investigator

---

affect the potential participant's decision. Thus, disclosure of any risk to the physical or mental health of the participant is considered necessary information, for we can reasonably expect health risks to alter a decision to participate. On the other hand, information describing the statistical analyses that will be used would probably not be considered necessary. The key element in informed consent is not the comprehensiveness of the information provided to the participant, but rather its relevance to the participant's decision (Parsons, 1969). See Box 3.1 for a sample informed consent form.

Clearly, any research project in which voluntary participation is undermined is also one in which the participants are not given the opportunity to exercise informed consent. Although the two issues are related, there are some not-too-subtle differences between them. One difference, for example, involves the *amount* of information presented to potential participants. A researcher may inform the participants about some, but not all, relevant aspects of the research procedures. Because these potential participants are unlikely to be aware that additional information is being withheld, their participation would be voluntary, but their consent would not be informed.

Participants may believe they are informed when the researcher knows otherwise. Thus, the researcher always bears the responsibility to inform participants of all relevant information (Veatch, 1982) and cannot expect potential participants to solicit such information. Sometimes this responsibility to inform participants is likely to interfere with the research project, as was the case in Humphreys's research. He believed that any information concerning the nature of his research would have negated his ability to observe the participants' behaviors. On the other hand, Humphreys did have a chance to provide the participants an opportunity to give informed consent in the second phase of his project, the data collection that was part of the health survey.

Humphreys believed that informing the participants about the nature of the tearoom project would have made it impossible to collect the demographic and attitudinal information without provoking biased responses or a refusal to respond. He also reasoned that providing information about the nature of his study after the fact—the tearoom observations were completed a year before the survey—could have produced psychological harm to the participants. Thus, Humphreys balanced his ethical considerations by providing information about the nature of the health survey but withholding information about the alternative use—the tearoom trade project—of the data. According to Humphreys, informed consent would have been more harmful than partial information.

Deception

Imagine that you have responded to an advertisement to participate in a research project. You arrive at a sophisticated laboratory to find another participant and a researcher waiting for you, and you are told the project will examine the effects of punishment on learning. After a bit of explanation, you find out that you are to play the role of a teacher, whereas your co-participant will be a learner. You are to present word lists to your compatriot and give him an electrical shock whenever he makes a mistake recalling the words. You are told the shock level you are to administer will increase with each mistake made by the learner. You are even given a sample of the shock you will be administering. The shock is not overly painful, but it definitely feels like an electric shock. Everything seems aboveboard; a little weird, maybe, but you believe that you and your compatriot have been fully informed, and he does not seem to mind the idea of receiving electrical shocks, even though he has said he has "a heart condition."

Such was the scene for Milgram's (1963) obedience experiments. Those of you familiar with this research know that the learner was a **confederate**—*someone who is apparently a research participant but is actually a member of the research team*—who did not receive any electrical shocks. Thus, Milgram engaged in **de-**

ception by *providing false information about the research project.* The deception involved presentation of inaccurate information about the purpose of the research—Milgram was studying obedience, not punishment—and the procedures of the project (no one was receiving electric shocks). Those of you familiar with the research also know that up to two-thirds of the participants complied with the experimenter's requests to "go on" and continued to increase the shock level until they administered what they believed to be electric shocks labeled Danger, Extreme Shock.

When he began his research project, Milgram was not interested in obedience per se; rather, he was conducting a pilot study in anticipation of investigating personality correlates relevant to those who were "only following orders" during the Nazi holocaust of World War II. A **pilot study** is *an abbreviated version of a research project in which the researcher practices or tests the procedures to be used in the subsequent full-scale project.* Milgram told the participants that the project involved learning because he believed that informing them of the true nature of the project would alter their reactions to the situation. Thus, he believed that deception was necessary to fulfill the obligation to collect information about human behavior.

Whether or not information about the true purpose of the project would have altered the participant's decisions to participate cannot be known. Some may have objected to the topic under study, others may have thought a fake electrical shock generator was a silly way to study the holocaust, and still others may not have given the matter any thought. The deception about the purpose of the study did, however, provide a rationale for the procedures.

Although similar deceptions have been used by a number of scientists over the years, the debate concerning the ethics of deception regarding the purpose of the research continues. After comparing the opinions of deceived participants with those who were not deceived, Smith (1981) concluded that participants are willing to accept deception when the consequences are not overly unpleasant, when they do not feel coerced into participation, and when the research seems justified by its scientific importance. Baumrind (1981), on the other hand, has argued that deception is unethical regardless of its acceptability by research participants. Baumrind's position is that deception, lying to participants, undermines their ability to make rational decisions.

The deception in the Milgram study would not seem to be related to coercion, for such deception would probably reduce, not increase, someone's inclination to participate. Being told to administer electrical shock might induce someone to refuse to participate, whereas someone who was not deceived might not object to pretending to shock someone. Milgram's procedures, however deceptive, overemphasized the unpleasantness of his study to potential participants. When Milgram asked colleagues at Yale to predict the outcome of his study (before he conducted the pilot study), everyone predicted that very few, if any, participants would agree to administer any but the most innocuous shocks. No one expected participants to experience anxiety over shocking another person because no one expected any participants to administer shocks severe enough to worry about. After Milgram began to collect his data, those expectations were quickly disconfirmed. Perhaps the majority of the controversy about Milgram's research was, and still is, related to the potential harm to the participants.

Physical Harm

A researcher cannot protect participants from all possible physical harm during a research project. The building may collapse, for example, or a session may be scheduled at a time when the pollen count is high enough to stimulate an allergic reaction. What a researcher is ethically bound to do, however, is protect participants from any physical harm that may be reasonably expected to result from the research project. The responsibility to protect participants from physical harm is weighed against the responsibility to obtain new knowledge about human behavior.

The aspect of Milgram's studies that generated the most vociferous complaints about ethical treatment was his own description of the physical symptoms experienced by the participants (Milgram, 1965). To prevent others from reaching the conclusion that his participants were cruel and sadistic, Milgram rather graphically described the range of behaviors related to the stress that accompanied their decisions to continue to "shock" the confederate. The stress was short-term and presumably produced no permanent injury to the participants, but it did constitute a form of physical injury (Baumrind, 1964). Particularly in research conducted after his initial study, Milgram resolved the ethical balancing act by determining that the amount of stress experienced by participants was not sufficient to outweigh what he considered to be his responsibility to more fully investigate obedience (Milgram, 1964).

Milgram's solution to the ethical balancing act in his research is similar to the solution of many researchers who must use animal participants. Some research involves procedures that one would never consider doing to human beings, procedures such as depriving newborns of light to study the development of the visual system, depriving young animals of social companionship in order to study social development, and so on. Protecting participants from unnecessary physical harm applies to all participants, not just humans. Of course, use of nonhuman participants also involves the issue of adequate housing and feeding. Regardless of the type of research participants involved in a study, the researcher has an ethical responsibility to balance, seriously and sincerely, the cost of physical harm with the benefits of knowledge to be gained from the procedures.

Psychological Harm

Just as we have an obligation to protect participants from physical harm, we have an obligation to protect them from psychological harm: worry, embarrassment, loss of self-esteem, failure, and so on. Such discomfort is more difficult to predict and observe than physical harm, but that does not reduce our obligation. Humphreys, for example, attempted to protect his participants from psychological (and, perhaps, physical) harm by publishing very few details about them and thereby concealing their identities. Humphreys also destroyed the list of license plate numbers used to identify his participants and conduct the health survey. Such procedures, however, did not alter that aspect of the balancing act that created the potential for psychological harm—his decision to collect data in the first place.

Milgram also attempted to protect his participants from psychological harm. First, Milgram's attempts to estimate (by surveying his colleagues) how many participants would administer "dangerous" levels of shock may be construed as an attempt to predict the amount of psychological harm to which he may have subjected the participants. After the sessions, Milgram took precautions against continued psychological harm by assuring the participants that they did not, in fact, shock the confederate. Milgram also had the confederate assure the participants that he held no ill will against them. Part of that assurance was information concerning the regularity with which other participants also administered high "shock" levels.

The responsibility to protect participants from psychological harm extends beyond attempts to rectify potential harm after the fact. To the extent possible, researchers have an obligation to protect participants before the fact by informing them of potential psychological impacts. The rather poor performance of Milgram's colleagues in predicting how many individuals would deliver high "shock" levels illustrates the difficulty of such predictions. None of Milgram's colleagues would have predicted that any of the participants would suffer a loss of self-esteem because none of them expected participants to engage in any activity that might produce such a psychological injury.

The ability to predict potential psychological harm involves being able to place yourself in the participant's frame of mind. In a study on reactions to public displays of affection, for example, Frank McPartland and I asked participants to rate the extent to which they would consider various displays of affection to be appropriate behavior in public places. We informed the participants that they would be asked to rate behaviors ranging from holding hands to sexual intercourse, and we indicated that they were free to refuse to participate if making such ratings would be offensive to them. We provided that information because we thought some participants might be offended by being asked to contemplate some of the behaviors.

What I did not realize until later—in fact, not until I began working on this chapter—is that we did not inform the participants that they would be asked to rate both heterosexual and homosexual behaviors. To the extent that some of the participants may have been offended by contemplating the propriety of homosexual intimacy, we neglected to protect them from psychological harm. After the fact, I very much doubt that such information would have affected decisions to participate, but it could have.

Self-Determination

One way or another, all of the above issues are related to the concept of **self-determination**—that *individuals have the right, and are assumed to have the ability, to evaluate information, weigh alternatives, and make decisions for themselves.* Much of the ethical balancing act involves conducting research without undermining individuals' self-determination. Preventing awareness undermines self-determination by preventing participants from knowing that a choice is available. Similarly, restricting informed consent undermines individuals' ability to evaluate information and weigh alternatives. Self-determination is also important once the research project is underway.

Ethical Issues During the Project

It is preferable to resolve all ethical dilemmas before starting a research project, but that is not always possible. Conditions during a project may change or, as in the case of Milgram's (1965) research, reactions to a procedure may differ from expectations. In this section, we consider a variety of ethical concerns that can surface after projects are underway.

Researcher's Identity

Part of a researcher's responsibility is to represent him or herself accurately. The researcher's identity and affiliations may affect someone's decision to participate and should be considered relevant to informed consent. Some people, for example, may be willing to participate in a project sponsored, by, say, Mercer University but would not be willing to participate in a project sponsored by the Ku Klux Klan.

As with other obligations, accurate representation of a researcher's identity and sponsoring organization is not always a straightforward matter. Consider, for example, some of the follow-up studies through which Milgram investigated additional influences on obedience. One possible explanation for his unexpected results was that the participants were overwhelmed by the prestige of Yale University. They may have obeyed Milgram's instructions because they believed that research conducted under the auspices of Yale must be important; they also may have believed that the administrators of Yale would not have allowed one of their scientists to conduct research in which someone could be seriously injured. To test this explanation, Milgram moved his laboratory to a rather seedy warehouse in Bridgeport, Connecticut, and did not inform the new participants that he was a member of the Yale faculty. Milgram misrepresented himself, but he could not have tested the "prestige" explanation otherwise. Maintaining a balance between obligations is even more difficult when one of those obligations—disclosure of the researcher's identity—is intimately related to the topic of research.

Behavior Changes in Participants

Although changes in behavior is part of participants' physical and mental health, it is of sufficient concern to merit its own discussion here. **Behavior change** refers to *any change in participants from which one may infer some alteration of behavioral style or capability.* Because we are obliged to maintain participants' self-determination, behavior change becomes a concern whenever the research situation affects participants' behaviors, and any but the most innocuous of observation procedures is likely to do exactly that.

Babbie (1979) described a study in which ministers in various churches distributed and collected questionnaires used to collect data. One of the ministers/research assistants read the completed questionnaires before returning them to Babbie and then used their content as the basis of hellfire-and-brimstone sermons. The minister told the congregation that they were all atheists and bound for hell. Although clearly unanticipated, the sermons may have led to some behavior changes among members of the congregation. The behavior changes were not under Babbie's direct control, but his research practices did affect the congregation, including members who had not participated in the study.

Whenever a researcher produces a setting different from the participants' normal social setting, the potential for behavior change exists. An ethical balance in research requires a distinction between behavioral changes due to the natural environment and those due to "unnatural" circumstances produced by the researcher. As you can well imagine, this distinction is not easily made.

Perhaps the most well-known example of behavior change is research conducted by Haney, Banks, and Zimbardo (1973), a study known as the Stanford prison experiment. To investigate the situational influences that might occur in prison, the researchers constructed a small prison at Stanford University. Informed, voluntary participants were assigned to be either guards or prisoners and were expected to spend two weeks playing their roles. The setting was realistic, as were the guards' uniforms and the prisoners' arrests, bookings, fingerprintings, and so forth. One of the purposes of the project was to determine whether or not college students placed in a prison setting would behave similarly to real guards and prisoners. It is difficult to imagine that anyone could have predicted the results before the project was underway.

Five of the participants who role-played prisoners had to be released due to "extreme emotional depression, crying, rage, and acute anxiety" (Haney, et al., 1973, p. 81). Symptoms appeared as early as two days into the project, when one of the prisoners developed a psychosomatic rash. The guards, who were admonished only to maintain order and to avoid assaulting the prisoners, began subjecting the prisoners to a variety of punishments for rule infractions. Blankets were taken away, buckets were substituted for traditional lavatory facilities, and the prisoners were repeatedly awakened at all hours of the night for head counts. In response the prisoners became hostile toward their guards, engaged in a variety of acts of civil disobedience, and eventually became hostile toward fellow prisoners whom they believed were responsible for the punishments inflicted by the guards. Keep in mind that before the study began, both prisoners and guards were college students very much like yourself.

As a result of the rather drastic behavior changes exhibited by the participants, the project was terminated prematurely, six days after it began instead of the scheduled two weeks. The question raised by a number of critics was whether or not the researchers waited too long to terminate the project. How long after the behavioral changes were noted should the researchers have terminated the project? Some would say immediately; others would say only after the prisoner-guard confrontations got out of hand; still others might say that the confrontations were a natural development of the environment and should have been allowed to continue until the scheduled completion of the project. The researchers' task in balancing ethical considerations was undoubtedly a difficult one, particularly in light of the value of the results for understanding behavior in prison settings.

The Stanford prison experiment also illustrates at least one other difficulty researchers encounter as part of the ethical balancing act: changes in their own behavior. Changes in the research procedures were seriously considered because it was rumored that the prisoners were contemplating an escape. Whether the contemplated escape was an act consistent with the participants' roles or was a genuine attempt to extricate themselves from what had become an uncomfortable experience cannot be known. But the researchers' effort to prevent the escape has clear implications for their attempts to maintain an ethical balance. The researchers' behaviors changed as they became involved in their roles as prison administrators, and once in those roles, it became extremely difficult to weigh calmly, rationally, and objectively the conflicting obligations to obtain knowledge about human behavior in prison settings and to respect the participants' rights to self-determination.

Considerate Treatment of Participants

The obedience and Stanford prison experiments clearly illustrate the extent to which researchers have an obligation to treat research participants considerately. Considerate treatment involves putting yourself in the participant's place. As part of the ethical balancing act, Milgram had to ask himself whether or not he would be willing to experience the stress undergone by his participants. Similarly, Haney and colleagues must have considered how they would feel in the prisoners' places while deciding to terminate their project. Of course, this sort of empathy is considerably more difficult when considering nonhuman participants. However, to the extent possible, considerate treatment requires such empathy for both human and nonhuman participants.

Few researchers ignore or intentionally decide to forgo considerate treatment before engaging in a research project. As conditions change in a study, however, researchers are obligated to continually put themselves in the participants' place and reexamine the extent to which the treatment is objectionable.

Retraction of Consent

Once an individual has volunteered to participate in a research project—regardless of whether or not the consent was fully informed—the participant maintains the right to reevaluate that decision in light of new information. Thus another ethical obligation of researchers is to allow participants to decide to quit the project at any time. This notion of retraction of consent may seem clear, but it can become clouded by a number of considerations.

The researcher may decide that his or her obligation to obtain knowledge is sufficiently strong to justify an attempt to convince a participant to continue. Another aspect of the balancing act might involve convincing participants to continue as part of the research procedure itself. Part of Milgram's procedure, for example, included telling participants who became reluctant to shock the confederate that the experiment must go on, or that procedures required them to continue. Once again, maintaining an ethical balance is particularly difficult when one of the ethical obligations is itself an aspect of the research procedure.

When a participant decides to retract consent, the retraction may well produce wasted time and effort for the researcher. If a participant quits in the middle of a lengthy, involved procedure, the time, effort, and (sometimes) money thus far invested may produce no usable data. It can be argued that such considerations ought not to be part of the ethical balancing act, but it is also certain that they will affect a researcher's willingness to try to change a participant's decision to quit. Wasted resources, although not part of the balancing act, make it considerably more difficult to consider ethical matters objectively.

Debriefing of Participants

Whenever a researcher has misled participants through omission or active deception, there is an ethical obligation to correct the participants' misperceptions. **Debriefing** is *a procedure by which any relevant information about the project that has been withheld or misrepresented is made known to participants.* Even though you believe the omission or deception was ethically justified, there is an obligation to "come clean" once the need for omission or deception no longer exists. As part of his debriefing procedure, Milgram made sure his participants learned that they did not in fact shock the confederate. Because there was no omission or deception in the Stanford prison experiment, Haney and colleagues had nothing to reveal when their study was completed.

The purpose of debriefing, however, extends beyond simply informing participants about any deception that may have occurred. In some cases comprehensive description of the research purposes may not be presented before the project begins, particularly if the purposes are not relevant to informed consent; in such cases, debriefing should include such descriptions. One purpose of debriefing is to provide participants with as much information about the project as they care to know. Particularly in an academic setting, research should be a learning experience for participants and researchers alike. Debriefing sessions are the ideal time to complete the learning experience that began with agreeing to participate.

Sometimes debriefing conflicts with another of the researcher's ethical obligations. Consider Humphreys's decision not to inform his participants after collecting the survey data. Humphreys reasoned that the potential for psychological harm caused by the debriefing was a greater concern than informing the participants about the purpose of the research. According to Humphreys, the obligation to protect the participants from harm was stronger than the obligation to debrief them. At other times, the debriefing may be uncomfortable, but not necessarily harmful, for participants and researchers. Bachrach (1981) wrote about one project in which some participants felt as though they had been duped after discovering they had received false feedback about their personalities. One of the participants refused to speak to the researcher after learning about the deception.

Debriefing involves more than simply explaining some of the information that was omitted or misrepresented. A researcher shouldn't simply state, for example, that the project is now over and this is how we fooled you. Debriefing involves explaining why the omission or deception was considered necessary and ensuring that the explanation is understood. The participant may not agree with the explanation, and there is no need to argue or try to persuade the participant that the procedure was justified, but you should make sure the participant understands the explanation. Debriefing also includes ensuring that the participant does not feel cheated by the experience.

Alleviating Harmful Aftereffects

Providing omitted or misrepresented information is not the only ethical obligation researchers have concerning participants' reactions. Researchers have an obligation both to alleviate discomfort resulting from the project and to prevent discomfort that may later arise from the experience. Preventing harmful aftereffects was the primary consideration in Humphreys's decision not to inform his participants about their participation in the tearoom trade project.

The potential for harmful aftereffects is particularly great when the conditions of the project change during the study. For example, both Milgram and Haney and colleagues were surprised by their participants' reactions. When unexpected, harmful effects occur in a research project, researchers are obligated to take special precautions to eliminate them. Milgram not only debriefed his participants; he later contacted many of them to determine whether or not they were experiencing any delayed effects from their participation. Haney and coworkers conducted follow-up examinations for an entire year to determine whether or not any of the observed behavioral changes continued beyond the encounter sessions they held after the premature termination of their prison project.

One danger to be avoided is considering other obligations less seriously as a result of believing that you can alleviate any harm after the study has been completed. Needless deception cannot be justified merely by including a debriefing session; nor can the potential for harm be minimized simply by telling participants to call you if they have any problems. Alleviating harmful aftereffects is an obligation that must be included in the ethical balancing act, but is not a reason to bias ethical considerations in favor of continuing a project when other ethical obligations require its termination.

Ethical Issues After the Project

As you may have suspected from Milgram's and Haney and colleagues' attempts to monitor their participants for a year after participation, a researcher's ethical responsibility does not end once the data have been collected. Even though researchers may never see the participants again, their responsibility to continue to treat them in an ethical manner remains.

Anonymity of Participants

When sensitive information about participants is collected, it is desirable to ensure the anonymity of the participants. **Anonymity** *exists when no one, including the researcher, can relate a participant's identity to any information pertaining to the project.* When data are collected anonymously, no one knows which data came from which participant. In studies in which only one questionnaire is completed by each participant, anonymity can be accomplished by not collecting identifying information. Frequently, researchers will also avoid maintaining any order of the completed questionnaires, thus making it impossible to identify a participant by the ordinal position of a questionnaire in the file cabinet.

In some projects, however, some form of identification is required. When the project design requires more than one data collection session and the researcher needs to relate data across sessions, participant codes are frequently used to ensure anonymity. In a study of juror orientation sessions conducted as part of the Kansas Jury Project (Dane, 1979), it was necessary to administer an attitude questionnaire to jurors before and after they served on a jury. To maintain anonymity, we developed a system of identification codes. During the first data collection session, each participant was given a business card on which an identification number was printed. The questionnaires were identified by this number only, and only the juror knew his or her number. No record of which number referred to which participant existed so that it would be impossible to determine which data came from which participant.

Confidentiality

Although it is sometimes considered to be the same as anonymity, confidentiality is different. **Confidentiality** *exists when only the researchers are aware of the participants' identities and have promised not to reveal those identities to others.* Obtaining participants' names during data collection and then destroying the record of their names upon completion of the project is one way to maintain confidentiality. Humphreys noted that he was lucky that no one asked him to reveal his list of participants' names and license plate numbers until after he destroyed it, for he probably could not have withstood a concerted effort on the part of law enforcement officials had they wanted the list before he destroyed it. (During the course of his research Humphreys was a witness to felonies under existing state law.)

Mead (1969) noted that confidentiality imposes obligations upon all researchers, regardless of the research model they adopt. Even under the anthropological model, in which individuals are considered informants or partners, researchers have an obligation to prevent negative consequences to participants as a result of their identification with the project. Monette, Sullivan, and DeJong (1986) noted that confidentiality is of particular concern in single-subject projects or those involving extensive observation. The obligation for informed consent can place the researcher in a "double bind": if the participant signs a form indicating consent, then a written record of participation exists. Although separate files for consent forms and data forms may prevent someone from relating a participant's name to specific data, some projects are sufficiently sensitive—Humphreys's tearoom trade project, for instance—that mere status as a participant may be embarrassing or dangerous.

Recompensing Control Groups

In some research projects, the researcher attempts to determine whether a new treatment, such as an educational technique, a method for problem solving, or therapy, is better than an existing one. If the new treatment does in fact turn out to be better than the old, the researcher may have an obligation to offer the new treatment to participants in the control group—the group that received the old treatment or no treatment at all.

The United States Public Health Service, for example, initiated a study investigating syphilis treatments. Although the potential for coercion in recruiting participants may also have been a problem, the controversy over this study concerns the fact that participants in the control group, who had been infected with syphilis, were not treated for the disease even after a cure had been discovered. As early as 1940, it was public knowledge that penicillin could be used to cure syphilis, but treatment was withheld from control group members well into the 1970s. This is clearly an extreme example, but it does illustrate the obligation to recompense control group members when appropriate and possible.

The ethical obligation to recompense control groups, however, also has limits. A researcher who does not know the identities of participants, for example, cannot be expected to contact and provide follow-up treatment to control group members. Similarly, even though educational research involving novel teaching techniques may lead to the discovery of an improved method of instruction, researchers cannot be expected to ask the students to repeat the class in order to benefit from the new techniques. When after-the-fact compensation is not possible, researchers have an obligation to provide control groups with adequate treatment from the start; in such studies, control groups should be given currently accepted treatment.

Data Analyses

Data analyses are not only tools we use to make sense of data collected in a research project; they are also a consideration in our ethical balancing act. Proper data analysis involves more than contributing to knowledge; it also involves treating other researchers ethically.

Other scientists use our research results as a basis for their contributions to knowledge; if our analyses are not correct, other scientists may waste time, effort, and money when relying on them. Perhaps of greater importance is that individuals who may be unfamiliar with data analysis techniques may also use our results to, for example, formulate social policies. Regardless of the purposes to which our research results may be put, we have an ethical obligation to ensure that we do not mislead anyone who may rely on them.

One study in which data analyses stimulated, and still stimulate, no small amount of controversy was Jensen's (1969a) compilation of the results of previous studies concerning the heritability of intelligence. The controversy centers on Jensen's calculation and interpretation of the **heritability index,** *an estimate of the proportion of influence that genetic factors exert upon a particular trait* (Anastasi, 1982). Jensen calculated a heritability index using data from studies that reported the correlations of intelligence-test scores for twins. By comparing correlations obtained from monozygotic (identical) twins with those from dizygotic (nonidentical) twins, Jensen arrived at the conclusion that about 80% of intelligence is due to genetic factors.

Calculating a heritability index for anything, including intelligence, is a very complicated matter. Anastasi (1982) noted that there are so many factors that may affect the correlations of scores obtained from either monozygotic or dizygotic twins that even a properly calculated heritability index may not be an adequate measure of the role of genetic factors. For example, any heritability index depends on the population from which and the environment in which the data are collected; if either the population or the environment changes, the index changes. It is inappropriate to generalize a heritability index, as Jensen did, from one population or environment to another.

Jensen himself was the victim of the unethical behavior of another researcher. Much of the data concerning the heritability of intelligence in twins was published by Sir Cyril Burt, a British psychologist. It was only after Jensen published his article that it became apparent that Burt had fabricated some of his results. Burt had also published studies with fictitious coauthors to create the appearance of replication (Hearnshaw, 1979). Years after he had committed what researchers consider an unpardonable sin, Burt's unethical behavior was still causing problems for other researchers.

Reporting Research Results

Another part of our ethical balancing act is to report our research as accurately as possible. Inaccurate reports do not contribute to knowledge; they detract from it. Ethical report writing is more involved than simply avoiding outright lies; it includes doing all you can to make sure your report is as clear as possible and contains all the information necessary for readers to understand what you have written.

The purpose of Jensen's (1969a) article was to examine the concept of intelligence in efforts related to **compensatory education—***attempting to raise the educational level of individuals whose education has been disadvantaged for one reason or another.* The article was published in the prestigious *Harvard Educational Review,* a journal read by many who were unfamiliar with the intricacies of either intelligence testing or heritability estimates. For this reason, Jensen devoted a considerable portion of his article to describing the key issues in these two areas.

A number of researchers (Anastasi, 1982; Kamin, 1974) have described some of the more controversial aspects of the manner in which Jensen presented his conclusions. For example, Jensen quoted from or summarized studies that may be used to refute his conclusions, but many of these studies were not included in his reference list. For the most part, however, criticisms of Jensen's writing deal with the material he presented and the potential audience for which he wrote.

One of the more questionable aspects of the way Jensen presented his conclusions involves his presentation of factors that limit the extent to which research on twins can be used to support his conclusions. Many of the studies Jensen cited involved comparing the correlations of intelligent-test scores of twins raised together with those of twins raised apart. The extent to which one can assume that twins raised apart actually experience different home environments is a matter of debate. Even though Jensen noted the practice of many adoption agencies to place separated twins in highly similar families, he appeared to ignore this limitation when he estimated a heritability index from studies involving the very comparisons about which he earlier cited limitations.

Jensen also noted that "all of the major heritability studies reported in the literature are based on samples of white European and North American populations, and our knowledge of the heritability of intelligence in different racial and cultural groups within these populations is nil" (1969a, p. 64). Twenty pages later, Jensen used heritability data to support the claim that genetic factors were the primary explanation of the differences in intelligence-test scores between Whites and Blacks in the United States. Jensen presumably believed that the qualifications he included in his article were adequate to prevent others from drawing the wrong conclusions from the data. Reactions to and interpretations of his article (see, for example, the "Letters" section in subsequent issues of the *Harvard Educational Review*) are indications that Jensen did not state those qualifications with sufficient clarity and emphasis.

The ethical obligations of a researcher do not end with an attempt to publish a research report. Participation in research should be a learning experience for all concerned: the researcher should learn something about the particular phenomenon under investigation, and participants should learn something about themselves. Thorough debriefing is one way to fulfill this obligation, but researchers have also distributed research reports directly to participants in order to accomplish this goal. Milgram (1964) sent a report summarizing his results to each of his participants. When using this method of informing participants, we should remember that participants may not be trained in psychology and should write the report in language that can be readily understood by the audience for which it is intended.

Although related to disseminating information to participants, the ethics of the use of research results by the public are more complex. The way in which the public uses a researcher's results is not something over which the researcher has any control. Baron's (1980) experience with the "Golden Fleece Award," discussed in Chapter 1, is but one example. Still, Warwick (1975) argued that doing research in a sensitive area engenders an obligation to avoid negative impacts on science itself. Those who do research in such areas have a special obligation to monitor the use of their research reports and to attempt to correct any misuse, whether apparently intentional or unintentional.

To some extent, every scientist has an obligation to prevent his or her research from having a negative impact on science. More than merely promoting knowledge, a scientist's obligation includes preventing others from attempting to misuse or otherwise limit that knowledge. Brazzill (1969), for example, noted that only five days after Jensen's research made headlines in Virginia newspapers, defense attorneys in a school integration suit were quoting from Jensen's article to support their claim that school systems should remain segregated. The defense attorneys and the newspaper article about Jensen's research appeared to have completely ignored the qualifications Jensen included in his article. Jensen, fulfilling his ethical obligation, wrote a letter to the editor in response to the misapplication of his results.

It is, of course, not possible for any researcher to ensure that no one will ever misuse his or her results or conclusions. However, it can be argued that all researchers have an obligation to attempt to correct misuse of any research, not just their own. Essentially, we all have an obligation to promote knowledge, regardless of the source of that knowledge.

Part of the obligation to promote knowledge includes an obligation to make one's writing as clear as possible. Clear writing makes it less likely that someone will unintentionally misinterpret results and conclusions. Clear writing also makes it more likely that someone's intentional misuse of information will be noticed by others and corrected. Disclaimers such as those offered by Jensen (1969b) in response to his critics might better be placed in the original publication, but it is always easier to second-guess someone else's writing than to edit our own. To whatever extent we are capable, each of us has an ethical obligation to make our writing as clear and as accurate as possible.

Formal Ethical Guidelines

The research problems discussed above provide an overview of ethical concerns with which most of us must deal when conducting research. A considerable number of formal guidelines concerning the ethical practice of research also exist, including legislation dealing with researcher practices and codes of ethical conduct published by professional societies.

Legislation

The horrors that Nazi torturers inflicted upon concentration camp inmates in the name of research led to some of the earliest legislation concerning scientific research. This legislation, the Nuremberg Code of 1947, was primarily directed toward medical research. An abbreviated version of the code appears in Box 3.2.

In the United States, breaches of research ethics, again primarily in biomedical research, led to the passage of the 1974 National Research Act. The act included creation of the National Commission for the Protection of Human Subjects of Biomedical and Behavioral Research (Seiler & Murtha, 1981), the purpose of which was to recommend an overall policy for research with human participants. The commission provided a report that led to a number of changes in the ways in which biomedical and behavioral research is conducted.

BOX 3.2   The Nuremberg Code

1. The voluntary consent of the human subject is absolutely essential.
2. The experiment should be such as to yield fruitful results for the good of society, unprocurable by other methods or means of study, and not random or unnecessary in nature.
3. The experiment should be so designed and based on [previous research] that the anticipated results will justify performance of the experiment.
4. The experiment should be so conducted as to avoid all unnecessary physical and mental suffering and injury.
5. No experiment should be conducted where there is an a priori reason to believe that death or disabling injury will occur; except, perhaps, in those experiments where the experimental physicians also serve as subjects.
6. The degree of risk to be taken should never exceed that determined by the humanitarian importance of the problem to be solved by the experiment.
7. Proper preparations should be made and adequate facilities provided to protect the experimental subject against even remote possibilities of injury, disability, or death.
8. The experiment should be conducted only by scientifically qualified persons.
9. During the course of the experiment the human subject should be at liberty to bring the experiment to an end.
10. During the course of the experiment the scientist in charge must be prepared to terminate the experiment if . . . continuation of the experiment is likely to result in injury, disability, or death of the experimental subject.

One of the major changes involved the identification of the Department of Health, Education, and Welfare, currently called the Department of Health and Human Services (HHS), as the agency responsible for formulating and administering federal regulations concerning research involving human subjects. HHS proposed a set of regulations governing all those who received federal funds for such research. These regulations, the 1974 interim regulations, were preliminary and would be revised after a trial period. Among other things, the interim regulations required the establishment of an Institutional Review Board (IRB), whose function was to examine and approve all research conducted at any institution receiving federal funds. Because most institutions at which research is conducted were receiving (or hoped to receive) federal funds, the regulations affected almost everyone engaged in any type of research.

The regulations also recommended that all research, federally funded or not, should be subject to some sort of prior review. In principle, prior review for all research should have been relatively easily accomplished, and most institutions complied with this recommendation. After all, the IRBs existed to review funded research, and it seemed simple enough to have the IRBs review unfunded research as well. It soon became apparent, however, that reviewing all research proposals was a very heavy burden for workers on IRBs; prior review was becoming a paperwork nightmare.

One of the reasons for the nightmare was the sheer volume of research proposals that required processing. All research conducted at a university, for example, includes research with any methodology conducted by faculty members, administrative staff, or graduate and undergraduate students, as well as contract research. Under the interim regulations (1974–1981), even research you might conduct as part of a classroom exercise may have to be reviewed by an IRB at your campus. Members of IRBs were very reluctant to grant exceptions to prior review, and sometimes they appeared to have lost sight of the ethical balance concerning research. Seiler and Murtha (1981), for example, reported that one IRB required researchers to obtain written, informed consent from all members of one Native American tribe under study, whereas another IRB required researchers to obtain written, informed consent from all living descendants of an historical figure whose archives were to be examined.

Finally, in 1981, HHS announced the creation of the final regulations concerning research involving human subjects (*Federal Register,* 1981). For the most part, the final regulations were not very different from the interim regulations, although the final regulations include a number of exceptions to prior review that primarily affect psychologists and other social scientists. The final regulations require prior review by an IRB only for research funded by HHS. Also exempted from prior review, even if funded by HHS, is any research consisting of surveys, interviews, and observational studies in which the identity of the participants is not known or in which the risk of harm is minimal. There are also exceptions for research on public figures or public documents. One exception that made life on university campuses a great deal easier was the exception for educational research conducted on instructional practices. Research projects you and your classmates might conduct on each other in order to practice your research skills need not be submitted for prior review, unless your instructor is planning to have you conduct studies involving more than minimal risk.

The above summary is certainly not adequate to complete your understanding of the rather complex regulations about research involving human participants. The requirements for research involving animal subjects are even more complex, for they also include very detailed requirements concerning housing and feeding of animals. In addition to the official publication of regulations in the *Federal Register,* a number of other sources provide additional information. Perhaps the best source for information about research involving human participants is the newsletter of the Hastings Center, *IRB: A Review of Human Subjects Research.* Although the majority of articles and letters pertain to biomedical research, it contains a great deal of information about behavioral research. Other sources include the case studies on ethical practices published in the *American Psychologist* and the occasional articles in virtually every newsletter published by any professional society whose membership includes a sizable proportion of researchers.

Locally, the best source of information about HHS regulations is your own IRB. Your instructor should know who the members of the IRB are, or at least know who the contact person is. Some campuses also maintain an ethics board or panel. An ethics board is different from an IRB in that the purpose of an ethics board is not to approve research proposals but to raise and discuss with the researcher ethical issues pertinent to the project. As you undoubtedly noticed while reading this chapter, it is sometimes easier for someone outside a research project to point out areas of ethical concern.

Despite the existence of an IRB or ethics board, the responsibility for the ethical balance of a particular research project remains with the researcher. As is apparent from the projects we've discussed thus far, what one researcher considers ethical is not always considered ethical by another researcher. Each researcher must seek his or her own ethical balance. Approval from an IRB or consensus from an ethics board does not constitute ethical absolution; whether formal or informal, such approval is only advice. No one else can resolve ethical dilemmas for you.

Codes of Ethics

The advice we receive from IRBs and ethics boards is helpful, but it is not the only source of advice available to behavioral scientists. Virtually every organization of research professionals has established a code of ethical conduct. Membership in each of these organizations invariably constitutes acceptance of its code. More important, professional codes of conduct provide preliminary guidelines for anyone concerned with ethical research. An excerpt of the code of research ethics of the American Psychological Association (APA), published in 1981, appears in Box 3.3. If you compare the Nuremberg code to that of the APA, you will realize that they are essentially the same. Although the Nuremberg code contains more detail about physical harm and the APA code covers psychological harm and confidentiality in greater detail, such differences reflect the different types of research, biomedical versus behavioral, covered by the codes.

Although organizations may have slightly different wording for explicit ethical principles concerning the practice of research, each code includes the principle that the individual researcher is responsible for ethical research practices. Whether or not one believes it is possible to legislate morality, it is clearly very difficult to enforce ethical behavior. As John Stuart Mill (1806–1873) so appropriately wrote (1965, p. 253), "It is not the fault of any creed, but of the complicated nature of human affairs, that rules of conduct cannot be so framed as to require no exceptions, and that hardly any kind of action can safely be laid down as either always obligatory or always condemnable."

In the final analysis, the individual researcher is responsible for ethical research practices. As scientists, we offer advice to and seek advice from other scientists concerning research ethics, but we must engage in the ethical balancing act ourselves. Just as we expect others to fulfill their obligations to us, others look to us to fulfill our obligations to them.

Summary

• Conducting research ethically can best be described as a balancing act. Researchers must balance their general obligation to promote knowledge with the general obligation to treat others fairly. These obligations exist before, during, and after the actual research project.

• Research participants have the right to voluntary participation (which includes a lack of coercion), the right to be aware that they are participating, and

BOX 3.3 American Psychological Association
Research with Human Participants

a. In planning a study, the investigator has the responsibility to make careful evaluation of its ethical acceptability.

b. Considering whether a participant in a planned study will be a "subject at risk" or a "subject at minimal risk" . . . is of primary ethical concern to the investigator.

c. The investigator always retains the responsibility for ensuring ethical practice in research.

d. Except in minimal risk research, the investigator establishes a clear and fair agreement with research participants, prior to their participation, that clarifies the obligations and responsibilities of each.

e. Methodological requirements of a study may make the use of concealment or deception necessary. Before conducting such a study, the investigator has a special responsibility to (i) determine whether the use of such techniques is justified . . . (ii) determine whether alternative procedures are available . . . and (iii) ensure that the participants are provided with sufficient explanation as soon as possible.

f. The investigator respects the individual's freedom to decline to participate or to withdraw from the research at any time.

g. The investigator protects the participant from physical and mental discomfort, harm, and danger that may arise from research procedures.

h. After the data are collected, the investigator provides the participant with information about the nature of the study and attempts to remove any misconceptions that may have arisen.

i. Where research procedures result in undesirable consequences for the individual participant, the investigator has the responsibility to detect and remove or correct the consequences, including long-term effects.

j. Information obtained about a research participant during the course of an investigation is confidential unless otherwise agreed upon in advance.

the right to information that may affect their decision to participate. Participants also have the right to be protected from physical and psychological harm.

• Unobtrusive observation of, withholding information from, or active deception of research participants may be ethical research practices only to the extent that the knowledge to be obtained from the research outweighs the consideration of participants' voluntary participation. Preventing physical or mental harm may be other justifications for limiting participants' opportunity to provide informed consent.

• Researchers have a responsibility to accurately represent themselves and their sponsors. Because most research involves situations in which behavior change is highly likely, researchers have an obligation to ensure that such changes do not restrict participants' rights to self-determination.

• Considerate treatment of research participants includes the researcher's obligation to protect the participants' right to retract consent at any stage of the project. Considerate treatment also includes comprehensive debriefing at the conclusion of research procedures. Debriefing includes presentation of omitted information, clarification of deceptive information, and a full explanation of the purposes of the research.

• Should participants experience any harmful effects as a result of the research, whether or not such effects were foreseen by the researcher, the researcher has an obligation to make every possible attempt to alleviate such harmful aftereffects.

• Researchers have an obligation to protect the anonymity or confidentiality of research participants, particularly when the topic of research is sensitive.

• When research involves testing new treatments and the results indicate that the new treatments are beneficial, researchers may have an obligation to make the new treatments available to participants who were denied treatment as a result of the research procedures.

• Researchers have an obligation to ensure that data analyses are both appropriate for the data collected and accurately completed and reported. Reports of research should be written as clearly as possible, and particular care should be taken to make readers aware of any qualifications or limitations that apply to the conclusions reached. The obligation to report the results of research includes, at a minimum, providing participants with information about the outcome of the research.

• Beginning with the 1947 Nuremberg Code, federal legislation concerning the ethical practice of research has been implemented and changed, mainly in response to apparent violations of ethical research practices. Together with codes of ethical conduct adopted by professional organizations, they serve as guidelines for researchers. Institutional review boards and ethics boards also provide guidance for researchers. It is the individual researcher, however, who is ultimately responsible for the ethical treatment of research participants and consumers.

CHAPTER FOUR

Literature Review

*The known is finite, the unknown infinite; in-
tellectually we stand upon an islet in the midst
of an illimitable ocean of inexplicability. Our business . . . is to reclaim a little more land.*

—T. H. Huxley (Sagan, 1980, p. 3)

Overview

The purpose of this chapter is to acquaint you with the techniques involved in
reviewing research literature related to your project. You will learn why beginning
a literature review before collecting any data will help you avoid unnecessary duplication of research and errors others may have made in their research projects.
You will also learn about searching for particular journals or books and using indexing or abstracting services in your search. Finally, you will learn how to organize the search process and the introduction of your research report.

Introduction

Every time I announce to a new class that I expect each of them to complete a
literature review as part of their research project, the same question is raised:
"How many articles must be included?" It is a legitimate question. Unfortunately,
the only legitimate answer is "As many as necessary." Quite expectedly, this answer is not very satisfying; pointing out that reviewing the literature is a process
that continues throughout a research project makes the answer no more satisfying
but somewhat more understandable. Reviewing the literature related to your re-

search project is best begun shortly after you develop the research idea. A number of advantages accrue from beginning the literature review as early as possible, not the least of which is the potential for finding information about how to implement your idea.

A great deal of information exists about most behavioral phenomena. Conducting a high-quality research project involves being aware of as much of that information as possible. In the best of all possible worlds, we would become familiar with all existing information about a phenomenon before doing any research on it. Such comprehensive knowledge is not practical, nor is it the primary purpose of a literature review. A good literature review should accomplish three main goals: obtaining a scientific perspective, avoiding duplication of effort, and avoiding conceptual and procedural problems.

Goals of a Literature Review

The first goal of a literature review is to place the current research project into a scientific perspective. As we noted in Chapter 2, science involves the accumulation of knowledge. As Huxley suggested, we try to claim a little more land from the ocean of inexplicability without losing ground already gained. Existing research and theory—the current literature—enable you to determine how your project adds to the current knowledge base. As a writer of research reports, your grasp of the literature will also enable you to introduce your project so that others can discover its worth as an addition to the body of knowledge.

Just as you would not want to enroll in an advanced course without completing at least some of the prerequisite courses, it is unwise to engage in research without being aware of others' research on, as well as the formal and informal theories relevant to, the phenomenon in which you are interested. Similarly, readers would have a difficult time understanding your research report without having some idea about why you think your research is important. Placing your research into perspective relative to what is already known avoids that difficulty.

The second goal of a literature review is to avoid duplication of effort—conducting the same old investigations without making them better. Replicating research is important, for replications establish the reliability of research results, but at some point we must be willing to say "enough is enough." Once researchers no longer provide new information about a well-researched phenomenon, we assume it to be reliable and should seek new efforts directed toward not-so-well-established phenomena. Different ways to operationalize the phenomenon or different applications are not considered to be the "same old thing." If you are aware of what others have done in their research, you can avoid duplication of effort.

The third goal of a literature review is even more pragmatic. A literature review can be used to avoid or solve problems others have encountered in their research. Undoubtedly, other researchers will have done something relevant to your research idea, and their work may give you clues for avoiding some of the pitfalls of research, which may be related to operationalizing the theoretical concepts, developing reliable and valid measurement instruments, or determining appropriate statistical analyses. If you use existing literature to identify the problems encountered by others, you are better able to avoid many of those same problems.

Deciding Which Information Is Relevant to Your Project

Regardless of the phenomenon you decide to investigate, others will have been there before. Some may have only mentioned an idea in passing, others may have proposed a theory, and still others may have collected data. I tend to get anxious when it appears that no one has written anything about a topic in which I am interested, for this probably means that I have not looked very hard for material or that I am looking in the wrong places. That others have been there before you does not reflect a lack of creativity on your part; it's just that there is an over-whelming amount of information about human behavior. The problem is not the existence of information, but deciding which information is relevant to your project.

Information Concerning Theory

The most obvious type of relatedness involves theory. As we noted in Chapter 2, all research stems from some sort of theory; explicit or implicit though it may be, theory is always present. For example, I am interested in how jurors make decisions in criminal trials. One of my implicit theories is that jurors rarely need to be convinced that the defendant is guilty. If any persuasion goes on during a trial, my implicit theory predicts that the persuasion entails convincing jurors that the defendant is *not* guilty; the prosecution attempts to prevent such persuasion. Re-lated to this interest are formal theories about decision making in general, as well as theories on persuasion, first-impression formation, and a number of other processes.

Whatever informal theory you may hold about your research idea, it will be related to at least one formal theory, and formal theories are the best way to start your literature review. Determining which formal theory, or theories is related to your idea may require in-depth thought about your idea, and such thinking often helps to clarify your interests. Of course, if your research interest is derived di-rectly from a formal theory, you're already on your way in your literature review.

Information Concerning Methods

One of the more common errors I've noticed is the tendency to think that previ-ous research is not related to one's project unless the other researchers used the same research method. This is simply incorrect. The phenomenon you are inves-tigating is usually more important than any particular method used to investigate it. If others have done some research on the phenomenon in which you're inter-ested, chances are that research is related to yours. In research on jury decisions, for example, some researchers interview jurors after the trial is completed, whereas others create simulated trials and ask participants to make decisions as though they were actual jurors. Both research methods may yield results related to my implicit theory.

Sometimes others' work is related to yours even if they did not investigate the same phenomenon. For example, research on how business leaders make de-cisions about investing company profits may have some relation to how jury members make decisions. As you progress through your career in research, you will discover an increasing number of ways to implement any given research idea. Some of these methods are standard; some are not. If you think a method not typically used by others fits your interests, you may want to collect some information about the method. You would then be able to use that information to explain and justify your choice of that method for your research. One way to view this text, for example, is as a general literature review of research methodology. As you delve deeper into your own research, you will undoubtedly need to go beyond this text and read some of the original material cited here.

Information Concerning Data Analysis

If you've already taken a course in statistics, you know that there are several different ways to analyze any set of data. (If not, you'll have to take my word for it.) Most of the statistical analyses you will use are like research methods, fairly standard. For such statistical analyses, you don't need to conduct a thorough literature review. As you read empirical and theoretical articles, however, it helps to pay attention to the types of analyses others have used. Some of these may involve relatively novel ways of dealing with data, and you may want to learn more about them. At the very least, paying attention to the analyses used by others will provide hints about how to analyze your own data.

Avoid at all costs the position of having collected data without any plans for their analysis. As you read about research related to your interest and encounter references to articles that concern data analysis, at least skim the referenced articles. If the articles don't seem to make a great deal of sense, consider this a warning sign. If you don't understand a statistical technique, don't use it until you do understand it. This doesn't mean that all of your research should be limited to whatever statistics you currently understand, but rather that you may need to review some statistical literature before deciding which analyses are appropriate for your study.

Now that you've begun deciding which information is relevant to your project (see Figure 4.1), it's time to turn to examining the sources of information available to you.

Finding Sources of Information

Knowing that an abundance of information exists is not enough. Before you can determine whether or not specific information is related to your research topic, you need to be able to examine that information. In this section, we'll examine how to find sources.

Published Sources

Some of the best, as well as some of the most overlooked, sources for literature are introductory textbooks. They contain a great deal of information, some of

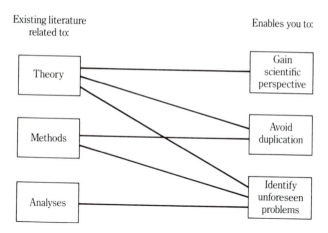

Existing literature
related to:

Enables you to:

Theory

Methods

Analyses

Gain
scientific
perspective

Avoid
duplication

Identify
unforeseen
problems

Figure 4.1   The relationships among the body of literature
and the goals of a literature review

which you may have forgotten since you last took that course, and the good ones
have several pages of references. Granted, the information is usually discussed at
a superficial—introductory—level, but there's usually enough information to decide whether or not a particular theory or empirical study is related to your research idea. Once you have identified relevant information, you can use a text's
reference section to determine where to find the original article or book.

Other good sources for published material are general content journals, such
as *Behavioral Science, Psychological Bulletin,* or *Psychological Review.* These journals include material on a variety of theories and research topics, and they usually
include a combination of theoretical and empirical articles. If you page through
these journals, you are likely to find a fair amount of information related to your
research idea. You can also peruse somewhat more specialized journals, such as
Journal of Personality and Social Psychology, Journal of Social Issues, and *Law and
Human Behavior.* Your library maintains a list, probably a computer printout, of
the periodicals it holds. The list will provide the call numbers that enable you to
locate current and back issues.

Journals are not the only sources for relevant literature, although they are
likely to be the major sources. Every year, Annual Review, Inc. publishes a series
of volumes, entitled *Annual Review of . . . ,* for most of the major disciplines dealing with human behavior. Other review series, often titled *Advances in . . . ,* can
be found by perusing the card catalog, or its computer equivalent, in your library.

Card catalogs are also useful for locating professional and trade books on specific topics. Some of these books present new theories, and others may be edited
volumes that review a variety of different but related research programs. You
might also want to locate and peruse Sheehy's (1976) *A Guide to Reference Books,*
which contains a list of reference volumes on almost any subject you can imagine.
Don't let the 1976 copyright date deter you from using it; annual supplements
keep it current.

Finally, the bookshelves of willing faculty and graduate students may be one of the best starting points for your search. When you ask them for potential sources on a topic, be as specific as you can. For example, I wouldn't know what to suggest to someone who wanted information about the general topic of jury decisions; there are too many places to begin. You need to have given your research idea some thought and narrowed the topic before someone else can provide useful suggestions.

Skimming through new issues of journals or annual series is one way to develop your research idea and find information related to it. Indeed, you have probably taken enough courses to have a good idea about which journals or series are likely prospects for perusal. Let's move on, then, to some very specific tactics for tracking down information you have decided you need.

Key Topics

One of the best tactics for locating relevant literature is searching for specific topics. Once again, textbooks are a great starting point: a glance at the table of contents and the index will let you know whether or not there's anything in the book that is relevant to your research.

When you know some of the key topics relevant to your research idea, there are even faster methods for locating related literature. You are probably familiar with a few indexing or abstracting services, such as the *Reader's Guide to Periodical Literature*. The *Reader's Guide* is organized by topics, under which can be found citations for published articles dealing with each topic. However, it covers a wide range of topics, and the articles contained in it reflect such general coverage. You will need to deal with more specific indexes.

In 1964, the United States Office of Education established the Educational Resource Information Center (ERIC), which is currently maintained by the National Institute of Education. ERIC is an indexing and abstracting service, available in most libraries through a computer link, that deals specifically with research on educational topics. Although originally established to reference only educational topics, ERIC now indexes an increasingly wider range of topics related to human behavior. With a little creative use of synonyms for topics of interest, you should have little difficulty using it. It's best to consult the reference librarian for the best way to use ERIC because each library's link involves a number of local options.

Perhaps the most appropriate indexing and abstracting service for behavioral research is *Psychological Abstracts*. Published monthly and accumulated in annual volumes, *Psychological Abstracts* includes both a topical index for locating references and an abstract for each reference. The topical index includes key words followed by a list of numbers that are used to locate the abstracts in the back half of each issue. In addition to an abstract, each entry contains a complete reference for the article, which enables you to locate the original article if, on the basis of the abstract, you decide it's relevant to your research. As with most indexes, the key-word listings in *Psychological Abstracts* are limited; you'll need a little creativity to comprehensively search for abstracts related to your research project.

Another extremely useful index is the *Social Science Citation Index* (SSCI). The SSCI is organized into four separate sections, but the Permuterm Subject Index is the most useful for finding material related to key topics. The Permuterm Subject Index is a listing of key topics, under which you will find references for articles dealing with the topic published during the year. The limitation of the Permuterm Subject Index is that entries are dependent on article titles; an article will be listed under a topic only if the author(s) happened to have included the key term in the article's title. Again, creativity is the solution to this potential problem.

The indexes and abstracts described above are the main ones you are likely to find useful, but they're certainly not the only ones that might be useful. Some libraries maintain their own computerized indexes for both general and specific topics. It's not possible for me to describe, or even list, all of the available indexes, nor would it do much good for me to try to guess which, in print or on computer, your library might have. The easiest way to find out what's available to you is to talk to one of the reference librarians.

I've not provided very many details about how to use any of the indexes or abstracts because it's much better to either find out for yourself or learn from a person rather than a textbook. Local options vary so much on most computerized indexes, even if it's officially the same index, that my telling you about how my library's index works could be a waste of time. It is worth your effort to get the information from your local reference librarian. I've been assured that most reference librarians really do enjoy showing people how to use the services they offer. One reference librarian likened it to showing off one's favorite toys; another said that reference librarians enjoy talking about their reference services almost as much as psychologists enjoy talking about their research—now that's enjoyment.

Key Authors

In almost all but the newest areas of research, there are likely to be key researchers—people whose names are known and who do a great deal of writing in the field. Milgram is a key researcher in obedience, Baron in aggression, Jensen in intelligence, and so on. If you have exhausted your key topics or cannot think of any key topics, one way to continue your literature search is by examining the work of key authors. You may discover key authors from perusing textbooks or general journals, or by reading whatever material you were able to discover through a key topic search.

Chances are, however, that the research of key authors will be "dated," just as the research by Milgram, Baron, or Jensen is relatively old by research standards. You may have to go back several years in a journal before noticing the regular appearance of any individual. After you have a key author's name, however, you can use the index issue of more recent journals to determine whether or not the author has published in that journal for the volume(s) included in the index issue. The index issue is usually the last issue in a given volume or the last issue of the calendar year.

Of course, the farther back in time you have to go to find a key author, the more likely it is that the author is no longer researching in the topic in which you're interested. Milgram, for example, is no longer alive, and so is obviously not currently publishing on the topic of obedience. Even if one or more of your key authors is no longer publishing on your topic, pursuing a particular author may lead you to a key study.

Key Studies

Sooner or later in your search you will find an article that seems perfectly related to your research idea—a key article. Once you've found them, key articles are one of the most effective bases for a comprehensive literature search. The reference section of the key study will list relevant research reports published before that study was published. Consulting those references provides the means for discovering related research in the relative past.

Key articles are a great find, but I can imagine you asking "What if my key article is ten years old?" I'm glad you asked that question. The Citation Index portion of the *Social Science Citation Index* provides the answer. Like the other portions of the SSCI, the Citation Index is published quarterly and collected in annual volumes, and it allows you to find related articles published after your key article.

The Citation Index consists of a list of key articles arranged alphabetically by the first author's last name. The publication dates of the key articles vary and are not limited to the date of the volume in which you happen to be looking. Under each key article entry is a list of additional articles, all of which are published in the same year as the Citation Index volume. Each of the articles listed under a key article have included the key article in the reference section or in a footnote. Because the author(s) of the listed article included the key article in its references, you are almost guaranteed that the listed article is in some way related to your key article. By locating and reading the articles listed under one or more of your key articles, and by systematically tracking down those articles in the Citation Index, you can very quickly bring yourself up to date on research related to your idea, even if the initial key article you used was 20 years old.

Unpublished Studies

Not all of the empirical and theoretical work related to your research idea can be found in published sources. One reason is that books and journals are subject to a publication lag. The author obviously wrote the material before it was published and collected the data before the article was written. And even after an article or book is accepted for publication, it will not appear in print for at least four months, and sometimes it may take as long as two years to appear in print. Thus there will always be research more recent than that contained in any given published article. Unfortunately, as a beginner in research you will have to accept this limitation; checking the most recent issues of appropriate journals is about as current as you can get. After you have been conducting research for a while, you will become

BOX 4.1   A Summary of Citation Indexes

Reader's Guide to Periodical Literature
 Broadest possible range of topics and widest range of entries; contains more general summary articles on topics than empirical or theoretical articles; contains citations but not abstracts
Educational Resource Information Center (ERIC)
 Topics generally limited to educational issues; entries typically not published but available from National Institute of Education; contains citations and abstracts
Psychological Abstracts
 Most directly related to behavioral research and theory; entries published in generally available journals; contains both citations and brief abstracts
Social Science Citation Index, Permuterm Index
 Topics within social science in general; entries limited to articles that include key term in title; contains citations but not abstracts
Social Science Citation Index, Citation Index
 Entries are articles that have included key article in reference list or footnotes; contains citations but not abstracts

acquainted with others who do research in the same field. Talking to your professional colleagues is about the only way to find out about the very latest research.

Some of the references you obtain in your search will be found in either *Dissertation Abstracts International* or *Masters International.* These publications contain abstracts of doctoral dissertations and masters theses, respectively, and have indexes through which you can find dissertations and theses related to various topics. In both publications, however, the abstracts are very short, about 300 words, and you will have to write to University Microfilms to get a copy of the entire research report. Before writing, however, check with faculty and graduate students; they may already have a copy and may be willing to loan it to you.

Organizing the Literature: Parting the Sea of References

Finding sources is not the end of the literature review process. You must still extract information from those sources. You may want to make a photocopy of very important reports, but you will generally have to rely on note-taking for the majority of sources. You have taken many notes in your college career, so there's no point in rambling on about how to take notes. Perhaps the best advice I can give you—and the only advice I'll offer here—is get it all the first time. It's extremely frustrating to have to make an additional trip only because you forgot to write down something you were sure you would remember but didn't.

Depending on which stage of your project you are working on, different types of material will be differentially important. Early in the project, information about theory, design, operationalization, and similar matters will be most important. Do not, however, neglect the rest of the information in any given article. Read the entire article; you never know when material you may not be interested in at that time will be useful at some other point in your project.

Very often, after you have begun finding material related to your research idea, you quickly find yourself adrift in a sea of research reports. The list of things to read next keeps growing, and it's difficult to organize all that you have. I have found it most useful to arrange the material on a continuum from specific to general; that is, first read reports that appear to be related to the specific procedures you intend to use, read material related to your working hypotheses next, read material on theory after that, and so on.

If you organize your reading from specific to general, you will acquire the information you need to get started on design implementation and data collection as quickly as possible. Even though you begin your literature review before designing your study, you don't have to complete the entire review before designing and implementing data collection procedures. The specific-to-general organization will also be helpful if you have a deadline for completing the project because searching for and reading specific material usually takes more time and is more difficult than searching for and reading general material. If you do the more difficult and time-consuming work first, you may not feel as much pressure as your deadline approaches.

Writing a Literature Review

Depending on how much you enjoy writing and the specific requirements of your instructor, you may wish to begin writing the introduction of your research report before or during the data collection phase of your project. Although report writing is covered comprehensively in Chapter 12, I'll briefly describe here how to write an introduction. I'll let you know immediately, however, that you will very likely need to do some major rewriting after you have completed your data analyses and interpretation.

The most important aspect of the introduction is its organization; from general to specific topics. The content of the introduction should resemble an inverted triangle or the top half of an hourglass; it should begin by placing your particular project into the broadest possible context. It's best to start with a general example of the phenomenon about which you are conducting the research. The remainder of the introduction leads the reader from that general example to the specifics concerning your project.

After the general example, present the available information concerning the theory related to your project; next comes research related to the theory, followed by research directly tied to your hypotheses. Finally, the introduction should provide a hint as to what comes next in the article—the specific methods you used to test your hypotheses.

If you organize the introduction properly, it will serve a purpose analogous to taking your readers by the hand and leading them along a path that begins with a general phenomenon and ends at your specific research procedures. That path should be only as long as necessary to get from the beginning to the end and as straight as possible. You also need to have a concrete notion about who your audience is. Your course instructor may have some specific requirements, but generally research reports are written for other researchers. You don't need to try to impress them with your knowledge of jargon, but you can assume that your audience will understand at least some of the few technical terms you might have to use.

At this point in your research career, the best audience for your report may be your classmates. You should have at least one of them read your introduction, and in turn, you should be willing to read at least one of their introductions. If a classmate understands your report, you are probably on the right path. When reading others' introductions, keep in mind that the purpose is constructive criticism. Simply telling someone that their writing is "very good" or "very bad" tells them nothing; tell them which parts are confusing and which parts are clear, and let them know exactly what you liked and disliked, and why.

When someone else is giving you feedback about your own writing, remember that you asked them to do so. More important, remember that the reader is always right: no matter how brilliantly you write, if the reader cannot understand what you've written, then you have failed to get your point across. Don't argue about whether or not something is unclear; find out why it's unclear. Ask the reader to explain what he or she read; the response will help you discover where you went wrong. After you understand what your reader believed the passage meant, explain what you were trying to convey; the reader may have some helpful suggestions.

The more constructive criticism you get from others, the better your writing will become. You must first, however, get the constructive criticism before you can improve, which means that you must write before you can get better. For example, I think of myself as a pretty good writer, but I always seek out a friend, colleague, or editor (not mutually exclusive categories, by the way) to give me some feedback. (That's one reason why the beginning of this book contains acknowledgments and thanks for the people who provided feedback.) Because you'll need to incorporate this feedback into your report, I strongly urge you to become familiar with at least one word processing software package. Editing and rewriting on a computer is infinitely easier and more enjoyable than typing everything over several times.

Finally, proofread what you expect will be "the final product," and consider asking someone else to proofread it, too. And then proofread it again. Whether you use a word processor or a manual typewriter, it's much better to spend some time correcting errors than to receive a bad review, or a bad grade, simply because you allowed too many typographical errors to remain in the report.

Summary

- Reviewing the literature is a process that should be started shortly after you have decided on a research topic and should continue throughout the entire project.

• A literature review serves three purposes: it places your research in a context related to existing research and theory, it enables you to ensure that your research will contribute to a better understanding of the phenomenon, and it helps you to avoid mistakes made by others.

• Existing research may be related to the theory on which your study is based, the methods you intend to use in your project, and the data analyses you intend to use to help you to interpret your data.

• Introductory textbooks are a good starting point for your literature review, as are general journals or review books.

• After you have some idea about the topics involved in your research, indexing and abstracting services can be used to locate additional research and theory relevant to your project.

• Although it has limitations, locating publications by particular individuals who have conducted research on a related topic is one way to add to your collection of source material.

• Finding an article highly related to your research idea can ease your search considerably. The references in the key article enable you to track research back through time, and the *Social Science Citation Index* can be used to track research published since the key article appeared.

• When taking notes from published sources, take all the notes you can, and make sure they are complete and correct.

• The introduction to a research report should be organized from the most general to the most specific. It should lead the reader from a point in his or her general experience to your specific research procedures. Any introduction written before you collect your data will help you organize your thoughts and plan the project, but it will most likely need to be revised after you interpret your data.

PART TWO

Design

CHAPTER
FIVE

Experimental Research

That [continuity and progress] have been tied to careful experimental and theoretical work indicates that there is validity in a method which at times feels unproductive or disorganized.

—Aronson (1980, p. 21)

Overview

The purpose of this chapter is to provide you the information you need to conduct experimental research, specifically research designed to test cause–effect hypotheses. You will learn about a variety of problems that must be considered, and avoided if possible, when designing an experiment. For each of the major designs discussed, appropriate data analyses will be suggested, and general considerations for report writing will be addressed. Specific criticisms of each design will also be examined. In the final section of this chapter we will review some of the ethical considerations specific to experimental research.

Introduction

To some people, experimental research is the highest peak of scientific research. To others it is the valley of darkness through which promising scientists must walk before they can do "meaningful" research. To most people, **experimental research** is *the general label applied to methods developed for the specific purpose of testing causal relationships.* Like Aronson, I sometimes feel that experimental research can be unproductive and disorganized, and at other times I feel that exper-

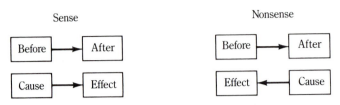

Figure 5.1   Sensible and nonsensible temporal priority

imental research is the best possible design for almost anything. I never feel it's the valley of darkness, but whatever negative feelings I may sometimes have are more than offset by the thrill of demonstrating that a cause–effect relationship exists where I predicted one would be. Experimental research may be the most complicated research design—that is, until one gets the hang of it—but it's the only way to obtain a definite answer to the question of why something happens. That's because experimental research is the only way to test causal hypotheses directly.

Causal Analysis in Experimental Research

Causal analysis—the logical process through which we attempt to explain why an event occurred—should not be new to you. It is, for example, the basis for explanatory research (see Chapter 1). Within the framework of experimental research, causal analysis includes a combination of three elements—temporal priority, control over variables, and random assignment—the presence of which enables us to test cause–effect hypotheses.

Temporal Priority
One of the requirements of causal analysis is knowledge that the suspected cause precedes the effect. Even though the simplicity of this requirement is readily apparent—something that will happen tomorrow cannot cause something that happens today—the concept can sometimes get a little confusing. For example, the unemployment figures that will be released tomorrow cannot affect today's decision to invest in the stock market; on the other hand, *speculation* about what tomorrow's unemployment figures might be *can* affect that decision. It is not tomorrow's event that affects today's behavior, but today's speculation about tomorrow that affects today's behavior. **Temporal priority,** *the requirement that causes precede their effects,* is a stringent requirement, and we must be careful to understand exactly what is being considered a cause. Figure 5.1 illustrates temporal priority.

Because the requirement of temporal priority is obvious, it is often assumed that temporal priority exists when in fact it may not. Consider, for example, the temporal priority involved in Jacobs's (1967) research on suicide notes discussed in Chapter 1. Jacobs's content analysis of suicide notes led him to conclude that people committed suicide because they believed the uncertainty of what might happen after death was preferable to the perception of certain, continued depression in their lives. One question Jacobs was not able to address directly was "Which came first?": did people decide to commit suicide because they preferred the uncertainty of death, or did they decide to commit suicide and then justify that decision by writing notes about the uncertainty of death? There is, of course, no way to answer this question using Jacobs's data; and there may be no ethical way to answer this question with any data, for in order to do so we would have to conduct a study in which we exerted control over someone's level of depression.

Control Over Variables

Because temporal priority is often difficult to establish through logic alone, experimental research invariably involves exerting some control over the research environment. Some of that control involves keeping certain things constant, such as the form used to collect the data or the setting (whether in or out of a laboratory). Some things cannot be held constant, and they are called, sensibly, variables. One way to establish temporal priority is to manipulate the **independent variable—** *the suspected cause under consideration.* In order to experimentally test Jacobs's hypothesis, then, we would have to be able to depress a group of people to the point at which they were suicidal and then compare them to a group of people who were not depressed. Obviously, such research would violate just about every principle of ethics discussed in Chapter 3. Let's continue this discussion with a more feasible experiment.

In a study investigating the effects of the judge's instructions concerning reasonable doubt on a trial's verdict, different types of instructions were presented to different groups of students role-playing jurors (Copenhaver & Dane, 1987). All of the students watched a videotape of a trial, which included instructions from the judge. Different groups of students saw a different version of the videotape. Some students received the standard instructions concerning reasonable doubt, whereas others received instructions that included a percentage, something like "Reasonable doubt means you must be at least 90% sure the defendant committed the crime." Each of the students was then asked to vote either guilty or not guilty and to answer a few other questions. The independent variable was instructions concerning reasonable doubt, and it was controlled by manipulating the videotape presentation.

We were primarily interested in whether or not subjects given the "percentage instructions" would return verdicts different from those returned by subjects given the standard instructions concerning reasonable doubt. *The effect under investigation* is the **dependent variable,** which in this example is the verdict. The dependent variable (verdict) is dependent on the suspected cause (instructions concerning reasonable doubt). Because we used videotape to present the trial, we were also able to control all of the other aspects of a trial—the attorneys' opening statements, witnesses' testimony, and so on—by keeping them constant. The only aspect of the trial that differed from one group to the next was the instruction concerning reasonable doubt, the independent variable. The research hypothesis is illustrated in Figure 5.2.

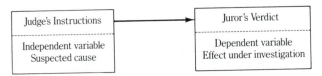

Figure 5.2   An example of an experimental research hypothesis

Random Assignment

Despite the use of videotape to control all aspects of the trial, there remain other, equally plausible explanations for the different verdicts that resulted. For example, perhaps one group of jurors just happened to be lenient, or perhaps another group was composed mainly of people who believed that defendants are always guilty. To attempt to control all of these other possible causes by manipulating them and including them as additional independent variables would soon require more groups of people than would be possible. Instead of attempting to manipulate all other possible explanations, we relied on **random assignment**—*any procedure that provides all participants an equal opportunity to experience any given level of the independent variable.* Thus, every subject had an equal chance of being assigned to the group that received the standard instructions or to one of the groups that received "percentage instructions."

Because random assignment ensured that each participant was equally likely to experience any given level of the independent variable, there should be just as many lenient jurors in one group as in any other group, just as many "hanging jurors" in each group, and so on for any other variable we might be able to imagine but cannot control by making it constant, and thus no longer a variable. Random assignment does not involve actually controlling extraneous variables; instead, it enables us to equalize their effects across all levels of the independent variable. The lenient jurors were, for example, still lenient, but the potential effect of lenient jurors was spread equally across all groups. Thus, the only thing that systematically differed among the groups was the independent variable, instructions about reasonable doubt.

Demonstration Versus Demography

The combination of temporal priority, control of variables through manipulation, and random assignment make it possible to test cause–effect hypotheses. That same combination, however, tends to produce a somewhat artificial environment. In real trials, jurors rarely see a videotape of a trial, as did the students in Copenhaver and Dane's experiment, and although jurors are randomly selected to sit in the jury box, attorneys are able to challenge any juror and have that juror removed if it is apparent that the juror is strongly biased about the case. Copenhaver and Dane allowed any biased students to remain as jurors, although they equalized such effects through random assignment. Does the fact that the experimental jury is not exactly like an actual jury mean that the experiment has nothing to do with jury behavior? The answer is a resounding no.

Experimental research is not supposed to produce an exact replica of natural phenomena. That's not heresy, but rather a recognition that experimental research has a very specific purpose—to test cause–effect hypotheses—and conclusions drawn from experimental research are drawn about the cause–effect relationship. In Copenhaver and Dane (1987), the conclusions we drew concerned how the different instructions produced different verdicts. We were not attempting to draw conclusions about whether or not our students would arrive at the same verdicts as actual jurors. On the other hand, we did expect that the differences apparent in our experiment—the effects of the instructions—would also be apparent with a sample of actual jurors.

The issue here is the difference between demonstration and demography. In our experiment, we demonstrated that "percentage instructions" concerning reasonable doubt produced different verdicts than did the standard instructions. Demography involves the question of how often we can expect those same differences to occur in courtrooms. Demonstration relies on the extent to which the independent variable is the only systematic difference among the groups. If the verdicts are different and the instructions are the only variable that could have caused those differences, then we have demonstrated a cause–effect relationship.

Demography, on the other hand, relies on **mundane realism**—*the extent to which the experience of the participants is similar to the experiences of everyday life.* If actual jurors heard and saw the same evidence we presented in the videotape and received the same instructions from the judge, then we would expect those jurors to behave much as our students behaved. But different trial evidence, different attitudes among the jurors, different instructions from the judge, and other variables would detract from the mundane realism of our experiment. We can claim that "percentage instructions" *can* cause different verdicts, but we cannot claim that they *always* will. Of course, replicating the experiment—for example, with a different set of evidence or with a different group of people role-playing jurors—and obtaining the same set of results would add to the generalizability of the cause–effect relationship we demonstrated in the first experiment. Eventually, enough replications with the same results would lead to the conclusion that different instructions usually produce different verdicts. Because there are no absolute truths in a scientific approach, however, we could not change "usually" to "always," no matter how many replications we completed.

Alternative Explanations of Research Results

When the purpose of research is explanation—testing cause–effect hypotheses—every effort must be made to ensure that the independent variable is the only systematic influence on the dependent variable. The results of experimental research typically involve detecting differences among groups as measured by the dependent variable. Therefore, we need to be sure that the independent variable is the only preexisting difference among those groups. Temporal priority, manipulation of variables, and random assignment are the general requirements of an experimental design, but there are specific preexisting differences, called alterna-

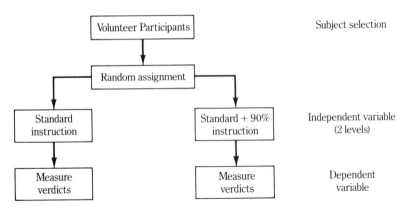

Figure 5.3   Controlling history effects through random assignment

tive explanations, that must be eliminated in order to make valid inferences from experimental research. Campbell and Stanley (1963) literally wrote the book on alternative explanations, and much of the following discussion relies heavily on their classic volume.

History Effects

A **history effect** is *produced whenever some uncontrolled event alters participants' responses.* Usually the event occurs between the time you manipulate the independent variable and the time you measure the dependent variable. Sometimes a history effect is caused by a truly historical event, but more often than not it is produced by more commonplace events.

Generally, random assignment enables you to eliminate the likelihood of a history effect. If, for example, there had been a great deal of publicity about crime during the time we were conducting our experiment examining the effects of the judge's instructions on a trial's verdict, random assignment would ensure that, whatever the effects of that publicity might be, the effects would be equalized across the different levels of the independent variable. Figure 5.3 depicts an experimental design that can be used to eliminate history effects in that experiment.

Maturation Effects

In some sense, maturation is a catchall alternative explanation. **Maturation** refers to *any process that involves systematic change over time, regardless of specific events.* From a causal point of view, the passage of time is not the cause of the process but is merely the most convenient indicator of whatever process may be affecting participants. Most experiments do not last long enough for maturation to occur in the everyday sense of the word—people growing older—but maturation also includes such things as fatigue, boredom, thirst, hunger, and frustration. If, for example, the "percentage instructions" were considerably longer than the standard instructions, then participants may have become bored or tired, and a systematic difference between groups other than that produced by the independent variable would have been introduced into the experiment.

The design involving random assignment illustrated in Figure 5.3 would provide some protection against maturation, but not necessarily enough protection. Maturation effects could remain an alternative explanation of results if we did not ensure that the videotapes representing the different experimental conditions were the same length.

At this point, you should realize that control over much more than the independent variable is necessary for good experimental research. Not only did Copenhaver and Dane need to control the independent variable, they needed to control the type of trial presentation and the length of the trial as well. The need to control so many factors made it impossible to conduct our experiment in a real courtroom, for the legal system just does not allow people to play around with trials that way. The need for even more control will become apparent as we continue to consider additional alternative explanations of research results.

Testing Effects

Recall from Chapter 2 that measurement always involves some sort of error. How you phrase questions, for example, can affect the responses you receive. In experimental research, **testing effects** are *changes in responses caused by measuring the dependent variable.* Testing effects can occur in a variety of ways. You might, for example, measure the dependent variable more than once, thereby creating the possibility that responses on the second measurement reflect memory of the first responses. Similarly, testing effects can occur when there is more than one dependent variable: you cannot measure all of the dependent variables simultaneously—you have to measure one of them first—and participants' responses to the first dependent variable might alter their responses to subsequent measures of that variable.

As the study concerning judges' instructions about reasonable doubt was described earlier, testing effects should not have presented a problem. The dependent variable—verdicts—is measured only once. Although there were other dependent variables, the primary one was verdict, and it was measured first. Of course, the participants' choice of verdict probably did affect their responses to other, secondary measures, but those secondary measures were not critically important to the research hypothesis. For example, participants who decided the defendant was guilty suggested considerably harsher punishments than did those who indicated the defendant was not guilty. Such testing effects make the dependent variable "punishment" suspect, simply because the participants may have suggested punishments merely to be consistent with their verdicts instead of on the basis of some other reasoning process.

The most obvious means for eliminating testing effects are to measure dependent variables only once and to measure the primary dependent variable before any other measures. Testing effects may also be avoided through random assignment if you cannot avoid multiple measurements of the dependent variable. Suppose, for example, that we measured each juror's verdict separately, then had them deliberate as a group, and then measured each's verdict after deliberation. Comparing the postdeliberation verdicts to the predeliberation verdicts would enable us to assess the extent to which verdict preferences changed during deliberation. However, that assessment of change is subject to testing effects. Jurors could have in fact changed their preferences during deliberation but reported no change in order to appear consistent or nonconformist, or because of some other aspect of self-presentation. But if participants are randomly assigned to the different groups, then such self-presentation effects, or any other effects for that matter, are likely to be equalized across the groups.

Instrumentation Effects

Beginning researchers, and even some experienced ones, can become confused about the difference between testing effects and instrumentation effects. Such confusion likely occurs because the two terms seem to refer to the same problem. They are not the same, however, and should be considered separately. **Instrumentation effects** are *changes in the manner in which the dependent variable is measured;* they are problems caused by inconsistent operationalization of the dependent variable or by inconsistently measuring participants' responses. Testing effects, on the other hand, are produced by the act of measuring something, even if the measurement itself is consistent.

In the context of the current example, instrumentation effects would be a viable alternative explanation if we had used different forms to record verdicts for the different groups of participants. Similarly, offering some, but not all, of the participants an alternative decision, such as "guilty but insane," would have introduced instrumentation effects.

To avoid instrumentation effects, control over operationalization of the dependent variable is critical. The logic of experiments may fall apart completely if those who experience different levels of the independent variable also experience different dependent variables. It may seem obviously foolish to use different versions of the dependent variable for different groups, but there are circumstances that might make such foolishness relatively easy to overlook. Even something as apparently innocuous as differences in the quality of copies of the form used to record the dependent variable can cause instrumentation problems. If one group has copies that are more difficult to read than the other group's, that discrepancy violates the logic involved in having the independent variable be the only systematic difference between the groups.

More often than not, instrumentation effects become a problem when the operational definition of the dependent variable depends on someone's judgment. Subjective measures, such as someone's rating of the quality of an essay, are subject to maturation problems. For example, the person making the judgments may grow tired, bored, or careless, and such changes are, in fact, changes in the dependent measure. In this case, because the "instrument" is the person making the rating, maturation effects upon the rater become instrumentation effects. Randomizing the order in which the ratings are made, perhaps by mixing the essays such that they are not grouped according to levels of the independent variable, is usually sufficient to equalize the likelihood of such maturation effects as fatigue.

Similarly, not allowing raters or judges to be aware of the level of the independent variable experienced by the participant reduces the likelihood of instrumentation effects. A **blind rater** is *someone who is unaware of either the research hypothesis or the experimental group from which the responses came.* When you read research reports containing such phrases as "the observers were blind to conditions" or "blind raters were used," it doesn't mean the observers had a vision deficit. Rather, it means the observers did not know to which group those being observed belonged.

Statistical Regression Effects

In the context of alternative explanations of research results, statistical regression effect does not refer to a particular type of data analysis; rather, **statistical regression effect** is *an artifact of measurement that occurs when extreme scores are obtained.* Someone who scores extremely high or extremely low on a measure is likely, if tested again, to obtain a second score that is closer to the average than was the first score. The person's score is said to regress toward the mean because the score moves back to the average score, either from an extreme high or an extreme low. Because Copenhaver and Dane used a dichotomous measure of verdict—guilty versus not guilty—their study is not subject to statistical regression effects.

On the other hand, most continuous variables, such as a rating from 1 to 10 or an IQ score, include the assumption that the overall distribution of responses should conform to the normal distribution, the bell-shaped curve. Most scores bunch together near the mean of the distribution, and the frequency of scores decreases as the scores become more distant from the mean. Therefore, the probability of obtaining extreme scores is lower than the probability of obtaining scores closer to the mean. Think of the distribution of grade point averages at your school. Most students have a grade point average somewhere between a 2.0 and a 3.0; the number of students with a 4.0 or a 0.5 is relatively low. Thus the probability of your running into someone with a 4.0 is considerably lower than the probability of your encountering someone with a 2.5.

The statistical theory gets a little complicated, but the essential point is that extreme scores, whether high or low, probably result from random measurement error—are an artifact or a fluke—rather than from a truly extreme level of whatever is being measured. Because extreme scores in a normal distribution are, by definition, unlikely to occur, the more reasonable explanation for an extreme score is that it was produced through measurement error. Thus, when someone with an extreme score is tested again, chances are that the random measurement error will not recur and that the person's second score will not be as extreme as the first score. If I took an intelligence test and scored an IQ of 145, most people (including me) would declare that score an artifact, a fluke, and would demand a retest. The retest would likely produce a lower score, one rather closer to the average IQ of 100.

Statistical regression effects, like testing effects, are a problem only when the dependent variable is measured more than once. Only random assignment can be used to avoid them. However, statistical regression effects can become a problem even when an implicit measure of the dependent variable is used. For example, a teacher might select students he or she believes to be the brightest and give them special assignments designed to further improve their abilities. If subsequently the students exhibit no change in their abilities, perhaps as measured by paired examination, then the lack of difference could be due to the fact that the assignments were ineffective, or due to statistical regression. That is, some of the "brightest," as measured by the teacher's perceptions, are probably not as bright as the teacher perceived them to be. Subsequent measurement would produce a score closer to average. But if the special assignments are actually making such students brighter, then the net result would be no change. Statistical regression brought the scores down, and the assignments brought them back up again, leaving the scores right where they started. Of course, the students did receive some benefit—improved abilities—from the assignments, but statistical regression prevented that benefit from being reflected in their scores. Note that such an experiment would also be subject to instrumentation effects; a teacher's perception and a written examination are not the same operational definition of the dependent variable.

Selection Effects

Statistical regression effects are a specific example of alternative explanations known as selection effects. A **selection effect** is *produced by the manner in which the participants were recruited or recruited themselves.* That is, selection effects occur because some characteristic of the participants differs systematically across the experimental groups. Once again, random assignment eliminates selection effects because the characteristic is equally distributed across the randomly assigned groups. In Copenhaver and Dane's experiment, some of the students may have believed that in general defendants are guilty and may therefore have decided before the videotape was shown that the defendant in the specific trial was guilty. If more of such students ended up in one group or the other, their verdicts would produce a difference that was not related to the independent variable—instructions concerning reasonable doubt. By now you should be getting the idea that random assignment is an integral part of any experiment.

Sometimes, however, random assignment is practically or ethically impossible. In such cases, a technique called matching provides a second-best alternative. **Matching** is *assigning participants to groups in order to equalize, across groups, scores on any relevant variable.* If, for example, we were conducting a study in an actual courtroom with real jurors, we would not be able to randomly assign jurors to conditions—whatever they happen to be—because doing so would mean we would undermine the defendant's right to due process. We might, instead, try to measure their beliefs about defendants and consider those beliefs as part of the research design. We could then compare those who were biased against defendants with those who were not and assess the extent to which biases affected their verdicts.

The problem with using matching to overcome selection effects is, very simply, that you can never be sure you have included all of the relevant variables in the matching process. We might, for example, have to match jurors on bias against defendants, experience with crime, number of crime shows they watch on television, level of intelligence, and so on. There is no limit to the number of different things that might affect their verdicts, and so there is no limit to the number of different variables on which the participants would have to be matched. Even though matching does provide an alternative when random assignment is not possible, it is not as effective as random assignment and should be used only when random assignment is truly impossible.

Mortality Effects

Borrowed from animal research terminology, **mortality effects** are *caused by the loss of participants during a project*. Those of us who use human participants prefer the term *attrition*, but mortality remains the official term. Mortality is a specific type of selection effect, one due to participants choosing to leave, rather than join, the research project. In Copenhaver and Dane's study, mortality effects were not an operant consideration, although they could have been if any students had opted to retract their consent to participate in the study.

Random assignment is considered a safeguard against mortality effects because the number of participants likely to retract their consent is considered to be roughly equal across different groups. Random assignment, however, cannot be considered a *cure* for mortality effects, for one experimental group could in fact contain a disproportionate number of dropouts. Suppose, for purposes of illustration, that ten students in the "percentage instruction" condition dropped out but only two students in the standard instruction condition did so. It would be difficult to interpret any differences between the two conditions because we would have no idea which verdict the students who dropped out would have returned. Any interpretation could be qualified by the phrase "for those who remained in the study," but it would be appropriate to wonder about the reason for the differential dropout rate. The reason could be, for example, that people are not willing to decide on verdicts when given a "percentage instruction" concerning reasonable doubt, or it could be something else related to the research hypothesis.

If you plan a study in which mortality is likely to be a factor, either because the procedure is long or there are multiple sessions, the best protection is a combination of random assignment and some preliminary measure of the dependent variable. Such a design is illustrated in Figure 5.4. The design will not prevent participants from retracting their consent, but it will enable you to determine the extent to which those who dropped out differed from those who stayed. Comparing scores on the preliminary measure will provide some indication—but not conclusive proof—about any differences that may exist. If the dropouts were different from those who stayed, then you have a potential problem with mortality effects. If the two groups score the same, then there probably are no problems. Furthermore, you can use change scores—the difference between the preliminary measure and the dependent variable—to assess effects due to the independent variable.

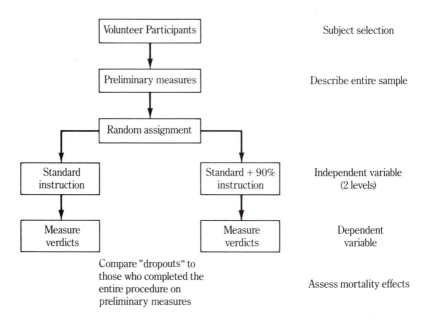

Figure 5.4   Assessing mortality effects through experimental design

Participant Bias

We have already noted that research participants can be affected by self-presentation, their concern about the perceptions the experimenter and others may form about them as a result of their responses in the project. This is one example of **participant bias**—*any intentional effort on the part of participants to alter their responses.* Another example may involve participants' concerns about revealing sensitive information about themselves simply because they believe it's none of the researcher's business what they think. Generally, any evaluation apprehension—concern about being observed—can produce participant bias.

Random assignment helps to reduce such types of participant bias because, as usual, random assignment equalizes the distribution of apprehensive participants across experimental groups. The only way to completely avoid participant bias is to prevent the participants from being aware that they are being observed, but such a practice brings in the ethical problem of justifying disregard of informed consent. The ethics involved in such justification were discussed in Chapter 3 and are reviewed later in this chapter.

In addition to evaluation apprehension and related forms of participant bias, participants may intentionally attempt to help or hinder your research efforts. The **beneficent subject effect** *occurs when participants are aware of the research hypothesis and attempt to respond so as to support it.* Suppose, for example, that students role-playing jurors became aware of the purpose of Copenhaver and Dane's study. Some of them may have believed that we preferred the "percentage instructions" and may have provided verdicts they thought would help support that idea. Perhaps some of them attempted to predict what actual jurors would decide in the case, instead of making their own decisions about the verdict. Although such an effect might be interesting in its own right—why would these "jurors" care what we preferred?—it would certainly have made our study worthless for its original purpose.

The opposite, the **maleficent subject effect,** *occurs when participants are aware of the research hypothesis and attempt to respond so as to undermine it.* In this case, jurors might alter their verdicts to make it seem as though the "percentage instructions" are less effective than the standard instructions, or they might attempt to predict what actual jurors would decide and then return the opposite verdict. Again, participants' interest in the project might be an interesting topic of study, but interest so expressed is not conducive to the purposes of the research. The only way to prevent either effect is to prevent participants from becoming aware of the research hypothesis. This is known as "keeping the participants blind" and is analogous to keeping raters of subjective dependent measures in the dark about the hypothesis. In some projects, a *double-blind procedure* is used; that is, both raters and participants are unaware of the research hypothesis.

Blind and double-blind studies may involve concealment of the research hypothesis by preventing awareness of participation itself or they may involve some sort of deception. Both procedures pose ethical problems and should be considered only after it has been determined that simply withholding information about the specific research hypothesis will not prevent participant bias. Once again, efforts to attain methodological rigor must be balanced with consideration of the ethical treatment of participants.

Experimenter Bias

Participants are not the only people who may alter their behavior during an experiment. **Experimenter bias** refers to *the experimenter's differential treatment of experimental groups.* In the jury experiment, there was considerable potential for experimenter bias. As much as we wanted to remain objective scientists, we had some definite ideas about what differences might result in response to the standard instructions and the "percentage instructions," and it would have been extremely difficult to keep those ideas from having some sort of subtle influence on our behavior during the project.

The logic of the experiment required us to treat all groups exactly the same; the only systematic difference between the groups was supposed to be the manipulated independent variable—the instructions concerning reasonable doubt. About the only way for us to be sure we would not exhibit experimental bias would be to remain blind to experimental conditions. Thus, in order to control the length and quality of the trial across conditions and our awareness of the independent variable condition for any given group, we decided to present the trial via videotape. By having one person code the videotapes and the other show the tapes to the subjects, the experimenter could remain blind to experimental conditions when showing the tape. Eventually, of course, the experimenter would hear which instruction was on the tape, but, by then, all he had to do was pick up the data collection forms as the participants walked out the door.

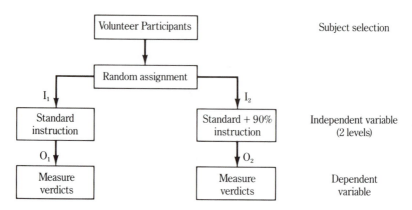

Figure 5.5   The experimental design of Copenhaver and Dane (1987) in design notation; this design is also known as the basic design

Experimental Design

Fortunately, not every experiment is subject to every alternative explanation described above. On the other hand, every alternative explanation must be considered a potential problem until logic, control, or experimental design enables you to rule it out. In this section we'll consider the various experimental designs that can be used to rule out alternative explanations. **Design** refers to *the number and arrangement of independent variable levels in a research project*. Although all experimental designs involve manipulated independent variables and random assignment, different designs are more or less efficient for dealing with specific alternative explanations.

The design you decide to use for your own experiment depends on your research hypothesis. However, being familiar with a variety of different designs enables you to be a little creative when deciding how to test your research hypothesis. The major factor in choosing a design is not its complexity, but the extent to which it provides internal validity. **Internal validity** refers to *the extent to which the independent variable is the only systematic difference among experimental groups* (Cook & Campbell, 1979). That is, the internal validity of an experiment allows you to conclude that the independent variable is the cause of the effects you measure with the dependent variable. Just as every poker hand either wins or loses the pot, every design is either a winner or loser at internal validity, depending on the specific research hypothesis you are testing.

In an effort to keep diagrams simple and easy to read, an "I" and subscripts will be used to denote levels of a single independent variable, and an "O" with subscripts will denote dependent variables. Thus, the design of Copenhaver and Dane (1987) would be diagrammed as in Figure 5.5.

The Basic Design

The basic design is the simplest design that still qualifies as a true experimental design. Campbell and Stanley (1963) refer to it as the Posttest–Only Control

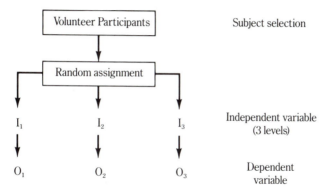

Figure 5.6 The basic experimental design with three levels of one independent variable

Group Design, and it is essentially the design used by Copenhaver and Dane (1987). In the basic design (Figure 5.5), participants are randomly assigned to one of two different levels of the independent variable, and the dependent variable is measured only once. Coupled with careful control over procedures, this design effectively avoids most alternative explanations and provides a comparison between control (I_1) and treatment (I_2) conditions by comparing the dependent variable responses of the two groups, O_1 and O_2.

Data analyses for the basic design include any analyses in which central tendencies for two groups (O_1 and O_2) can be compared. These include a simple chi-square for categorical dependent measures such as verdicts; the Mann-Whitney U test for dependent measures composed of ranks, such as best-to-worst drawings in an art contest; or a t-test or analysis of variance for continuous variables that do not involve ranks. (If you are unfamiliar with these or subsequently mentioned statistical tests, you may want to consult Chapter 13 for more information.)

When attempting to describe this design in a research report, you need simply point out that participants were randomly assigned to different groups. You might write the following, for example:

> Participants were randomly assigned to receive one of two instructions defining reasonable doubt. In the standard condition, participants received instructions currently used in most jurisdictions. In the "percentage condition," the phrase "beyond reasonable doubt means you must be at least 90% certain the defendant committed the crime" was appended to the standard instruction.

The basic design is not necessarily limited to two groups, as can be seen in Figure 5.6. Different levels of the same independent variable, such as percentage instructions using the words "50% certain," "60% certain," and so on would also qualify for the basic design. In fact, Copenhaver and Dane included eight different levels of their independent variable: standard instructions plus percentage instructions ranging from 50% to 99%.

The basic design is most efficient for research in which the premanipulation state of participants—what they are like before they experience a single indepen-

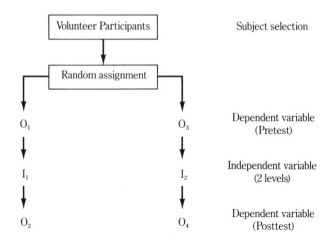

Figure 5.7 The basic pretest design, in which the dependent variable is measured both before and after manipulation of the independent variable

dent variable—is either not of interest or can be assumed to be unrelated to the independent variable. Neither change over time nor differential reactions to the independent variable as a function of some preexisting characteristic can be studied with the basic design, simply because you don't have any way to know anything about the participants before they experience the independent variable.

The Basic Pretest Design

The basic pretest design, as the name implies, involves adding a pretest measure to the basic design. The obvious reason for adding a pretest measure is to examine how much the independent variable causes participants to change. The basic pretest design, illustrated in Figure 5.7, is the design Campbell and Stanley (1963) call the Pretest–Posttest Control Group Design. In Figure 5.7, O_1 and O_3 refer to the pretest measure, the dependent variable measured before the manipulation of the independent variable, and O_2 and O_4 refer to the dependent variable measured after the manipulation. Although not depicted in the figure, the basic pretest design can include more than two levels of the same independent variable.

Suppose, for example, that we were interested only in knowing what jurors thought the phrase "beyond a reasonable doubt" meant. We might first ask them to indicate, say on a scale from 0% to 100% certainty, where reasonable doubt lies. Then we could ask participants to view one of the videotapes used by Copenhaver and Dane and have them again indicate where reasonable doubt lies on the same percentage scale. Because the only differences among the videotapes were the instructions concerning reasonable doubt, we could use the data to determine the extent to which such instructions change individuals' perceptions about reasonable doubt. We would analyze the data by subtracting each participant's pretest response from his or her posttest response ($O_2 - O_1$ and $O_4 - O_3$) and, treating the difference as though it were the only dependent variable, we could use repeated measures analysis of variance.

The obvious advantage of the basic pretest design over the basic design is the ability to obtain information about the premanipulation state of the participants—to examine the change in scores. The disadvantage is that the pretest measure may affect participants' reactions to the independent variable; that is, asking participants to first provide their impressions about reasonable doubt could sensitize them to the instructions they will later see in the videotape.

Random assignment enables us to overcome the possibility of general testing effects, but the combination of pretest measures and manipulation of the independent variable may create another alternative explanation for the results. Campbell and Stanley (1963) call this alternative explanation a **testing–treatment interaction** in which *participants experiencing one level of the independent variable may be more sensitive to testing effects than participants experiencing a different level of the independent variable.* Essentially, the pretest measure may make one of the levels of the independent variable, such as the percentage instructions concerning reasonable doubt, more forceful than it would have been without the pretest. This increased forcefulness of that particular level of the independent variable, then, is an artifact rather than a true test of the variable's impact. The dependent variable in such cases measures both the effect of the independent variable and its combination with the pretest, instead of measuring the effect of the independent variable only. It is also possible that the pretest measure may make participants wonder about the purpose of the study and increase participant bias.

The Solomon Four-Group Design

If the possibility of a testing-treatment interaction exists in your research project, the most effective design for dealing with the problem is the Solomon (1949) four-group design, illustrated in Figure 5.8. It is important to realize, however, that this design does not eliminate the testing–treatment interaction, but rather enables you to determine whether or not it has occurred and, if it has, assess its impact. This design also enables you to determine whether or not overall testing effects have occurred; that is, it enables you to assess the effectiveness of your random assignment procedure.

If the I_1 level of the independent variable represents a control condition—the absence of the manipulation—then comparing O_2 with O_6 provides a test of the overall testing effect. The only difference between these two groups is the existence of a pretest measure, and any difference between these two groups would be due to the pretest. Comparing the difference between O_4 and O_8 with the difference between O_2 and O_6 provides an estimate of the testing–treatment interaction effect. If there is no interaction between testing and treatment, then the upper half of the design can be analyzed in the same way as the basic pretest design. If, however, there is a testing–treatment interaction, you can use the interaction to adjust statistically the size of the effect of the independent variable.

Unfortunately, the Solomon four-group design is not, in general, a very efficient design. It requires twice as many groups as the basic pretest design to ex-

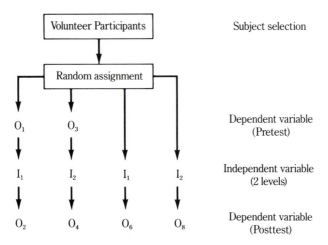

Figure 5.8 The Solomon four-group design. Although there are only two levels of the independent variable, four groups are required to assess the extent to which testing effects have occurred.

amine essentially the same cause–effect hypothesis. The four groups depicted in Figure 5.8, for example, include only two levels of a single independent variable. The loss of efficiency is related to the need to test for the testing–treatment interaction. In general, the more you need to know, the more groups or participants will be required—an important rule to keep in mind when deciding how many questions you want to answer within your research project.

Factorial Design

Many research questions require inclusion of more than one independent variable in your design. For example, I am currently planning a study in which I want to assess the extent to which jurors rely on witnesses' nonverbal behavior (apparent nervousness and so on) in deciding on a verdict. I also want to know whether it makes any difference if the witness is undergoing direct examination (questioning by the attorney on their side) or cross examination (questioning by the other side's attorney). This situation requires two independent variables—one for nonverbal behavior and one for type of examination.

Designs that include more than one independent variable are called **factorial designs.** In terms of our diagram scheme, a simple factorial design is illustrated in Figure 5.9, in which "A" refers to one independent variable and "B" refers to a second independent variable. Within the design, participants experience all possible combinations of the two independent variables, but each participant experiences only one of these combinations. As with other designs, each of the independent variables can have two or more levels.

More often than not, the notation used in Figure 5.9 is not applied to factorial designs. As you probably discovered while attempting to decipher Figure 5.9, the

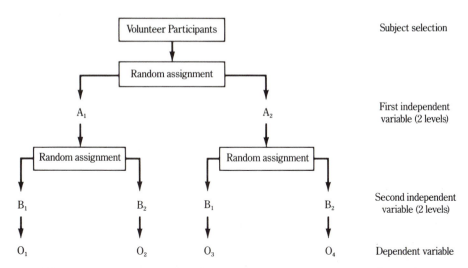

Figure 5.9 The factorial design for two independent variables. Each of the two groups created by manipulating the first independent variable is randomly assigned to receive one of the two levels of the second independent variable, creating a total of four groups of subjects.

notation is a little cumbersome. Instead, the notation used in Figure 5.10 is more acceptable for factorial designs. Figure 5.10 illustrates the study I am currently planning. I've added identification numbers to the groups, called "cells" in the design, to make it easier to refer to them in further discussion. Usually, means, standard deviations, or some other summary statistic are presented in the cells when reporting research results.

In cell 1, participants will see a videotape of an obviously nervous defendant undergoing questioning from the defense attorney. In cell 2, different participants will watch the same videotape, but they will be led to believe that the attorney is the prosecutor. In cell 3, a calm-looking defendant will be questioned by his attorney, whereas in cell 4 the calm defendant will be questioned by the prosecutor. In order to control for such things as other physical characteristics of the witness and attorney, all participants will see the same attorney and the same defendant, but they will be told that the attorney is either the defense attorney or the prosecuting attorney. In order to control for what is being said—I'm only interested in nonverbal behavior—the sound will be turned off while the participants view the tape. The design depicted in Figure 5.10 is called a 2 × 2 factorial design—two levels of one independent variable combined with two levels of another independent variable.

The advantage of a factorial design is that interactions between independent variables can be tested. An **interaction** *occurs when the effect of one variable depends on which level of another variable is present.* In the study just described, perhaps a nervous defendant will be evaluated as more believable when undergoing cross examination than when undergoing direct examination. Because most people expect someone to be nervous when they are being challenged, it would be

Type of examination (A)

Direct (A₁)   Cross (A₂)

	Direct (A$_1$)	Cross (A$_2$)
Nervous (B$_1$)	Cell #1 A$_1$B$_1$	Cell #2 A$_2$B$_1$
Calm (B$_2$)	Cell #3 A$_1$B$_2$	Cell #4 A$_2$B$_2$

Nonverbal behavior (B)

Figure 5.10 Typical representation of a factorial design. Instead of cell numbers or condition labels, means, standard deviations, or some other summary statistic are presented for each cell in a research article.

reasonable to expect someone to be nervous under cross examination, but it would not be reasonable to expect a defendant to be nervous when being questioned by the defense attorney. On the other hand, a calm defendant would be more believable when undergoing direct examination than when undergoing cross examination; someone being challenged and appearing calm might seem too rehearsed and so might be perceived as less believable. Thus, we expect an interaction between type of examination and nonverbal behavior; the effect of being nervous will depend upon whether it occurs under cross examination or direct examination.

The easiest way to illustrate an interaction effect is with a graph such as that depicted in Figure 5.11. The dependent variable, credibility, is represented on the ordinal or vertical axis of the graph, whereas one of the independent variables, nonverbal behavior, is represented on the abscissa or horizontal axis. Two different lines representing two aspects of the other independent variable, examination

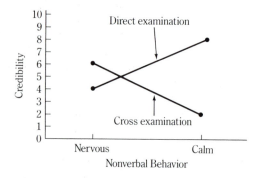

Figure 5.11 Illustration of an interaction between examination type and nonverbal behavior. The effect of one variable, examination type, depends on the level of the other variable, nonverbal behavior.

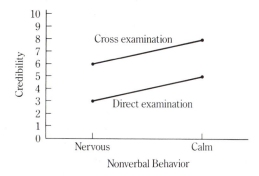

Figure 5.12 Illustration of a main effect for nonverbal behavior. Whether undergoing cross or direct examination, nervous defendants are perceived as less credible than calm defendants.

type, complete the graph. Notice that the lines representing type of examination cross or intersect; this is the *sine qua non* (the essential characteristic) of an interaction effect.

It is not always the case, however, that including two independent variables in a research design will produce an interaction effect. It could be, for example, that a nervous defendant will always be less credible than a calm defendant, regardless of who is doing the questioning. If so, we would observe a **main effect**—*an effect produced by a single independent variable.* Figure 5.12 illustrates a main effect for type of examination; nervous defendants are always less credible than calm defendants. Notice that the lines in Figure 5.12 do not cross; they remain parallel. Parallel (or nearly parallel) lines on a graph such as those in Figure 5.12 are the hallmark of a main effect.

When data analyses, usually analysis of variance, indicate that the interaction is significant or reliable, it may not be important to interpret main effects that are part of the interaction. The interaction invariably makes the conclusion one would draw from the main effect wrong at least part of the time. For example, the data illustrated in Figure 5.11 reflect both a main effect for examination type and an interaction effect. The main effect is that, combined or averaged over nervous and calm defendants, the overall rating for cross examination (4) is lower than the overall rating for direct examination (6). However, it is clear from the figure that claiming the defendant is perceived as more credible under direct examination would be wrong when the defendant is nervous.

Instead of trying to interpret the main effect, I would simply acknowledge its existence and then describe the interaction effect. I would write something like "an analysis of variance produced a reliable main effect for examination type, but it was superseded by the interaction between examination type and nonverbal behavior" and then proceed to describe the interaction or refer the reader to a graph that is similar to Figure 5.11. Of course, the quote is fictional—I haven't yet collected any data—but it does give you some idea about how to report interaction and main effect results. The temptation to interpret main effects that are superseded by an interaction is a rather strong one to which even seasoned researchers fall prey (Dane & Thompson, 1985). Like so many other temptations, it's best to avoid it.

The ability to detect and interpret interactions is the primary advantage of factorial designs. However, they can become methodological nightmares if you try to accomplish too much with any one design. With ten participants in each cell of the design, a 2×2 factorial requires 40 participants. If you include a third independent variable, the resulting $2 \times 2 \times 2$ design requires 80 participants. Including more than two levels of any of the independent variables also further increases the number of participants required. Again, trying to accomplish too many things in a single research project creates more trouble than it's usually worth in the long run. Determine what questions you want to answer, and then limit the study design to examine only those questions.

Repeated Measures Design

Sometimes it is necessary either to expose participants to more than one level of an independent variable or to measure the dependent variable more than once for each participant. The basic pretest design, for example, is the simplest form of repeated measurement design, but that design does not involve exposing any participant to more than one level of an independent variable. A **repeated measures design** is *a specific factorial design in which the same participants are exposed to more than one level of an independent variable.* Repeated measures designs are also called "within subject" designs because the independent variable is manipulated within the same subject instead of between or across different subjects. Whether or not repeated measures is an option in your own research depends on the type of independent variables you use and, of course, the hypothesis you are trying to test. For some types of experiments, exposing participants to more than one level of an independent variable is illogical or impossible, and repeated measures designs also require some additional groups to test for order effects.

Type of examination (A)

		Direct (A_1)	Cross (A_2)
Nonverbal behavior (B)	Nervous (B_1)	Subject numbers 1–10	Subject numbers 11–20
	Calm (B_2)	Subject numbers 21–30	Subject numbers 31–40

Figure 5.13 Subject numbers for a 2×2 between subjects factorial design. Each subject experiences one and only one level of each of the two independent variables. Such a design requires 40 subjects to meet the chosen criterion of ten subjects per condition.

Type of examination (A)

	Direct (A$_1$)	Cross (A$_2$)
Nervous (B$_1$)	Subject numbers 1–10	Subject numbers 11–20
Calm (B$_2$)	Subject numbers 11–20	Subject numbers 1–10

Nonverbal behavior (B)

Figure 5.14   Subject numbers for a 2 × 2 repeated measures factorial design. Each subject experiences two levels of both independent variables. Such a design requires only 20 subjects to meet the chosen criterion of ten observations per condition, but may suffer from order effects.

Suppose, for example, that I decide to use ten participants in each of the four cells of the witness credibility study described earlier. Such a design is represented in Figure 5.13, in which participant identification numbers are entered in each cell; each participant experiences one and only one combination of the two independent variables. Such designs are also called "between subject" designs because the manipulations of the independent variables occur between participants.

If I were to use a repeated measures design—expose any given participant to more than one level of an independent variable—the design of the resulting experiment would appear as in Figure 5.14. Each participant would see a nervous defendant undergoing direct examination and a different, calm defendant undergoing cross examination. I would be able to test more or less the same hypothesis with half as many participants. The "more or less" in the previous sentence refers to the different experiences in the two experiments: in the "between" design—illustrated in Figure 5.13—participants would see only one defendant; in the "within" design (Figure 5.14), participants would be exposed to two different defendants.

More important, the repeated measures design depicted in Figure 5.14 would not be adequate for testing my original research hypothesis because the illustrated design would suffer from **order effects**—*changes in participant responses resulting from the order in which participants experience multiple levels of an independent variable.* The potential for order effects exists because participants would be exposed to the two defendants in different orders: participants 1–10 would first see a nervous defendant and then a calm defendant, whereas participants 11–20 would experience the opposite order. Whatever the order, part of their reaction to the second defendant would be due to their reaction to the first one. For participants 11–20, for example, the nervous demeanor of the second defendant might appear even more nervous coming after exposure to a calm defendant.

To correct for the alternative explanation of order effects, we would have to add additional participants and groups to the design. A corrected repeated mea-

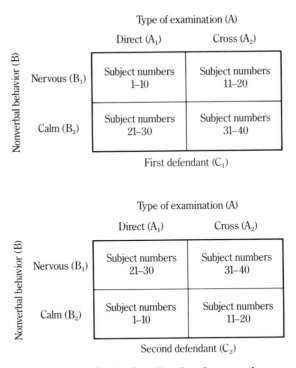

Figure 5.15 Design for a 2 × 2 × 2 repeated measures factorial design. Each subject experiences two levels of the nonverbal behavior independent variable. Notice that this design allows us to test for the order effect that would have gone undetected in the design illustrated in Figure 5.14.

sures design for the witness study might look like the design illustrated in Figure 5.15. Notice that all possible orders of nervous and calm defendants are covered in that design. Notice also that once again 40 participants are included in the design. The design in Figure 5.15 allows us to test the same research hypotheses tested in the design illustrated in Figure 5.13, as well as an additional hypothesis about the potential effects of viewing one defendant after viewing a second defendant.

For some variables, repeated measures designs are simply not possible. Some independent variable effects may last so long that they interfere with later, different levels of the same variable. Consider, for example, an experiment in which two different teaching techniques are being compared. A repeated measures design could not be used because students may learn so much material with whichever technique is used first that further learning under a second technique would be too slight to be measured. Whether or not you will encounter such problems when considering a repeated measures design depends, of course, on your selection of independent variables. Like any other design, repeated measures designs make sense for some research hypotheses, but not for all research hypotheses.

Participant Characteristics

Before we leave design and move on to a review of some of the ethical considerations involved in experimental research, let's consider the use of participant characteristics as independent variables. **Participant characteristics,** *sometimes*
called subject variables, are variables that differentiate participants but cannot be ma-
nipulated and are not subject to random assignment. Participant characteristics include such variables as gender, age, race, amount of formal education, height, and
so forth. They can be included in an experimental design, but because they are
not subject to manipulation or random assignment, they cannot be considered true
independent variables in an experimental design. When reading research reports,
however, you will often find that they are described as independent variables.

   In the witness study, for example, I could (and probably will) include participant gender as a variable in the overall design. This would involve treating men
and women as though they represented two different levels of an independent variable, gender. If I were to analyze the data and observe a main effect for gender,
however, it would be ludicrous to interpret such a finding to mean that being male
(or female) caused people to view witnesses as less credible. Instead, it would be
more reasonable to conclude that some other systematic difference between men
and women caused the effect, but I would have no experimental basis for declaring
what that systematic difference might be. It could be attitudinal, hormonal, per-
ceptual, or any other potential difference.

   When participant characteristics are included in an experimental design,
conclusions about cause–effect relationships cannot be drawn from any effects
associated with such variables. Despite this restriction, you would not have to
look very long before finding a research article in which the author(s) did exactly
that. Drawing cause–effect conclusions about participant characteristics seems
to be an almost irresistible temptation to many researchers. When this happens,
it usually results from a very logical consideration of the effect and the researcher's knowledge about related research. Suggesting potential explanations for a
gender effect, for example, is certainly within the realm of scientific research. But
concluding that a gender effect results from differential attitudes when attitudes
have not been manipulated in the design falls outside the logic of experimental
research.

Ethical Considerations in Experiments

Although ethical considerations for research are covered in Chapter 3, it is important to review some of those considerations as they apply specifically to experimental research. Manipulating independent variables and randomly assigning
participants to conditions are not in and of themselves questionable research procedures. However, the power differential between researcher and participant is
often greater in experimental research than in other research methods, if for no
other reason than the experimenter can manipulate some aspect of the participant's environment.

Random Assignment of Participants

Because it eliminates so many alternative explanations, random assignment is essential to true experiments. It also creates some very specific ethical considerations that must be included in any researcher's ethical balancing act. The witness credibility study, for example, could not be conducted in an actual courtroom with a real trial: it is neither legal nor ethical to randomly assign jurors to different courtroom trials.

The witness credibility experiment might seem to present a fairly trivial ethical consideration, but differential treatment of participants resulting from random assignment can sometimes take on very nontrivial proportions. For example, a psychologist testing the effectiveness of a new and presumably more effective therapy must decide to randomly assign some clients, the control group, to receive a (presumably) less effective therapy or no therapy at all. Similarly, a social worker testing a new program for helping disadvantaged children would have to randomly assign some children to a condition in which they would not experience the program.

Of course, providing a currently acceptable therapy or some other version of the status quo is not exactly unethical treatment, unless, of course, the status quo is extremely undesirable. When there is sufficient evidence that some treatment will benefit participants but that treatment must be withheld in order to provide an experimental test of the treatment, the researcher has an obligation to attempt to provide the treatment after the conclusion of the experiment if the treatment turns out to be beneficial. Whenever different levels of an independent variable include the possibility of differential benefit or harm, the use of random assignment involves striking an ethical balance between treating participants fairly and testing cause–effect relationships.

Manipulating Variables

Whenever you intentionally manipulate the experience of another individual, you are exerting control over that person's life. Most of the time such control is trivial, as in the case of presenting participants with either a nervous or calm defendant in a simulated jury trial. At the other end of the spectrum is the very nontrivial example of yelling "Fire!" in a theater to test people's reactions to an emergency.

Between the clearly trivial and the clearly unethical there exists a wide range of manipulations in which control over participants must play a major role in the ethical balancing act. In addition to the effects discussed in Chapter 3, controlling other people can reduce the degree to which those people believe they have control over their own experiences. Loss of that belief with respect to an important area of their self-concept can constitute psychological, and sometimes physical, harm (Schulz, 1976). Of course, the best way to resolve this aspect of the ethical balancing act is to be a little creative in finding nonthreatening means by which to test whatever research hypothesis interests you.

Blind Procedures

As noted earlier, one of the best ways to eliminate participant bias is to keep the participants blind—unaware of the research hypotheses. We also noted that informed consent is an ethical responsibility of anyone who conducts research. If your research hypotheses require you to keep the participants blind, you must be sure to provide them with enough information to enable them to make an informed decision about participation.

Avoiding participant bias through blind procedures involves balancing the internal validity of the experiment, an ethical responsibility in its own right, with the requirement for informed consent. How much information needs to be withheld to avoid participant bias is a decision only the researcher can make, preferably after consulting others. That judgment is made from the viewpoint of a researcher attempting to produce an internally valid experiment.

How much information a participant needs in order to give informed consent is also a judgment made by the researcher after consultation, but the judgment about sufficient information must be made from the viewpoint of the participant. The two decisions are theoretically independent, but because they must be made by the same person, they cannot be truly independent in practice. If the two decisions are not in conflict, there is no ethical dilemma. If they do conflict, you should seriously consider finding another way to implement your study. You need not abandon your research hypothesis, but you may need, for example, to find alternative ways to operationalize your independent or dependent variables.

Demonstration Versus Demography Again

Earlier in the chapter the primary purpose of experimental research was described as testing whether or not a cause–effect relationship can be demonstrated. This purpose does not automatically rule out generalizing the results of the experiment, but generalization (demography) is secondary to testing the relationship (demonstration). If generalizing well beyond the experimental environment is an important part of your research intentions, you need to ensure that your efforts in that direction do not undermine the internal validity of the experimental design. If random assignment is not consistent with generalization, you cannot forgo random assignment in favor of some other, more "natural" procedure; without random assignment, you have no experiment from which to generalize.

Overgeneralization is also something to avoid. Although overgeneralization is a potential problem in any research method, experimental research seems particularly prone to the phrase "research has proved." Random assignment is critical to experimental research, but experimental research is a process that also depends on replication for its effectiveness. Like any procedure based on probability theory, random assignment works "in the long run" but may not be effective on a one time only basis. Any research requires replication before we can rely heavily on the results.

You should realize that a single experiment does not prove that a cause–effect relationship exists; rather, it demonstrates the existence of the relationship under the conditions created by the experimental procedures. Those conditions include the specific experimenter, participants, operational definitions, and a host of other potential factors that differ from one experiment to another. A demonstration that something can happen does not mean it always will happen. The more carefully you attempt to eliminate alternative explanations, the more likely your demonstration will be replicated by others. Conducting a valid experiment requires paying attention to all aspects of experimental research.

Summary

• Experimental research methods are the only methods designed specifically to test cause–effect hypotheses. Experiments are accomplished by manipulating the independent variable, randomly assigning participants to the various levels of the independent variable, controlling or eliminating alternative explanations, and measuring responses via the dependent variable. The independent variable is the suspected cause; the dependent variable is the effect.

• Generalizing the results of an experiment well beyond the experimental situation is logically impossible, for the major purpose of most experiments is to demonstrate that the cause–effect relationship *can* occur, not that it always occurs.

• The logic of experimental research is that any difference between groups of participants as measured by the dependent variable is caused by their different experiences with the independent variable. Therefore, an experimenter must maintain internal validity—must rule out alternative explanations of any obtained differences.

• Alternative explanations are generally ruled out through the use of random assignment to conditions created by manipulating the independent variable. These alternative explanations include history effects, maturation effects, testing effects, statistical regression effects, selection effects, and mortality effects.

• Control over the experimental situation can be used to rule out instrumentation effects, participant bias, and experimenter bias.

• The basic design of an experiment includes different groups representing different levels of a manipulated independent variable to which participants are randomly assigned. Adding a pretest to this design enables us to measure change as a function of the independent variable. Care must be taken, however, to avoid an interaction between treatment and testing.

• The Solomon four-group design can be used to measure testing effects, including a testing–treatment interaction. This added ability to test effects decreases the efficiency of the design with respect to testing the research hypothesis.

• When more than one independent variable is necessary, factorial designs must be used to assess both main effects and interaction effects. Main effects are simple effects due to one variable, whereas interaction effects are those caused by a combination of two or more independent variables.

• Repeated measures may be used with any experimental design, but only if the effects of an independent variable are not so long lasting as to interfere with subsequent levels of the same or another independent variable. Designs with repeated measures must also take into account the possibility of order effects.

• Although often used in experimental research, participant characteristics cannot be considered true independent variables. Also called subject variables, they may indicate the presence of a systematic difference, but they are not themselves considered to be causal agents.

• Experimental research involves potentially serious ethical questions concerning benefits withheld from participants, level of informed consent, and control over participants' experiences. All of these must be included in the ethical balancing act.

CHAPTER SIX

Quasi-Experimental
Research

 *Participants were randomly assigned to the high
and low IQ groups.*

—Confused Student's Paper

Overview

Quasi-experimental research, as the name implies, includes research methods that
approximate but are not truly experimental methods. In this chapter, you will
learn about the major types of quasi-experimental designs and will also be exposed
to the types of statistical analyses appropriate for these designs. The mathematics
may be complex, but the principles are not. You will also learn about designs that
involve only a single participant.

Introduction

For a variety of different reasons, many of which were not understood by the
student quoted at the beginning of this chapter, it is simply not possible to randomly assign participants to the different levels of many independent variables. It
is also not possible to manipulate many independent variables. You cannot, for
example, manipulate participants' levels of intelligence; even if you found a way to
make such a manipulation, doing so would be well beyond the boundaries of ethical
research. On the other hand, you can manipulate their knowledge about specific
topics—which is what the confused student did—but that's not the same as ma-

nipulating levels of intelligence. Similarly, you cannot assign participants to different gender categories. For these and other variables that cannot be controlled, true experimental research is not possible. It is possible, however, to test research hypotheses with approximations of experimental research.

In this chapter, we will concern ourselves with quasi-experimental designs— research designs that approximate experimental designs but do not include random assignment to conditions (Cook & Campbell, 1979). Although quasi-experimental designs do not involve so rigorous a test of cause–effect hypotheses as do experimental designs, they do provide worthy alternatives when experiments are impossible, impractical, or unethical. Many of the designs discussed below can be used to avoid a number of alternative explanations fully described in Chapter 5. Quasi-experimental designs cannot, however, avoid all of the alternative explanations that threaten internal validity; instead, logical analysis replaces random assignment.

In their roles as alternatives to experimental designs, quasi-experimental designs ask nearly the same questions as those asked by true experimental designs. Testing cause–effect questions—explanation—is also the main purpose of quasi-experimentation. Although the questions are pretty much the same, the specificity of the questions differs greatly. Recall from Chapter 5 that experimental research involves asking whether the independent variable can be demonstrated to cause the dependent variable—whether, for example, judge's instructions concerning reasonable doubt can cause jurors to arrive at a particular verdict.

In quasi-experimental research, the cause–effect aspect of the question remains, but its emphasis changes. Instead of asking whether the independent variable *causes* the dependent variable, the question becomes whether an independent variable *is an indicator* of whatever the real cause may be. You cannot sensibly ask, for example, whether gender causes verdicts; gender per se is not a legitimate cause. Instead, you must ask whether verdicts differ as a function of gender—whether gender is an indicator of some unknown true cause, whether whatever may be causing verdicts to change is strongly associated with gender. Observing that males and females systematically differ with respect to the unknown cause is not the same as claiming gender is the cause.

A more realistic example of quasi-experimental research is the study I am currently conducting on community reactions to field tests of genetically altered organisms. (Dane, 1988a). Genetically altered organisms are bacteria created in a laboratory through gene splicing or through some other form of recombinant DNA technology. Field tests of such organisms involve placing the organism in a natural environment outside the laboratory in which they were created. One manufacturer of these organisms is currently field testing an organism to determine how well it survives winter and multiple-crop planting. I am interested in the reactions of people living in and around the community where the field test is being conducted.

By measuring attitudes on a variety of issues before, during, and after the field test takes place, I hope to be able to draw some conclusions about attitudinal changes that coincide with the field test. Reactions to the field test are indicators of whatever changes may take place, but I cannot conclude that the field test caused any of the changes that do occur. It is reasonable to assume that the field

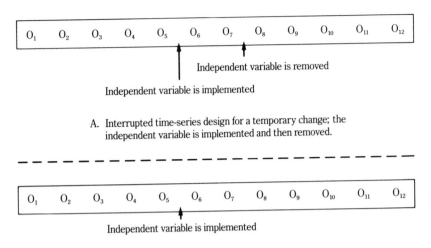

A. Interrupted time-series design for a temporary change; the
   independent variable is implemented and then removed.

B. Interrupted time-series design for a permanent change; the
   independent variable is implemented and remains in effect
   for the duration of the study.

Figure 6.1   Time-series designs for (a) a temporary independent variable and
(b) a permanent independent variable

test is causing some change, but observed changes may also be due to coincidental
changes in weather patterns, employment opportunities, or any number of other
potential factors that happen to coincide with the field test. As you learn about the
various designs available for quasi-experimental research, you will also learn about
some strategies for limiting the number of possible alternative explanations.

Time-Series Design

Time-series designs are a type of extended repeated measures design in which
the dependent variable is measured several times before and after the introduction
of the independent variable; that is, a series of measures are taken over a period
of time. There are two types of time-series designs: interrupted time-series and
multiple time-series.

Interrupted Time-Series Design

Interrupted time-series designs take their name from the notion that the independent variable is an interruption of ongoing activities, a change in the normal
stream of events. For example, the field test mentioned earlier is a change in the
ongoing experiences of the people living in the vicinity of the test. Figure 6.1 contains two examples of an interrupted time-series design.

In the research diagrammed in Figure 6.1a, each "O" represents a set of measurements of attitudes toward a variety of different issues. The field test will continue for a period of time, but it will not be permanent. However, because the
effects of the field test may last considerably longer than the physical presence of

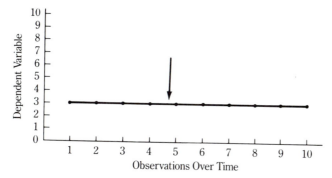

Figure 6.2 Results for a permanent time-series design
in which the independent variable appears to have no effect
on the dependent variable. The independent variable was
implemented between observations 4 and 5 (as indicated by
arrow).

the test, it may be more appropriate to consider the field test to be associated
with a permanent change, as depicted in Figure 6.1b. Another relatively permanent change might be a change in the requirements for graduation at your college;
the change, although not permanent in any absolute sense, would be permanent
relative to your period of matriculation.

Whatever the research hypothesis under consideration, the measures obtained before the introduction of the independent variable (O_1 through O_5 in Figure 6.1) provide a way to determine the extent to which maturation and testing
may be alternative explanations. If the results of those measures remain fairly
stable, then testing and maturation are not likely alternative explanations. On the
other hand, time-series designs are subject to history effects. If, for example,
another chemical leakage incident such as that which occurred in Bhopal, India
happened during the field test I am studying, I could not determine whether any
change in attitudes was associated with the field test or with the chemical leakage
incident.

The analyses that are appropriate for time-series designs are forthrightly
called time-series analyses. The mathematics of time-series analyses is beyond
the scope of this book, but there are readable references you can consult on this
topic (McDowell, McCleary, Meidinger, & Hay, 1980; Ostrom, 1978). Before doing so, however, you should have a solid background in multiple regression techniques. The essential basis of time-series analyses is a comparison between the
preindependent-variable observations and postindependent-variable observations.
For example, the preindependent- and postindependent-variable trends in Figure
6.2 are the same, indicating that the independent variable had no effect or that its
effect was canceled out by some history effect.

In Figure 6.2, whether or not the independent variable represents a permanent change does not alter the conclusion, although it does make a difference in
the actual calculations of the time-series statistics. The results displayed indicate
no effect at all for the independent variable. However, this interpretation must be
qualified by the possibility that some history effect canceled what may have been a

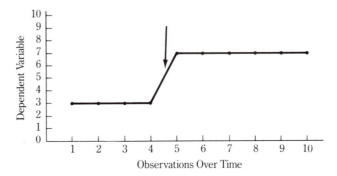

Figure 6.3 Results for a permanent time-series design in which the independent variable clearly has a dramatic effect on the dependent variable. The independent variable was implemented between observations 4 and 5.

very effective independent variable. If the preindependent-variable trend is different from the postindependent-variable trend, then you may conclude there was an effect, which again must be qualified by the possibility that the effect was a history effect rather than a true effect of the independent variable. Figure 6.3 provides an example of a time-series study in which an effect was observed.

Drawing conclusions from a time-series design is not always as easy as Figures 6.2 and 6.3 suggest, for quasi-experimental data are not always as straightforward as those presented here. More often than not, the trends observed before and after introduction of the independent variable cannot be described by a straight line. One reason for this difficulty is the lack of control one has in such research; because you cannot manipulate the independent variable, you may not be able to control other variables that may coincide with it. Consequently, the data become more difficult to interpret. The results illustrated in Figure 6.4 are far

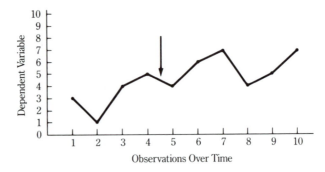

Figure 6.4 Results for a permanent time-series design in which the independent variable, implemented between observations 4 and 5, may have had an effect on the dependent variable. Time-series analyses would be required to determine whether the increase in the dependent variable was statistically significant or merely a result of random instability.

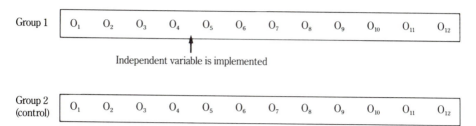

Figure 6.5 Multiple time-series design for a permanent change. The independent variable is implemented between observations 4 and 5 in Group 1 only. Group 2 never experiences the manipulation, although observations are taken at the same time for both groups.

more representative of typical time-series data. Deciding whether the data shown in Figure 6.4 represent an effect for the independent variable or merely the continuation of an unstable trend requires a statistical decision, which is why we must rely on time-series analyses to interpret data from such designs.

Multiple Time-Series Design

One variation of the interrupted time-series design is the multiple time-series design. In this design, two sets of observations are compared. As illustrated in Figure 6.5, one set of observations includes the manipulation, whereas the other set, which serves as a quasi-experimental control group, does not. The existence of the control group (Group 2 in Figure 6.5) guards against a history effect, but only if the corresponding observations are obtained simultaneously. Analyzing multiple time-series data is considerably more complex in practice than is analyzing interrupted time-series data, but the theoretical basis for the analysis is the same.

Returning to the community reaction to a field test as an example, Group 1 in Figure 6.5 would be composed of people living in the community where the field test is being conducted. Group 2 would include people in some other community, preferably a similar one that is unaware of the ongoing field test. If I measure the two groups at the same time, then it is less likely that a history effect will occur for one group but not the other. Of course, I could not be as sure about it as I could be if I could randomly assign participants to the two groups, but that's a problem I can't solve. However, with careful monitoring of the research environment and some common sense, you can all but eliminate history, maturation, instrumentation, and testing effects as alternative explanations for time-series designs.

Regression-Discontinuity Design

Time-series designs are **longitudinal designs**—*the same participants are repeatedly measured over time.* For some research projects, however, it is too expensive or otherwise undesirable to make repeated measurements. In such instances,

Group 1 O_1 ⎫
Group 2 O_2 ⎬ Groups 1–4 do not experience
Group 3 O_3 ⎪ the independent variable
Group 4 O_4 ⎭

Group 5 O_5 ⎫
Group 6 O_6 ⎬ Groups 5–8 do experience
Group 7 O_7 ⎪ the independent variable
Group 8 O_8 ⎭

Figure 6.6   A regression-discontinuity design with eight groups. The first four groups do not experience the manipulation, whereas the last four groups do experience it. It is assumed that the groups differ along some relevant, preexisting dimension, such as age or amount of time resident in a community.

cross-sectional designs are more appropriate. A **cross-sectional design** involves *one measurement of different groups that represent different time periods.* It might involve, for example, grouping participants according to the number of years they have lived in the community where the field test is occurring. Such a design, called a regression-discontinuity design, is illustrated in Figure 6.6.

The underlying logic of the regression-discontinuity design is the same as that for the time-series design: the different groups represent different amounts of experience with the independent variable. In Figure 6.6, for example, Group 8 could contain residents who have been living in the community for the longest period of time, and presumably the field test constitutes the greatest amount of change for them by virtue of the existence of more experience with the status quo. Group 1 would then contain residents who have lived in the community the least amount of time and therefore have less basis for comparison for the changes that may result from the field test.

The design is called a regression-discontinuity design because the groups that do not experience the manipulation (Groups 1 through 4 in Figure 6.6) are used to project expected values by way of multiple-regression analyses. These expected values are then compared to the actual values obtained from groups that experienced the independent variable (Groups 5 through 8 in Figure 6.6). The expected values are what would be expected if the independent variable had no effect.

Figure 6.7 illustrates the results from a regression-discontinuity design in which the independent variable apparently increased scores on the dependent variable. The line with solid squares represents actual scores, whereas the line with open squares represents the scores that would be expected if the independent variable had no effect. The difference between the two lines represents the effect of the independent variable.

Although the regression-discontinuity design may seem to be more efficient than the time-series design, the relative efficiency of being able to obtain all measures at the same time is offset by the requirement of additional assumptions

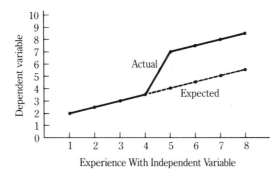

Figure 6.7 Ideal results from a regression-discontinuity design. The line labeled Expected depicts the values one would expect if the independent variable had no effect. The line labeled Actual represents the actual results obtained, indicating that the independent variable did have some effect on the dependent variable.

about the participants. Experience with the independent variable may be determined equivalently under both designs, but the regression-discontinuity design requires you to assume that the independent variable has not changed during the time period of interest. If, for example, a major incident occurred during the field test, such as a demonstration by an environmental group, the independent variable would also change. It may also be that some of the more recent residents, who are assumed to experience less change in the community because they haven't lived there as long, moved to the community because they wanted to live someplace that was environmentally stable. Without careful monitoring of the ongoing activities and without attempting to measure the previous experiences of the participants, you cannot be sure the groups in a regression-discontinuity design differ only in amount, and not in kind, of the independent variable they have experienced.

Data analyses for regression-discontinuity designs, as you might expect from the name, involve regression analyses. Multiple regression analyses are used to determine whether the equations for the two lines in Figure 6.7 are the same. If the statistical analyses indicate that the two equations are not the same, then you can conclude that the independent variable had an effect, provided you can logically rule out alternative explanations. Like time-series analyses, the mathematics associated with multiple regression is beyond the scope of this book, but Kerlinger (1979) is an excellent source for this topic. For illustration purposes, however, you don't need to understand the math to understand the principle; either the two lines are the same or they're not.

Nonequivalent Groups Basic Pretest Design

When it is not possible to make multiple measurements over time, to measure a relatively large number of different groups of participants, or to assign participants

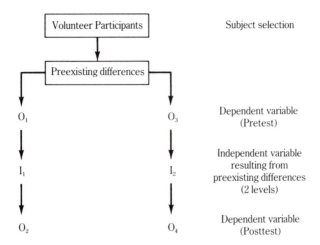

Figure 6.8 The nonequivalent groups basic pretest design. The independent variable is a result of preexisting differences among the subjects, such as gender or some other variable that cannot be manipulated.

randomly to different levels of an independent variable, then an abbreviated combination of time-series and regression-discontinuity designs may be used. The design in Figure 6.8 should remind you of the basic pretest design described in Chapter 5. Except for the fact that participants are not randomly assigned to different conditions (a very important exception), the nonequivalent groups basic pretest design is identical to the basic pretest design. The use of pretesting (O_1 and O_3 in Figure 6.8) enables you to determine whether any change exhibited by those experiencing the independent variable also would have occurred in its absence.

Of course, the nonequivalent groups basic pretest design, like the time-series and regression-discontinuity designs, is subject to selection effects because it lacks random assignment to conditions. When it is necessary or otherwise desirable to use this design, alternative explanations must be ruled out through logical analysis rather than through random assignment and control over variables. Because it is highly similar to the basic pretest design discussed in Chapter 5, the statistical analyses used for the nonequivalent groups design are essentially the same: these include analysis of variance, the Mann-Whitney U test, and chi-square (Nowaczyk, 1988).

Matching, discussed in Chapter 5, provides an alternative to random assignment but is not as effective as random assignment for dealing with selection effects. Matching, you should recall, involves measuring the extent to which two or more groups differ on some preexisting characteristic, such as intelligence or experience, and adjusting the size of the independent variable effect accordingly. There is no end, however, to the number of potential variables that may require matching, and therefore you can never be sure you have matched participants on all relevant characteristics.

Self-Selection

Although it may seem that random assignment is always preferable to quasi-experimental designs, such is not the case. There are a number of situations in which self-selection is the rule rather than an alternative explanation to be avoided. Self-selection refers to any circumstances in which the participants are already at different levels of an independent variable, usually because they have some desire to be at that level. Your own experience with class scheduling is an example. Unless you are very different from most undergraduates, you would rather be in a position to choose your courses than to have them randomly assigned to you by the registrar's office. If your research hypothesis involves a similar self-selection component, then a quasi-experimental design provides greater **external validity**—*the relationship between the research experience and everyday experience*—than does an experimental design. Self-selection is not always an alternative explanation; it may sometimes be the independent variable.

The key distinction between experimental and quasi-experimental research is the manner in which the participants experience the independent variable. Experimental participants are randomly assigned to conditions, whereas quasi-experimental research capitalizes on preexisting differences among participants. Whenever such preexisting differences are the focus of research, quasi-experimental designs may be more appropriate than their experimental counterparts. We next turn to considering designs in which there is only one participant.

Single-Participant Design

Known also as single-subject design, **single-participant design** is a *design specifically tailored to include only one participant in the study*. Whenever your research interests center on a single person, perhaps a client experiencing therapy, single-participant designs are appropriate. They are also appropriate when the population of interest is so highly homogeneous that studying more than one member of the population is redundant. Learning studies involving experimental animals, for example, generally involve the assumption that one animal's reaction to the independent variable will be the same as any other animal's reaction. There are three types of single participant designs: case study, baseline, and withdrawal.

Case Study Design

As the name implies, a **case study** involves *intensive study of a single participant over an extended period of time*. The most common example of such designs is a therapist monitoring a client's responses to therapy. By definition, therapy begins as soon as the therapist and client meet, so there is usually no opportunity to monitor the client before the independent variable—therapy—is experienced. Of course, self-reports from the client provide some information about pretherapy experiences, but that is not the same as directly measuring the dependent variable prior to the initiation of therapy. Using traditional design notation, a case study is illustrated in Figure 6.9. Of course, there is only a single participant and therefore no reason to include group numbers in the notation.

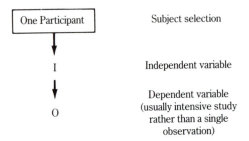

Figure 6.9 The case study in design notation. Because there is only one participant,
no group numbers are assigned to either the
independent or the dependent variable.

By now you should realize there are a host of alternative explanations to this design, which is essentially the basic design without random assignment. However, a series of logical assumptions may enable you to rule out some alternative explanations. For example, in a therapy situation, it is reasonable to assume that a problem existed before the therapy began or the client would not have sought therapy. Thus, a measure of the dependent variable before initiation of the independent variable is not always necessary, although it can be used when appropriate and possible. More important, a case study involves a series of intensive, in-depth observations, and many of those observations may provide information that can be used to rule out additional alternative explanations.

For the most part, case study designs should be considered when you are interested only in the specific individual serving as the participant. Similarly, conclusions drawn from a case study should be limited to that participant. Although it is certainly possible to generalize from a case study, it is most often unwise to do so. The major assumption underlying generalization is that the research participants represent the individuals to whom the generalization is applied, and a single participant rarely represents any larger group of people. Animals bred for research may be sufficiently homogeneous to allow generalizations, but people are rarely that homogeneous.

On the other hand, a case study can certainly be used to develop research hypotheses to be examined in later studies. Indeed, hypothesis generation is probably the most common purpose of case studies. Piaget's (1984) famous theory of child development, for example, came about through his case studies of individual children. Since he first began proposing hypotheses generated from case studies, many of his theoretical formulations have been supported empirically through a variety of different methods. There may be rare times, however, when you can reasonably generalize from a single participant, in which case you may want to use a baseline design.

Baseline Design
The baseline design is really an elaboration of the case study. In a **baseline design,** *preindependent variable measures are compared with postindependent mea-*

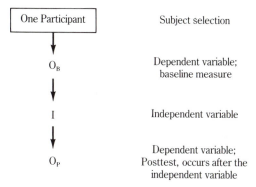

Figure 6.10 The baseline design for a single subject. The dependent variable is measured before (the baseline measurement) and after (the posttest measurement) a change in the independent variable. Usually, but not always, the independent variable is manipulated by the experimenter.

sures. Illustrated in Figure 6.10, the baseline design is very similar to a time-series design, except that only one participant is included in the study. Multiple baseline measures may be taken, and you can use repeated measurements after a change in the independent variable regardless of whether or not the independent variable is manipulated.

Just as with time-series designs, the measures taken before a change in the independent variable are compared to those taken after the change. If you can assume that the single participant does indeed represent another group of people and can establish sufficient control over the research environment to rule out alternative explanations, then the baseline design is nearly as powerful as any of the designs discussed in this or any other chapter. Laboratory rats raised in a controlled environment, for example, can generally be assumed to be so homogeneous as to make each rat representative of other laboratory rats. Testing the effect of an independent variable, such as the addition of sucrose to the animal's water, would enable you to demonstrate a cause–effect relationship between the presence of sucrose and the animal's drinking behavior. If you measured consumption of water prior to adding the sucrose and again after adding the sucrose, you have a very powerful test of the effects of sucrose. Indeed, baseline designs using laboratory rats to test addiction to cocaine are the basis for a number of anti-drug television commercials that claim that rats prefer cocaine to food and will eventually starve to death before giving up cocaine in favor of food.

The strength of the baseline study is that the measures of the dependent variable before the change in the independent variable enables you to assess its effects. With the case study, for example, you can only guess about the preexisting state of the individual participant, even if that guess is based on self-reports from the participant. The baseline design allows you to measure premanipulation levels directly. Despite their strength, baseline studies should be replicated to allow you to assert the generalizability of the results with greater confidence. Remember that if you are only interested in that specific participant, there is no need to generalize.

Withdrawal Design

Despite the strength of the baseline design, it is not the most powerful among the single-participant designs. That distinction belongs to the **withdrawal design,** *in which the treatment is presented and removed several times.* Known also as an A-B-A-B design, the withdrawal design involves measuring the dependent variable before the independent variable is manipulated, after it has been manipulated, again after the manipulation has been removed, and so on for as many repetitions as seems appropriate. The withdrawal design is illustrated in Figure 6.11, wherein it is easy to see why the design is also known as an A-B-A-B design.

Usually, the "A" condition refers to the baseline state of the participant—the state without the treatment—and the "B" condition refers to the state of the participant while experiencing the treatment. At some point the treatment is withdrawn and the participant returns to baseline, after which the independent variable is manipulated again. Of course, this design may be used only if your

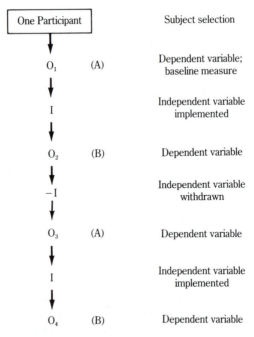

Figure 6.11 The withdrawal design. The treatment is introduced and removed in alternation, with measures of the dependent variable taken at each change in the status of the subject. Only independent variables that can be manipulated and have no permanent effects can be used in the withdrawal design.

independent variable is manipulable and does not create a permanent change in the participant.

Using the study of cocaine addiction in laboratory rats as example, you could measure food consumption, replace the food with cocaine, measure consumption, return the food, and so on so long as you think is necessary in order to demonstrate the effect. The same procedure could be used to measure reinforcement using a reinforcer other than cocaine. On the other hand, you could not use a withdrawal design to study the effect of hypothalamic lesions, for once you induce lesions in an animal you cannot remove them, and thus you could never return to the baseline state. The same problem would be encountered in a therapy study with a human participant; although you can remove therapy, doing so does not necessarily negate all of the effects therapy has had thus far. It's not enough to remove the manipulation; the withdrawal design requires the removal of the *effects* of the manipulation, as well as its physical presence. You must also be able to control alternative explanations, such as history, before drawing a cause–effect conclusion from a withdrawal study.

Data Analyses

Data analyses for single-participant designs tend to be extremely simple and straightforward. Because there is no variation among participants, there is no need for statistical procedures such as analysis of variance or regression. In general, single-participant data analyses tend to be "interocular trauma" tests; either the effect is so apparent it hits you between the eyes or it is not there. You might, for example, graph the daily consumption of food in the rat study or graph a client's self-reported behavior problems. The graph should clearly demonstrate the effect, much as the graph of ideal time-series results in Figure 6.3 does. Because there is only one participant, there is little need for examining the margin of error associated with your conclusions; either the effect is there or it's not.

Summary

• Although experimental designs provide the best way to test cause–effect relationships, there are times when true experiments are not possible. At such times, quasi-experimental designs are a preferred approximation. Quasi-experimental designs lack random assignment.

• Time-series designs are longitudinal designs involving repeated measures of the dependent variable before and after implementation of the independent variable. The repeated measures can be used to assess maturation and testing effects.

• History effects can be assessed through multiple time-series designs, which involve simultaneously measuring more than one group of participants.

• Regression-discontinuity designs involve a single measure of the dependent variable across groups that differ along a dimension defined by the independent variable. They are cross-sectional designs that can be used when longitudinal designs are not feasible.

• When repeated measures or a large number of groups cannot be included in a research project, the nonequivalent groups basic design may be used to approximate an experimental design. In this design, two or more groups that have not been randomly assigned to conditions are measured before and after implementation of the independent variable.

• All quasi-experimental designs are subject to selection effects as an alternative explanation. Selection may, however, be considered a function of the independent variable if self-selection is part of the phenomenon being studied.

• There are also research hypotheses that can be tested with single-participant designs, but these are limited to hypotheses about the specific participant or involve the assumption that the participant represents a homogeneous group of others.

• In a case study, the participant is observed after the independent variable is introduced. A baseline design involves measuring the dependent variable before and after the independent variable is manipulated. In a withdrawal design, measures are taken sequentially with successive presentation and removal of the manipulation.

• If the independent variable can be manipulated and the research environment controlled, single-participant designs may be used to test cause–effect hypotheses, but such tests lack the generality of more traditional experimental designs.

• Data analyses for single-participant designs typically involve graphic presentations instead of complicated statistical analyses. The effect of the independent variable is either apparent or not.

CHAPTER SEVEN

Survey Research

The latest research on polls has turned up some interesting variables. It turns out, for example, that people will tell you any old thing that pops into their heads.

—Caption from a Cartoon by Saxon

Overview

The purpose of this chapter is to introduce the main issues and procedures of survey research. Survey research includes methods in which participants are asked questions directly. The questions may be part of an interview schedule or a questionnaire and may be asked through one of several different procedures. You will learn which research purposes are most effectively accomplished via surveys, as well as some specific techniques for preparing survey instruments. You will also learn how to administer a survey face-to-face or via the telephone (interviewing) and how to administer a survey through the mail (questionnaires). The relative merits of each technique will be discussed, and sampling issues specific to each technique will be examined. Finally, you will learn about general conventions for data analysis for survey research.

Introduction

Survey methods are probably the oldest methods in the researcher's repertoire, and they are the methods with which the general public is most familiar. All of us have asked people for information, and all of us have been asked by others to provide information. As humorously illustrated in the opening quote, however, there is more to survey research than simply asking other people to provide information. How to conduct and evaluate scientific surveys—how to avoid getting "any old thing"—is what this chapter is all about.

Survey research is a general label applied to a variety of different research methods that share a common purpose. **Survey research** involves *obtaining information directly from a group of individuals.* More often than not, it includes interviews or questionnaires, but it is important to keep in mind that the use of an interview or a questionnaire does not, by itself, define survey research methods: the procedure is not what defines the method, but rather the manner in which the procedure is carried out.

Survey research methods involve obtaining information directly from the participants by posing questions. The questions may be presented orally, on paper, or in some combination, but the response comes from the person to whom the question is addressed at the time the question is asked. Thus you and the participant are working together to collect the data; you ask and the participant answers. Even when questions are written on paper, you need to keep in mind the interactive aspect of survey research. Responses must be interpreted in terms of potential self-presentation effects and other effects related to recollection.

Although interviewing and questionnaires may be part of any type of research project, the sample size helps to distinguish survey research from other methods. The sample size in survey research is generally large, although it is not possible to provide an exact range. A survey research project may include as few as 100 participants or as many as 250 million.

As you might expect, directly obtaining information from a group of participants is more efficient for some research purposes than others. Survey methods are most appropriate for description and prediction, although they may be used less efficiently for exploration and action. Because surveys rarely involve manipulation of independent variables or random assignment to conditions, they generally are not used for testing cause–effect hypotheses.

Description is perhaps the most frequent purpose for survey methods. The classic example is the United States Decennial Census, which includes a sample of hundreds of millions of participants. The relative frequency data obtained from the census are often used by other researchers as a basis for their sampling procedures, particularly those who want to obtain a sample representing a particular region of the country. On a smaller scale, the examinations you take in class can be considered a form of survey research. Your instructor, through a questionnaire called an exam, attempts to assess the relative frequency of information you can correctly recall about the subject matter. Examinations, however, are missing at least one important ingredient of scientific research: the results are rarely reported to the scientific community.

The predictive survey research with which you may be most familiar is the use of college entrance examinations to predict first-year grades in college. The results of the research are reported, although their circulation is somewhat limited. A more traditional use of survey methods is the work of Hill, Rubin, and Peplau (1976), who attempted to determine the characteristics that predict the continuation or break-up of romantically involved couples. Although a number of variables were related to the status of the relationship, the predominant predictor was the general similarity of the two people. The more similar the two individuals in the relationship, the more likely they were to remain a couple during the two-year period of the study. We will come back to Hill and colleagues' research, but first we'll briefly examine why survey research is inefficient for exploratory and action purposes.

Although survey research invariably involves either a questionnaire or an interview, you will soon learn that there is more to survey research than simply putting together a collection of questions. Surveys can be used for exploratory research, but not with any degree of efficiency. One of the first rules of survey research is to know what kind of information you want to collect. The survey instrument should be designed on the basis of a research hypothesis, a condition antithetical to exploratory research. More often than not, designing a good survey study involves too much time and effort for exploratory research purposes.

If the intended effect of action research is to change the opinions of a large group of people, survey methods are an appropriate means by which to accomplish such research. Back (1980), for example, described the important role of surveys in an extensive program of research concerning population control. The surveys were used to assess the effectiveness of information campaigns designed to change attitudes about population control in general and birth control as a specific means. In the majority of action research, however, systematic observation or indirect measurement (see Chapter 8) is probably more appropriate. In the population control study, for example, the best measurement of the intended effect might be the birthrate in a selected target area. Survey methods may help to pinpoint reasons for a behavior change, but surveys may not be the most efficient way to measure the change itself.

In general, any question that can be expressed in terms of the relative frequency of information can be addressed through survey research. Put another way, whenever you want to know what a lot of people are thinking but don't necessarily need to determine why they are thinking that way, survey methods can be used.

Survey Content

There are three different types of information that may be obtained from survey respondents, the participants in a survey research project: facts, opinions, and behaviors. Although most surveys include all three types of information, we'll examine them separately. The words used to label the different types of information may be familiar, but they have very specific meanings in the context of survey research.

A **fact** is *a phenomena or characteristic available to anyone who knows how to observe it.* Often called sociological or demographic characteristics, facts include such variables as age, race, gender, income, and years of education. Facts are anything that can be verified independently. Hill et al. found that couples who were similar in age, education, and physical attractiveness were much more likely to remain in the relationship than were couples whose facts were not similar.

In most surveys, "fact" is a somewhat misleading label because respondents' self-reports are usually accepted without independent verification. That a survey fact can be verified doesn't necessarily mean that it will be, and respondents have been known to misrepresent themselves on a variety of different facts. Don't confuse the label as it is used in survey research with its use in everyday speech; just because someone says it's so don't make it so.

An **opinion** is *an expression of a respondent's preference, feeling, or behavioral intention.* Opinions can be objectively measured, but they cannot be verified independently. Thus, my behavior, as I wrote this text, including my stated intentions, may have led my publisher to believe that I intended to complete this book. But there is no way that my publisher could have verified that my intentions truly were to finish this book. I could have been going through the motions to make people think I was busy, for example, while having no real intention of bringing the project to completion. As you read this now, however, you can verify the fact that I did complete and have this book published, but at the time I wrote this you could not have verified my intentions.

The major difference between facts and opinions concerns agreement about the ways in which the two can be operationally defined. You can operationally define my age in terms of the date of birth on my birth certificate, for example, and encounter little or no disagreement about your operational definition. However, there may be considerable disagreement about whether my sitting in front of the word processor as I write this is a good operational definition of my intention to complete this book. That differential consensus about operational definitions exists does not necessarily mean that facts are more valid than opinions, but agreement is one measure of validity.

Using agreed-upon operational definitions of opinions concerning closeness, love, traditional sex roles, and religiosity, Hill and coworkers found that all these variables were related to a successful relationship. In general, the more similar the couple's opinions on these topics, the more likely the couple was to remain in their relationship.

The third type of survey content, **behavior,** refers to *an action completed by a respondent.* A typical behavior question may be worded something like "How many times did you attend your research methods class this week?" Like facts, behaviors can be verified, but only if a witness or indirect evidence can be obtained. Hill et al., for example, included in their survey questions about such behaviors as frequency of sexual intercourse and cohabitation. Clearly, the former is more difficult to verify than the latter. Interestingly, respondents' self-reports of these behaviors were not related to the success of their relationships.

Although opinions may contain a behavioral component, opinions involve intentions—How many times will you attend your class next week?—rather than actual completion of the behavior. Without verification, behaviors (and facts) can only be measured through self-reports. You must keep in mind that self-reports are not the same as verified, independent evidence; information from the two sources doesn't always agree.

Within any categorization system, there always seem to be things that do not fit cleanly. Knowledge is one of these things. Because most of their respondents were college students, Hill and coworkers attempted to assess knowledge through SAT math and verbal scores. Other researchers may measure knowledge in other subject areas, but the problem involves determining whether for the purposes of analysis knowledge should be considered a fact (an SAT score is verifiable) or a behavior (an attempt to remember information) or an opinion (a belief that the knowledge area is important). The resolution to the problem depends on your purposes: if you are using knowledge as an operational definition of a behavior, then treat the variable as you would any behavior measure.

Because most surveys include all three types of content, there is a tendency to disregard distinctions among them. Do not fall prey to this tendency. As you will learn later in this chapter, some types of content are best given precedence over other types of content. If you don't pay attention to the type of content in your survey, you may introduce considerable error into your data. The nature of self-report information already introduces some error into survey research (Phillips, 1971), and there is no point to adding more error through careless handling of survey content.

Survey Instruments

Just as the dials, gauges, and lights on the instrument panel of an automobile provide the means by which a driver obtains information about the car, the items on a survey instrument provide the means by which a researcher obtains information about respondents. The item topics, instructions, item formats, and arrangement of the items can all have an effect on the information you obtain. In this section, you will learn how to deal with such effects when designing and implementing a survey. The discussion is equally appropriate for interviews and questionnaires, with the exceptions that interviewers can be trained to overcome some instrument shortcomings and questionnaires cannot be altered once given to respondents.

Survey Topics

Every survey instrument should have a topic—a central issue to which most of the items are related. Which topic is addressed, of course, depends on your interests and research hypotheses. The items included on a survey should be at least partially derived from theoretical interests. Although such advice may seem obvious and unnecessary, it is too often the case that researchers include items, sometimes create entire questionnaires, without giving enough thought to what questions are to be answered by the data. Such shotgun approaches, as I call them, rarely provide the wealth of informative data expected by those who use them, and I strongly suggest you avoid them. If you can't think of a good reason to include an item, don't include it.

Some topics will be perceived as sensitive by your respondents, and questions dealing with such topics are likely candidates for responses based on self-presentation instead of accuracy. Data from such questions may be incomplete or reflect beliefs about what is appropriate. Respondents are generally unwilling to admit to illegal or socially deviant activities, for example, but they may also be unwilling to report even what seems to be innocuous information. In a recent survey (Dane, 1988a), for instance, respondents were unwilling to identify their employer. They had no reservations about revealing what they did for a living, but did not want to tell us for whom they did it.

That certain topics or items may be sensitive, however, does not automatically mean that you will not be able to obtain information. Anonymity or confidentiality can facilitate respondents' willingness to reveal such information. Kinsey and co-workers (1948, 1953) were able to obtain interview responses on a topic as sensitive as sexual practices, and Hunt (1974) was able to obtain questionnaire responses on the same topic. If you include sensitive topics in your survey instrument, you must be especially concerned about the validity of the data, but that does not mean you cannot obtain valid data. Following ethical guidelines (Chapter 3) and treating respondents as you would want to be treated usually is sufficient to obtain cooperation.

Survey Instructions

The instructions for completing the survey instrument can be used to eliminate some of the response biases mentioned above through assurances of anonymity or confidentiality. Of course, you must be careful to be sure that you can guarantee anonymity or confidentiality if you promise to do so. False claims are unethical and usually cannot be justified simply in order to produce better response rates or more accurate responses.

The first part of any set of instructions should be a brief introduction to the study. If you are using a questionnaire, place the instructions on a cover sheet or in an accompanying cover letter. If you are conducting an interview, the introduction of the study should be the first statement you make. Explain what the survey is about, how the results will be used, why the individual respondent's data are important to the study, and the level of anonymity or confidentiality with which the data will be treated. If you use any identifying numbers on a questionnaire, explain what they are. You might also make some mention of how respondents were selected to be included in the survey, such as random selection from the telephone book. You don't need to go into great detail about the sampling procedures, but most respondents are interested in finding out how they came to be respondents.

More specific instructions about how to complete survey items should be included throughout the instrument. Inclusion of sample items that illustrate the type of response or the length of responses for open-ended items tend to reduce the amount of unusable data. If more than one topic is covered by the survey, the items for each topic should be separated by brief explanations about the kind of information desired. Something as simple as "In this section, you are being asked to provide your opinion about several political issues" would be an adequate transitional explanation. In general, any point at which the topic or response format changes is a good point at which to insert a transition instruction. Such instructions need not be extensive; they should provide a transition to avoid surprising respondents and should inform them how to provide the information desired.

Survey Formats

The general layout of any survey instrument should, of course, be neat. One characteristic that contributes to neatness is space between items. Spacing prevents a cluttered appearance, and makes it less likely that a respondent or interviewer will skip an item. Do not be tempted to make the instrument appear shorter than it is by "crunching" the items together. The respondent who begins to tire before turning the first page (or before noticing the interviewer turning the first page) is probably going to decide that the remainder of the instrument will require too much time and effort. Short is not necessarily better; what is better is anything that makes it easier for the respondent to understand.

Response formats for specific items are discussed in detail in Chapter 15, the resource chapter on scaling. Before constructing specific items and formats for any survey instrument, you should examine the material in that chapter. However, some general guidelines can be addressed here. Regardless of the format you select, be sure your respondents and interviewers understand how to use the format. If you ask an open-ended question—the kind of question asked on essay exams—be sure to allow sufficient space to write a response. If the respondent is to choose from among multiple choices, they should represent the range of possible responses and be mutually exclusive. If the response involves choosing a point on a continuum, then clearly label the endpoints of the continuum. Be sure your respondents understand the labels you are using.

You may be tempted to consider that last bit of advice as very obvious. But Crew (cited in Babbie, 1983), for example, has pointed out that the word "very" has varied uses in different parts of the United States. In most parts of the country, "very" is an intensifier; it implies more of some quality. In some parts, however, "very" serves as a limiter; it implies less of some quality. The first sentence of this paragraph, then, could mean that the advice is something everyone would know about. But it could also be interpreted to mean that the advice was something only a few people would know about. Be aware of regional speech patterns and alter the wording of items and their labels accordingly. Don't assume that everyone knows the same idioms, phrases, and forms of speech with which you are familiar.

Arrangement of Survey Items

The arrangement of items within the instrument can also be used to reduce response bias or other forms of unusable data. Within a section dealing with a particular topic, for example, the more sensitive items should be placed toward the end of the section. Respondents should be gently led toward more sensitive items, not hit over the head with them.

For questionnaires, the first set of items should deal with the most interesting but least threatening topic and should be directly related to the overall purpose of the survey. At the beginning, you are trying to get the respondent interested in completing the instrument, and one way to do this is to create the impression that the instrument actually does accomplish the purpose outlined in the cover letter. Dillman (1978) suggests creating one or two questions specifically for this purpose, if necessary. Such "dummy" questions would not be analyzed, but the impression they create may make analyses of other items more worthwhile. Save the factual items—age, race, and so forth—for the end of the questionnaire.

For interviews, nonthreatening factual items—length of time at current address, age, and so on, but not income—are best placed first. They allow the interviewer to establish rapport without having to challenge the participant. Factual items help the interviewer to appear genuine and increase the likelihood that the respondent will indeed begin to respond; once begun, an interview is likely to be completed. As with a questionnaire, threatening items, even if they are factual, should be placed near the end of the interview.

In many survey instruments, some form of contingency item is necessary. A **contingency item** is *an item relevant only if a certain response was provided for a previous item.* A loan application, which is essentially a survey of your credit history, often requests a previous address if you have been at your current address for less than three years. Similarly, an item for which the respondent indicates that he or she is a registered voter might be followed by a contingency item such as "In what year, then, did you last vote in a national election?"

If only one or two contingency items follow a particular item, you can offset them simply by using different margins. Different margins indicate that the item is special in some way, much the same way that different margins for extensive quotes in a manuscript indicate that the material is from a different author. If a series of contingency items is appropriate—say, ten items for registered voters and ten different ones for those not registered to vote—it is best to instruct the respondent or interviewer to skip to the appropriate section. When instructions to skip items are included, be sure to indicate the item number to which the respondent should proceed, as well as the page number on which the item can be found.

The order of items is important when leading respondents into sensitive topics and when dealing with contingency items. Order, however, can both create and eliminate response bias. People have a tendency to want to appear consistent, and a series of items on the same topic may lead respondents to alter their responses to later items just to be consistent with their earlier responses. Not many people are willing to admit that they haven't voted in the last ten years, for example, after they've indicated that voting is an important responsibility of every good citizen. Similarly, a series of items on one topic may influence responses to items on a different topic. Responding to 20 items dealing with the threat of communism, for example, is likely to alter responses to a subsequent series of items dealing with the defense budget. Response bias can occur as a result of the order of the items, even if the items themselves are not biased.

Unfortunately, there is little one can do to prevent response bias due to the order of items. Randomizing the order of items may reduce the bias, but it's also likely to confuse respondents. Few people enjoy being questioned when the topic of inquiry is constantly changing. What can be done, however, is to estimate the extent to which order bias exists. If there is reason to suspect order bias, prepare different versions of the instrument and compare the responses. This procedure is best done when pretesting an instrument, but different versions of the final instrument may be required under some circumstances.

Pretesting Survey Instruments

I'll go out on the proverbial limb and state that pretesting is the most important phase of survey research. It's a sturdy limb; no survey data can be trusted unless you can be sure the respondents understood the instrument and provided appropriate responses. In addition to editing the instrument to avoid various forms of bias, pretesting is required to ensure that assumptions made while editing were reasonable.

Pretesting—*administering research measures under special conditions, usually before full-scale administration to participants*—involves giving a draft of the instrument to a relatively small group of people. Pretesting allows you to fine-tune the instrument in much the same way that a bench check allows a technician to evaluate a part before installing it. Pretesting is not exactly the same as a pilot test, however, because you are not trying to make a test run of the entire research procedure; you are only trying to test the measures you will use. Regardless of how you proceed with the actual survey, pretesting should involve interviewing some of the pretest respondents. Some may only receive a part of the final instrument, such as instructions and a few items, whereas others may receive the entire instrument. Depending on the length and complexity of the instrument, you might interview some pretest respondents about every item, some of them about a single series of items, and still others about the instructions only.

During a pretest, you first want to determine how well your instructions were understood. Did the cover letter and opening remarks convey the meaning you intended? Did the instructions for completing particular response formats actually help? Examine the pretest responses to determine whether there are clear indications of misunderstood items or instructions. Check to be sure that the pretest respondents completed what they were supposed to complete, skipped the right parts, circled all that needed to be circled, filled in the correct blanks, and so on.

If you construct instruments with different orders of items, you should randomly assign pretest respondents to the different versions. By statistically comparing the different groups you can determine what effect the different orders created. Random assignment, you should recall, ensures that whatever difference is obtained resulted from the different order. You may not be able to eliminate bias, but pretesting can provide an estimate of its impact.

Pretesting can also be applied to the people who are going to conduct the research—the interviewers. If the final instrument is to be administered by interview, you can pretest the interviewers to ensure that they are smooth and efficient. Do they quickly establish rapport, correctly record responses, follow the correct order of items, and do all the other things they are supposed to do? Pretesting provides an opportunity to evaluate the training you gave to the interviewers.

Essentially, pretesting should be used as an opportunity to investigate every aspect of the survey project. Surprises during pretesting may be annoying and may require additional preparation, but even major problems can be corrected. It was during pretesting (fortunately) that I discovered that respondents were unwilling to identify their employers, even though they were willing to provide their job titles. I had to rewrite that part of the survey instrument, but rewriting was better than getting no data at all. Surprises during the actual survey, even very minor surprises, often turn the full-scale administration of a survey into a very large and very expensive pilot project. It's always better to do a series of pretests than to waste a great deal of time, effort, and money to get nearly worthless data.

Depending on the procedures you will use, you may also want to conduct a pilot project—a small-scale administration of the survey using the exact procedures you plan to use for the full-scale project. Normally, however, survey procedures are planned well enough to make a pilot test unnecessary. Unless your procedure involves some sort of manipulation to create different groups—an experiment using survey procedures to measure the dependent variables—there is usually no need to conduct a pilot project in addition to pretesting.

Administering Surveys

Every method for administering surveys has advantages and disadvantages, regardless of the amount of pretesting completed to facilitate proper administration. It is impossible to declare categorically that one method is better than any other. Research purposes, intended respondents and report audience, instrument length, and staff availability all enter into decisions about administrative procedures. Before conducting any survey research, carefully weigh the relevant aspects of the alternative procedures.

Face-to-Face Interviews

In what was probably the first instructional volume on face-to-face interviews, Bingham and Moore (1924) described an interview as a conversation with a purpose. For our purposes, we can define an **interview** as *a structured conversation used to complete a survey.* The survey instrument provides the structure for the conversation, and collecting the data is the purpose.

The amount of structure in an interview depends on the amount of structure in the survey instrument. *Survey instruments that are essentially orally administered questionnaires* are called **schedules,** and they impose a high degree of structure on the interview. In some cases, schedules may consist of cards given to respondents; all the interviewer does is establish rapport, provide instructions, record responses, and answer the respondents' occasional questions (Gorden, 1969). Of course, establishing rapport, providing instructions, and answering questions are probably the most important things an interviewer does. Given the increased mistrust of strangers, however, a highly structured interview will probably produce a better response rate if administered through a mailed questionnaire or a telephone interview (Nederhof, 1981).

When items are likely to produce questions or the sequence of items is complicated, a structured interview is the most effective means for ensuring responses based on an accurate understanding of the questions. Structured interviews are also very effective when particular members of a household, such as the oldest person or employed individuals only, comprise the sample. In such cases, the interviewer will be able to ascertain the propriety of a potential respondent.

In a partially structured or **focused interview,** *the interviewer poses a few predetermined questions but has considerable flexibility concerning follow-up questions* (Merton, Fiske, & Kendall, 1956). Focused interviews are typically used when respondents consist of a specific group chosen for their familiarity with the research topic. A focused interview might be used to survey graduating seniors as part of an evaluation of the quality of a major program, or for some other type of exit interview. As you might expect, it is also important that the interviewer be somewhat familiar with the topic; otherwise, the interviewer will be at a loss when the time comes to generate follow-up questions. The primary emphasis of a focused interview is gaining information about the subjective perceptions of respondents.

The major advantage of a focused interview is its flexibility, but that is also its major disadvantage. The flexibility enables the interviewer to explore more fully the opinions and behaviors of respondents; thus the total collection of responses should contain more and varied detail than would the data from a structured interview. On the other hand, because not every respondent will be asked exactly the same questions, it is more difficult to interpret differences obtained when responses are compared. Thus because some questions (and therefore some responses) will be unique to a given respondent, comparisons across respondents are best limited to the predetermined questions to which everyone responds.

Consider an exit interview, for example, in which everyone is asked why they are leaving their jobs. Some might say they were dissatisfied with their position, which would naturally lead to a follow-up question about specific aspects of the position. Others may say they are leaving to take advantage of a better offer, which would lead to questions comparing the new offer with the current position. Still others may be leaving to make a career change, which leads to entirely different follow-up questions. Although everyone has been asked why they are leaving, it would make no sense to compare the three groups' responses to follow-up questions. The entire set of responses from each participant, however, may be subjected to a content analysis in order to determine the main themes underlying the responses. Comparisons may then be made across respondents on the basis of the themes, rather than on the exact responses. When the *wording* of responses cannot be compared, the *issues* addressed by the responses may be comparable.

The least structured kind of interview is the unfocused or **nondirective interview,** in which *the interviewer encourages the respondent to discuss a topic but* *provides little or no guidance and very few direct questions.* I've included nondirective interviews here to provide the full range of structures available for interviews, but I do not recommend you try to use one to conduct a survey. With little or no guidance from the interviewer, responses from a nondirective interview are likely to be so idiosyncratic as to make analysis impossible. Nondirective interviews may be used to gather data in a single-participant design (see Chapter 6) or with a larger sample of extremely homogeneous respondents, but they are generally inappropriate for survey research.

Still, it is certainly reasonable to use a combination of interview structures within a single study. A combination of structures both ensures that at least a portion of the responses are based on the same questions and provides an opportunity to pursue a promising line of questioning with less structured probes. A **probe** is *a phrase or question used by the interviewer to prompt the respondent to elaborate on a particular response.*

If you were conducting a survey of psychology majors, for example, about the relationship between satisfaction with research methods courses and intended career plans, one item on your schedule might involve having respondents rate, say on a ten-point scale, the overall utility of their most recently completed methods course. If a respondent rated the course toward the "useful" end of the continuum, you could follow up with a focused question, such as "What about the course did you find useful?" Such nondirective probes as "What else?" or "Can you tell me more?" could be used to obtain more comprehensive information. Often, however, the most useful nondirective probe involves simply keeping your pen on the paper and waiting for the respondent to continue talking. Should a respondent begin to drift off the topic, a probe such as "That reminds me, I wanted to ask you about . . . " will usually get the interview back on track.

Have you ever felt as though you were being interrogated by someone? Did you enjoy the experience? Unless you are remarkably fortunate, your answer to the first question is yes; unless you are remarkably weird, your answer to the second question is no. Most respondents would provide these same answers after being subjected to a poorly trained interviewer. An interview is a conversation with a purpose, but it is not an interrogation. First impressions are extremely important, and the impression you want interviewers to create is that of a trustworthy, pleasant, and competent individual. Indeed, you want interviewers to in fact be trustworthy, pleasant, and competent. When conducting face-to-face interviews, you are asking potential respondents to open their doors and perhaps even allow you inside their homes. Aside from avoiding looking strange, you want to provide a greeting that both very quickly establishes your purpose and legitimacy and begins the survey instrument. For example, you might say

> Good morning, I'm conducting a survey on college athletics for Research University. Your name was selected randomly from the phone book, and we'd like to include your ideas in the survey. For example, do you attend Research University's football games?

Longer introductions are usually not necessary and may actually create suspicion.

Remember that the interview is a conversation; be pleasant and remain neutral. You should record any and all responses without reacting to them. If the respondent asks questions, answer them if you are able to do so or simply say you don't know the answer. Regardless of the respondent's demeanor, remain polite. Some people appear to be rude without actually intending to be rude; if you return apparent rudeness, you can forget about the rest of the interview. Also, a stiff or uncomfortable conversation is unpleasant and is very likely to be terminated. Be sufficiently familiar with the survey instrument to bring each item into the conversation smoothly. Don't memorize the instrument, but know it well enough to be able to move on to the next item without having to search for it.

Part of an interviewer's competence involves being able to present every item to every respondent exactly as it appears on the instrument. Rewording should be used only when it is clear, after one or two repetitions, that the respondent does not understand. The items should be presented in the same order as they appear on the instrument; rearranging or needlessly rewording items is only likely to undermine all of the work that went into pretesting the instrument.

A competent interviewer must particularly avoid presenting his or her own viewpoints on the topic. If the response to the sample opening question is "Yes, I've attended every football game since 1954," it would be inappropriate to comment either positively or negatively. Even a seemingly innocent remark such as "Good for you" can introduce bias; the respondent may infer you have a particular response set in mind and provide that response set instead of responding sincerely. If you are asked to provide your own viewpoint, the best response is to nonchalantly tell the respondent that his or her viewpoint is more important than your own and move on to the next question.

In addition to avoiding bias resulting from providing your views, it is also important to avoid bias by making sure you accurately record the respondent's views. Record all responses as they are provided, and avoid the temptation to correct the respondent's grammar or discard seemingly irrelevant comments. If the respondent says it, write it down, and write it verbatim.

Finally, the best way to make an interviewer competent is to conduct interviews. Practice interviewing others on your research team or practice interviewing friends. Practice, practice, and practice some more; practice until you feel comfortable doing the interview and others agree that you are doing it well.

Telephone Interviews

The telephone interview is an alternative to face-to-face interviews that has had a justifiably bad reputation for many years. At one time the primary problem with telephone interviews was, very simply, that not enough people had telephones. The size of the potential sample was relatively small, which introduced a fair amount of error into results obtained through telephone surveys. Today, however, the proportion of homes with telephones is sufficiently large to obviate the problem. According to the United States Bureau of the Census (1979), about 97% of homes in the United States have at least one telephone. Furthermore, Klecka and Tuchfarber (1978) used a telephone survey to replicate a survey done via face-to-face interviews and found no appreciable differences between the results of their survey and those of the original interviews. It thus appears that the bad reputation of telephone interviews is no longer justifiable.

The technique used to obtain respondents in Klecka and Tuchfarber's survey, and indeed in most telephone surveys, is known as random digit dialing. **Random digit dialing** is *a sampling procedure in which a valid telephone exchange is sampled from a region and the telephone number is completed with four randomly selected digits.* For national surveys, area codes are randomly selected; then valid exchanges within each area code are randomly selected, and then the final four digits are randomly selected from a random number table or generated by a computer program. Nonworking or invalid numbers (such as a business instead of a residence) are removed from the list of generated numbers as soon as their invalid status is determined.

Random digit dialing can be entirely computerized, and equipment that can both generate and dial the telephone number is available. Indeed, I have received calls—usually attempts to sell me land—that even include a computer-generated message. Of course, you would not want to use a computer to generate the opening remarks in a survey, but computer dialing is easier on the fingers. One of the disadvantages to random digit dialing is that it is extremely difficult to obtain a specific sample, such as members of a particular economic, religious, or political group. You may have to make many phone calls before you reach enough of the right type of respondents for your purposes. On the other hand, random digit dialing does overcome the problem of unlisted phone numbers.

One of the major disadvantages of face-to-face interviews—generally low response rates—can be overcome through the use of telephone interviews. Steeh (1981), for example, observed a trend of declining response rates for face-to-face interviews. Since the 1950s, willingness to be interviewed in person has steadily decreased, making it more difficult to complete a sample. Hawkins (1977) studied face-to-face interview response rates in the Detroit area and noted a decline from an 85% response rate in the 1950s to a 70% response rate in the early 1970s. On the other hand, Dillman, Gallegos, and Frey (1976) obtained very good response rates for telephone interviews.

Another major disadvantage of face-to-face interviews is their cost (Dillman, 1978). Nederhof (1981) noted that some face-to-face interviews can cost as much as $100 per respondent. Hawkins (1977) pointed out that interviews can require as many as 17 repeated attempts to locate and talk to a given respondent. Of course, using the telephone won't necessarily reduce the number of attempts to locate a respondent, but a phone call is certainly less expensive than a drive to the respondent's home.

There are other advantages to telephone interviews. Although not necessarily a major advantage, telephone interviewers do not have to concern themselves with their physical appearance. Also, calls made from a central office allow the interviewer to consult with a supervisor if a problem develops or a question arises that the interviewer cannot handle. An interviewer in the field must deal with such matters without supervision, which makes it more difficult to implement a consistent strategy for such occurrences.

Telephone interviews, however, are not a miracle cure for problems encountered with face-to-face interviews. Indeed, if the interview schedule is very long or complex, a face-to-face interview is more appropriate than a telephone interview. It is generally accepted that telephone interviews ought not to exceed 15 minutes, which is not much time to complete a lengthy instrument. Similarly, focused and nondirective interviews are more difficult over the phone.

Another disadvantage to telephone interviews is the relative ease with which the respondent can break off the interview (Institute for Social Research, 1976). It is considerably easier to refuse to begin or continue an interview when not facing the interviewer. Furthermore, the telephone interviewer must obtain all information through direct questions. You cannot unobtrusively measure such variables as race, age, or relative economic status over the telephone.

Before we leave interviewing, I want to mention what I believe the predominant way in which most interviews will be accomplished within the next few decades. Known by the acronym CATI, **computer-assisted telephone interviewing** involves *reading questions from and recording responses directly into a computer file.* The computer can be used to accomplish random digit dialing and can even maintain a file of invalid numbers for reference during future surveys.

CATI also avoids having to print the interview schedule on paper, and the computer can be programmed to produce a variety of different orders for the items if desired. Invalid response codes, such as "7" on a four-point scale, can be identified and corrected immediately, and daily summaries can be obtained to keep track of the progress of the survey. The data may be analyzed as soon as they are collected, without the delays typically associated with coding and transcribing. Using a computer, however, cannot compensate for a poorly trained interviewer, unless we get to the point where people are willing to listen to a computer-generated voice asking them questions.

Mail Surveys

Distributing survey instruments through the mail to a predetermined sample is an example of a **self-administered survey**—*a survey in which respondents complete the instrument without intervention by the researcher.* Self-administered surveys provide greater privacy for the respondent, but they also increase the likelihood of misunderstood items or incomplete responses. There is no opportunity to follow up a seemingly inconsistent response, which makes instructions for a self-administered survey more important than those for an interview.

Any instrument sent through the mail should, of course, conform to size and weight restrictions established by the postal authorities. Determine what those restrictions are before printing the final version of the instrument. Also, return postage should be included—don't expect respondents to pay for returning your questionnaire. If possible, prefolded covers should be used because return envelopes can be misplaced. Also include a preprinted, identifying code number on the questionnaire.

Preprinted code numbers allow you to monitor returns. When a questionnaire is returned, the respondent can be removed from the mailing list to avoid duplication on subsequent mailings. As soon as the questionnaire has been returned and the respondent removed from the mailing list, the preprinted code can be replaced with a chronological code. The chronological code enables you to determine the influence of a suspected history effect by comparing questionnaires returned before and after the suspected event.

As a means by which to *reach* a specific sample, a mailed survey is the least expensive, least time-consuming, and most effective administration method. However, mailed surveys also rank lowest among administration methods with respect to response rates, for reasons we'll discuss next.

Surveys administered through the mail lack one very important ingredient—an interviewer. No one is there to answer questions about the items or explain instructions. It's also a great deal easier to throw a survey in the trash than to say no to an interviewer. Essentially, the more distant—physically and psychologically—the maker of a request, the more likely it is that the request will be refused. A survey researcher at the other end of a mailed questionnaire is about as distant as one can be. For this reason, a variety of practices have been developed to increase response rates by making the instrument, which is not distant, as inviting as possible.

Dillman (1978) has provided the most comprehensive set of practices designed to increase response rates. Known collectively as the Total Design Method (or TDM for those who like acronyms), these practices have been supported by empirical research (Nederhof, 1981). Some of the individual practices may seem to be mere gimmicks, but they do enhance response rates.

Dillman views the survey research process as a **social exchange**—*an interpersonal relationship in which an individual's willingness to enter or remain in the relationship depends on expectations of rewards and costs* (Kelley & Thibault, 1978). From that viewpoint, a researcher must make completing and returning a questionnaire worthwhile for the prospective respondent. Dillman's Total Design Method involves making the instrument well-organized and easy to complete, and it attempts to reward respondents by offering them copies of the research results.

To make the instrument well-organized, Dillman suggests it be printed in booklet form, about the size of an examination bluebook. It should contain no more than ten interior pages of items. The front cover should contain an interesting title (to capture the respondent's attention), the name and address of the sponsor (to convey legitimacy), general instructions (to provide an overview), and one or more graphic illustrations (to make it attractive). That's a great deal to put on a booklet cover, and careful planning is obviously necessary.

Within the booklet, the first item should be easy to complete—not an open-ended item—and should be applicable to everyone in the sample. It should also be neutral and directly related to the topic of the survey. Dillman suggests creating an item just for this purpose if an actual item does not qualify.

The remaining items should be arranged in descending order according to their relationship with the topic. Items about respondent characteristics—age, race, and so on—should appear at the end of the instrument. Items of similar content should be grouped together, and instructions should provide transitions so that each section follows from the previous one. Within any given topic, sensitive items should appear toward the end of the section. The back cover of the booklet should be reserved for comments from the respondent and should be labeled as such.

There are a variety of other specific recommendations incorporated into the Total Design Method, and I suggest you read Dillman's book if you are interested. As a student, however, you are not likely to have an opportunity to conduct the kind of full-scale mailed questionnaire survey to which Dillman is referring. Nevertheless, the ideas and intentions underlying the Total Design Method can be incorporated into any survey research project. Essentially, getting a good response rate boils down to making respondents feel as though they are doing something worthwhile that also happens to be enjoyable, and making sure respondents know that you appreciate the effort they made.

Comparisons Among Administration Methods

As mentioned earlier, each survey method has some advantages and some disadvantages. Box 7.1 contains a summary of those discussed thus far. The comparisons are grouped into four major areas: sampling, instrument construction, validity, and efficiency.

The ratings given to each method in each category are based on the assumption that the method is competently administered. A poorly done survey, regardless of which method is used, is not likely to provide any advantage at all, except, perhaps, as an example of what not to do next time.

Mixed-Method Surveys

After perusing Box 7.1, you should be able to conclude that there are only a few instances in which face-to-face, telephone, and mail surveys are equally effective for a given research purpose. Just because one method is better in one or another category, however, does not mean that you must necessarily accept shortcomings in your own research project. Mixing methods, normally not a good idea in research, can be extremely beneficial in survey research. You can, for example, call respondents who have returned a mailed instrument to obtain clarification on incomplete or seemingly inconsistent responses.

Certain circumstances may lead to intentionally mixing administration methods. If it were necessary, for example, to use a complex instrument that also dealt with sensitive topics, you might consider adopting a proctored questionnaire approach. By allowing respondents to complete the questionnaire privately, you would be in a better position to avoid bias due to self-presentation. By having a proctor available for questions, you also avoid problems that might arise from the complex format. A ballot box or similar receptacle for completed questionnaires could be used to further assure respondents of anonymity.

When it is possible for respondents to assemble in one place or when captive audiences (such as students in a class or a regular meeting of a civic group) are available, group administration is more convenient than a mailed questionnaire. An advertisement placed in a local newspaper or announcements to appropriate groups could be used to attract respondents. However, such techniques involve **accidental sampling,** *selection based on availability or ease of inclusion,* which limits generalizability. An accidental sample of students in a large class, for example, is a fairly homogeneous sample, and it would be difficult to generalize results

BOX 7.1   Face-to-Face, Telephone, and Mail Surveys Compared

Category	Face-to-face	Phone	Mail
Sampling			
Availability of a complete sample			
Completely listed population	+	+	+
Incompletely listed population	+	0	0
Ability to select respondents	+	+	0
Ability to locate specific respondents	0	+	+
Response rates			
For heterogeneous sample	+	+	0
For homogeneous sample	+	+	+
Ability to avoid volunteer bias	+	0	−
Instrument construction			
Tolerance for length	+	0	0
Tolerance for complexity	+	−	0
Success with open-ended items	+	+	−
Success with screening items	+	+	0
Sequence control/contingency items	+	+	0
Success with tedious items	+	0	−
Avoidance of incomplete responses	+	0	−
Flexibility of format	+	0	−
Validity			
Avoidance of self-presentation	−	0	+
Avoidance of interviewer bias	−	0	+
Avoidance of interference from			
nonrespondents	0	+	0
Avoidance of misunderstood items	0	−	0
Efficiency			
Small staff requirements	−	+	+
Implementation speed	−	+	−
Low cost per respondent	−	0	+
Low cost for geographical dispersion	−	0	+

obtained from them to a group of, say, retirees. Furthermore, the possibility of volunteer bias is much greater with such an accidental sample.

The most important aspect of survey administration methods is to understand your research needs before deciding on a method or a sample. If your project both requires a very high response rate, low costs, and some open-ended responses and contains some boring and sensitive items, then a combination of face-to-face and mail methods may be best. Boring or complex items could be administered in the face-to-face interview, and the interviewer could leave a printed questionnaire containing the sensitive items for the respondent to complete and return by mail. As with all research, a little creativity tempered with knowledge is very helpful in survey research. See Box 7.2 for a compilation of checkpoints for preparing a survey instrument.

BOX 7.2 Checkpoints for Preparing a Survey Instrument

_____ *Purpose*

Exploration
• Inefficient use of surveys because surveys should have a specific set of hypotheses to be tested.

Description
• Most frequent use of surveys because of variety of questions that can be included allows you to describe a variety of concepts.

Prediction
• Another frequent purpose for surveys because length of a survey instrument allows you to measure more than one concept and relate them using correlational analyses.

Explanation
• Inefficient use of surveys because of difficulty inherent in manipulating the independent variable(s) and controlling the environment in which the survey is administered.

Action
• Somewhat inefficient use of surveys unless the dependent variable involves attitudes or other, similar measures.

_____ *Content*

Facts
• What objectively verifiable information is to be included?

Opinions
• What preferences or behavioral intentions are to be included?

Behaviors
• What actions are to be included?

_____ *Instrumentation*

Topic
• What subjects are to be covered? Be sure to have a good reason for including each and every item on the survey.

Instructions
• Do the instructions explain why the survey is being done? the conditions for anonymity or confidentiality? how to respond to each item, including examples?

Format
• What is the best way to display the survey items? Which items require open-ended responses? multiple choices? Are endpoints of continua clearly labeled?

Arrangement
• Are more sensitive items placed near the end of the instrument? contingency items clearly identified? directions about which items to answer next clear?

_____ *Pretesting*

Respondents
• What is their reaction to the topic? the instructions? the format(s)? the arrangement?

Interviewers
• Do they establish rapport? know the instrument? understand the items? know how to record responses?

(continued)

BOX 7.2   Checkpoints for Preparing a Survey Instrument (*continued*)

_____ *Administration*

Face-to-face interview	• Do you need to talk to the respondents in person?
Telephone interview	• Is the instrument short enough for a telephone call?
Mailed survey	• Is the instrument sufficiently interesting for people to want to complete and return it? Are the items sufficiently understandable for people to complete them unassisted?

Data Analyses in Survey Research

How you analyze your data depends on your research hypotheses and the types of measurement scales you use. There are three general types of analyses appropriate for survey data: description, association, and elaboration. Within each of these types, you may have either categorical or continuous data. We'll examine each type of analysis in this section, but not in sufficient detail for you to be able to immediately analyze data. If you are unfamiliar with these analyses, read Chapter 13, which provides considerably more detail about data analyses. Also, the various references cited along the way are excellent sources for expanding your statistical knowledge.

Description

The analyses best suited for descriptive purposes are generally referred to as summary or exploratory statistics. They include frequency displays and measures of central tendency and variability. Tukey (1977) and Hartwig and Dearing (1979) are two of the many excellent volumes that describe these analyses in more detail.

Nominal data yield categories rather than amounts, which is why they are also called categorical data. Gender, religious denomination, and voting preferences are some examples of nominal variables. Frequency distributions are a good way to begin to describe such data; simply determine the number of respondents in each category for each variable. Frequency distributions may also be expressed as percentages, such as "75% of the respondents were in favor of the Equal Rights Amendment." You may want to determine the modal response—the most frequently chosen response alternative—for variables with more than three categories.

If you have obtained a representative sample, you may also want to use frequency distributions to make inferences about the population from which the sample was selected. If that is your purpose, you should use inferential statistics appropriate for nominal data. The most common of these, chi-square, usually involves a goodness-of-fit test. A **goodness-of-fit test** is *a test in which data values* *obtained from one sample are compared to theoretical values to determine whether or not the two sets of values are equivalent.* The ultimate outcome of a goodness-of-fit test is a probability value—the probability that the obtained data fit the theoretical data. Chi-square tests are particularly appropriate for survey data in which comparisons to earlier data are to be made, or when comparisons between subsamples are necessary.

One example of a chi-square goodness-of-fit analysis is when the network newspeople declare the winner of an election based on only 2% or 3% of the election returns. They are really saying that the obtained returns do not fit distributions of returns that would enable any of the other candidates to win the election. The actual returns are the survey data; the predicted distributions are the theoretical values to which the actual data are fit. The probability associated with the obtained data (the declared winner) fitting the theoretical values (one of the other candidates winning) is so low that the network is willing to claim that the obtained data could never fit the theoretical data in which one of the other candidates is a winner. Of course, they don't say all of that when they report the projected winner; they just say so-and-so is projected to be the winner on the basis of scientific polls (surveys).

Frequency distributions and goodness-of-fit analyses may be appropriate for continuous data, but they are not the most efficient way to analyze such data. Continuous data reflect amounts—more or less of whatever is being measured— such as temperature, annual income, and so forth. For such data, a stem and leaf display is more informative and efficient than a simple frequency distribution. If you are unfamiliar with stem and leaf displays, you may want to consult Chapter 13 or read Tukey's (1977) volume on exploratory analyses. It would be appropriate to include a stem and leaf display in a report to be read by other researchers, but probably not in a report for the general public, because most of the public does not know how to read a stem and leaf display.

You may also want to calculate the mean for each variable, as well as determine the variability by calculating the standard deviation or variance. The mean and standard deviation are usually the most efficient way to describe continuous data distributions.

For inferential purposes, the standard error of the mean can be used to determine the probability that a theoretical population mean falls within a range about the sample mean. If you are unfamiliar with the concept of the standard error of the mean, consult Chapter 16. The standard error provides an indication of what the population mean should be if your sample is a random sample from the population. When the sample mean is very different from the theoretical mean, you may conclude that your data are not from the theoretical population. It is essentially the same concept as a goodness-of-fit test except that it is based on sample means instead of categorical distributions.

When the United States Bureau of the Census reports that the population is getting older, for example, it is really indicating that the mean age of the latest sample is considerably higher than the mean age of the previous sample; that is, the probability that the two sample means came from the same population is very low, and the Bureau is confident that the two means could not have come from the same population. A probability smaller than .05—less than a 5 in 100 chance—is usually low enough to make such a decision. When several groups are being compared, it is preferable to use an analysis of variance test, which is also based on the standard error of the mean.

Whatever statistics you use to report group differences, you must keep in mind that you are trying to describe the fact that the groups are different. Unless you have met the condition of random assignment and a manipulated variable, you cannot do much more than speculate about why the differences are there. Speculation is, of course, permitted, so long as you clearly label it as such.

Association

Surveys for which association analyses are desirable are those for which the hypotheses involve relationships between variables. One of the appropriate association analyses for categorical data is, again, a chi-square statistic. The procedure for association analyses, however, is a contingency analysis. **Contingency analyses** are *used to determine the probability that the results for one variable are related to the results for another variable.* Recall Hill, Rubin, and Peplau's (1976) survey of romantically involved couples in the Boston area. They performed contingency analyses to determine whether remaining a couple was related to living together. If the two variables were associated, the researchers expected a greater proportion of one kind of couple to have lived together than another kind of couple. They did not find evidence for that association; the proportion of intact couples who had lived together was not sufficiently different from the proportion of unsuccessful couples who had lived together.

Another way to word the above conclusion is to report that the probability that an intact couple had lived together was the same as the probability that an unsuccessful couple had lived together. Similarly, you might report that breaking up was not related to cohabitation. All three statements are different ways to convey the same idea—that remaining a couple and living together were not associated in their sample.

The most common association statistic for continuous data is the correlation coefficient, also covered in Chapter 13. Hill et al. calculated a number of correlations from their data. They found, for example, that the correlation between the age of one member of a couple and the age of the other member was positive, $r = .19$, meaning that couples tended to be composed of individuals of about the same age.

Writing about correlational analyses is fairly straightforward—you report the correlation coefficient and the probability associated with it, along with the degrees of freedom for your sample size. Going beyond your results, however, can be very tempting but should be avoided. If you report that parents' income and children's income are related, $r(98) = .50$, for example, you might be tempted to conclude that wealthy parents tend to give their children more money than do poor parents. Although such a conclusion makes sense, you cannot draw that conclusion from your data. Unless you have somehow managed to randomly assign parents to different levels of wealth, you have not met the necessary conditions to claim a causal relationship. You know that parental and child wealth are related, but the data you've collected don't allow you to know why they are related.

Elaboration

The difficulty of being able to draw conclusions about causal relationships from survey data is one of the reasons why Lazarsfeld and his colleagues at Columbia University developed the elaboration model for analyzing survey data (Merton & Lazarsfeld, 1950). **Elaboration** is *a process in which data analyses are used to explore and interpret relationships among variables.* The logic of elaboration enables you to dissect a relationship by examining how it changes when additional variables are included in the analysis. The original outline of the method makes interesting reading, but a later volume by Lazarsfeld, Pasanella, and Rosenberg (1972) is a better source from which to get information.

The starting point in elaboration is an observed relationship between two variables. For illustration, let's assume you have conducted a survey and found a relationship between parents' and children's wealth; at age 22, wealthy respondents are more likely to have wealthy parents. You don't believe this relationship exists merely because parents are giving money to their children, but you would like to examine that and other hypotheses in order to more fully understand what's going on:

Why?

Parents' Wealth   ⟶   Children's Wealth

Luckily, you have been paying attention and thought about the design of your survey instrument. You have some data with which to test some of the hypotheses you suspect explain the relationship:

Education?
Employment?
Direct Support?

Parents' Wealth   ⟶   Children's Wealth

Using the logic of elaboration, you might first determine whether respondents with college degrees exhibit the same relationship between parental and respondent wealth as those who do not have college degrees. That is, could the relationship exist because wealthy parents can better afford to provide a college education for their children? If the relationship remains unchanged after you separate your sample into those with and those without college degrees, then you can rule out education as one of the explanatory variables. If the relationship is different for the two subsamples, then education becomes part of the underlying mechanism:

Parents' Wealth   ⟶   Education   ⟶   Children's Wealth

Essentially, elaboration enables you to statistically control variables that may contribute to (elaborate on) the basic relationship identified in the initial data analyses. Again, keep in mind that statistical control is not the same as actual control through manipulation. Just as matching is only a second-best alternative for random assignment, statistical control is only a second-best alternative for manipulating the independent variable in a true experiment.

Despite the remaining inability to draw fully supportable causal explanations from your survey data, elaboration has a decided advantage over simply guessing about underlying mechanisms. The hypotheses that remain viable after elaboration are more likely to be supported by additional research; that is, the data you have already collected support the hypotheses, and it makes sense that additional data will likely provide additional support.

When writing about elaboration, or about any analysis dealing with association, you should avoid falling into the trap of ex post facto explanations. **Ex post facto explanations** are *untested causal statements applied to observed relationships.* (The phrase is Latin for "after the fact.") Suppose, for example, that you determined through elaboration that parental wealth was related to respondent wealth more strongly for males than for females. If you proceeded to explain this elaboration by concluding that males are more likely to inherent the family fortune, you would be guilty of an ex post facto explanation. The difference between the genders is real, but the underlying mechanism, inheritance, is not something you have tested with your data. An ex post facto explanation recently resulted in a "color expert" claiming that men who drove red cars had unfulfilled sexual desires. The "expert" had read somewhere that male owners of red cars were more likely to be single than married and had jumped to this conclusion about sexual desires. Whether or not male owners of red cars are more likely to be single, the existence of that relationship provides no information at all about their sexual desires, fulfilled or otherwise.

Elaboration and ex post facto explanation are often mistaken for the same process, but there is one very important difference between them. Applying the logic of elaboration provides a test of the proposed hypotheses; ex post facto explanation is nothing more than speculation. Granted, the test of a proposed hypothesis through elaboration is not as rigorous a test as would be obtained through a true experiment, but it is a test.

There also exists a chi-square analysis known as hierarchical chi-square, which can be used for elaboration when the variables are categorical. Haberman (1978, 1979) has written two very technical books that require considerable math background. Lindeman, Merenda, and Gold's (1980) chapter on contingency analyses is somewhat less mathematically oriented, but still rather technical. I would suggest you not consult these sources without at least one basic course in statistics, preferably two.

Elaboration can be accomplished using correlation coefficients for continuous data in much the way as that described in the example concerning parental and child wealth: separate the samples and recalculate the coefficient. For continuous data, however, multiple regression analyses are more efficient and more statistically correct. **Multiple regression** is *a statistical technique for estimating simultaneous correlations among any number of predictor variables and a single, continuous response variable.* When multiple regression is used, the coefficients are called regression coefficients, and they can be interpreted in much the same way as correlation coefficients. Kerlinger (1979) has an excellent chapter on multiple regression, one that doesn't require an extensive math background to understand.

With elaboration analyses, you may find that some of the variables you would like to include are categorical and some are continuous. When you have such mixed data, multiple regression is appropriate if the response variable is continuous. Such is the case with children's wealth in the previous example. If the response variable is categorical, such as religious denomination, then a technique called discriminant analysis is best. **Discriminant analysis** is *a statistical technique designed to estimate the relationship between any number of predictor variables and one or more categorical response variables.* The logic of discriminant analysis is the same as that for multiple regression, but considerably more complex calculations are necessary.

Discriminant analysis involves finding a set of predictor variables that can be used to categorize respondents into groups defined by the response variable. A series of repeated estimations, called iterations, is used to determine discriminant function weights (analogous to regression or correlation coefficients) for the predictor variables. The iterations continue until the computer program determines the best combination of predictors that, literally, predict responses on the categorical response variable. By comparing the computer-generated responses with the actual responses in a type of goodness-of-fit test, the relative effect of the predictor variables can be estimated. Kerlinger (1979) also includes a chapter on discriminant analysis, although you probably want to have more than just a basic course in statistics before tackling it. Multiple regression and discriminant analysis are especially complex statistical techniques; although you should be aware of them, it is not necessary for you to fully understand them at this point in your research career. Figure 7.2 contains an overview of various analyses appropriate for different types of data, samples, and research purposes.

Summary

• Survey research methods are used to obtain self-report information from research participants, mainly in order to accomplish descriptive or predictive goals. Although less efficient for such purposes, survey methods can be used for exploratory and action goals, but rarely for explanation (because it is usually too difficult to randomly assign respondents to different conditions produced by manipulating variables).

• The items contained in a survey instrument are used to measure facts, opinions, and behaviors. Facts are verifiable characteristics of respondents; opinions are preferences expressed by respondents; behaviors are reports of completed actions. Care must be taken to avoid response bias or incomplete responses to sensitive topics. Anonymity or confidentiality generally alleviates such bias.

• Instructions and formats should make it easy for respondents to complete the instrument. Pretesting should be used extensively to accomplish this goal.

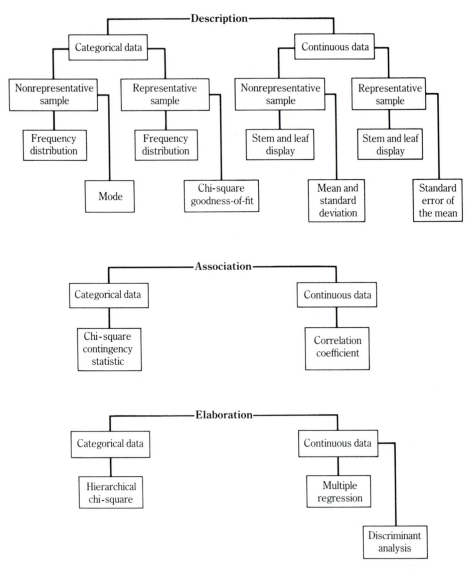

Figure 7.2 A summary of the types of data analyses that can be applied to survey data. The types of analyses that should be used depend on the types of data collected and the purposes of the analyses. More information about all of these analyses can be found in Chapter 13.

Pretest respondents and interviewers should be interviewed to assess the need for alterations in procedures or in the instrument. Any major change should be followed by additional pretesting.

• The face-to-face interview is the preferred method for administering relatively unstructured instruments, although it is also the most expensive method. Probes may be used more effectively with this than with any other method.

• Telephone interviews are less expensive than face-to-face interviews, but the acceptable length of a telephone interview is considerably shorter. The one-time problem of limited availability of samples because potential respondents lacked telephones is no longer relevant, but random digit dialing is necessary to reach respondents with unlisted numbers.

• Mail surveys can be used for relatively structured instruments, but care must be taken to ensure that the items and instructions can be understood by respondents. Mail surveys also produce lower response rates than interviews.

• The Total Design Method has been successfully used to increase response rates for mail surveys, and recent research indicates that it is more successful than merely offering incentives. The Total Design Method involves a collection of procedures that make the instrument pleasant to complete as well as worth the respondent's investment of time and effort. As the need arises, various administration methods can be mixed to obtain the best combination of advantages.

• Data analyses used for surveys depend on the purpose of the research and the type of data collected. Summary statistics are most appropriate for descriptive purposes. Association statistics are used for data analyses when predictive goals are to be met. Care must be taken, however, to avoid unsupportable cause–effect conclusions from association analyses.

• Elaboration is a logical process for analyzing data that enables you to test tentative hypotheses about relationships among variables, but it is not as rigorous a form of causal analysis as a true experiment. Ex post facto explanations are untested assumptions about association data. Although similar to elaboration analyses in the final outcome, elaboration involves a statistical test of the hypothesis, whereas ex post facto explanations are nothing more than speculation.

CHAPTER EIGHT

Field Research

 Observation is a skill over and above passive reception of the raw data of sensory experience.

—Weimer (1979, p. 21)

Overview

In this chapter you will learn about methods that enable you to conduct research on everyday events. You will learn about systematic observations—a method designed to examine behavior without actually being a part of it—and you will learn about participant observation, in which you do become a part of the event you are observing. You will also learn about the advantages and disadvantages of intruding into the action being observed. As with other methods described in this text, you will learn about appropriate data analyses and conventions for writing reports about field research.

Introduction

One of the continuing themes of this text is that every one of us conducts research every day but that scientific research is more objective and systematic than the informal research that merely satisfies our curiosity. In this chapter you will learn about research methods that are more similar to those of informal research than any other methods. Just because field research methods are similar to informal practice does not mean that they are less scientific in any way. The principles and practices of field research provide you with the skills necessary to move beyond the notion of passive reception of everyday experience. However, don't let the label, field research, lead you to believe the methods described in this chapter can be used only outside the laboratory, or to believe that research conducted outside the laboratory can be accomplished only through these methods. The label is an accident of tradition and not very descriptive.

Field research is *the general label applied to a collection of research methods that include direct observation of naturally occurring events.* The first characteristic of field research, direct observation, means that you examine the event as it happens, which sets it apart from the collection of retrospective data in survey research (Chapter 7). What is observed in field research, however, need not necessarily be "live" events; part of our discussion will include various techniques available to record events for later examination. Still, whether live or on tape, the emphasis is on observing events as they unfold.

The second characteristic of field research, naturally occurring events, involves a continuum of naturalness rather than a natural/artificial dichotomy. A **natural event** is *an event that is not created, sustained, or discontinued solely for research purposes* (Tunnell, 1977). The viewpoint used to assess naturalness is that of the research participant, which is why naturalness needs to be conceptualized as a continuum: the more the participant perceives the event to be part of the normal stream of experiences, the more natural the event is. The emphasis on natural events in field research is why field methods are sometimes called naturalistic methods.

Events may be artificially created by the researcher and still be perceived as natural by the participant. The research on helping behavior conducted by Piliavin, Rodin, and Piliavin (1969), discussed later in this chapter, is a good example of events that were artificially created for the purpose of conducting an experiment but were perceived as natural by the participants. Of course, events such as earthquakes or terrorist attacks are also considered natural, even though they may not qualify as part of the participant's normal stream of experience.

In Chapter 1 you learned that research methods may be used to address a variety of questions about our world, questions that were categorized in terms of exploration, description, prediction, explanation, and action. You also learned that certain research methods were more appropriate for some questions than for others. The naturalness of field research makes it difficult, but definitely not impossible, to randomly assign participants to different levels of an independent variable. Most explanatory questions, therefore, fall outside the purview of field research. For similar reasons, including the difficulty of extending hypotheses outside the preexisting situation, prediction is also somewhat inefficient when accomplished through field methods. Field research typically involves collecting data in order to form new hypotheses and is particularly suited to exploratory and descriptive goals (Butler, Rice, & Wagstaff, 1963).

As attempts to answer exploratory questions, field methods are very similar to the informal research of everyday living. More specifically, the method known as participant observation is ideally suited for the development of hypotheses about existing events. Participant observation generally involves studying events while simultaneously taking part in them, something we do as a part of life itself. On the other hand, the method known as systematic observation is more likely to lead to the discovery of new empirical relationships. Systematic observation involves studying events without participating in them, remaining all the while as unobtrusive as possible. We'll more carefully and more comprehensively cover each of these methods later, but first let's address the general issues of validity and intrusion as they apply to field research.

Validity of Field Research

That field methods are most appropriate for exploratory and descriptive purposes does not necessarily mean that they cannot be used to address questions about relationships between variables. Rather, the limitation of field methods is that they cannot easily be used to test causal relationships—explanations—unless the field research is based on previous experimental research. Recall from Chapter 5 that testing causal relationships involves manipulating the independent variable and randomly assigning participants to the different levels of the independent variable. Random assignment and manipulation are rather difficult in a natural setting.

The way in which field research is typically used to test causal relationships involves taking an already experimentally tested phenomenon and applying it in a natural setting. Berkowitz and his colleagues (Berkowitz & Donnerstein, 1982), for example, have conducted numerous experiments through which they demonstrated that the presence of weapons (and other cues for violence) can cause people to become more aggressive. The causal relationship between the presence of violent cues and aggression, therefore, has been well-established. Diener and Crandall (1979) used field research methods to evaluate the reverse of the causal relationship—the effects of removing cues for violence—in a natural setting in Jamaica. Anticrime legislation in that country included gun control regulations and banning gun-related segments from television shows and movies. Diener and Crandall measured the effects of this natural event and found rather dramatic decreases in crime rates, particularly for crimes involving firearms. The experimental research by Berkowitz and others tested the causal relationship, but the field research by Diener and Crandall described the impact that that relationship can have in everyday life.

Internal Validity

Fassnacht (1982) noted that many people believe field research to be less valid than other methods, particularly experimental methods. If one defines internal validity solely in terms of testing causal relationships (see, for example, Cook & Campbell, 1979), then this belief is somewhat correct. If, however, internal validity is defined as the extent to which research procedures enable one to draw reasonable conclusions, then field research is no more or less valid than any other method.

Diener and Crandall's (1979) research on the effects of gun control legislation in Jamaica is a valid test of what can happen when such laws are enacted. If they had gone so far as to conclude that censorship of gun segments on television is what *caused* the reduction in crime, however, they would have gone beyond the limits of their research design and would have drawn an invalid conclusion. The experiments by Berkowitz and others make it reasonable to conclude that removing the cues for violence had something to do with the reduction in crime, but the Jamaican legislation involved more than removing cues for violence. As with any other research, conclusions drawn from field research methods should be limited to effects actually tested in the research.

External Validity

Internal validity is only part of the overall validity of a research project. We must also be concerned with external validity—the extent to which the data may be generalized beyond the research project. Field research generally suffers from a lack of external validity, mainly because either the setting studied is often unique or the common components of the setting cannot readily be demonstrated to be related to the results of the research. One could hardly claim, for example, that enacting the Jamaican legislation in another country would produce the same results. We do not know what aspects of Jamaican society may have contributed to the effectiveness of the legislation, aspects that may not exist in some other country. On the other hand, whenever a researcher is in a position to define the relevant aspects of the situation under investigation, field research probably has greater external validity than any other method because the naturalness of the situation more closely approximates everyday life.

Intrusion in Field Research

Earlier I described a natural event as one in which the researcher does not create, maintain, or restrict behavior for research purposes, but also noted that naturalness must be determined from the viewpoint of the research participant. Intrusion is anything that lessens the participants' perception of an event as natural (Tunnell, 1977). Intrusion can involve any aspect of an event; the behaviors that comprise the event, the setting in which it takes place, and the treatment of the participant by the researcher.

Intrusion into Observations of Behaviors

Connecting participants to a polygraph machine and measuring their physiological reactions to a violent movie is behavioral intrusion, as is handling each participant a questionnaire in order to measure attitudes about violence. More natural ways to observe behaviors might involve unobtrusively watching physical reactions to a violent movie in a theater or eavesdropping on conversations about violence. Between the ends of the continuum is a host of "moderately obtrusive" ways to study behavior; the key element is the degree to which those engaging in the behavior are aware that they are being observed as part of a project.

Studying behavior naturally does not always exclude observation of artificially induced behavior. A study on helping behavior by Latané and Darley (1968) began with participants completing questionnaires in a waiting room, a procedure that is intrusive. Each participant was either alone in the room or with two others who were actually confederates of the experimenters. After a while, white smoke began to pour through an air vent. At first, puffs of smoke escaped at somewhat irregular intervals. Eventually, enough smoke was discharged to fill the room. The behavior in which Latané and Darley were interested was whether or not participants would report the smoke to someone. Although certainly not an everyday event, to the extent that participants did not suspect that the smoke was part of the research procedure, the behavior was natural (and the observation of it was unobtrusive). For those of you not familiar with this rather important experiment, participants who were alone were much more likely to report the smoke than were those who shared the room with two passive confederates.

Intrusiveness of Settings

The degree of intrusion into the setting is determined by the extent to which the event takes place in an environment the participant believes is a research setting. Laboratories, as in Latané and Darley's study, are clearly intrusive settings. Natural settings include those normally frequented for purposes other than participating in research. In a very different study, Piliavin, Rodin, and Piliavin (1969) used the Eighth Avenue subway in New York City as a natural setting in which to study helping behavior. A "victim" collapsed on the floor of the subway car, and observers were on hand to record the reactions of others in the car. By varying the apparent problem and race of the victim, Piliavin et al. were able to discover some rather clear differences in participants' behavior between their more natural setting and the intrusive setting used by Latané and Darley. These differences led to considerable theoretical development as to why and under what circumstances people are willing to help others (Dane, 1988b). Note that both studies involved experimental research that took place in the field; naturalness and experimental design are not necessarily mutually exclusive.

Intrusiveness of Treatments

Intrusion with respect to treatment refers to the extent to which the event could have occurred without the researcher's presence or influence. In the Latané and Darley study (1968), the treatment of the participants was intrusive; they would not have encountered the smoke if the researchers had not been manufacturing it. Indeed, a number of the participants later explained their failure to report the smoke by stating that they believed that the experimenter wanted them to experience a smoke-filled room. Piliavin et al.'s treatment was also intrusive, but not as much. That particular "victim" would not have collapsed without the influence of the researchers, but I know from experience that sooner or later in one or another subway car, there would have been a real victim. Diener and Crandall's (1979) treatment clearly qualifies as natural. Unless they have a great deal more power than most researchers, Diener and Crandall's absence would not have prevented the crime control legislation from being enacted by the Jamaican government.

The naturalness of the events being studied is a continuum, not a dichotomy. Participants' perceptions of naturalness can vary from one end of the continuum to the other. Also, the mixture of behavior, setting, and treatment makes some events more or less natural than others. Natural behaviors do not always occur in natural settings; they can arise from intrusive treatments, or arise under unusual settings, and so forth. The key to determining the naturalness of an event is attempting to understand what is going on from the participant's point of view. With this in mind, let us move on to discuss specific field research methods.

Systematic Observation in Field Research

Unless you live in a sensory deprivation chamber, most of your waking hours are spent as an observer. You watch activity, listen to sounds, feel objects, taste flavors, and smell odors. Merely paying attention to sensory inputs, however, is not scientific—is not systematic—observation, although it does satisfy curiosity. **Systematic observation** is *a research method in which events are selected, recorded, coded into meaningful units, and interpreted by nonparticipants*. Because this is a rather long and involved definition, let's take it apart and separately deal with each component.

Selecting Events

When you select events, you must first decide which events are of interest, and then you must decide how to sample the specific events you will observe. The first decision, of course, depends on the general kinds of behavior you wish to explore and the hypotheses you wish to examine. The second decision is dependent on the first, for the sampling procedures cannot be determined until you decide which events to investigate.

Deciding which events to observe is not as simple as you might think. You should not, for example, decide to go out and observe everything, for that's not, well, systematic. It is also not possible. If you concentrate on nothing in particular, that's pretty much what you will observe—nothing. Weick (1968) has categorized events on the basis of behaviors in which field researchers are most interested: nonverbal, spatial, extralinguistic, and linguistic.

Nonverbal behaviors are body movements that convey information. They may include facial expressions, eye contact, hand movements, posture, and so on. Spatial behaviors involve maintaining or altering distances among people or between people and objects; again, such behaviors convey information or reactions to another's behavior. Extralinguistic behaviors include rate, tone, volume, and other similar characteristics of speech. Spoken in a normal tone and at even speed, for

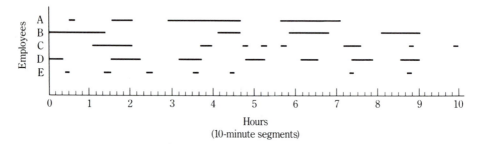

Figure 8.1 Continuous time sampling: The amount of time each of five employees spend at the coffee pot during a ten-hour workday. In order to obtain these results, someone or some equipment must be observing the coffee pot during the entire workday. A solid line represents a person's presence at the coffee pot; absence of a line means they are elsewhere. Measuring the total length of the solid line for each person enables one to determine the total amount of time each person spent at the coffee pot.

example, "Hey, Frank" means "Hello Frank, how are you?" (at least in the South); spoken loudly with a pause between the two words, "Hey, Frank!" may mean anything from "wait for me" to "turn around and catch the softball about to hit you in the head." Finally, linguistic behaviors refer to the content of speech or written material. Which type of event is of interest to you as a researcher is a decision that must be made for each study; interest values of events vary as a function of hypotheses. If your hypothesis involves observing people from a distance in order to attain a high level of naturalness, for example, you will be limited to nonverbal and spatial behaviors (unless you happen to have a long-distance, directional microphone on hand). The general principles of measurement (see Chapter 14) should be used to guide you in these decisions.

Deciding how to select the actual events you will observe involves the general principles of sampling (see Chapter 16), but there are a few aspects specific to systematic observation. Generally, sampling events involves either time or event sampling. Time sampling, as the term implies, refers to selecting a specific interval of time during which observations will be made. It is used whenever duration of the event is of interest. If you want to know how much time people spend lingering at the table after a restaurant meal, for example, then you need to use time sampling.

In **continuous time sampling,** *the researcher observes every instance of the behavior for the entire duration of the event* (Figure 8.1). Continuous time sampling is usually limited to studies involving very short events or to studies in which measuring absolute duration is required. It is analogous to making a videotape of the entire event. Studies of the total time devoted to coffee breaks in an industrial setting, for example, may require continuous time sampling; you need to know exactly how much time people spend on their coffee breaks. More often than not, however, only relative measures of frequency or duration are required, such as whether people spend more time at the coffee machine than at their desks, and under such conditions you can use either time-point or time-interval sampling.

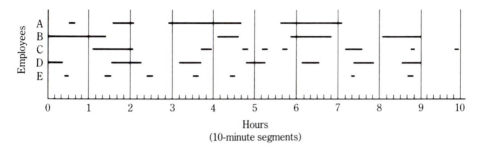

Figure 8.2 Time-point sampling: Results for five employees of the time spent at the office coffee pot. Each long vertical line represents a "snapshot" observation, which occurs every hour on the hour. The horizontal lines represent the actual amount of time each employee was at the coffee pot. Note that some employees would not be observed during the brief "snapshot" interval because they had just left or were about to arrive at the coffee pot.

Time-point sampling involves *selecting only those behaviors that occur at the end of a specific time interval within the duration of the event* (Figure 8.2). Continuing with our coffee machine example, you could observe the coffee machine at the top of the hour and note which employees were present. Time-point sampling is analogous to photographing the participant and making your observations from the photograph. Indeed, still photography is one of the ways in which permanent records of time-point sampled events are created. With time-point sampling you cannot measure every trip to the coffee machine or the total amount of time spent there, but you can determine whether one employee visited more often than another.

Time-interval sampling involves *observing whether a behavior occurs during a specified interval within the duration of the event* (Figure 8.3). You could, for example, observe the coffee machine for the last ten minutes of each hour and record whether each employee was there at that time. Time-interval sampling is

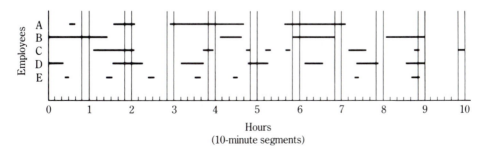

Figure 8.3 Time-interval sampling: Results for five employees of their presence at the office coffee pot. The pairs of long, vertical lines represent the sampling interval—the last ten minutes of every hour. If an employee's horizontal line, which represents the complete history of coffee pot activity, falls within the pair of vertical lines representing the sampling interval, the employee was observed at the coffee pot.

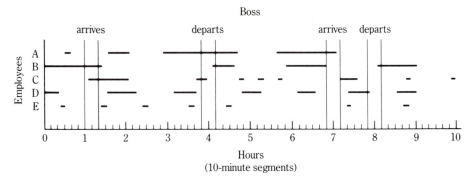

Figure 8.4 Event sampling around the office coffee pot. Observations were made for each twenty-minute period after the boss arrived at or departed from the office. Note that employee B's presence at the coffee pot seems to be governed by the boss's presence or absence.

analogous to making a videotape of part of the entire event. You get more than just a "snapshot" of the event, but not the entire event. As with time-point sampling, only relative measures are possible with time-interval sampling.

Whether you use time-point or time-interval sampling depends on the duration of the event you want to observe. If the behavior is very brief, time-interval sampling will probably be required, and longer intervals will be required for infrequent behaviors. If the behavior is long-lasting, time-point sampling is more appropriate, particularly if the duration of the behavior is not relevant to your hypothesis.

Event sampling involves *observing one behavior contingent upon the presence of another behavior* (Figure 8.4), and is usually used for hypotheses about relationships between two variables, or when knowing the duration of the behavior is not necessary. You may not, for example, be interested in how long people spend on their coffee breaks, but you may be interested in whether they take more coffee breaks when the boss is away from the office. Event sampling provides only relative information; only continuous time sampling will enable you to make absolute measurements of the behavior. Regardless of the sampling procedure you select, the key is to sample systematically: every X minutes or every time behavior Y occurs. Devise a sampling strategy and stick to it.

Recording Events

After you have decided which, how often, and under what circumstances events are to be selected for observation, you need to decide how to record your observations. Although often done simultaneously, we will discuss recording and coding as separate processes. **Recording** refers to *the manner in which a permanent copy of the observation is made.* Taking photographs or video recordings, making notes, or making marks on a checklist or scale are all examples of recording observations. **Coding** involves *attaching some sort of meaning to the observation.* Deciding whether a baby's smile means the baby is happy or has intestinal gas is part of the coding process. Deciding how to record your observations depends on your research hypotheses and the resources you have available. Generally, previous research is the best guide.

Recording, like any other measurement process, introduces some error. Even film or videotape involves error due to the camera angle, lighting, film speed, and other aspects of photography. If you cannot focus a camera on the behavior, you cannot record it. Therefore, recording is best accomplished with multiple observers so you can estimate error through the amount of agreement between the observers. If six people make the same record of an observation, the record is more reliable than if only one person makes the record.

Coding Events

As noted above, coding involves interpreting what has been recorded, and it is very often accomplished at the same time as recording. You may observe a baby's smile, interpret it as being happy, and simply record that the baby was happy. Sometimes, coding is used to more efficiently represent a behavior—as a kind of shorthand system for recording observations. Leventhal and Sharp (1965), for example, developed an elaborate system of symbols used to record facial expressions. LaFrance (1979) used a similar system for arm positions in her study of the similarity of posture and its relation to attitude similarity. The symbols used are a shorthand for the actual behavior, but they don't necessarily ascribe any meaning to the behavior.

More often than not, however, coding involves both recording and interpreting an observation. The most well-known of such systems is the interaction process analysis (IPA) system developed by Bales (1950, 1970). IPA allows observers to record inferred meanings for linguistic, extralinguistic, and nonverbal behaviors among groups, using the categories listed in Table 8.1. As you can see from the table, IPA requires the coder/observer to decide not only whether the behavior

Table 8.1   Categories for Interaction Process Analysis (IPA)

Positive Actions	1. Seems friendly
	2. Dramatizes
	3. Agrees
Answers	4. Gives suggestion
	5. Gives opinion
	6. Gives information
Questions	7. Asks for information
	8. Asks for opinion
	9. Asks for suggestion
Negative Actions	10. Disagrees
	11. Shows tension
	12. Seems unfriendly

has occurred but to attach meaning to it. The IPA is one of many examples of **checklist coding schemes**—*coding systems for which the behaviors and their meanings are determined prior to making observations.*

An alternative to checklist systems is the unstructured or ethological system, also known as natural history. The **ethological system** involves *a detailed and comprehensive recording of behaviors with little or no inferred meaning.* With an ethological system you might simply note that Ralph stuck out his tongue at Mary instead of checking the "seems unfriendly" category of the IPA. The emphasis is on making as few assumptions and interpretations as possible, hence its sometime name—natural history. McGrew (1972) used an ethological system to categorize 110 different behaviors of nursery school children's social interactions. Ethological systems, however, are not for the impatient. McGrew spent 15 hours coding each hour of videotape and another five hours coding each hour of audiotape. The advantage to an ethological system, however, is that you have a permanent record that can be coded different ways if later hypotheses require it. With a checklist system, all you have recorded are the codes themselves, not the behaviors that produced the codes.

Interpreting Events

Unless you have invented infallible recording equipment and discovered an infallible operator, interpreting observations may begin before the behavior is recorded. **Interpretation** refers to *the process whereby recorded observations are used to describe events, generate hypotheses, or test hypotheses.* Any time you edit or otherwise impose meaning on the event, you interpret the event. Recording involves interpretation, if for no other reason than you must decide what to record and what to leave out of the record.

Coding, too, involves some degree of interpretation, particularly when checklists are used for coding and recording. Refer again to Table 8.1 and notice that the IPA categories require considerable interpretation. In one context, sticking out one's tongue may seem unfriendly, but a different context may require that same behavior to be coded under "seems friendly" or "gives opinion." The observer/coder must first determine whether the action took place (recording interpretation) and then decide how to code it (coding interpretation).

When checklists or rating scales are used to simultaneously record and code actions, at least some interpretation occurs before any observations are made. Choosing the categories to be included on the checklist, or choosing an existing checklist, involves interpreting what will and will not be important before any observation occurs. When using the IPA, for example, you are deciding that the 12 categories are relevant and that other actions or codes are not relevant. Using more than one checklist may help solve the problem but may also introduce problems of its own. Gellert (1955) and others have noted that the number of different categories and the number of coding errors are directly related. Similarly, category abstractness and error are directly related: the more a coder/recorder must do in terms of interpretation, the more likely it is that he or she will make a mistake.

Sources of Error

You may have realized that interpretation, whenever it occurs in the research, involves two concepts with which you are now rather familiar—reliability and validity. If observations are not measured reliably—measured consistently—then you cannot describe the event or generate and test hypotheses about it. Similarly, if the observations are not valid—don't measure what they are supposed to measure—then only invalid or meaningless interpretations can be made. Dunnette (1966) described four sources of error that reduce reliability: inadequate sampling, chance response tendencies, changes in the participant, and changes in the situation.

The first of Dunnette's sources of error, **inadequate sampling,** *occurs when only a subset of events is recorded and the sampling process is not systematic.* When using IPA, for example, you must focus on linguistic, extralinguistic, and nonverbal behaviors. If you focus on one type of behavior during part of the observation interval and focus on a different behavior at another time, your observations are subject to inadequate sampling error. Comparing data obtained from the same observer at two different times will allow you to assess the extent of this type of error, which may be corrected through additional training.

Also correctable through additional training are **chance response tendencies**—*replacing formal category definitions with idiosyncratic definitions.* The most frequent source of chance response tendencies involves changing your mind about what to observe after you have begun making observations. If you begin observing smiling, for example, and then decide to include head nods in the same category, you have introduced chance response tendencies. By including head nods you have changed the measure from smiling to "friendly nonverbal behaviors." The observations you made before the change are no longer valid, and the measure is therefore not reliable.

Dunnette noted that chance response tendencies are more likely to occur when using abstract categories in a checklist system, although complex categories of any kind are generally sources of error. Essentially, the more confusing a coding or recording system is, the more likely the coder or recorder is to become confused when using it. When more than one participant is being observed, randomly splitting the sample into halves and comparing the two halves will enable you to estimate the extent to which chance response tendencies are operating for a single observer. If you randomly split the sample, the two halves should be more or less equal on all measures; if they are not equal, you have some reliability problems due to chance response tendencies.

Dunnette's other two sources of error refer to potential changes in the event being observed. Changes in the person being observed affect the consistency of observations, as would changes in the environment in which the observations are being made. If you are observing smiling behavior and something happens to put the participant in an especially good or especially bad mood, the behavior is going to change. If you are not aware of the event that caused the mood change, you cannot account for it when later interpreting the observations.

Correlating data from two independent observers provides a test of changes in the event. If something has changed, data from both observers should reflect the change. Of course, a high correlation between observers doesn't necessarily mean that no change has occurred, only that both observers have consistently detected the change. If changes in the event are not consistent with your research hypotheses, agreement between the raters will not correct such a failure to meet the conditions you have established for the research protocol.

Validity

You should be aware that reliability alone does not make good measurement. Categories for observation must be consistent, but they must also be valid; that is, they must measure what you want them to measure. The validity of observational measures becomes more difficult to establish as the observation categories become more abstract. It is easier to be sure that an observation fits the category "clapping hands" (McGrew, 1972) than that it fits the category "seems friendly" (Bales, 1970). Determining whether or not any particular measure is valid is covered in more detail in Chapter 14, and you should consult that chapter before attempting to use any categorization system for observation.

Participant Observation

Depending on your research hypotheses and the opportunities for observation, systematic observation may not be the most effective method for completing your research project. It is often impossible to merely sit back and watch events as they unfold. In such instances, participant observation is the method of choice. **Participant observation** is *an observational research method in which the researcher becomes part of the events being observed.* It differs from systematic observation not only in terms of the amount of researcher participation, but also in terms of hypothesis formulation and data collection tactics.

Levels of Participation

Whenever you engage in field research, you must decide how much you will participate in the sequence of events. For systematic observation, participation is minimal and the researcher usually qualifies for Gold's (1969) label of **complete observer**—*one who observes an event without becoming part of it.* The participants may not be aware of the researcher at all. Depending on the level of intrusion, participants may not even be aware the researcher is conducting research. Gold has labeled three other points on the participation continuum: observer-as-participant, participant-as-observer, and complete participant (Figure 8.5).

According to Gold, the **observer-as-participant** *is known to the participants as a researcher but does not take an active part in the events.* In this capacity, your role is analogous to an announcer at a sporting event. Everyone knows the announcer is paying attention to the game, but the announcer is not one of the players. Because the observation is not entirely unobtrusive, some reactivity effects—changes in the participants' behaviors because they know they are being

A researcher whose status
as a researcher is not
known to the participants

A researcher whose status
as a researcher is
known to the participants

A research
participant

A. The complete observer is one who does not take part in the activity
and whose status as a researcher is unknown to the participants.

B. The observer-as-participant is one who does not take part in the activity,
but whose status as a researcher is known to the participants.

C. The participant-as-observer is one who does take part in the activities.
Status as a researcher is also known to the participants.

D. The complete participant does take part in the activities, but his
or her status as a researcher is not known to the participants.

Figure 8.5   The four levels of participation according to Gold (1969)

watched—may occur. In this role, however, reactivity should be avoided, and the
researcher is more likely to be conducting systematic observation than participant
observation.

Being a **participant-as-observer** involves *being known as a researcher but
fully participating in the ongoing activities.* One classic example of this role is Liebow's (1967) study of low-income individuals in the ghetto area of the District of
Columbia. Liebow was known to his participants as a researcher, but he also involved himself as much as an outsider could. He sat through and testified at legal
hearings, visited employment agencies, and generally became a friend to a number
of his participants.

Liebow did not, and probably could not, adopt the complete participant role in
his research. A **complete participant** is *a researcher who fully participates in the
events but is not known to the other participants as a researcher.* A complete ob-

server is analogous to an undercover agent; no one knows his or her true identity as a researcher. Because Liebow was White, it would have been extremely difficult for him to have gone undercover in the predominantly Black D.C. ghetto. Whether pretending to participate or actively participating, the complete participant appears to be just another person in the sequence of events. One example of complete participation with which you may already be familiar is Humphreys's (1975) study of homosexual activity in public restrooms (Chapter 3). He served as a lookout while gathering data and the participants were unaware of his status as a researcher. Ethical issues concerning complete participation are covered in Chapter 3, and I strongly urge you to review that material before attempting to engage in observation as a complete participant.

Aside from reactivity, any level of participation has some effect on the events you are observing. Whether such effects are intentional or not, you should be aware of them and their potential influence on your observations. Even remaining neutral during a group discussion, for example, has some effect. You may be creating the impression that not all participants in the decision process have a preference, which may make it more likely that other participants will alter their preferences. Making suggestions may also influence others, even if the suggestions are not adopted. Care must be taken to objectively consider your own influence when interpreting any data collected through participant observation.

Selecting Settings

Whereas systematic observation involves selecting behaviors, participant observation is more likely to involve selecting a setting in which to observe the events of interest. Liebow's (1967) study of low-income individuals was set in the D.C. ghetto, for example, whereas Humphreys's (1975) research was set in public restrooms in St. Louis. The research in both cases was about people and their behaviors, but the selection of participants was based on the settings in which they behaved.

Given the emphasis on settings, sampling in participant observation is very different from sampling in systematic observation. Primarily, you must first select the group of people you wish to observe and then attempt to locate settings in which those people can be found. Random selection or random assignment is rarely possible. Liebow, for example, could not randomly assign some participants to live in the ghetto and some to live in the suburbs. He could have obtained a list of all ghettos in the United States and randomly selected some of them to be observed, but that would have been incredibly inefficient for his research purpose.

More often than not, participant observers rely on informants for participant selection. An **informant** is *anyone who is knowledgeable about the participants to be observed.* Informants may or may not be co-participants, and, as you might expect, you are rarely in a position to randomly select informants. After learning about your target group from an informant, including suggestions about the best settings in which to find a reasonable number of participants, you may elect to use one of three types of sampling suggested by McCall and Simmons (1969): quota, snowball, and deviant case.

Quota sampling—*selecting sampling elements on the basis of categories as-sumed to exist within the population,* involves purposefully searching out partici-pants who fit your requirements. You may want to include a certain number of men and women, young and old, Blacks and Whites, and so on. Once you have enough of one type of participant young men, for example, you avoid observing additional members of that subgroup. For each of the identified subgroups you may need to find different informants, who then lead you to other members of the subgroup and so on until you have enough observations. Sometimes you may not become aware of the existence of a subgroup until you begin your research, in which case you may need to alter your sampling plan to include members of the newly discovered group.

More often than not, participant observers use a snowball sampling technique. **Snowball sampling** involves *obtaining suggestions for other participants from those you have already observed.* Also called key informant sampling, snowball sampling is analogous to a salesperson asking the most recent customer for names of prospec-tive customers. If your research role is participant-as-observer, snowball sampling is fairly straightforward: all you have to do is ask the person you are interviewing for suggestions as to who you might interview next. As a complete participant, however, great care must be taken not to arouse suspicion while looking for key informants, particularly if some degree of secrecy surrounds membership in the group you are studying. However, as a complete participant you can more easily engage in passive sampling; you can allow the participants to make themselves known to you through the normal activity of the group.

McCall and Simmons's third sampling method, deviant case sampling, is not some weird sampling procedure. Rather, **deviant case sampling** involves *observ-ing individuals who do not seem to fit some pattern exhibited by others you have observed.* Insights into reasons for engaging in an activity can often be discovered from those who choose not to engage in the activity. In a study of religious cult membership, for example, you might want to interview those who considered join-ing but did not, or those who joined but later quit. Deviant case sampling depends on finding people who do not seem to fit a group pattern, which in turn depends on your ability to detect patterns. You can sometimes learn about patterns that enable you to identify deviant cases from participant observations conducted by others. Or you may have to observe and detect patterns for yourself, which is what we turn to next.

Recording Observations

When using systematic observation methods, recording techniques such as check-lists, video recorders, and other devices for creating permanent records are usu-ally available. When conducting a participant observation study, your equipment will probably consist of little more than paper and pencil (and perhaps a word pro-cessor). From time to time you may need to rely on memory, but even the best memories are fallible.

The research tool of greatest importance in participant observation is the **field journal**—*a notebook into which you enter your observations.* Entries in field journals fall into two categories—certain and uncertain—and it is essential that you make notes about which kind of entry you are making. For so-called certain entries you might, for example, write "Mary told Ralph to sit down and shut up." You can be fairly certain about such an entry. You might also note that Ralph appeared to take the comment as a joke, but Mary seemed to be fairly angry. These latter entries would be less certain; Ralph may have been trying to save face by treating it as a joke, or you may not know Mary well enough to be able to tell whether she was angry or normally behaves that way. The intentions of others, as a general rule, are things about which we have little certainty. New information may lead you to believe that Mary was joking, and it would be easier to incorporate the note about her anger if you had indicated that you were uncertain about the observation.

As easy as distinguishing between certain and uncertain events may seem to be, keep in mind that recording even seemingly straightforward events is often little more than logically filling in blanks in what we have observed. A number of researchers (Forgas, 1982) have provided a very impressive amount of evidence about "blank filling" in recollection. If I tell you, for example, that I grabbed my motorcycle key and helmet and went for a ride, you would probably infer that I took that ride on my motorcycle. Of course, you have no direct information that I took the motorcycle, but it seems logical given the other information. At a later time, you could perhaps become certain that I had indeed taken the ride on the motorcycle. That's the way our memories work; assumptions we make today become the certain conclusions of tomorrow. In everyday life, assuming I used my motorcycle is probably of little consequence. After all, who cares what I drive? But in participant observation research, such assumptions can have disastrous effects. Your field notes are your data, and you don't want to make assumptions about them any more than you would want to assume a participant would have obtained a certain score on the dependent variable in experimental research. Collecting data involves measuring variables, not assuming values for them.

As with taking notes in the classroom, participant observers must decide how much detail to include in their field journals. Contrary to what your instructors may tell you about taking notes in the classroom, you should try to write down "everything" when conducting participant observation research. Because you may be formulating additional hypotheses after completing your observations, you cannot be sure what will and will not be important at the time you make your observations. The rule for participant observation research is simple: if it happens, make a note of it. The bother of spending a little extra time making notes at the end of the day will never outweigh the frustration you would experience if you can only vaguely remember something that you later decide is extremely important.

Finally, maintain your field journal as often as possible. Take time at every opportunity to record whatever observations have been made up to that time. You may not have time for anything more than a few key words and phrases, but such sketchy notes are often the difference between remembering and forgetting an event. At the end of each day, rework any notes into complete journal entries, but hang onto the sketchy notes as well. If at all possible, use a word processor for making field journal entries. Eventually you may want to incorporate some of your notes into a research report, and you will already have them on file for such use. A word processor also makes coding your observations considerably easier.

Coding Observations

After you have a complete copy of your field journal, it is time to begin tearing it apart; that is, you make copies of the journal and cut and paste the copied entries in order to organize them into logical (rather than chronological) patterns. (If you have used a word processor, this becomes considerably easier.) It is during this phase, coding your field journal entries, that you may notice the development of conceptual patterns, the stuff of which hypotheses are made.

Rework entries along whatever line of reasoning seems promising. You are likely to generate more than one working hypothesis during this process, and you will want to construct a different organizational pattern for each working hypothesis. Don't spend a great deal of time worrying about whether each hypothesis can be supported by your observations; instead, organize all relevant observations for each hypothesis you develop. Continue to generate additional hypotheses until the possibilities seem exhausted. Attempting to logically determine whether or not the data support any particular working hypothesis during the coding process will make generating additional working hypotheses more difficult. *Generating and revising working hypotheses* is known as **dynamic hypothesis formulation.** Essentially, it involves searching for patterns among your notes. You should pay equal attention to things that fit together and things that don't fit together; differences are as important as similarities.

Whatever background information you collected prior to making your observations should be maintained separately from your field notes. Separating files for background information will later enable you to determine whether a conclusion you drew originated with your observations or with the background material you consulted. Comparing the background information to your own observations will also provide an indication of how much influence you may have exerted on the group.

Interpreting Observations

When you have a collection of working hypotheses, it is time to begin testing them. Testing hypotheses, particularly hypotheses involving some aspect of causality, requires differentiating between necessary and sufficient causes. A **necessary cause** is *something that must be present in order to produce the effect.* Carbon, hydrogen, oxygen, and nitrogen are all necessary causes for life as we know it; the absence of any one of these elements for an extended period of time precludes life. Certainly, other causes must also be present before someone or something is alive, but that does not diminish the extent to which these very simple elements are necessary causes for life. On the other hand, a **sufficient cause** is *something that will produce the effect.* The earth's atmosphere is a sufficient source of oxygen, but other sources serve equally well. The sometimes confusing aspect of causation is that necessary causes are not always sufficient; imagine trying to stay alive in a room full of carbon dust, water, and nitrogen gas. Similarly, sufficient causes are not always necessary: you can stay alive with SCUBA tanks; you don't need the earth's atmosphere.

When attempting to formulate causal hypotheses, the key is finding causes that can qualify as both necessary and sufficient. One method for doing this is **negative case analysis**—*searching for data that disconfirm a tentative hypothesis, revising the hypothesis to include the disconfirming data, searching for more data, and so on.* Whatever hypothesis survives this procedure is very likely to contain both necessary and sufficient causes. You cannot conclude that the remaining hypothesis is true, nor can you place as much faith in it as you could had you tested it with experimental research. However, negative case analysis is about as close as you can come to providing empirical support for a hypothesis short of experimental or quasi-experimental research.

Numerical Data Analyses

You may have gotten the impression that field research, whether systematic or participant observation, does not lend itself to numerical data analyses. If so, it is time to correct that impression. Natural observations are often analyzed qualitatively, but it is just as often the case that they can be subjected to quantitative analyses. Some researchers might consider the use of numerical analyses for ethnographic or participant observation research to be a sacrilege (Schwartz & Jacobs, 1979), but the key to proper analysis of any data is to consider numerical analyses as supplements to logic, not as replacements.

Description

As long as you observe more than one person, regardless of the manner in which you collected the observations, you can always conduct descriptive analyses to summarize the sample. Such analyses may include mean or median ages; frequency histograms of racial, economic, educational, and ethnic backgrounds; or even a sociogram of relationships among participants. Which of these analyses, if any, you conduct and include in your research report depends on the number and characteristics of the people in your sample. If you only had three participants, for example, it would be foolish to calculate a mean age. In general, if it takes less trouble or space to describe your participants in narrative form, do so. Otherwise, summary statistics may save you and your reader a considerable amount of time.

Frequency histograms may also be used to present summary information about the various types of activities you observed. Again, do not rely on numerical analyses to describe the activities, but do rely on them to summarize information about frequency of activity.

Correlation

Correlational analyses are always part of systematic observation research, if for no other reason than to assess interobserver reliability. (For more information on reliability analyses, consult Chapter 14.) It is also possible to use correlational analyses to assess reliability for participant observation research. Such analyses can provide useful information about the relative comprehensiveness of field journal notes.

It is nearly axiomatic that one gets better at participant observation the longer one does it, provided one is doing it correctly (Johnson, 1975). The are a number of different correlational analyses you can use to gain insight into the progress of your note taking. You could, for example, simply correlate the day of your activity (1, 2, 3, and so on) with the length of your notes (number of lines per entry or some other measure). Although crude, the results would enable you to determine whether you changed the thoroughness of your note taking during the course of the study. Similarly, you could correlate the number of certain and uncertain entries, in which case each day's entry would provide a pair of data points. Or, you or another person could rate each day's notes on a subjective scale of "detailedness" and correlate one-half of your notes with the other half. This analysis would provide information about your consistency with respect to including detail in your notes.

The above analyses are only a few of the many possible correlational analyses you could use to learn about the way in which you conducted your research. They don't necessarily prove anything, but they can make you aware of changes in the procedures or some other aspect of your study. The ways in which you can use correlations to learn about your data are limited only by your imagination. If you don't care to take the time to calculate correlation coefficients, you can use scatterplots to provide a graphic representation of patterns within your observations.

When you use correlational analyses, however, remember that you are using them for descriptive, not inferential, purposes. Don't get caught up in calculating statistics for the sake of obtaining numbers. Instead, use the statistics to help you understand what trends and patterns may exist in your observations. Statistics are not a required part of observational studies, but they can be helpful when there are too many data to comprehend in narrative form.

Report Writing

Recording, coding, and interpreting observations do not define the limits of field research. The final phase of a field research project, or any research project for that matter, is reporting your results and conclusions. As with any other phase of research, the starting point for report writing is paying attention to what others have done. Read reports written by others whose methods, topics, or hypotheses are similar to your own. In addition to the methodological and theoretical information you can obtain from such reports, you can also obtain information about style and content of research reports.

It is not possible to tell someone what to include and what to leave out of a research report without being familiar with the research itself. By now you should be aware that Chapter 12 contains general guidelines for report writing. The remainder of this section includes guidelines that are specific to field research but are not necessarily specific to your research project.

When more than one observer recorded or coded observations, describe the procedures and results of any reliability analyses you completed. Also, any training you conducted should at least be mentioned if not fully described. The extent of the description depends on how unusual the procedures were. If, for example, you used the IPA, you probably need only mention that you used the IPA and trained the observers accordingly. If, on the other hand, you developed your own checklist, you need to provide enough detail to enable the reader to understand, and preferably be able to recreate, your procedure.

You should also, of course, describe how you obtained your research participants—your sampling procedure. Let the reader know how you contacted informants, what your role as participant might have been, and so on. What you told the participants about your study may have affected their behavior, and the reader needs to know about such things as well.

Finally, be careful not to generalize beyond or otherwise mistreat your data when drawing conclusions; that is, do not be so concerned with proving something that you fall into one or another of the logical pitfalls surrounding data interpretation. Ask yourself whether you are (1) using a narrow viewpoint when examining the data, (2) ignoring alternative conclusions that make equally good sense, (3) indeed measuring what you thought you were measuring, (4) ignoring data that should be included, and (5) setting up straw hypotheses in order to lead the reader to your own conclusions. (Straw hypotheses are hypotheses you never intended to relate to the data but are included in order to make yourself appear to be considering all points of view.) All five of these problems should be avoided.

Each time you write the equivalent of "it seems reasonable to conclude," consider the five points listed above. If you cannot rule out all five of these mistakes, the reader will probably not consider your conclusions to be reasonable. You will have lost credibility, which may affect the reader's appraisal of other conclusions. When you write a research report, you have but two purposes: to inform the reader about your research and to ensure that the reader accepts your information as valid. If you fail to achieve either one of these, you have failed to successfully complete your research project.

Summary

- Field research includes any research applied to natural events—those not created, sustained, or discontinued solely for research purposes. How natural an event may be, however, must be determined from the viewpoint of the participant.
- Intrusion undermines naturalness, and can affect the behaviors of participants, the settings in which the behaviors occur, and treatments presented to participants. In general, anything perceived by participants as foreign to their normal experience may be intrusive.
- Field research methods are best applied to exploration, description, and action. They generally lack the external validity required for prediction and the internal validity required for explanation.

• Systematic observation involves observing activities without taking part in them. Events are selected on the basis of the types of behavior to be observed: nonverbal, spatial, extralinguistic, and linguistic. Selection usually involves choosing a sample of time periods during which the behaviors occur, or choosing specific activities on the basis of some criterion related to the research hypothesis.

• Recording and coding events in systematic observation are often simultaneous processes. The former involves creating a permanent record of the activity, whereas the latter involves assigning to the activity meaning that is relevant to the research hypotheses. Regardless of the technique used for either process, recording and coding always involve some degree of measurement error.

• Participant observation involves making observations while taking part in the event sequence, sometimes while being recognized as a researcher and sometimes not.

• Sampling procedures in participant observation generally involve selecting a setting in which the activity occurs and then attempting to observe participants as a group or individually. If an activity of interest is not completed by all participants, deviant case sampling may be used to formulate hypotheses about participants' reasons for engaging in the activity.

• The primary research tool in participant observation is the field journal, a notebook into which all observations are entered. It is advisable to keep the field journal as contemporary and accurate as possible because it contains the data that will be used to test research hypotheses.

• Coding and interpreting participant observations often involve rearranging chronological observations into patterns related to the research hypotheses, a process called dynamic hypothesis formulation. Necessary and sufficient causes should be differentiated when interpreting field journal entries.

• Negative case analysis involves attempting to find data that disconfirm a working hypothesis. When such data are found, the hypothesis should be revised so as to include the disconfirming cases. Eventually, one or more hypotheses will be retained that can be used to account for all of the data.

• Although field research does not usually involve numerical analyses, they can be used to summarize information or to search for patterns related to research hypotheses.

• As with any research, field research is not complete until a report has been written. The report should contain enough information about sampling, measurement, and interpretation procedures to enable a reader to recreate the research.

CHAPTER NINE

Archival Research

> ... *but there is still no [person] who would not accept dog tracks in the mud against sworn testimony of a hundred eye-witnesses that no dog passed by.*
>
> —*Prosser (1964, p. 216)*

Overview

This chapter is about archival research—methods in which the sources of data are various types of documentation. You will learn about content analysis, a method for determining the meaning of recorded communication, as well as some special sampling problems relevant to content analysis. You will also be exposed to some of the techniques used to quantify information derived from content analysis. You will learn about the uses of existing data—measures that have been obtained by other researchers—as well as some ways in which such data may be used and analyzed. Finally, you will learn about research methods for investigating trends within a collection of related studies.

Introduction

The label *archival research* may suggest an image of an elderly scholar (with bad eyes, of course) bent over an ancient, dusty manuscript in the decrepit basement of a library. Indeed, many behavioral scientists have some disdain for archival research, the type of disdain reflected in the opening quote from Prosser (1964). One of the early reviewers of this text, for example, commented, "I prefer to leave archival research to librarians and historians." Such images and comments not withstanding, archival research has been firmly established as a research tradition in the behavioral sciences. One reason why archival research has gained acceptance may be that there are times when a researcher cannot find any "tracks in the mud" and must rely on the testimony of others. Such testimony may be found in dusty old manuscripts, but it is also found in newspapers, songs, novels, memoirs, movies, magazines, government reports, research reports, and a variety of other sources.

Archival research, like field research, is something every one of us does informally every day. We all read, watch, and listen. We may even be exposed to such statistical summaries as the gross national product, crime rates, or the batting averages of our favorite baseball players. Formal archival research, however, involves systematic examination of archives in order to formulate or test hypotheses and theories. For our purposes, then, **archival research** is *any research in which a public record is the unit of analysis.* What distinguishes archival research from other methods is that the researcher deals with information generated before the research began, and archival researchers deal with people's products rather than with the people themselves.

Archival research involves attempting to answer questions about people by investigating a portion of the seemingly infinite amount of recorded information they generate. Specific methods have been developed to allow researchers to find such records, obtain a sample of them, transform the collected information into usable data, analyze those data, and use the results to draw conclusions. Sometimes, research was not a consideration of those who originally compiled the information; in other instances the original information was gathered through the use of some research method. Literally any record of information is fair game for archival research.

Systematic archival methods can be separated into two types: content analysis and existing data analysis. Content analysis may involve interpreting any communication medium, whether written, pictorial, oral, or audiovisual. By studying such archives you can test and formulate hypotheses about a variety of different behavioral phenomena. Existing data analysis generally involves using data for purposes other than those for which the data were gathered. Various archives, for example, may contain information about trends that could not have been detected when the data were first collected. Because the above descriptions are very general, more specific discussions follow.

Content Analysis

The amount of communication each of us experiences throughout a typical day is incredible. We converse with others, read what others have written, listen to live or taped conversations and songs, watch the actions of others on a television or movie screen, and pay attention to the various signs that surround us. All of this communication has some meaning for us, and content analysis is one research method that can be used to study that meaning.

The "stuff" of content analysis has been described very succinctly by Lasswell, Lerner, and Pool (1952, p. 12) in the question "Who says what, to whom, how, and with what effect?" Holsti (1968) adds "Why?" for the sake of completeness, although discovering why a particular message was sent is not always a part of content analysis. More formally, **content analysis** is *a research method used to make objective and systematic inferences about theoretically relevant messages.* Let's examine this formal definition in order to appreciate the potential power of content analysis as a research method.

As noted above, our world is full of messages—communication directed by someone to someone else for a specific purpose. These messages are the observations we investigate in content analysis. Messages contained in any medium can be analyzed, although the medium chosen for analysis depends on both theoretical and practical concerns. Content analysis is best used to test research hypotheses, and the content of archives serve as operational definitions of theoretical concepts. Some media are easier to analyze than others, however, and practical concerns also become part of the planning process.

Like all research, content analysis should be used to make inferences about events related to theory. In turn, your ability to make inferences depends on the sample you study. If you want to investigate the violent content of television programs during the last ten years, for example, it would be rather difficult to analyze all of the decade's programming. The messages you decide to sample systematically should represent the entire decade's programming, and you need to be able to use a sampling procedure that ensures such representativeness (for more information about sampling, see Chapter 16).

In addition to being systematic, inferences must be objective; the inferences you make about messages should be similar to the inferences someone else would make if he or she had access to the same information. Part of this objectivity is accomplished through careful construction of the operational definitions you use in your research; another part of objectivity results from the consistency with which you use the operational definitions you construct—that is, the reliability of measurement. Although reliability and validity are important in any research project, the ease with which communication can be misunderstood makes reliable measurement more difficult in content analysis.

The range of potential topics for content analysis is considerable but finite. Just because any question of the form "Who says what to whom, how, with what effect, and why?" can be answered through content analysis does not mean that content analysis is always the most appropriate method for such questions. Specifically, content analysis is best used as a comparative technique. It cannot, for example, be used to measure how conservative a particular newspaper's editorial policy is, but it can be used to determine whether one newspaper is more conservative than another.

"Who": The Source of Messages

When the research question involves the "who" part of Lasswell et al.'s question, you are concerned with describing the individual(s) who created the archives. The research hypothesis may concern disputed authorship or may involve making inferences about characteristics of the author(s). One example of disputed authorship was resolved by using content analysis of *The Federalist,* a series of 85 essays originally published under the nom de plume Publius. Alexander Hamilton, James Madison, and John Jay wrote the essays to persuade people to throw over the Articles of Confederation in favor of the Constitution. The authorship of 12 of the essays (essays 49–58, 62, and 63) was uncertain; either Madison or Hamilton could have written them.

Mosteller and Wallace (1964) compared the relative frequency of certain common words—*and, in, the,* and *enough*—in essays known to have been written by the two authors with the same words in the disputed essays; their results clearly indicated that Madison was the author. They demonstrated that even in the least convincing paper (No. 55), the odds were 80 to 1 in favor of Madison's authorship. Subsequently, Rokeach, Homant, and Penner (1970) compared values expressed in the papers—freedom, honor, equality, and comfort—and arrived at the same conclusion concerning authorship.

In both research projects, the researchers were able to address the question of authorship only because they had access to material known to have been written by Hamilton and Madison; without the undisputed essays, authorship could not have been settled. Using content analysis in the absence of comparative standards can cause a number of problems. Morton (1963), for example, used seven characteristics of an author's style to analyze the Epistles of St. Paul and concluded that there were at least six different authors for the Epistles. Responding to Morton's published challenge to others to repudiate his results, Ellison (1965) used the same procedure to demonstrate that Morton's own articles exhibited multiple authorship. Morton was repudiated, rather cleverly. Attempting to determine authorship in the absence of comparative standards usually leads to more ambiguity than clarity.

Rather than attempting to describe a single author's characteristics, Seider (1974) investigated ideologies and value systems of a group of authors—U.S. business executives. When Seider began his research, the predominant view was that most business executives shared a common ideology (Sutton, Harris, Kayson, & Tobin, 1956). Seider, however, hypothesized that different priorities among different industries would be mirrored in the language used by the executive officers.

By analyzing business speeches published in *Vital Speeches* from 1934 to 1970, Seider found support for his hypothesis. Three major ideologies were identified among the speeches: classical, social responsibility, and nationalistic. Classical ideology included such themes as free enterprise, profit, and self-regulation; social responsibility included solving social problems and improving conditions for employees and communities; and nationalism included themes protecting the United States and downgrading competing countries. The three ideologies appeared in 52%, 19%, and 31% of the speeches, respectively. Even though the classical ideology was prevalent, preferred ideologies did indeed differ across industries. Corporate officers in the aerospace industry, for example, emphasized the nationalism more than did the other two ideologies.

"Says What": The Content of Messages

Perhaps the most prevalent use of content analysis has been to investigate the content communicated in a message. Holsti (1968) separated this question into three distinct components: (1) changes in content over time, (2) the relationship between author characteristics and content, and (3) the extent to which content conforms to some external standard. Research by Zimbardo and Meadow (1974) provided a simultaneously encouraging and disconcerting example of the first of these components. The starting point for their research was the phenomenon known as **unconscious ideology,** *a prejudice that has lost its label as prejudice and has become an implicit assumption that strongly affects the roles of certain members of a society* (Bem & Bem, 1970). For example, a man would consider the expectation that his male roommate would do all the cleaning to be unfair but would be perfectly willing to expect a female roommate to do the same. That there is apparently nothing wrong with expecting a female to do all the housework is an unconscious ideology.

Zimbardo and Meadow reasoned that humor may be the most effective medium for preserving prejudicial attitudes and that therefore changes in the content of humor should reflect the prevalence of a specific prejudice. They focused on stereotypes about women and analyzed the content of jokes taken from the "Cartoon Quips" and "Laughter, The Best Medicine" sections of *Reader's Digest* from 1947–48, 1957–58, and 1967–68. After identifying jokes with anti-women bias, they discovered that the frequency of such jokes had declined over the 20-year period. Approximately 28% of the jokes were anti-women in the 1940s, followed by 10% and 6% respectively, for the 1950s and 1960s. The total number of jokes in the sections increased over the years, but the proportion and absolute number of prejudicial jokes decreased. That's the encouraging aspect of Zimbardo and Meadow's research: general sexism declined over the years.

The disconcerting aspect of their research involves the analyses of specific stereotypes represented in the anti-women jokes. Table 9.1 contains a list of the negative traits ascribed to women in the jokes and a representative quip for each trait. Zimbardo and Meadow's content analysis indicated that the amount of anti-women sentiment decreased over the years, but the sentiments themselves remained relatively constant.

Using content analysis to investigate what is said can involve any one of three components outlined by Holsti (1968). Zimbardo and Meadow's study is just one example of temporal trends in content. Jacobs's (1967) content analysis of suicide notes (described in Chapter 1) is an example of archival research in which the content and author's characteristics were related. In the next section, the focus shifts from originators to receivers of messages.

"To Whom": The Audience of Messages

It is no great revelation that people communicate different messages to different audiences. We all, for example, talk about different topics with fellow students than with nonstudents, and we talk about different topics with friends than with strang-

Table 9.1   A partial list of negative traits assigned to women

Stupid, incompetent, foolish:

("**sweet young thing**" **to husband**) "Of course I know what's going on in this world! I just don't understand any of it, that's all."

Domineering, selfish:

(**wife to husband picking out a three-piece suit**) "Well, go ahead and please yourself. After all, you're the one who will wear the suit." (**meek husband's reply**) "Well, dear, I figure I'll probably get to wear the coat and vest, anyway."

Exploiting men for their money:

(**woman trying on a hat, to the salesperson**) "It's nice, but it's a little less than he can afford."

Jealous, catty:

(**one woman to another**) "I've been wondering, my dear, why you weren't invited to the Asterbilt's last week?" (**other woman**) "Isn't that a coincidence? I was just wondering why you were."

Spendthrift, financially irresponsible:

(**husband to guest**) "The decor is Helen's own blend of traditional, modern, and twenty-five hundred dollars."

Gossipy, nagging:

(**one woman to another**) "I like her. She just gives you the straight gossip, without slanting or editorializing."

Manhunting, overanxious to marry:

(**young student explaining her choice of colleges**) "Well, I came here to get went with, but I ain't yet."

---

ers. One purpose of content analysis is to determine the extent to which audience-specific messages really are different.

Berkman (1963), for example, analyzed the content of advertisements in *Life* and *Ebony* magazines and found that the major difference was the presumed economic status of prospective buyers. *Life* included a greater proportion of higher-priced products among its advertising. However, within any given price range for products, the only difference in the ads in the two magazines was the race of the models: Whites for *Life* and Blacks for *Ebony*. In all other respects the content of the advertisements was similar.

Differences among messages directed to different audiences can also be used to investigate theoretical issues. Levin and Spates (1970), for example, used content analysis to investigate Parson's (1951) propositions about the importance to subcultures of instrumental and expressive values. According to Levin and Spates, what had been labeled the "hippie" movement of the 1960s should be a prime example of an expressive subculture—one characterized by an emphasis on feelings over accomplishment. They compared the content of various publications of the 1960s underground press to that of *Reader's Digest*, a much more traditional publication.

They found that 46% of the content in underground publications included expressive themes, whereas only 10% of the content included instrumental themes. On the other hand, *Reader's Digest* included 23% expressive themes and 42% instrumental themes. Clearly, the communications directed toward "hippies" emphasized expressive themes, whereas the more traditional press emphasized instrumental themes. The communication of different messages to different audiences, although nothing new in and of itself, did provide supporting evidence for Parsons's theory.

"How": Communication Techniques in Messages

Investigating the "how" of communication is a relatively rare application of content analysis, although the few investigations into this matter have been highly informative. Holsti's (1968) work, for example, provides an excellent starting point for research on propaganda, as does that of Crano and Brewer (1973). A more recent example is the work of McHugo, Lanzetta, Sullivan, Masters, and Englis (1985), which involved an analysis of Ronald Reagan's communication techniques.

McHugo et al. analyzed the content of a number of videotaped Reagan speeches, but they did not limit themselves to analyzing only the verbal content. Using a panel of judges, they separated videotapes into four groups based on Reagan's facial expressions: neutral, reassuring, threatening, and evasive. In order to examine the "how" of communication, McHugo et al. did something unusual for content-analysis researchers: they brought the videotapes into a research laboratory and monitored viewers' reactions to the tapes.

Some people viewed the tapes intact (both picture and sound), whereas others watched only the video portion of the tapes. By comparing the two groups, McHugo et al. were able to demonstrate that Reagan's facial expressions were more influential than the verbal content of his speeches. The only exception to this general effect occurred among those whose attitudes were strongly anti-Reagan—these viewers were not affected by Reagan's reassuring facial expression, particularly when the content of the speech was not reassuring. This research illustrates the combination of content analysis and experimental methods, and it also demonstrates that content analysis of the "hows" of communication need not be limited to the manner in which people put words together.

"With What Effect": The Effect of Messages

Assessing effects through content analysis can be approached in one of two ways. One way involves examining the effects of some phenomenon by analyzing the content of documents related to the phenomenon. A content analysis of interviews with first-grade children (Kounin & Gump, 1961), for example, provided evidence that the attitudes of children's teachers affected the children's perceptions of inappropriate behaviors. The other way to assess effects is to examine the effects produced by the content of the documents themselves. An example of this approach is Levin and Spates's (1970) analysis of the impact of the 1960s underground press on traditional publications.

Kounin and Gump (1961) studied the effects of teachers' styles through their pupils' beliefs about misbehavior. Using consensus among raters, they categorized teachers as either punitive or nonpunitive. The children were then asked to answer two questions: "What's the worst thing a child can do at school?" and "Why is that so bad?" The results clearly demonstrated that children who had punitive teachers were much more likely to consider fighting and other physical behaviors to be misconduct, whereas children with nonpunitive teachers were more likely to consider behaviors such as lying to be misconduct.

Of greater relevance to our educational system, children with punitive teachers were much less likely to consider poor academic performance to be misconduct. The authors concluded that a punitive teaching style is less likely than a nonpunitive style to produce high levels of academic performance. You may be thinking to yourself "So what else is new," but you should realize that the research was completed in 1961, when punitive teaching styles were considered the norm. This content analysis was influential in leading others to conduct research that has since made this conclusion "old hat."

"Why": The Reasons for Communications

Attempting to discover why various archives were created deals with one of the most difficult questions to answer using content analysis. Most research dealing with "why" has to do with biographical material and investigations of individuals' motivations for various actions. Using content analysis for such purposes has been variously labeled life history analysis, case study methodology, psychobiography, and psychohistory. Proponents of these different labels differ only a little in their specific methods and purposes but for the most part are highly similar (Runyan, 1982).

One use for investigating the "why" of archives is gaining an understanding of the social and political motives of biographers. Runyan (1982), for example, provided an insightful look at the motives of the Nixon administration through his analysis of two different archives concerning biographical material on Daniel Ellsberg. Ellsberg leaked to the U.S. press the Pentagon Papers, classified documents that provided evidence of the deceitful and otherwise unethical activity of the Nixon administration during the Vietnam War.

In summary, content analysis can be rather effectively used to answer a variety of questions. Understanding the variability of applications, however, is not the same thing as understanding the technique itself. For this reason, we turn next to procedural issues concerning content analysis.

Methodological Issues in Content Analysis

The first step in any content analysis research is deciding what part of the "who says what to whom, how, with what effect, and why?" question you will address. That decision, of course, depends on your interests in human behavior, the theory with which you are working, and the research hypotheses you have developed. Making that decision, however, is only the beginning of content analysis. You must also make a series of decisions concerning units of analysis, units of observation, sampling techniques, and coding before you can begin to collect data.

Suppose, for example, that you decided to investigate the degree of sexism displayed on television, as did Ellis (1988). Your next decision would concern *the objects about which you would like to answer your question*—the **units of analysis.** You could not, for example, analyze everything on television. Even if you chose to select a relatively small period of time—say, a day or two—you would still have a great deal of programming given the number of channels across the country. You would have to choose a sample of programming that included network broadcasts, a small number of independent channels, daytime programming, children's programs, news shows, commercials, and so forth to limit your research observations.

Deciding on units of analysis then enables you to choose the **units of observation**—*the specific material to be measured.* After deciding to use television commercials, for example, you must refine your choice by deciding which of the myriad of commercials you will actually examine for sexist content. Will you deal only with a specific type of commercial, such as cleaning products? Or commercials presented at specific times of the day—say, during prime time? Or commercials aired during specific programs, such as during the news? You must refine your choice until you have a concrete description of the archives you will be examining.

Seider (1974), for example, decided to use speeches as units of observation in his study of corporate ideologies. He wanted to obtain a cross-section of business leaders, and he decided that *Vital Speeches* sufficiently represented the range of material of interest to him. At the risk of second-guessing Seider, it may be that the annual reports of the various corporations would have served equally well as units of observation. Of course, it would have been more difficult to obtain copies of annual reports from the variety of businesses he wanted to include; copies of *Vital Speeches* were readily available in the library and were therefore more convenient. The point is not that there may have been better units of observation, just different units. Once you have selected your units of observation, you must be aware that there are other units that also could have been observed.

Deciding on the units of observation leads to a series of decisions about sampling—about how you will select some representative group of the units. If, for example, you decided to examine commercials presented during network news programs, you could probably look at every commercial during every newscast on every network for some specified period of time, but it would be unnecessary to do so. You could instead, for example, plan a procedure that involved sequentially and randomly choosing a day of the week, a time period, a network, and a newscast you would observe for any given data collection session. If you had a programmable video recorder, you could set the machine to tape the newscasts you randomly selected and then view the commercials at a convenient time.

The reason for establishing a systematic sampling procedure is to avoid having to observe everything included in your units of observation. A systematic sampling procedure provides you a representative sample from which you can generalize to the entire set of observational units. You don't have to watch every television commercial to be able to draw conclusions about television commercials in general. Chapter 16 contains more detail about specific sampling procedures.

Having defined your sample, you then must decide how you are going to measure the variables contained in your research hypothesis. This, of course, involves determining the operational definitions you will include in your research. You might, for example, simply decide to categorize commercials as either sexist or nonsexist, but even such a simple measure requires an operational definition. What makes a commercial sexist? Is there more than one way to define sexist? If there are different types of sexism, are you going to consider all types or only some of them? How many examples of sexism must a commercial contain in order to categorize it as sexist? When dealing with content analysis, you must decide between two different levels of content: manifest and latent.

Manifest content—*the physical or noninferential material that makes up an archive*—is usually coded in terms of words or letters in written material, words and pauses in audio material, concrete actions in visual material, and so forth. Kounin and Gump (1961), for example, used manifest content in their study of children's impressions of misconduct. Such words as "hitting," "pushing," and "kicking" were coded as assaultive behaviors; such phrases as "talking out of turn," "yelling at someone," or "lying to someone" were coded as nonassaultive. Manifest content is usually relatively easy to code reliably; few people would disagree about the presence or absence of a word or an action in an observation.

Latent content refers to *inferred, underlying, or hidden meaning in material that makes up an archive*. It may be coded in terms of words or actions, and it usually involves inferences from sentences, paragraphs, facial expressions, and tone of voice, as well as other indications of meaning. When someone says "Nice try" during a softball game, for example, they may be complementing me on my effort, or they may be making a sarcastic appraisal of my relative incompetence. Cultural propriety, too, plays a role in coding latent content. When I moved to the South, for example, it took some time before I was comfortable with being greeted by the word "hey." In the North, saying "hey" is usually a warning or a threat, depending on the tone of voice. In the South, however, "hey" simply means hello.

Because coding latent content involves making inferences about the manifest content of an archive, latent content is generally less reliable than manifest content. On the other hand, latent content may be the only way to operationalize some concepts. Advertisers are not likely, for example, to come out and straightforwardly say "Women are inferior decision makers" in their commercials. They may, however, show women deciding to buy a car because of its color and show men basing their decisions on gas mileage or investment value. Coding manifest content and coding latent content are not mutually exclusive practices. The same archive, *The Federalist*, was coded for manifest content by Mosteller and Wallace (1964) and for latent content by Rokeach et al. (1970); both research teams arrived at the same conclusions but used different coding practices in the process.

To summarize, a number of different, related decisions must be made in order to turn your research idea into a research hypothesis (see Figure 9.1). You must decide what archives to analyze and which specific documents among those archives you will actually observe or measure. You must also decide how to obtain a representative sample of your archives and how to operationally define the vari-

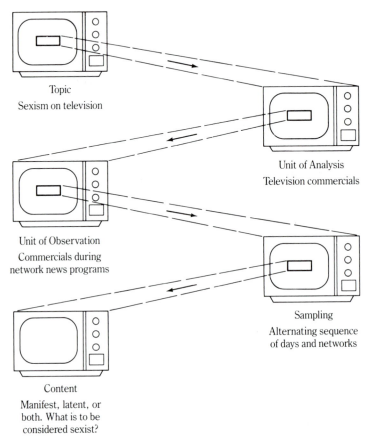

Figure 9.1 An example of the decisions involved in a content analysis of sexism on television in which the final research plan involves assessing both latent and manifest content of television commercials that air during network news programs on a variety of days and networks. What remains is the decision concerning what exactly will and will not be classified as sexist.

ables included in your hypotheses. Having made all these decisions, you are then in a position to begin to collect data—to measure the variables you have defined.

Quantification in Content Analysis

Virtually anything is quantifiable, provided the principles and procedures of measurement are followed correctly. Measurement in general is covered in Chapter 14, but some measurement issues are specific to content analysis. It is these specific issues to which we turn our attention in this section. The type (or types) of quantification procedure you select for your content analysis project depends on the units of observation and the coding procedures you have selected; one or more of the procedures outlined below will be appropriate for your study. As the procedures are discussed, we'll consider an example from my own research to illustrate the differences among the procedures.

The most common method of quantifying variables in content analysis involves measuring frequency—counting the number of times a given variable appears in the observational unit. In a study of simulated jury deliberations, for example, I counted the number of times jurors mentioned an item of evidence, a personal experience, the judge's instructions, and a few other variables in an effort to examine the relationship between the content of deliberations and the final verdict. By tallying the frequency with which each topic was discussed, I was able to determine that jurors made more remarks about evidence than about any other topic. I also discovered a relationship between the amount of evidence-related discussion and the verdict: more talk about evidence was associated with a greater likelihood of conviction.

One common difficulty associated with the frequency method of quantification, however, is deciding what to do with repetitions. One juror may say "We have to remember that he had a knife" and another juror may echo that with "Yeah, a knife." Do both statements count or only the first, or should there be a separate category for repetitions? If you want to measure the number of times a certain word occurs, as did Mosteller and Wallace (1964), then repetitions are no problem. But if you want to measure the number of times an idea is presented, repetition becomes a question that must be resolved. There is no single solution, for the decision depends on your hypotheses and other considerations. I decided not to count repetitions, partly because I was interested in counting how many times evidence was discussed, not simply how many times someone referred to any particular piece of evidence.

An alternative to frequency counts—one that also overcomes the potential problem of repetitions—involves measuring the amount of space (for written material) or time (for audio and visual material) appropriated to the variable. Using the same deliberations, I compared the amount of time jurors spent discussing evidence and other topics. With the temporal measure, however, I discovered that less time was devoted to evidence, despite the fact that the frequency measure indicated that evidence statements were most frequent. That is, the jurors mentioned evidence more often than any other topic, but the amount of time spent discussing evidence was relatively brief. More to the point, using temporal coding resulted in no apparent relationship between discussion of evidence and verdict.

Different operational definitions of the variable produced different results, which is not unusual. One reason for the difference was that my unit of analysis was the sentence. There were more sentences about evidence than about any other topic, but the evidence-related sentences were also shorter than sentences about any other topic.

To avoid the problem introduced by differential sentence (or other unit) length, some researchers use a technique first developed by Osgood and colleagues (Osgood, Sporta, & Nunnally, 1956; Osgood, 1959). The technique, called evaluative assertion analysis (EAA), involves breaking down statements into one of two structural forms: subject–connector–descriptor or subject–connector–object. Using EAA, the sentence "There are people who are unbalanced and pick up a knife" can be separated into two statements: some people–are–unbalanced and unbalanced people–pick up–a knife. The first statement, according to my coding scheme, was categorized as general knowledge; the second was categorized as a remark about the defendant's character.

Of course, when you use EAA you cannot measure the amount of time devoted to a topic. When I used EAA on jury deliberations, I obtained essentially the same results as when I used simple frequency counts. Evidence was the most frequently discussed topic and was related to verdicts.

Perhaps the most difficult quantification method to use is the intensity method. Whenever the units of analysis might vary in intensity—some statements have more meaning or more relevance than others—it is often the case that simple frequency or space/time enumeration are insufficient. A number of different techniques can be used for intensity analysis, all of which involve using some sort of rating scale. For example, one of the coding categories I used in the content analysis of jury deliberations was verdict preference, an indication of the juror's intention to vote guilty, not guilty, or undecided. There are different ways, however, to indicate a preference. One juror might say "I think he's guilty," whereas another might say "He's definitely guilty." Clearly, these two jurors are expressing the same belief with different intensities.

Although there are a number of different ways to scale intensity (see, for example, Chapter 15), I decided to ask several individuals to rate each statement on a scale from 1 to 10; the more intense the statement, the higher the rating. The first statement quoted above received an average rating of 5, and the second received an average rating of 8. I discovered that intensity ratings of statements about the incriminating nature of evidence—"No matter what his reasons, he still stabbed someone"—was the variable most strongly related to final verdicts, even more strongly related than were initial statements about verdict preferences.

Different quantification methods may lead to different results, although that does not mean that one method is necessarily better than another. In the above examples, the research question addressed by each method was slightly different. With frequency analysis, the analysis dealt with the relationship between frequency of occurrence and verdict; for the space/time analysis, the relationship examined was between verdicts and time spent discussing topics; the intensity method assessed the relationship between verdicts and strength of opinion. Once again, the questions asked have a great deal to do with the answers obtained. In your own research, you need to decide on a method that enables you to answer the question you want to ask.

Existing Data Analysis

Up to now our discussion has dealt with creating data from existing archives. In this section we consider research in which the data already exist. **Existing data are** *the archived results of research accomplished by someone else.* They are typically found in one of three formats: raw data, aggregate or summary data, and the results of completed data analyses (statistical results).

The raw data format generally contains measurements in the original units of observation. Thus using existing raw data is analogous to hiring someone else to collect your data, except that you don't have the latitude to determine which data are collected. Your instructor's record of examination scores, for example, are raw data. Your instructor collected the data and, if you can obtain access to them, they are yours to analyze however you see fit. Archived raw data are the most flexible of the forms of existing data.

Aggregate or summary data are not nearly as flexible as raw data. They typically are archived as one or more combinations of the original measures. For example, if your instructor only kept a record of the average score on each exam, those average or mean scores would be considered aggregate data. The original units of observation were the individual examination scores, but they have been combined into a higher-order unit of analysis, the mean. Because you don't have access to the original units of observation for aggregate data, your use of them is somewhat limited. You could not, for example, use the mean examination scores to investigate an individual's improvement during a given semester, although you could use them to determine the extent to which the class improved.

The third format for existing data, statistical results, is the format with which you are probably most familiar. The statistical results included in research reports are a form of existing data, although this format has the most restrictions. Consistent with the previous examples, the statistical result format would be analogous to your instructor saving only correlations between exam scores, not the scores themselves or any other descriptive summaries of the scores.

Applications of Existing Data Analysis

Regardless of their complexity or the format in which they are stored, all existing data have one thing in common: someone else was responsible for their collection; all of the decisions about measurement have already been made. If those decisions match your purposes, then you can use the data as they are. At other times, however, you may need to build upon the decisions made by the original researcher. In this section, you will learn about how to accomplish such building by reading about examples of research completed with existing data.

In January 1973, the firm of Louis Harris and Associates conducted a survey of leisure activities and opinions in the United States. The raw data were archived at the Louis Harris Political Data Library of the Institute for Research in Social Science at the University of North Carolina. A number of years later, Marsden, Reed, Kennedy, and Stinson (1982) made use of those same data to investigate potential lifestyle differences between the northern and southern sections of the country. Their major intent was to determine the extent to which the considerable anecdotal and stereotypical information about North–South differences could be supported by empirical data.

The original survey data included responses on participation in 40 different leisure activities, far too many variables on which to measure North–South differences. To create a more manageable data set, Marsden et al. used **cluster analysis,** *a statistical technique that groups variables according to the degree of similarity* *exhibited among the variables.* The mathematics of cluster analysis are well beyond the scope of this book, but the principle is simple. Categories of activities were formed on the basis of the extent to which people participated in the activities. For example, if many of the people who participated in spectator sports such as watching car races also participated in competitive sports such as softball, the two activities were grouped together in the same category. Table 9.2 contains a list of the various activities and the categories into which they were grouped.

Table 9.2 Examples of activities categorized by Marsden et al. (1982)

Category Label	Activity
Outdoor Activities	Spectator sports
	Competitive sports
	Rock music
Social Activities	Yoga
	Fashions
	Collecting things
	Nature studies
	Weekend trips
Cultural Activities	Lectures
	Reading
	Museums
	Theater
	Concerts
	Dance recitals
Arts Participation	Playing musical instrument
	Acting
	Performing for others
	Painting
	Dancing
	Singing
Music Listening	Opera
	Classical
	Broadway
	Jazz
Crafts	Sewing
	Gourmet cooking
	Gardening
	Country–western music
	Popular music
	Religious music

One way to interpret Table 9.2 is to consider the relative proximity of activities. For example, spectator-sport participants are likely to participate in competitive sports but are not as likely to visit museums. On the other hand, those who collect things are equally likely to enjoy yoga and weekend trips. Category boundaries should be considered to represent "distance" as well. For example, those who play musical instruments are more likely to act than they are to attend dance recitals. The three activities at the bottom of the table—country–western, popular, and religious music—stood out as separate categories. People who listen to those three types of music are not any more or less likely to engage in any of the other activities.

Using the categories as dependent variables, Marsden et al. discovered that Northerners participated more than Southerners in every type of activity except two: Southerners were more likely to listen to country–western and religious music. Thus, even though the original data were not collected for such purposes, Marsden et al. were able to use them to demonstrate empirical support for anecdotal evidence about North–South differences—for the notion that Northerners are more active with respect to leisure activities.

Taking full advantage of the comprehensive nature of the original data set, Marsden et al. looked into some possible reasons for the North–South differences. The original survey included a great deal of demographic information, and Marsden et al. found that taking demographic variables into account reduced but did not eliminate the North–South differences. They concluded that "Southerners do less of almost everything—or at least almost everything it occurred to the [data collectors] to ask people about" (p. 1040).

The qualification in their conclusion points out one of the difficulties that arise when analyzing existing data: using existing data limits you to information that others consider important, not necessarily the same information you may consider relevant to your purposes. Marsden et al. may have wanted to examine other types of leisure activities but were unable to do so because such activities were not included in the original survey. They were also required to use some rather sophisticated statistical analyses to adapt the original data to their purposes. Although the raw data format is the most flexible of the formats for existing data, existing data are rarely as flexible as those you collect yourself—for your own purposes and for testing your own hypotheses.

The classic illustration of the use of aggregate data is Durkheim's (1951; originally published in 1897) research on environmental correlates of suicide. In an effort to address the question of why people take their own lives, Durkheim obtained and analyzed suicide rates and other demographic statistics from a number of different European countries. Although he identified a number of patterns in the suicide rates—including information that refuted the then-accepted explanation of uncomfortably hot weather—the most intriguing aspects of the data were the associations of suicide rates with both political activity and religious affiliations. Durkheim noted, for example, a dramatic increase in suicides during 1848, a particularly tumultuous year politically for many European countries. He also noted that countries with larger proportions of Catholic residents exhibited consistently lower suicide rates.

But Durkheim did not have access to information on the religious denominations of individuals who committed suicide. Instead, he investigated the religious connection by using the relative number of Catholics and Protestants within various countries. For example, predominantly Catholic Bavaria exhibited one-third fewer suicides than predominantly Protestant provinces. Generally, the greater the proportion of Catholics in a given region, the lower the suicide rate.

Taken together, the associations of suicide rates with both religious affiliation and political turmoil led Durkheim to conclude that **anomie**—*a general sense of instability or disintegration*—was an important contributory factor in suicide. Political changes led to instability in everyday life, which in turn produced anomie. Fewer suicides among Catholics may have been due to the fact that Catholicism in the 1800s was more structured and more authoritarian than were Protestant denominations, and the structure available to Catholics may have provided stability and prevented anomie.

Another example of the use of aggregate data is a study by Travis (1985), who used aggregate health statistics to demonstrate gender biases in elective surgery. Travis showed that hysterectomies were much more likely to be elective than other types of surgery such as appendectomies (for men and women) or prostate removal (for men). More important, Travis was able to demonstrate that physicians were estimating risks and benefits in different ways for female and male patients.

In Chapter 4, you learned how to conduct a review of the existing literature, a process analogous to a qualitative content analysis. It is also possible to engage in a quantitative analysis of previous research using statistical results as data. When statistical results are the source of existing data, the research is called **meta-analysis,** *integrating research findings by statistically analyzing the results from individual studies* (Glass, McGraw, & Smith, 1981). Meta-analysis has become a means by which to determine how strong a particular empirical effect may be.

For example, Wrightsman and I completed a qualitative review of research on the influence of defendant and victim characteristics on jury verdicts (Dane & Wrightsman, 1982). One of our conclusions was related to the finding that attractive defendants are generally treated more leniently than unattractive defendants. However, most of that research involved simulations of trials—legal and ethical restrictions on manipulating independent variables in actual trials made simulations necessary—and there has been considerable controversy about whether simulations can be generalized to actual trials (Bray & Kerr, 1982).

One of the major criticisms of the use of simulations is the limited amount of information presented to mock jurors. The amount of material ranges from half-page summaries to complete transcripts or videotapes of trials. Opponents of simulation claim that incomplete simulations overemphasize the influence of defendants' physical attractiveness and other independent variables. For example, viewing photographs of the defendant paired with a half-page summary of evidence might have a greater impact on jurors than seeing the defendant as one of many individuals in a videotape of a trial.

The controversy involved some very good arguments on both sides. But without a reasonable amount of empirical evidence, the debate could not advance beyond the equivalent of a shouting match. Rather than add more voices to either side, Linz, Slack, Kaiser, and Penrod (1981) used meta-analysis to provide the required empirical information. Their meta-analysis included 15 studies on the effects of defendant's physical attractiveness, and their results led them to estimate the odds that the effect was due to chance alone at less than one in a million. Of greater importance was the finding that the impact of manipulating physical attractiveness tended to increase with the amount of material included in simulations. Rather than being lost among the legitimate items of evidence presented in a full-scale simulation, physical attractiveness appears to have stronger effects. Thus, the controversy surrounding trial simulations was stilled, at least for physical attractiveness of defendants as the independent variable of interest.

Methodological Issues in Existing Data Analysis

Just as with content analysis, research that uses existing data requires a specific purpose. Marsden et al. wanted to investigate stereotypes about leisure time, Durkheim's purpose was to consider environmental correlates of suicide, Travis wanted to examine gender bias in surgical procedures, and Linz et al. assessed the impact of defendants' physical attractiveness on verdicts. Each of these research projects had a specific hypothesis to be tested with existing data. Although a necessary first step, a specific hypothesis is not sufficient for analyzing existing data.

You may have noticed the rather wide range of units of analysis illustrated by these investigations. Marsden et al. analyzed individual responses to questionnaires, Durkheim analyzed regional suicide rates, Travis analyzed rates of surgical procedures, and Linz et al. analyzed the results of statistical analysis. Great care must be taken to ensure that the units of analysis chosen are appropriate to your hypotheses. Durkheim, for example, analyzed regional suicide rates but drew conclusions about individual suicide rates. *A mismatch between units of analysis and the research hypothesis* is known as an **ecological fallacy.** Durkheim's data dealt with groups, but his hypotheses were about individuals. Consider his conclusion regarding religious affiliation: Catholics committed fewer suicides because their religion reduced anomie. That hypothesis was tested by comparing the suicide rates in predominantly Catholic regions with the rates in predominantly Protestant regions. As Babbie (1983) has suggested, it may be that Catholics committed just as many suicides as Protestants but did so in predominantly Protestant areas. Certainly, Durkheim's explanation seems more plausible than the notion of Catholics (but not Protestants) traveling to faraway regions to commit suicide. On the other hand, neither hypothesis can claim to have clear empirical support from Durkheim's data. Effects identified through research on aggregate data cannot be used to test hypotheses about the individual units that produced the aggregate.

Linz et al. did have a match between their hypotheses and their units of analysis; both dealt with research studies. However, someone might be tempted to conclude that Linz et al.'s findings also mean that attractive defendants may be treated more leniently in longer trials than in shorter trials. After all, the effect of attractiveness was stronger in the more complete (longer) simulations. This conclusion, however, would involve **reductionism,** *the logical fallacy of drawing conclusions about individuals' behaviors from units of analysis that do not deal with individuals.*

As noted earlier, one of the problems inherent in conducting research with existing data is that the hypotheses you can test are limited to the data you can find. In addition to not being able to find relevant data, you may also encounter a problem with the age of the data. Existing data, obviously, were collected in the past, and old data may not be appropriate to your hypotheses. The data used by Durkheim is now about a hundred years old. Although ancient by research standards, they can still be used for valid tests of hypotheses, provided the hypotheses are about what happened a hundred years ago. You could not, for example, use those data to predict next year's suicide rates in Europe.

Another threat to validity is the quality of the data. Consider Linz et al.'s meta-analysis. The essential aspect of meta-analysis involves comparing the size of effects across different studies. But the size of the effect in any given study depends on the quality of the study. If, for example, the studies that involved less complete simulations were also poorer in quality, the relationship identified by Linz et al. would be spurious. I should point out that such is not the case—the research included by Linz et al. was good research—but the potential effects of poor research procedures must be considered whenever you decide to use existing data.

Just as you must rely on the original collectors of existing data for the data's validity, you must also rely on them for the data's reliability. Again, consider Durkheim's study. At the time the data were collected, suicide carried a much greater stigma for Catholics than for Protestants, and thus it is possible that some suicides in Catholic regions were mislabeled as accidental or due to some other cause. The suicide rates on which Durkheim depended for his research therefore may not have been reliable. Durkheim did not have direct experience with the data collection procedures, nor do most researchers who use existing data. Before using existing data, carefully examine the research procedures to ensure sufficient reliability and validity for your purposes.

Summary

• Archival research includes any project in which existing documents or data are the units of observation. These may include novels, music, movies, and other reports, as well as raw, aggregate, or statistical data collected by others.

• Content analysis may be used to answer questions of the general form "Who says what to whom, how, with what effect, and why?" Although any communication medium can be content analyzed, it is more appropriate to compare two or more messages than to draw conclusions about a single message.

• Coding in content analysis can involve either manifest content or latent content. Coding manifest content—concrete denotations—usually results in more reliable data because the coding is more objective. Although sometimes less reliable, coding latent content may be the only way to operationalize complex theoretical concepts.

• Quantifying data in content analysis can involve recording either the frequency of variables or the amount of time or space devoted to a topic in the message; either may be used for manifest content or latent content. Evaluative assertion analysis can also be used for messages that contain complex statements.

• Archival research involving existing data relies on data collected in the past, usually by other researchers. Analyzing raw data is the most flexible procedure, provided the operational definitions used to collect the data match those in your hypotheses. Aggregate data may be less flexible but may provide better operational definitions of complex concepts. Meta-analysis of statistical results limits you to hypotheses about research studies but may be used to support conclusions drawn from qualitative literature reviews.

• The analysis of existing data includes the potential problems of ecological fallacy and reductionism. The former occurs when there is a mismatch between the units of analysis and the research hypotheses, and the latter occurs when conclusions about individuals are drawn from aggregate data.

• When using data collected by others it is sometimes more difficult to determine their reliability and validity. Because you lack direct experience with the data collection procedures, a careful reading of the original procedures is the only way to determine whether the data fit your purposes.

CHAPTER TEN

Data Organization

The Law of the Too, Too Solid Data Point: In any collection of data, the figure that is most obviously correct . . . is the mistake.

—Dickson (1981, p. 86)

Overview

The purpose of this chapter is to provide information about how to plan a structure for your data. You will learn some of the principles of effective and efficient data storage, including the different ways in which data are stored on a computer. You will learn about the mechanics of storing data on various computer media and ways to ensure data accuracy throughout the storage process. Finally, you will learn about preliminary analyses that can be used to check the accuracy of stored data.

Introduction

"All the questionnaires are filled out. I want to do correlations but I have too many. How do I put these numbers in the computer?"

"Frank, I need a repeated measures analysis, but can't do it the way I've set up my data file. Can I reorganize it without putting all my data in the computer again?"

"Groups? I didn't write down a group number. I thought the participants' names would be enough. What do you mean I can't do the analysis?"

These remarks are a sample of statements made by people who have come to me with, according to them, questions about analyzing their data. The first person had some ideas, but didn't know how to execute them. The second knew exactly how to analyze the data but hadn't thought about what was required to do it. The third was really in trouble; no thoughts at all about what to do after collecting the data. Even though they came to me for help with "data analysis," the questions they asked were really about data organization.

The process of **data organization** involves *designing a system for the accurate storage and retrieval of the information obtained during a research project.* Information obtained through research is called data. (Data is plural; the singular is datum.) Every researcher needs a plan for dealing with data, a plan that should be made before the data are collected. Data need to be stored so that you can analyze them, interpret them, and save them for future reference or additional analyses. Storage may be accomplished through any one of a number of media, including data sheets, computer cards, magnetic tapes, and computer disks. The specific structure of the data depends on the medium, but the structure should be systematic. You need to be able to find certain parts of the data efficiently, and you should be able to understand the system long after you first stored the data.

I can't think of a more frustrating research situation than that of the third person quoted above. The months invested in the project were almost a complete waste of time. The only reason it was not a total waste was that a valuable lesson was learned: data organization is an integral part of any research project. Of course, that's learning the hard way. You have a chance to learn the same lesson more easily.

Data Storage Terminology

Before we go too far, we need to consider some terms that pervade discussions of data organization. The terms are not unusual, but their meanings differ from everyday use. The reason for learning this jargon is that it is used in almost every manual ever written about computer programs and packages used for data analysis. There's no need to use this jargon in everyday language, or even in research reports, but knowing the meanings of the words will make it considerably easier to understand computer program documentation.

In everyday language, we use a code to disguise or simplify something. Shortwave and citizens' band radio operators use the code "10-20" as a simplified reference for location or position. When people discussing data organization use the term **data code,** they mean *the symbol or number used to represent a specific value for an operational definition.* For example, according to the usual measured operation of age, my data code would be "35." Similarly, the data code for my gender might be "male," "M," or "1" depending on the chosen coding system.

In everyday language, a field is an open area in which you plant crops, play a game with a ball, or frolic to your heart's content. A **data field** is *an area set aside to hold data codes for a specific measurement.* Instead of crops or frolicking individuals, the open areas of data fields contain data codes. The term comes from reserving a specific place in a computer. If one of the variables is age, then sufficient space must be set aside for the computer to store the highest age. Such data fields are called fixed fields because the space reserved for each value is always the same size, even if some of the values don't require all the room. For example,

when	I	make	these	five	lines
of	text	conform	to	a	fixed
data	field,	with	each	word	being
a	value	in	a	different	field,
the	text	looks	very	strange.	

Each word field has been fixed at ten characters, the amount of space needed for the longest data value, the word "different."

One of my favorite trivia questions involves the number of grooves on one side of a record. The answer is one; the groove on each side of a record is continuous from beginning to end, regardless of the number of songs, or cuts, on the album. In the jargon of data storage, a **data record** is *a collection of data fields that is only one line long*. Each line in the text example above is a record. Due to inherent limitations in early computer storage media, the longest a data record could be was only 80 characters. Now, however, the limit varies depending on the storage media.

In everyday language, "case" has a number of different meanings. To an attorney, it is a set of facts about a specific trial. To elementary-school students, it's the thing that keeps all the pencils in one place. To a researcher, a **data case** refers to *all the data values corresponding to a single participant*. In the research involved using Wrightsman's (1974) philosophies of human nature scale, for example, one data case would include responses to all 84 questions on the scale, as well as whatever identification and demographic information was collected. Depending on the number and size of the measures you use, a single case may contain more than one data record.

In everyday use, a file is a collection of information relevant to a specific topic, usually contained in some sort of folder. Similarly, a **data file** refers to *all of the data for a single research project*. More specifically, it refers to all of the collected data that have been organized and stored on some medium.

In summary, a data file consists of all of the codes (values) for each of the fields (variables) arranged according to cases (participants). Enough jargon; let's move on to learning about storing the data.

Data Storage Media

A number of different media can be used to store data. Which medium best suits your purposes depends primarily on the facilities at your institution, but it also depends on the kind of data you have. If you don't have a particular medium available, you can't use it; if you have several media from which to choose, one may match your needs better than the others.

Computer Cards

Computer cards, *thin paper cards in which holes may be punched and read by machine,* are almost an anachronism. There are only a few computer facilities at which they are still used, partly because they are among the most inconvenient forms of data storage. Each computer card contains 80 columns in each of which up to three holes can be punched to represent characters. The pattern of the three holes in each column serves as a code for a character, a code that is read by the card reader and transmitted to the computer.

One of the inconvenient aspects of computer cards is that data storage requires a three-stage process. First, codes are typically written onto data sheets. You might, for example, code gender such that males receive a "1" and females a "2." Second, the computer cards are prepared with a keypunch machine, which has a keyboard much like that of a typewriter. The operator types the codes, and the machine punches the appropriate pattern in the card. Finally, a machine called a verifier is used to ensure that the codes are punched and aligned correctly. A verifier has a keyboard much like the keypunch machine, but it merely shines a light through the card to "read" the pattern of holes. If what is entered at the keyboard does not match the pattern of holes, a light goes on to indicate an incorrectly punched card. If there is an error, a new card must be punched; you cannot correct a computer card.

As a storage medium, computer cards have been traditionally used whenever the data file is large. Cards, however, are not easily stored and are easily damaged by changes in temperature and humidity. If a card becomes warped, for example, the card reader will either interpret the pattern incorrectly or will not be able to read the card at all. Cards are bulky. I remember days in graduate school when I would have to lug two, sometimes three, boxes of computer cards, each weighing about ten pounds, to and from the computer center. If you must use computer cards for data storage, I strongly suggest reading the cards into some other storage medium, and then using the secondary medium for analyses. Keep the cards in case you need them again, but use them as little as possible.

Computer Disks

If you have ever used the mainframe computer on your campus or have used a personal computer, you have used computer disks. A **computer disk** is *a thin, round piece of plastic on which magnetic impulses are stored.* The disk spins rapidly while the reading and writing heads move over its surface. A disk head works much like a phonograph stylus, except that the head does not actually touch the disk. On a large disk drive, anywhere from five to 100 disks may be stacked in a single disk pack. If you have used a personal computer, you have used diskettes, 5.25 or 3.5-inch versions of the larger disks used for mainframes.

Disks are also subject to changes in temperature and humidity, although they are considerably more resistant to damage than cards. Disks, however, need to be written and read using the same format—the specific organizational pattern for storing the magnetic impulses. Disks written for one format usually cannot be read by using a different format. Despite potential format changes, however, disks are the most versatile and portable form of storage.

More often than not, data storage on disk involves entering data codes from the terminal, and the codes are initially stored in the memory of the computer until you specifically execute a command to store the data on the disk. Before entering the data at the terminal, however, you need to plan the structure for the data. Mainframe machines usually have a program called an editor for data entry, and you need to learn how to use the editor before you can store your data. There are many different programs equivalent to a mainframe editor for storing data on a personal computer. Which program you need to learn depends on the brand name and the operating system of the personal computer you have available. Unfortunately, computer disks can hold only relatively small amounts of data; still, for most of your purposes as a student, disks will provide more than enough storage space. But if you collect very large data sets, you may need to consider using magnetic computer tapes.

Magnetic Tapes

Chances are you have seen magnetic tapes in movies or television shows that involve computers. If you have ever seen two reels, each about ten inches in diameter, spinning on a machine about the size of a file cabinet, you've seen a tape drive. Magnetic tapes work the same way that cassette and reel-to-reel tapes work for music: separate heads are used for reading and writing the tapes.

Storing data on magnetic tape is usually accomplished by transfer from some other storage medium—files stored on cards or disks are transferred onto tape. Because data files large enough to make using tapes convenient are incredibly large—thousands of cases, for example—the data file is built a portion at a time. You might enter a few hundred cases onto a disk, transfer those to a tape, enter a few hundred more cases to the disk file, append those to the tape, and so on until all the cases are on the tape. Terminals that are tied directly to tape drives do exist, but they are relatively rare and you probably wouldn't encounter one on your campus.

Regardless of which medium you decide to use for computer storage—cards, disks, or tapes—you first need to plan an organizational structure for your data file and decide which codes you will use for the values inherent in the variables you measured. For this reason, data coding is the topic to which we next direct our attention.

Data Coding

Imagine that your campus is located at the edge of a small town and that the majority of students live in dormitories. Many students do not have automobiles but would like to be able to get around town to shop and take advantage of various opportunities for entertainment. Unfortunately, about the only ways for many of the students to accomplish such things are walking, bicycling, riding with someone who owns a car, or borrowing someone's car. The latter two options are sometimes not very safe given that the predominant entertainment opportunities in town involve alcohol. Imagine also that your student government is considering a proposal to implement a shuttle service, but the members of the student legislature don't know how many students would use it or whether students would be willing to bear the financial burden of operating the service. The situation is complicated because the cost of the service depends both on the number of users and the size of the geographic area to be served by the shuttle.

What I have described is essentially the situation with which students at Clemson University were faced several years ago. A few of the students in my research methods class decided to implement an action research project, one they hoped would provide the student legislature with the information needed to make decisions about the shuttle. Through a telephone survey, they asked a sample of students the questions listed in Table 10.1. As you can see, most of the questions involved multiple choices, but some of them incorporated open-ended responses.

The researchers knew they had to do two things before they could enter the data into the computer. First, they had to choose a storage medium. Because all of them wanted to have access to the data at a variety of times of the day, they chose to use disks and to store the data on the mainframe. Second, they had to determine a set of codes for the responses to the questionnaire.

Numeric Representation

The first part of any coding process is deciding what codes to use—how to translate responses into characters to be stored in the computer. Because computers deal more efficiently with numbers than with any other characters, most codes involve numeric representation—using numbers to represent data values. When you examined Table 10.1, you probably noticed three different types of responses. Some already consist of numbers, such as respondent number and dollar and cent amounts. If the respondents and researchers followed directions, no coding is required for such items.

Some of the other items do not contain numeric codes but may still be easily coded. All of the yes/no responses, for example, can be coded by assigning a "1" to a "yes" response and a "2" to a "no" response. What code is actually assigned to such responses makes little difference, so long as the codes are assigned consistently. It is a good idea, however, to develop a plan and stick with it for all such responses. That way, regardless of which of your data sets you are analyzing, you can always correctly encode and interpret such yes/no responses.

A few of the items involved open-ended responses, and these require the greatest amount of effort to code. Think, for example, of all the possible responses to item 7 in the survey. Respondents could drive their own cars, walk, ride with others, borrow cars, ride bicycles, use motorcycles, hitchhike, ride skateboards, and so on. One way to develop codes for open-ended items is to decide, before collecting the data, to categorize responses in some meaningful way. When that is not possible, you can use content analysis (Chapter 9) to decide how best to categorize the responses.

In the shuttle survey, for example, the various means of transportation could be categorized as "unassisted," "owned," or "borrowed." Walking would be cate-

gorized as unassisted, driving one's own car or motorcycle as "owned," and borrowing a car or hitchhiking as "borrowed." Such a priori categorization, however,
requires a number of assumptions about the variables and their relationships. Including hitchhikers and car-borrowers in the same category would also mean assuming that their responses to the other questions would be similar.

Although making such assumptions is not always invalid, it is generally a good
idea to avoid making too many assumptions when coding data. Even though the
assumptions may seem reasonable at the time, there may come a time when such
assumptions become unreasonable. If you needed to change those assumptions,
you would have to recode and reenter the data file. The best way to avoid such
problems is to code every unique response with a unique code, and then use data
analysis software to create combined categories. That way, you still have the orig-

Table 10.1   Response sheet for the campus shuttle survey

1. Interviewer _____

2. Respondent number _____

3. Should student government implement a shuttle service?   Y   N

4. If a shuttle were available, would you use it?   Y   N

5. Where do you live? _____

6. Do you own your own car?   Y   N

7. When you go somewhere in Clemson, how do you usually get there? _____

8. There are three proposals for funding the shuttle:

    1. Raise the student activity fee paid with tuition;

    2. Raise the price of photocopying on campus machines;

    3. Charge for each ride on the shuttle.

  Which of these three do you most prefer?   1   2   3

9. If the shuttle were to be funded by raising the student activity fee, how much
extra would you be willing to pay, in dollars? _____

10. If the shuttle were to be funded by raising the price of photocopying, how
many extra cents per copy would you be willing to pay? _____

11. If the shuttle were to be funded through a charge per ride, how much would
you be willing to pay for each ride? _____

12. Would you prefer some other way to fund the shuttle?   Y   N

13. (If YES to #12) What other kind of funding would be agreeable to you?

inal codes should you decide to recategorize the data at a future time. Whenever possible, follow the first rule of data storage: never throw anything away.

Regardless of the type of response format for a given variable, the codes assigned to that variable should include a code for missing data caused by a refusal to answer, a recording error, or any other reason. The code for missing data should be an "impossible" code—something that does not resemble any of the valid codes for that variable. When zero is not a valid response, I use "0" as a missing data code; otherwise, I fill the field with nines—9, 99, 999, whatever— or some other appropriate number. When using a computer for storage and analysis, avoid using a blank as the missing data code; most computers read blanks as zeros.

Codebooks

More often than you might think, researchers decide to reanalyze their data or may spend months ferreting out relationships in a large data file. In order to do this, you need some way to remember which codes you used for which values; you need a codebook. A **codebook** is *a record of the codes assigned to the measures and contains information about the storage structure of the file.* The format of the codebook depends on the storage medium, but it should contain enough information so that someone who knows little about the project could understand and know where to find the codes. Table 10.2 contains a portion of the codebook for the shuttle survey. Even though you don't know much about the protocol involved in collect-

Table 10.2 A portion of the campus shuttle survey codebook

Column Number	Variable Description and Code

1	Interviewer identification number:
	   1. John Smith
	   2. Mary Jones
	   3. Mark Miller
	   0. missing

2–4	Respondent identification number 0. missing

5	Do you want student government to implement a shuttle service?
	   1. Yes
	   2. No
	   0. missing

6	Where do you live?
	   1. campus dormitory
	   2. within city limits
	   3. outside city but within five miles
	   4. between five and 30 miles from city
	   5. more than 30 miles from city
	   0. missing

ing the data, you could understand what the data meant by looking at the code-book. I suggest that you always create a codebook; you may think you'll never forget the codes you used or the order in which the variables appear in the file, but sooner or later you will forget.

Coding Mechanisms

Once you have planned a coding strategy and have written the codebook, you still have to create and store the data on the chosen medium. There are several ways to do this, including direct transcription, edge coding, transfer sheets, optical scan forms, and direct entry.

If your data set is relatively small and doesn't contain many complicated codes, the most efficient way to enter your data is to read from the original de-pendent measure forms: read the responses, type them into the terminal, and you're done. However, if your data set is very large or you have a complicated coding system, paging through the codebook while sitting at the terminal will be somewhat frustrating, not to mention costly if you have to pay for your own com-puter time.

For complicated coding systems, edge coding is slightly more time-consuming but more convenient than direct transcription. **Edge coding** involves *writing the data code in the margin of the dependent variable form before entering the codes into the data file.* Edge coding can be accomplished anywhere you have the codebook and the dependent measures—at home, at the coffee shop, wherever. It requires extra time to write all the codes in the margin before entering them at the termi-nal, but it saves time at the terminal.

For large data sets, the most commonly used coding mechanism is **transfer sheets**—*preprinted data sheets onto which codes are written before entry.* Transfer sheets are the most time-consuming because they are analogous to entering the codes twice: once on the sheets and again at the terminal. The advantage to transfer sheets is that you don't have to carry the entire data set with you; all you need are the transfer sheets. If you lose the transfer sheets, you must redo them; but if you lose the dependent measure forms, the data are gone forever. Also, if you are part of a research team, you can split the coding and entry tasks.

An improvement on the transfer sheet system is the use of optical scan forms. If you have ever pencilled in circles or ovals on a computer answer sheet, you have used optical scan forms. As a form of transcription, optical scan forms can be prepared the same way transfer sheets are prepared; then they can be read into the computer using an optical scanner. The scanner replaces sitting at the termi-nal and entering the codes by hand, which saves a great deal of time.

It is also possible to use optical scan forms as the dependent variable forms. Your respondents, raters, or interviewers can fill in the circles and you can thereby avoid the task of transcription. The apparent convenience, however, has a potentially severe disadvantage: you must make sure that whoever fills out the forms does so correctly. Some friends of mine decided to use optical scan forms in a large-scale survey, only to discover that about 3000 of the respondents failed to use a pencil. Their forms were unreadable and had to be redone. Of course, the measures you plan to use must also be amenable to optical scan forms.

Finally, you may use direct entry for data coding. With **direct entry,** *data are entered directly into the data file.* Respondents may read questionnaire items at a terminal and enter their responses on the terminal, or a telephone surveyor may enter the responses directly into the data file. A great deal more preparation for coding must be done, but direct entry eliminates all the intermediate steps—coding, transfer, and so on—in the data entry process. Direct entry requires access to a computer terminal at the moment data are being collected, but the increasing availability of personal computers and telecommunication programs may eventually make direct entry the preferred coding mechanism in the future.

Data Cleaning

After the data are entered into the data file, you need to clean the data. **Data cleaning** involves *identifying and correcting erroneous codes.* Simply getting the data stored doesn't do much good if the file contains errors that will make your analyses uninterpretable. No matter how carefully you entered the data, you'll still end up with the equivalent of five different codes for gender, and age of –2, or some other error. In addition to proofreading the data file, data cleaning can involve several different forms of data analysis.

Single-Field Analyses

Finding erroneous codes that were not detected through proofreading can be done through simple frequency analyses on each field or variable in the file. A **frequency distribution** is *a tabulation of the number of times a given observation is made; in single-field analyses, it is a tabulation of the number of times a given code is detected in the data file.* If one of your measures is gender, for example, and you have coded males, females, and missing data as "1," "2," and "0," respectively, then a frequency distribution for gender should contain only those codes; if you have a "5" in the frequency distribution for gender, you know it's wrong.

If you identify an erroneous code in a frequency distribution, you need to determine the correct code and enter it in the file. Correcting errors is one of the primary reasons for always including participant identification numbers in the data file. You can scan the file until you find the incorrect code, note the identification number, find the original data sheet for that participant and read the correct code, and then enter the correction in the file. Without identification numbers, however, you would have to search through all of the original data sheets to find the one with the wrong code. Worse yet, if you have two instances of the same error, without identification codes you may not be able to determine which correct code to enter for which respondent.

Multiple-Field Analyses

Some erroneous codes cannot be detected through single-field analyses. A code indicating 12 years of formal education, for example, would not necessarily jump out as an error when scanning a frequency distribution. If, however, you also found out that the same participant had an age of five years, then you would quickly conclude that something was wrong. To identify and correct such errors, you need to be able to relate one variable to another, which can be accomplished through cross-tabulation and scatterplots.

Cross-tabulation involves *counting the codes from one field that occur for each code in another field.* With a little imagination and common sense, many errors can be detected using this analysis. Consider, for example, a respondent in the shuttle survey who indicated ownership and use of a car to get around town. Suppose, however, that this respondent was erroneously coded as not owning a car. You could not detect the error through a simple frequency distribution; many of the respondents do not own cars. However, cross-tabulation would result in identifying one respondent who was impossibly coded as both not owning a car and driving an owned car around town. Presumably, this respondent would be the only one identified with such a combination, and you could identify the respondent number and then correct the error.

As a data cleaning technique, cross-tabulation is ideal for categorical variables but can be very cumbersome for continuous variables such as age or income. If the age of respondents ranged from 20 to 40 years and income ranged from $20,000 to $40,000, a cross-tabulation would produce 400 different categories. Instead of cross-tabulation, data cleaning for continuous variables can be more efficiently accomplished through **scatterplots**—*graphs in which corresponding codes from two variables are displayed on two axes.*

Figure 10.1 contains a scatterplot that might be obtained from a relationship between income and age. Notice the two points lying outside the main grouping, one in the upper left and one in the lower right. These two points could possibly represent valid codes, but they are much more likely to reflect errors in coding one or the other of the variables. Whenever points lie outside the main grouping in a scatterplot, it's a good idea to examine the original data sheets.

Data Reduction

Earlier we briefly discussed the possibility of combining certain codes in order to reduce the number of codes for any one variable. We also noted that you probably don't want to engage in data reduction until after the data are stored. To reduce the data before you have them stored in a file prevents you from either returning to the original codes or using a different reduction strategy. Further, data reduction should be postponed until after you have cleaned the data file.

Once you have a cleaned data file, reducing the data involves combining two or more codes for a single variable; sometimes it involves combining two or more variables into a single, new variable. Whatever way you choose to reduce the data, you should always maintain the original data file. For example, suppose there was only one respondent in the shuttle survey who indicated that he or she rode a motorcycle into town. That respondent could be grouped with other respondents who indicated they used their car, but the recoding should be done through another variable or field. If the original variable was named TRANS (for transporta-

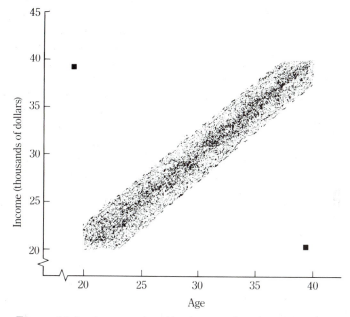

Figure 10.1   A scatterplot of income as a function of age. The errant points in the upper left and lower right are probably mis-coded data.

tion), you could retain that variable and create another one called TRANS2. The motorcycle rider would have a code for riding a motorcycle for TRANS, but would be coded as driving a car for TRANS2.

Most data analysis software makes data reduction rather simple: you need only decide how to reduce the data, and it can be done with only two or three statements. Reducing the data in order to make analyses more convenient, or simply possible, is a valid process, but it should be done in a way that maintains all of the information in the original file; that is, you reduce the data by actually expanding the size of the data file itself by adding new variables and fields to the file. Making the data file larger is rarely undesirable; the first rule of storing data is to never throw anything away.

Summary

• Data organization is a process through which the researcher designs and implements a system for maintaining the accuracy and availability of data. A data file contains all the data collected for a given project; it contains data codes for each field or measured variable obtained from each participant.

• Data files may be stored on computer cards, disks, or magnetic tape. Each medium has certain advantages and disadvantages, although disk is probably the most frequently used storage medium. Computer cards are nearly obsolete, magnetic tape is relatively slow and is reserved only for very large data files.

• Data coding involves transcribing the data as collected into a format appropriate for the desired storage medium. Each response included in the data should be assigned one and only one data code. A codebook should be prepared for every data file, and it should contain sufficient information to allow someone else to understand and locate the various codes used to represent the data.

• Direct transcription is a coding mechanism in which responses are read and coded directly from the original dependent variable forms. For large or complicated data sets, direct transcription may produce too many errors. Edge coding—writing data codes in the margins of the data forms before entering them into the file—is one way to reduce coding and entry errors.

• When coding and entry can be separated easily, preprinted data sheets are often used to provide a source for data entry. Optical scan forms can be used both as transfer sheets and original data collection forms. Optical scan sheets eliminate a number of steps in the coding and entry process.

• Direct entry involves using a computer terminal as the original data collection form. Although it is a somewhat uncommon coding mechanism now, the increased availability of terminals and personal computers may result in its becoming the most common coding mechanism in the future.

• Once entered and stored, a data file must be cleaned to ensure the accuracy of the data. Proofreading codes before and after entering them is necessary but rarely sufficient to remove all errors. Frequency distributions provide a means by which to detect incorrect and impossible codes within a field, such as a "9" for gender when the codes are "1" and "2."

• Incorrect but otherwise possible codes may be detected through multiple-field analyses, such as cross-tabulation for categorical variables and scatterplots for continuous variables. Not all apparently strange variable combinations will necessarily be incorrect, but each should be checked for accuracy.

• Data reduction involves combining two or more low-frequency codes into a new code, or combining two or more variables into a new field. Reduction should be accomplished only after the data have been cleaned and only in a manner that preserves the original codes in the file.

• Never discard any data. You can always decide not to use a portion of the data file, but it is rarely possible to be absolutely sure that you will never need data you may consider discarding.

CHAPTER
ELEVEN

Beyond Hypotheses

People don't usually do research the way people who write books about research say that people do research.

—First Law of Research (Bachrach, 1981)

Overview

In this chapter you will learn about some data transformations that may help you analyze your data correctly. More important, you will learn how to use your data to accomplish more than a test of your original hypotheses, for regardless of the intended purpose of any research study, the data collected can always be used for exploration. Part of the material covered in this chapter addresses ways to handle surprising results. Finally, you will learn how to deal with results that seem to be almost—but not quite—interpretable.

Introduction

In this chapter I want to break Bachrach's First Law of Research. Most of this textbook has dealt with research from a prescriptive point of view. I have presented the rules of behavioral research and have basically tried to convince you that they are the best rules to follow. I've not misled you, for following the rules is the best way to do research. What you may have already discovered yourself, however, is that following the rules does not always produce the very clean and easily interpretable data published in journals.

The reasons why other chapters have been included in this text are obvious; the reason for this chapter may not be so obvious. This chapter is designed to provide you some informal (and a few formal) rules for dealing with research results that are not exactly what you had in mind when you began your project. I don't mean the kind of tricks that led Disraeli to indict statistics and research methods by saying, "There are three kinds of lies—lies, damned lies, and statistics." Instead I mean some techniques that help you avoid the tendency to decide that there is something wrong with seemingly uninterpretable results. I will argue in the remainder of this chapter that, given the rules of research have been followed, it is far more likely that there is something wrong with the researcher whenever a study produces uninterpretable results. That is, the researcher who decides that results are not interpretable has probably not given them sufficient thought.

Data Transformations

Data transformation—*changing original data values through mathematical functions*—has traditionally had a bad name in many research circles. The argument most frequently touted is that a researcher would not need to change data if they were worthwhile in the first place. Indeed, there exist many examples of needless transformations that apparently were used only so that the data would get published. Such use of transformations may be the reason why some statisticians, such as Wike (1985), use the term *reexpression* to refer to data transformations.

If data transformations have such a bad reputation, why am I telling you about them? Like most other research tools, data transformation can be beneficial and valid when used properly and misinforming when used improperly. When used properly, a given transformation is applied to all values obtained for a particular variable, but only if there is reason to believe that the original values are inappropriate for data analysis. There are four main reasons for transforming data: outliers, skewed distributions, heterogeneous variances, and proportions.

Outliers

An **outlier** is *a data value that is widely discrepant from other values for the same variable.* Any data value that is more than about 2.5 standard deviations from the mean of the other values is an outlier. For example, an individual with an annual income of $100,000 in a group with a mean of $50,000 and a standard deviation of $20,000 is an outlier. One or more outliers in a group of scores may produce misleading central tendency (mean) values.

One method for dealing with extreme outliers is to simply eliminate those scores from the analysis. Although acceptable from the point of view of data analysis, eliminating data may not be acceptable if data are few or difficult to obtain. One alternative is to apply a logarithmic transformation to the data—either natural or base 10 logarithms are appropriate—and then conduct data analyses on the logarithms instead of the original values.

Skewed Distributions

There are times when your data will exhibit a skewed distribution instead of one or two outliers. A **skewed distribution** is *an asymmetrical distribution*. In a positively skewed distribution, the mean is considerably higher than the median, whereas the opposite occurs in a negatively skewed distribution. For any analyses that function better with normally distributed data, such as analysis of variance, transforming skewed distributions is entirely appropriate. One index of skewness was provided by Nowaczyk (1988):

$$\text{Index of skewness} = \frac{3\,(\text{mean} - \text{median})}{\text{standard deviation}}$$

Whenever the resulting value is greater than $+0.50$ or less than -0.50, the distribution can be considered skewed and may be transformed.

Several different transformations may be used to reduce skew, depending on the degree of skew. For extremely skewed distributions, expressing each score as a reciprocal (1/score) seems to work best; for moderately skewed distributions, a logarithmic transformation is best; for distributions with only a small degree of skew, a square root transformation is advisable. All of these functions have a greater effect on extreme scores than on scores near the mean, which is why they reduce skew. After completing the transformation, it's always advisable to recalculate an index of skewness with the transformed scores to make sure you actually have eliminated, or at least reduced, the skew.

Heterogeneous Variances

Analysis of variance (ANOVA) is one of the more common analyses used to detect differences among groups, and it is also one of the analyses that function better when group variances are approximately equal. **Heterogeneity of variance** refers to *any instance in which group variances are disparate*. Although ANOVA is fairly robust and small amounts of heterogeneity don't affect the results, extensive heterogeneity of variance reduces your ability to detect group differences. A square root transformation will reduce variance heterogeneity and thereby increase the efficacy of ANOVA or similar analyses.

Proportions

There are many instances in which data are best expressed as proportions. A question on a survey might require respondents to express how much time they spend on various activities in terms of the percentage of their overall time. Performance might be measured through the proportion of correct or incorrect responses whenever the number of total responses is not the same for all participants, and so forth.

Proportions, however, exhibit somewhat different characteristics than other measurement scales. They are practically and theoretically restricted to a specific

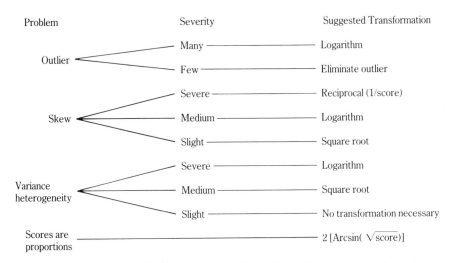

Figure 11.1 Strategies for data transformations. Any data transformation should be used only if it solves the problem (or at least makes the problem less severe than no transformation at all).

range—zero to one—whereas other scales—income, for example—are, at least theoretically, unlimited at one end. Proportions also involve known variance parameters; the population variance of a set of proportions is defined, in part, by the size of the sample.

When data values are expressed as proportions, it is generally advisable to transform them with arcsins. The traditional formula involves multiplying by two the arcsin of the square root of the data value. Winer (1971) and a few other texts contain tables for this transformation, although it is fairly simple to accomplish with a computer or a reasonably sophisticated calculator. The arcsin function eliminates the restriction on the range of original proportions, and the square root function helps to overcome the tendency for proportions to be skewed.

For a summary of the circumstances in which particular data transformations are appropriate, refer to Figure 11.1.

Informal Guidelines

Data transformations, like most suggestions in this chapter, must be attempted before you can determine whether they have accomplished what you want. A logarithmic transformation, for example, might eliminate some, but not all, of the outliers in a group of scores. Similarly, a square root transformation might reduce, but not eliminate, heterogeneity of variance. If you have good reason to transform your data, do so and compare the original distribution with the transformed distribution. If the transformation helps, use the transformed data in your analyses; if the transformation doesn't seem to help, forget it and analyze the original data.

If you use transformed data in your analyses, you should still analyze the original data. Regardless of the reasons for the transformation, there will always be some reader interested in knowing the result of an analysis of the original scores.

In your research report, a footnote describing the similarity between the transformed and original data analyses will usually satisfy such readers.

When discussing and interpreting results of central tendency analyses conducted on transformed data, it is best to "untransform" the measure of central tendency before interpretation. If you used a square root transformation and conducted ANOVA, for example, square the resulting group means before trying to make sense of the results. You will probably feel more comfortable thinking about the means in the original metric, and your readers will be better able to understand your discussion in the original metric.

Finally, because transformations are used to avoid potential problems in data analysis, they should therefore be used *before* you analyze your data. It is inappropriate to obtain results that are unimpressive and then hunt around for a transformation that will make the results seem more impressive. Such tactics may make you deserving of Disraeli's indictment for misuse of statistics and will probably be fruitless. Transformations are not likely to alter the direction of an effect or drastically change the size of an effect. In other words, data transformations won't make your data look better; they will just make them more interpretable.

When Surprising Results Are Obtained

With or without data transformations, you may encounter some surprises—relationships where you expected none, or no relationship where you expected one. In either case, don't panic. Instead, welcome surprising results as a puzzle to be solved. Regardless of the intended purpose of your study, surprising results provide a perfect opportunity to engage in exploratory research.

Check Your Analyses for Errors

One of the first things you should do upon discovering a surprising result is check your analyses. Such a result may not be a surprise at all, but rather the product of an undetected error. For example, after analyzing data from a very complicated experiment, I thought I had discovered an exception to a major theory about group decision making. The results made sense, I was certain I could find relevant literature that could be used tangentially to support the apparent exception, and I was ready to set the world on fire with my discovery.

Upon checking my analyses, however, I discovered that I had mislabeled some variables in my data file. The error led to interchanging one of the independent variables with one of the dependent variables. Once I corrected that error, the results were neither exceptional nor novel. Had I not checked my analyses, the incorrect results might have been published and I would have been extremely embarrassed. Worse, the results would have misled a number of other researchers and would probably have wasted a great deal of their time. Whenever you are surprised by your results, check your analyses to make sure it's a legitimate surprise and not an error.

Explore Reasons for the Results

If your surprising results survive the check for errors, attempt to interpret them. It is at this point that your study becomes exploratory, no matter what its original purpose may have been. Essentially, you begin to explore the possible reasons for the results you obtained.

What, for example, did you do in your study that others had not done? What did you not do that others had done? Differences in procedures are the most likely keys for unlocking the explanation behind the surprise. I am not implying that simply discovering a procedural difference between your study and previous research is the end of your exploration; rather, an exploration of procedural variation gives you a starting point. Ask yourself what there might be about the variation that could lead to the surprising results you obtained. Think about your research procedures from the participant's point of view, and think about other researchers' procedures from the participant's point of view.

If different questions were asked in your study, for example, think about what you might have been measuring with those questions. Obviously, your participants were different from the participants in previous research. Consider the possibility that demographic or experiential differences underlie the surprise. Carefully consider each and every way in which your study is different from previous research on the same topic, and when you do, ask yourself why that difference might have caused the surprise. You are conducting exploratory research, so don't worry about whether your method or design allows you to draw cause–effect explanations. Treat your surprising results as a mystery to be solved. Suspect everything, just like detectives in classic mystery stories.

Unlike such detectives, however, you should consider yourself one of the suspects. There may be something you did or did not do, or there may be some aspect of your demographics, that could account for the surprising results. If you were using an experimental or quasi-experimental design, for example, were you blind to the conditions?

Return to Your Data

One of the most important places to search for a reasonable explanation of your surprising results is within the data themselves. Do any of the measures exhibit bimodal distributions? If so, you may want to consider the possibility that you have two different kinds of participants. Bimodal distributions can be caused by participant characteristics, an overlooked threat to internal validity, systematically different treatment of participants, and so on. Very few behavioral measures exhibit naturally bimodal distributions, and such distributions are almost always a good indication that you overlooked something in your study.

If you have used more than one dependent variable, search for relationships between them for an explanation of the surprise. Does only one dependent variable exhibit the effect? If so, it may be that the measure you were using is invalid for the purposes you intended. Or, if more than one variable exhibits the effect, ask yourself what those variables have in common. Wike (1985) calls this activity "praying" over your data, but I prefer to think of it as "preying" on your data. Follow the tracks of your data to wherever they may lead, always thinking about the inferences you can draw from them to help explain the surprising results.

Return to the Literature

When you think you have found one or more reasonable explanations for your surprise, return to the research literature. Instead of reading the material you read to prepare for your study, read material specifically relevant to the reasonable explanations you are considering. Do not worry about similarities between your study and the new studies you are reading. You are not looking for support for your study as you planned it, but rather support for your potential explanation. After all, if a study had been published with results similar to your own, the results would not be surprising. Examine research articles on a variety of different topics related to your potential explanation. Rather than use the original purpose of your study as a guide for this literature review, use the concepts that are part of your potential explanation as a guide.

Develop a Curious Mind

Aside from the relatively general suggestions above, the only other advice I can offer to help you deal with surprising results, or any results for that matter, is to develop a curious mind. Unfortunately, about all I can do is offer the advice; I cannot tell you how to put the advice into practice. An important (perhaps the most important) aspect of behavioral science is curiosity. Become interested in the research you are doing. Think about what you or someone else has done. Engage in what I call "what-ifing": ask and try to answer the question "What if my research were different," and in the process examine any and all aspects of your research.

Nonsignificant Versus Insignificant

In the behavioral sciences, the accepted rule of thumb for concluding that something occurred at a rate or degree beyond what would be expected by chance alone is a probability less than .05. If the probability of incorrectly rejecting the null hypothesis is less than .05, we reject it. In the accepted jargon, we conclude that the obtained relationship or difference is "significant." In this section, we will consider the utility of nonsignificant results. You should have inferred from this section's title that the jargon label "nonsignificant" is not the same thing as "insignificant."

Horseshoes and Hand Grenades

There's an old saying that close only counts in horseshoes and hand grenades. To the strictest of logicians, a relationship is either significant or not; you either reject the null hypothesis or you don't. Labeling an effect "almost significant" is like declaring someone almost dead: the distinction can be understood, but it doesn't change the dichotomous nature of the decision to be made. On the other hand, an effect that yields a .06 probability of incorrectly rejecting the null hypothesis should not be labeled as insignificant and abandoned.

One of the more common misuses of statistics as a tool in research is to rely on statistical reasoning as though it were the only form of reasoning. There is nothing magical or sacred about the .05 probability criterion, or any other probability for that matter. The probability of falsely rejecting the null hypothesis is exactly that—the probability that you are wrong when you conclude what you have observed in your data is a real effect and not something that resulted from measurement error.

Trends—the more acceptable term for almost significant effects—probably ought best be treated as clues that effects are smothered in error variance. Sometimes trends really are nothing more than error variance masquerading as an effect, but to ignore trends in your data is to ignore an opportunity to learn something from your data. If the trends represent an important phenomenon, you have all the more reason to set aside statistical reasoning for the moment and consider the implications of your results as though you would not be wrong in rejecting the null hypothesis. In other words, treat trends in the data the same way you treat surprising results: investigate them, mull them over in your mind, engage in some what-ifing.

No Study Is Worthless

There are studies, more than most of us would like to admit, that produce results that do not even come close to being trends. With all due respect to some colleagues who insist they have evidence to the contrary, I claim that such studies are not worthless. Something can always be learned from any data collected, regardless of the lack of apparent results from statistical analyses.

In 1976, for example, I conducted a study on what I thought was a rather ingenious hypothesis derived from three different research areas in social psychology. The first of these areas dealt with the effects of physical attractiveness on liking. The general finding was, and still is, that liking another person is positively correlated with that person's physical attractiveness. The second area concerned Schachter and Singer's (1962) theory of emotions. Put briefly, they posited that emotions consist of physiological arousal and a label for the arousal. The greater the level of arousal experienced by a person, the stronger the emotional experience. Further, under certain conditions it is possible to cause someone to misperceive emotions. If someone experiences physiological arousal but does not perceive an obvious cause for the arousal, that person will search the environment for cues about the cause of the arousal. Therefore, someone may experience arousal for one reason but decide that the cause of the arousal is something else.

By using a simple factorial design, I attempted to get participants to experience arousal and attribute the arousal either to an attractive or an unattractive

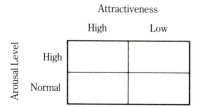

Figure 11.2 The 2 × 2 factorial design of the arousal–attractiveness experiment. Participants rated photographs of attractive or unattractive women while experiencing either high or low levels of arousal. Arousal was manipulated by the proximity of the experimenter.

individual. Physical attractiveness was manipulated by showing participants a photograph of an attractive or an unattractive person. The only photographs available to me at the time had been pretested for attractiveness but contained only women, so I decided to use male participants only.

I used the third area of social psychological research to manipulate the arousal level of the participants. The research on proxemics—also known as personal space—had clearly demonstrated that sitting too close to another person made that person experience an increase in physiological arousal. To create arousal in my participants, I placed my chair within three inches of their chair while they were rating the women in the photographs. In the normal arousal conditions, I sat halfway across the room while they rated the woman in the photograph. The design of the experiment is illustrated in Figure 11.2, and the dependent measures consisted of a series of rating scales dealing with first impressions.

The hypothesis was that the level of arousal experienced by the participant would interact with the attractiveness of the photograph they were rating. The attractive women would receive more positive ratings than the unattractive women, and that difference would be exaggerated when the participant was experiencing a high level of arousal. Those participants to whom I sat close were expected to attribute their arousal to the women in the photographs and therefore were expected to react more strongly—more emotionally—to them than would participants who were not experiencing a high level of arousal.

The results, at first glance, were a disaster. Not only did I not get the interaction I expected, the data did not exhibit any trends at all. Even the "sure" effect of a more positive first impression for the attractive women was not apparent. Rather than chucking the whole thing as too complicated and going on to some other study, I "preyed" on the data in order to discover what had gone wrong. I noticed that many of the participants in the high arousal conditions provided seemingly random responses. Qualities of the women that should have been related were not, and some that should not have been were related. A few participants simply rated all of the items at one end of the scale.

This rather weird effect led me to believe the participants were not concentrating on the women in the photograph. I called some of them, interviewed them, and discovered that indeed many of them were not concentrating on the women in the photograph. It seems that my results were caused by the participants' beliefs about what was being studied. Most of the participants in the high arousal conditions thought that because I was sitting very close to them, I was studying some aspect of homosexuality. They admitted to completing the ratings as quickly as they could so that they could get out of the room. Although this finding had nothing to do with the theories I was studying, it did lead me to the very interesting topic of homophobia—an inordinate fear of people and things related to homosexuality. I've since completed a couple of studies on homophobia, one of which is under editorial review as I write this chapter.

Summary

• Research involves considerably more than simply developing a hypothesis, testing it, and writing a report of the results. Sometimes, more can be learned from a research project gone awry than from a textbook-perfect project.

• Data transformations can be used very effectively to overcome some of the problems encountered when the data do not meet the requirements of whatever statistical analyses you want to use. Outliers, skewed distributions, heterogeneous variances, and proportions can be treated with appropriate transformations, but the transformations cannot be used to cause effects to appear magically when there are none.

• Surprising results can be viewed as an opportunity to engage in exploratory research. If your results are not what you expected, treat the results as a puzzle to be solved instead of simply rejecting them as research errors. The first step in finding a reason for surprising results should be to check the analyses to ensure that the results are not errors.

• If the surprise is not an error, concentrate on differences between your study and the studies that led to your original expectations for the results. Any difference in procedure, design, or method is a potential alternative explanation. When considering alternative explanations, adopt a participant's point of view.

• Trends—almost significant effects—should not be considered insignificant results. More often than not, a trend indicates the presence of an effect in the midst of measurement error or poorly controlled research conditions.

• Regardless of the outcome of a research project, there is always something to be learned from the project. The most effective tool a behavioral scientist can bring into the research setting is a curious mind. Always try to understand why you obtained your results.

CHAPTER
TWELVE

Writing a Research Report

Do not be afraid to seize whatever you have written and cut it to ribbons; it can always be restored to its original condition in the morning, if that . . . seems best. Remember, it is no sign of weakness or defeat that your manuscript ends up in need of major surgery. This is a common occurrence in all writing, and among the best writers.

—Strunk and White (1979, p. 72)

Overview

The purpose of this chapter is to provide you information about how to write a research report. You will learn about general style, as well as the difference between what is required, what is not required but allowed, and what is not allowed in a research report. You will also learn about the traditional organization of a research report.

Introduction

Good writing requires practice, thought, and awareness. The more writing you do, the more your writing will improve. The more you think about your writing, and the more you pay attention to the writing of others—good or bad—the more your writing will improve. To become a better writer, write more and revise what you write.

I strongly suggest you read and reread the writing of four people: Kilpatrick (1984), Safire (1984), and Strunk and White (1979). Kilpatrick and Safire are syndicated columnists. I rarely agree with their politics, but they know how to write and express what they know entertainingly. The volume by Strunk and White is a handbook of rules for good writing; if you buy any more books in your life, Strunk and White's is the first one you should buy. I recommend reading it often, perhaps as often as every six months.

That's about all I can include in this chapter about how to improve your writing, for to comment any more on your writing would require a sample of it. Instead, the remainder of this chapter deals with why and how to write a research report. There are some general (and a few specific) conventions adopted by those who write reports about research, and it's these conventions that we'll examine in this chapter.

The purpose of writing a research report is simple: to inform others about the research you have conducted. This simple purpose involves the assumption that others want to be informed about the research. Part of what writing a research report is all about is writing the report so that others will want to read it.

Bem (1981) noted that at least two reports can be written about every research project: one contains what you would have written when you designed your study; the other contains what is necessary to make sense of your research after the data have been collected and analyzed. These two reports are rarely the same, and it is the latter report you should prepare. Because the purpose of a research report is to inform others about your research, you should prepare your report so that others can make sense of and use your research results.

Preparing a report that informs others involves writing for a specific audience—the people you want to inform. This audience will most likely be other scientists interested in your research topic. Although the trials and tribulations of collecting data might make great stories around a campfire, other researchers don't want to read them in a journal. What they do want to read includes the theoretical and empirical background of your research, the procedures you used to collect the data, the results of the data analyses, and the conclusions you have drawn from the results.

Research Report Organization

The organization of a research report is fairly standard in the behavioral sciences. In psychology the standard is comprehensively described in the *Publication Manual of the American Psychological Association* (American Psychological Association, 1983). If you have not already done so, obtain a copy of the manual and adhere to the technical requirements described in it. Slightly different formats may be used to present the organized material, but every research report should contain an introduction, sections for method, results, discussion, and references, and a summary or abstract of the report. The major sections—introduction, method, re-

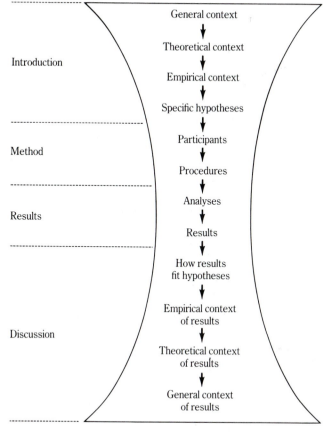

Figure 12.1 The hourglass analogy of the research report. The introduction begins leading the reader from very general issues to successively more specific issues until the results, the center point of the article, are presented. Then, the reader is led back from the very specific results to the most general implications of the results.

sults, and discussion—are often described as being analogous to an hourglass of information through which the author guides the reader.

As depicted in Figure 12.1, the report begins with one or more general statements that place the research in context, followed by increasingly more specific statements until the reader is informed of the intentions and hypotheses of the research. The method section includes information about how the data were collected, the results section contains what was found, and the discussion is used to bring the reader back to the general context. As the center of the hourglass, the results are the focus of the research report. For this reason, you cannot consider any part of the manuscript to be more than a working draft until you know the results.

Writing Style

The most important aspects of a research report are its accuracy and clarity: if it is not accurate, a report cannot inform others about your research; if it's not clear, it cannot be informative. Accuracy and clarity, however, are not the same as dry and uninteresting. Sentences should be simple and devoid of jargon as much as possible. Some jargon will be necessary, as in the statement "The interaction effect was reliable," but it should be kept to a minimum.

Voice and Person

Traditionally, research reports are written in the third person with passive voice (as is this sentence). Passive voice is less interesting than active voice, and many scientists are now breaking this tradition. Instead of writing "participants were instructed to provide a response to every question," try writing "the instructions admonished the participants to complete every item." Research is an activity, and an active voice conveys that notion.

The tendency to write in the third person remains stronger than the tendency to write in passive voice, but use of the third person is also no longer an unbreakable rule. Avoid the temptation to overuse the first person—"I randomly assigned participants to conditions, then I read the instructions, and finally I manipulated the independent variable"—but infrequent first-person statements are acceptable.

Tense

The tense of report writing is also traditional, but this tradition is more sensible than passive voice. When writing about the conclusions of others in the introduction, past tense is normally used. The reason for past tense is very simply that others' statements were made in the past. For example, "Dane (1985) concluded that the self-report method for measuring reasonable doubt was inaccurate" makes sense because Dane wrote that conclusion before the current sentence was written. Similarly, use the past tense for descriptions of your research procedures and data analyses. At the time you write the report, the procedures and analyses have already happened. The present tense is reserved for specific directions to the reader, such as "see Figure 2 for an illustration," and for general conclusions beyond the data, such as "it is clear that the solution to measuring reasonable doubt does not include self-reports."

Avoiding Stereotypes

The key aspects of research reports are accuracy and clarity. Perpetuation of stereotypes detracts from accuracy and clarity and should be avoided. Many of us seem to have particular trouble with sexism, so I'll concentrate on that in this section. If males and females participated, do not refer to participants with male pronouns only. Do not exclude groups when they should not be excluded; the statement "A scientist has an obligation to promote knowledge, but he must balance that obligation with fair treatment of others" excludes women from being scientists. Indeed, the example is intentionally ironic, for it involves denying fair treatment to females through the implication that scientists are male.

Avoiding exclusionary and stereotypic writing requires a bit of creativity. Continual use of inclusive phrases such as "he or she" becomes tedious, and artificial constructions such as "he/she" or "s/he" look terrible on paper and cannot be pronounced. If you need not refer to an individual, use plural pronouns. For example, the statement "Scientists have an obligation to promote knowledge, but they must balance that obligation with fair treatment of others" eliminates the exclusionary pronoun. If you must refer to an individual, avoid overusing "he or she" and similar phrases. For example, the statement "A scientist has an obligation to promote knowledge but must balance that obligation with fair treatment of others" is just as informative and meaningful without the male pronoun. However, when a male or female is specifically appropriate, use it. "Dane (1985) suggested . . . He also stated" is appropriate, but "Dane (1985) suggested . . . He or she also stated" is inappropriate and confusing.

Avoiding inappropriate gender references involves more than simply getting the pronouns right. Stereotyping is often subtle, and even such subtle stereotyping should be avoided. Sentences such as "Man requires more mothering than any other species" reflect stereotyping and exclusion. Unless the author is referring to males only and requirements that can be met only by mothers, it would be more appropriate to write "Humans require more nurturing than any other species." Similarly, phrases such as "man and wife" and "men and girls" convey unequal status. Use "husband and wife" and "men and women" or "boys and girls" instead. The use of examples can also convey stereotyping. If exemplary individuals are identified by gender, avoid using an overabundance of one gender or always using males at one end of a continuum and females at the other.

Avoiding inappropriate gender references requires creativity, as does conducting research itself. If you are creative enough to design and implement a research project, you are creative enough to avoid exclusion and stereotyping when writing the report (see Miller & Swift, 1980). Do not rely on others for justification to engage in sexist writing. Strunk and White (1979), for example, suggested the use of male pronouns exclusively. That they are correct about other elements of style does not necessarily make them correct about gender-specific pronouns.

Clarity

Every paragraph in your research report should convey an idea, every sentence in a given paragraph should be related to the idea, and every word in every sentence should add to the reader's understanding of the idea. These three "shoulds" are what clarity is all about. All unnecessary words, sentences, and paragraphs should be omitted. Sentences not related to the rest of the paragraph should be eliminated or moved to an appropriate paragraph.

Clarity means a reader will understand the message you intended to convey. Check the clarity of your writing by asking someone to read your research report and explain to you what you wrote. If the reader does not understand or misinterprets what you have written, then what you have written is unclear. Misinterpretation is not the reader's fault; it's the author's fault. Take the opening quote from Strunk and White to heart and revise unclear portions of your report. Using word processing software makes revising easier, but the lack of such software is no excuse for unclear writing.

Introducing the Project

Accurately and clearly informing others about your research includes providing some background information. Regardless of the purpose of your research, the reader is a stranger to your project and requires an introduction. The reader will need to know something about how your research fits into the general scheme of inquiry. You need to let the reader know why your research was done, and that context is provided in the introduction of the report.

Getting the Reader's Attention

Below is a portion of the first part of the introduction from the report Dane and McPartland (1985) wrote about research on judgments of the propriety of various public displays of affection:

> Intimacy between two people is often inferred from the manner in which they relate to each other at a nonverbal level. Since the publication of Hall's (1959) *The Silent Language,* research on nonverbal indicators of intimacy has grown at a geometric rate, and touch occupies a primary position within the literature. Coverage ranges from rigorous reviews and theoretical proposals (Patterson, 1976; 1982) through textbook summaries (Kleinke, 1975; Malandro & Barker, 1983). Throughout this literature, however, authors have focused on people directly involved in interpersonal exchanges. Observers' reactions have been neglected.
>
> Hall's volume, for example, is devoted almost entirely to interpreting nonverbal behaviors from the actors' viewpoints. He offers only a few examples in which the reader is asked to imagine amazement upon observing peculiar behaviors. Kleinke (1975) similarly devotes several pages to touching, but only from the perspective of involvement. Malandro and Barker (1983: 270) concluded "the sender and receiver recognize that touch carries messages that are often more dominant than the words we speak," but failed to mention inferences drawn by observers. A thorough review of the literature yields many more analyses of touch from participants' viewpoints, but no analysis of observers' viewpoints.

In two paragraphs, we presented the general area into which our research fit (nonverbal behavior), introduced the specific aspect on which we would concentrate (observer's reactions to touch), and provided several examples to buttress our argument that research is needed in this area. We established the hourglass pathway through which we would lead the reader.

Bem (1981) offered four rules for the beginning of an introduction, rules that make it easier for you to convince the reader that your research is worth reading.

The first of these is to write in prose instead of jargon. Some jargon will be necessary, but use it only when it actually is necessary. Although it is possible to rewrite the two sample paragraphs so that they contain little except jargon, it is far from desirable to do so. Excessive jargon will not impress anyone with your command of technical language; it merely makes your writing more difficult to understand.

The second rule is to avoid immediately putting the reader into the middle of your problem or theory. Bem suggested taking the time to introduce the research problem a little at a time. In the sample paragraphs, we did not immediately state, for example, "There is not enough research on observers' reactions to nonverbal indicators of intimacy." Although it's a legitimate statement, a reader's reaction is more likely to be hostile—"Prove it to me"—instead of understanding.

Bem's third rule is the one most often violated by beginning and experienced researchers alike: begin the introduction with a statement about human behavior instead of a statement about research. The first sentence in the introduction should describe the phenomenon as a behavior—something the reader can relate to experience. The first sentence in the example could have easily been left out, but then the paragraph would have begun with a statement about Hall's book instead of what the research was about.

The fourth rule is to use examples to illustrate, introduce, or expand the abstract or technical points you wish to make. The second sample paragraph is devoted almost exclusively to this rule. From a strict perspective of providing only absolutely necessary information, the second paragraph could be eliminated, or at least reduced considerably. But the introduction of a research report should do more than merely provide the minimum of information. The introduction should lead the reader to the statement you want to make with your research. Examples smooth the path that leads from the general behavior of people to the specific behavior examined in your study.

Reviewing the Literature

After you have gotten the reader's attention, you need to provide information about relevant research. You completed a review of the literature before starting your project, and that information was valuable to the conceptualization and design of your project. It will also be valuable to the reader who is trying to understand what you did and why you did it.

Reviewing literature does not mean bombarding the reader with everything you learned while conducting your literature search. The purpose is not to impress the reader with your knowledge, but to provide necessary information. Consider the following portion of a literature review:

> A decade ago, Hunt (1974: 11) dramatized the frequency with which observers were exposed to public displays of intimacy by noting "the unprecedented spectacle of sexually normal young people stripping off their clothes and having intercourse out in the open." Indeed, about 70,000 people in the U.S. were arrested for "sexual misconduct" in 1980 (Flanagan & McLeod, 1983). Somewhere along

the continuum from holding hands to sexual intercourse, observers' primary reactions to public touching change from a simple inference about intimacy to marked disapproval. At what point that change takes place is not known. For that matter, we can only assume the existence of general cognitive structures about reactions to interpersonal intimacy.

The paucity of research on observers' reactions to public touching involves only general attitudes. Excluding research on erotica presented through mass media, we found only one study on the topic. Crawford and Crawford (1978: 396) reported individuals' reactions to the statement "Public displays of affection are in poor taste" were highly correlated with items concerning public nudity, sexually explicit reading material, and so on. They concluded reactions to public intimacy are a subset of general attitudes toward sexuality. Conceptual leaps aside, it seems overly simplistic to assume reactions to observing public touching will mirror, in substance and form, reactions to engaging in the same behavior.

These two paragraphs from the center of our introduction (Dane and McPartland, 1985) accomplish three purposes. First, they provide the reader with information about existing research. Second, they provide some indication of the reasons that existing research is not sufficient. Finally, they lead the reader further into the hourglass to the point at which we presented specific information about our study:

The purpose of the present study is to assess individual attitudes toward the propriety of specific displays of intimacy in public. Relationships among different displays were explored to determine the extent to which attitudes reflect categorical reactions. Reactions to kissing and hugging, for example, may be considered similarly appropriate but distinct from reactions to mutual fondling or body contact *sans* clothing. In light of the issues addressed by Paul et al. (1982), attitudinal differences concerning heterosexual and homosexual couples were considered likely. It would seem straightforward to predict that a male kissing another male in public would be judged less appropriate than a male kissing a female. It may also be the case that categorical reactions differ for heterosexual and homosexual couples.

Little by little, we lead the reader from a very general statement about human behavior to a specific statement about our research. Notice also that the above paragraph—the last paragraph of the introduction—includes some predictions about what we expect to find in the research. Of course, these predictions are not really predictions; we had already analyzed the data and knew the outcome. The apparent prediction prepares the reader for what is to come. This is an example of writing for the results; it shows the difference between the report that would be written before the project begins and the report written after the results are known.

The introduction of a research report is not a vehicle for explaining the winding road that led you from your initial research idea to your results. Instead, it is a pathway on which you lead the reader, slowly but straightforwardly, from a common experience to the methods and procedures you used to obtain your results. The last paragraph of the introduction should serve as a transition to the specific details of your research, just as this sentence serves as a transition to the next section about methods.

Describing the Method

The method section of the report is the section wherein you describe what you did in sufficient detail to accomplish two purposes. First, you need to provide enough information for the reader to understand how you collected your data. In one sense, the method section is a secondary introduction, for it serves to guide the reader to your results. The second purpose involves providing enough information to enable someone to replicate your research. Thus, the method section is also an archive.

Describing Participants

The first subsection of the method section should be a description of the participants. It should include who they were, how they were selected, and any other pertinent information:

> The participants were 73 male and 113 female undergraduate volunteers attending a small state college in upstate New York. The median age was 19, and each received partial course credit for participating.

Brief though it may be, the above description provides the relevant information a reader needs to know about the people in our research. We included information about how many, gender, regional location, and age. Other than the label "volunteers," we did not include any specific information about sampling procedures, but the label says it all. By calling them volunteers and not providing additional information about sampling, the reader can infer that the sample was an accidental sample. Although information by omission may not be the best way to describe our sampling procedures, such is the convention in research reports.

Describing Sampling

If you obtained other than an accidental sample, you should explain the procedure you used. You might, for example, write "Random digit dialing was used to obtain a random sample of residents in South Carolina. Business and other nonresidential phone numbers were eliminated, which produced the final sample of 600 residents." There's no need to go into great detail, such as describing the computer program that generated the random phone numbers, unless your sampling procedure is so unusual as to require such explanation.

Describing Apparatus or Materials

The apparatus or materials subsection is included if you used any special equipment or materials in your study. Whether equipment or materials, you will need to include a brief description—in case readers want to replicate your study—and the function(s) served—so readers will better understand your procedures. Of course, common equipment need not be described; no one really cares what brand of pencil you used to record observations. We wrote:

The face sheet of the questionnaire contained instructions for completing the instrument, and items concerning age, gender, and religious preference. The second and third page contained a list of 26 behaviors, ranging from holding hands to sexual intercourse, with instructions that each behavior was to be rated as to its propriety as a public display of affection. The seven-point rating scale ranged from −3 (strongly inappropriate) to +3 (strongly appropriate), including a labeled neutral point. Separate ratings were made for a male-female, male-male, and female-female couple, and the items were listed on the page in a randomly determined order.

Included in this paragraph are examples of the types of items and a very explicit description of the response scale. Depending on the journal to which the report is to be submitted, an appendix containing a copy of the instrument might also be included with the report. Only those readers interested in replicating the research exactly would need to see the entire questionnaire, so there's no need to add such lengthy material to the body of the report. Of course, your instructor may require you to submit appendices with your report; such a requirement is an example of an editorial policy.

If the questionnaire had been described in a previous report, whether ours or someone else's, we would have provided a more general description of the instrument and referred the reader to the more detailed published description. You might, for example, write "The questionnaire used by Dane and McPartland (1985) was used to obtain attitudinal information about a variety of public displays of affection." Such a statement should then be followed by a general description of the questionnaire, a description that would enable the reader to understand what you did without having to look up the Dane and McPartland reference. If the reader wants to replicate your study, the original description of the scale could be examined at a later date.

Describing Procedure

The procedure subsection contains details about the specific manner in which the data were collected. Enough detail should be included to accomplish the archival purpose of this section, as well as to enable the reader to empathize with your participants. That is, write about the procedures from the participant's point of view. Empathy enables the reader to get a feel for the meaning of the data you collected. In our report, we wrote:

> To ensure anonymity, participants completed the questionnaire in groups of 10 to 20. For each session, a male researcher described the study as an investigation of reactions to public displays of affection. Participants were asked to rate the propriety of specific displays of public affection, for which public was defined as any location where one could reasonably expect to be observed by others. It was explicitly noted that those who believed they would be offended by the task should complete only the face sheet of the questionnaire, but no one exercised this option.

Notice how much information we packed into the above paragraph. We pointed out that the questionnaire was administered anonymously and in small groups. We summarized the instructions and indicated how we provided for informed consent. If the exact wording of the instructions had been important to the data collection process, we would have provided a direct quote. Because the procedure involved completing a questionnaire, there was no need to describe manipulations of an independent variable or to describe graphically the physical environment.

Describing Manipulations

If your research involved experimental manipulations, they should be described in sufficient detail for the reader to understand them, and again they should be described from the participant's viewpoint. For example:

> Three different feedback groups were created. In the Positive Feedback group, we told participants they correctly answered 45 of the 50 test questions. In the Negative Feedback condition, we said they correctly answered only 5 of 50 questions. Participants in the No Feedback group did not learn about their performance.

Notice that the labels given to the various groups are informative labels. The groups are not called Group 1, Group 2, and Group 3. Although such numeric labels do distinguish among the groups, they don't provide the reader with any aid for remembering the manipulation used to create the groups. If the procedure in the study is very complicated, it is also preferable to provide a brief summary of the method and design before moving on to the results section.

Describing Your Results

The results section is where you report the results of the data analyses you completed. It is the section around which the entire report is centered. You want to be sure the reader understands the results, and that requires following the rule of thumb used in oral presentations: tell them what you are going to tell them, tell them, and tell them what you told them. Following this rule, however, does not mean being redundant; instead, it means presenting information at three different levels. I'll provide examples as we move on to the preliminary and main subsections of the results section.

Describing Preliminary Results

Just as the overall research report requires an introduction to prepare the reader for what is to come, the results section may require an introduction to prepare the reader for the main results. Depending on your procedures, there may be any number of things you need to accomplish at the beginning of the results section.

If you used a manipulation or selected your participants on the basis of some pretest measure, you need to convince the reader that the manipulation or selection procedure did what it was supposed to do. The first part of the results should include the results of analyses that support your manipulation or selection procedure. For example:

> Participants rated their level of performance on a ten-point scale ranging from poor (1) to excellent (10). These ratings were used to determine whether the feedback manipulation was effective, and produced a main effect for Feedback when subjected to an Analysis of Variance, F (2, 59) = 10.25, $p < .05$, indicating that the manipulation was successful. Participants in the Positive Feedback group rated their performance (Mean = 8) reliably better than those in the No Feedback group (Mean = 5).

Included is information reviewing the manipulation, the result of the analysis, an interpretation of the result, and a clarification. The quote follows the rule: we told them what we were going to tell them, we told them, and we told them what we told them.

Other material in the preliminary results might include analyses of interrater reliability, descriptive statistics about the participants, information about data eliminated from the analyses, and any other results that move the reader toward your main results. How much information you include in a preliminary results subsection depends on the specific nature of your study and your data. In the public displays of affection report, we used the beginning of the results section to convince the reader that the participants' ratings were sensible:

> Table 1 contains the overall mean propriety rating for each of the 26 behaviors, according to type of couple. The participants clearly discriminated among the items, which are ordered from most to least appropriate within ratings for the male-female couple. Of particular interest is the trend for female couples' behaviors to be rated consistently less appropriate than the male-female couples and, also without exception, the trend for male couples' behaviors to be least appropriate. These trends are not overly surprising in light of Gross, Green, Storck, and Vanyur's (1980) findings concerning prevalent negative reactions to overt homosexuality.

I've not included the table from the article; it's too long to merit the space as an example here. The table in the report contained what the text said it contained and exhibited the properties described in the text. It is evident from the table that the participants rated holding hands, for example, as more appropriate than kissing, and so forth. The results are not surprising, but surprise was not the point. Rather the purpose was to convince the reader that the data make sense—that the participants did what they were expected to do.

Another part of the preliminary results subsection should be an overview of the statistical procedures used to analyze the bulk of the data. This part of the results section should be included in every research report because it serves to orient the reader—to enable the reader to develop expectations about the kinds of information to come. Any transformations performed on the data should be included at this point in the section. We wrote:

> To explore the potential structure underlying the ratings, separate factor analyses were conducted for each type of couple. Because the analysis was exploratory, all

factors yielding eigenvalues greater than one were retained prior to orthogonal rotation. For all three couple types, four factors emerged, accounting for 64%, 72%, and 67% of the variance for male-female, female-female, and male-male couples, respectively. The order of emergence was identical across couple type, although specific item loadings differed among couple types for the fourth factor.

The paragraph informs the reader that factor analysis was used for data analysis. Factor analysis is a statistical technique for investigating structure among a number of variables. Essentially, it can be used to group variables together based on their correlations in much the same way that those who write college admissions tests group items into separate subject categories. Even though this paragraph dealt with preliminary results, we began to discuss some of the main results of the study. We pointed out, for example, that each of the three sets of ratings produced four factors. Beginning to present main findings in the last paragraph of the preliminary results is one way to provide a transition from one subsection to the next.

Describing Main Results

When you describe the main results of the study, present the most central or most important results first; then present decreasingly important results. Use the same format for each result: a general description, more specific information, and finally relevant qualifications.

For each set of results, first remind the reader what question the result is supposed to answer. In the above paragraph from our report, for example, we reminded the reader that we wanted to explore the structure of the propriety ratings. Then we restated the result in terms of the specific operational definition used to measure the variable. This should be followed by a prose statement of the result, such as "The ratings produced four factors for each type of couple." Don't keep the reader in suspense about the meaning of the result until you have presented all the numbers. The statistics only support the conclusion, so don't provide support without also providing the conclusion.

Once you have presented the central aspect of the results, present any qualifications or elaborations using the same format: prose, numbers, and prose. For example, the excerpt below, which did not follow the above paragraph in the results section, concerns analyses conducted on the scores produced by the factor analyses mentioned above:

Additional exploration of the reactions involved determining whether the participants' characteristics were related to their reactions. Item loadings were used to create weighted factor scores ranging from -1 (inappropriate) to $+1$ (appropriate). These were then subjected to a 2 (Gender) $\times$ 4 (Religion: Catholic, Jewish, Other, None) $\times$ 4 (Factor Label) $\times$ 3 (Couple Type) Analysis of Variance.

The analysis yielded a reliable main effect for Gender, $F (1, 172) = 4.10$, $p < .05$. Males (Mean $= 0.07$) considered the behaviors to be generally more appropriate than did females (Mean $= -0.05$). The only other reliable effect was a Factor Label $\times$ Gender interaction, $F (3,516) = 8.27$, $p < .0001$, for which the means are presented in Table 6. As is evident from the table, women rated all but the Asexual behaviors as less appropriate than did men.

Each finding is first presented in prose, then in numbers, and then again in prose. Each statistical analysis is clearly identified, and each effect is accompanied by its level of statistical significance. For the simpler main effect, however, the means were included in the text. The table (labeled Table 6 because it was the sixth one we included in the report) was used to clarify the interaction effect because it was more efficient to present the eight means in tabular form than in prose. Notice, however, that a prose clarification of the interaction was included in the text. One should not simply refer the reader to a table and leave it to the reader to discern its meaning. The same rules apply to figures—graphs, pictures, and drawings—which you should use whenever the information you want to convey cannot be conveyed in text or in a table.

Notice also that each effect was accompanied by a small amount of interpretation, such as "males considered the behaviors to be generally more appropriate than did females." You should not simply state that the mean for males was higher than the mean for females and leave it at that. Use the qualifying result to remind the reader what it is you are trying to get across. A little interpretation—but only a little—in the results section is permissible, and it is one way to begin leading the reader toward the conclusions you will draw in the next section of the report.

Describing the Conclusions

The conclusions you draw from the results are placed in the discussion section of the report. This is where you begin to expand the hourglass, beginning with a restatement of the main results. In some respects, the discussion section is the reverse of the introduction: instead of leading the reader to your results (as you did in the introduction), you are leading the reader away from your results toward the general points you want to make. The conclusions you draw should logically follow from the results. You can't put just any old thing in the discussion section; the discussion is a discussion of the results.

It is best to begin the discussion with a restatement of your main research question and a summary of the relevant results. For example:

> In general, the data demonstrate that observers do make attributions about public displays of affection. Specifically, judgments about the propriety of the behaviors conform to expectations based on the level of sexual intimacy for the behavior. More important, the data show that propriety may be judged on the basis of categorical information about groups of behaviors.

This is a very full first paragraph for a discussion section. It includes a restatement of the research question: Do people react to intimate touching other than registering it as an intimate act? It also points out that observers' reactions may be categorical, and it limits the conclusions to the data collected. All this is done, however, without merely restating what has already appeared in earlier sections of the report. Even though it leads the reader along the path defined by previous sections of the report, the discussion section should not merely rehash what's already been said. The discussion section should add something to the reader's knowledge and understanding of the study.

Although we could not do it in the public displays of affection report, the discussion should also include your efforts to relate the results to previous research on the topic. We couldn't do it because there wasn't any previous research. You don't want to mention every study ever done on the same topic, but you do want to provide enough information to place the results in a theoretical context. Differences between your results and those of previous research should be noted, but not to the point of dwelling on every detailed difference between the two. Concentrate on what you believe to be the important implications of your results. If you have written the report with the results as the centerpiece, those implications will flow smoothly from the introduction through the discussion section.

Above all, keep the discussion section as brief as possible. Bem (1981) hinted, perhaps only somewhat facetiously, that there may be a $-.73$ correlation between the clarity of the results section and the length of the discussion section. The discussion should lead the reader from the data to their implications; it should not explain what should have been explained in the results section. Toward the end of the discussion section, but not at the very end, you should present what you believe to be some questions that remain unanswered despite your study, or questions that are raised because of the results of your study:

> Furthermore, research and theory that may be stimulated by the current exploration should include consideration of the discrepancies between heterosexual and homosexual behavior. For example, there is a considerably wider range of behavior considered sexual for homosexuals than for heterosexuals, even though the same behavior was rated for both couple types. It is clearly the case that observers process and react to the public behaviors of others, and it is time we began to include observers' inferences in our theories about the meaning of touch as a means of nonverbal communication.

Because the study was exploratory and the results may be limited to the sample we used, the suggestions about future research are rather general. The more specific the hypotheses with which you deal, the more specific the recommendations you will be able to make. Finally, lead the reader back through the hourglass at least as far as you led them into the hourglass; that is, don't stop writing after you suggest possible strategies for additional research. As Bem (1981) pointed out, suggesting additional research is a common ending point for reports, but a very dull one. Bring the reader back to a reference point that involves behavior, rather than research about behavior.

One last note about the discussion section needs to be made: The discussion section should not contain any surprises for the reader. It should be interesting, to be sure, but it should not take any detours from the path initiated in the introduction. If your results revolutionize the study of human behavior, or even if they just call into question one or two conclusions about previous research, that pathway should be established in the introduction. Revolutions about theory can be tolerated, but no one likes surprises in the discussion section.

Writing Other Sections

The introduction, method, results, and discussion sections constitute the bulk of the research report. There are, however, a few other sections of the report. Even though they may not be included in the limelight of report writing, they are equally important in terms of the information they provide the reader. They include the abstract, the references, and the appendices. Again, the American Psychological Association's (1983) publication manual is an excellent source for additional information.

Summarizing the Report

Regardless of the length of the report, you should prepare a summary of it. This summary is usually called an abstract, and it is usually printed at the beginning of a journal article. It is best, however, to write the abstract after the rest of the report has been written. An abstract should include about 100 to 150 words—not many words in which to summarize a research report that may be as long as 25 pages. Writing abstracts requires a great deal of practice and invariably requires many, many revisions. It also requires patience. Consider the abstract from the public displays report:

> The purpose of this study was to explore observers' reactions to public, intimate behaviors. College students rated the propriety of imagined behaviors ranging from holding hands to sexual intercourse for opposite- and same-sex couples. Behaviors for the heterosexual couples were consistently rated as most appropriate. Factor analysis of the ratings yielded four categories: genital contact, other erotic contact, asexual contact, and an inconsistent factor that varied with type of couple. Suggestions for [topics of] future research included potential underlying cognitive processes of observers and the need to incorporate such processes into current theories about nonverbal behavior.

The abstract contains the main points of the complete report but includes none of the qualifications and elaborations necessary to fully understand those main points. The abstract is essentially a teaser. Because readers will use the abstract to decide whether or not to read the full report, the abstract needs to be informative and brief. The restriction on the number of words and the importance of getting across the main points require very clear writing. They also require revision after revision until you get it right. The quoted abstract, for example, went through ten revisions before I was satisfied. Note that, even with all of my revisions, Alan Titche, the copyeditor for this book, was able to improve the abstract by inserting "topics of" into the last sentence. I do not make this point to frighten you away from writing the abstract, but rather to warn you about the need for patience and persistence.

Identifying Your Sources

Any published material to which you refer in the report should be referenced in what is called, straightforwardly enough, the references section. Styles for references vary somewhat from journal to journal, but the predominant style is that recommended by the American Psychological Association (1983) in its publication manual. You can also consult a short pamphlet by Solomon (1985) or examine the references listed in the back of this text. I strongly recommend, however, that you buy the APA publication manual; it's a source of information you will repeatedly consult, and it contains a long list of suggested readings for additional information about better writing.

Regardless of the style you use for references, be sure to provide a complete reference for every citation in your report. If a revision leads you to add more citations to the report, be sure the appropriate references are included in the proper location in the references section. If revision involves dropping a citation, remove it from the references. Above all, make sure each reference is correct— not just close, absolutely correct. Other researchers may rely on your references section to find an article. You would not want to hunt through many volumes because someone incorrectly referenced an article, and you should not subject your readers to similar frustrations. The three most important aspects of the references section are completeness, accuracy, and accuracy.

Including Appendices

If the materials you used in the study are too long to be included in the report, they should be included in one or more appendices. A copy of the questionnaire, a verbatim transcript of verbal instructions, or anything else one would need to replicate your study should be in an appendix. You probably have never seen a published appendix, but that's only because journal space is too expensive to use it for appendices. This does not mean that appendices are unimportant.

Whether or not your instructor requires one (or whether or not the journal to which you submit a report requires one), it is always advisable to prepare an appendix. If your report leads another researcher to a similar idea, or if you decide to follow up on your own research project, the appendix will enable you to provide the necessary details. It is much easier to prepare an appendix at the time you write the research report than it is to try to reconstruct your exact procedures long after the project is over.

Having Your Research Report Reviewed

If you are required to prepare a research report for your class, your instructor will be one of its reviewers. Your instructor should not, however, be the only reviewer, or even the first reviewer. The true test of the clarity of a report is the opinions of your readers. Unless you are writing entries in a personal diary, your own beliefs about clarity are only a first step in achieving true clarity.

Friends and classmates are excellent sources for feedback about your research report. Use them as reviewers, and be a reviewer for them. You need not blindly accept their comments and criticisms, but the fact that they have a criticism should alert you to the possibility that changes are necessary. The manuscript for this book, for example, was read by a number of reviewers. They made many suggestions for improvement, some of which were incorporated and some of which were not. Every criticism was considered, whether or not it led to revisions. As a result, this text is a great deal clearer than the first draft of the manuscript.

Enough. The only way to improve your own writing is to write and pay attention to your readers' reactions. So go and write your research report (but first read the summary).

Summary

• Good writing requires practice, thought, and critical examination of others' writing. The more you do of any of these things, the more your writing will improve.

• The purpose of writing a research report is to inform others accurately and clearly about your research. Because the results are the focal point of the research, the final draft of the report cannot be written until after you have analyzed the data.

• Research reports are organized in an hourglass fashion. You first present information about the general phenomenon, then more specific issues related to the phenomenon, next the details about the research procedures, then the results, and finally you lead the reader back from the results to general conclusions.

• Although succinct, the style of the report should not be dry. Using active voice, limiting the use of first person, and using the appropriate tense will make the report more interesting. Sexist and other exclusionary language should be avoided.

• The introduction should begin with a statement about the behavior of interest; then it should lead the reader logically and straightforwardly to the specific hypotheses of the study.

• The method section should describe the way in which the data were collected. It should contain enough detail to enable someone to empathize with your participants and to replicate your study.

• The results section should include a preliminary exposition of the major types of analyses used. It should also include all results obtained from your data, ordered so that the most important results are presented first.

• The discussion section should begin with a brief summary of the major hypotheses and the results relevant to those hypotheses. Further generalization from the results should proceed in the same logical and straighforward organization used in the introduction.

• Although usually printed at the beginning of a report, the abstract should be written last. It should include the main points of the complete report but should be extremely brief.

• Styles for references vary, but every reference should be complete and accurate. Every citation used in the report should have a reference in the references section, and only citations used in the report should be referenced.

• Appendices should be prepared, even if they are not required for publication. It is easier to prepare an appendix when you write the research report than it is to try to reconstruct details long forgotten.

• Stop reading now, and write something.

PART THREE

Resource
Chapters

CHAPTER
THIRTEEN

Conceptual Overview of
Statistical Analyses

Aristotle could have avoided the mistake of thinking that women have fewer teeth than men by the simple device of asking Mrs. Aristotle to open her mouth.

—Bertrand Russell (Peter, 1980, p. 457)

Overview

The material presented in this chapter is a follow-up to the research strategies presented in Chapter 1. In addition to learning more about the strategies—exploration, description, prediction, explanation, and action—you will be given an overview of statistical analyses appropriate for each strategy. For those of you who have yet to complete a course in statistics, the material will serve as an introduction to the concepts of statistical analyses. Although basic theory and principles of inferential statistics will be covered, formulas and calculation procedures will not be presented.

Introduction

The first part of this book describes the nature of research—its definitions, limitations, philosophies, and ethics—as well as idea generation and literature review. The second part of the book presents the principles and procedures of specific research methodologies. This chapter begins the third part of the text, in which additional details are provided on specific topic areas common to all research methods.

As I've said so many times, research involves asking and attempting to answer questions. How the questions are asked determines the methods used to answer them, which in turn partly determine the answers. Another aspect of research that partly determines the answers is the statistical procedures used to analyze the data.

Research design and data analyses are interdependent; one makes little sense without the other. And one situation you should always avoid is having data without a way to analyze them. It is tremendously frustrating. Your data may contain the answers you want, but you don't know how to get at those answers. Worse, you may have spent a great deal of time and effort to collect data, only to find that they cannot be used to answer the questions you want to answer. The purpose of this chapter is to help you avoid such situations by providing an overview of current research strategies and the analyses most appropriate to them. The chapter is organized around the major research strategies: exploration, description, prediction, and explanation.

Exploratory Research

As defined in Chapter 1, exploratory research is an attempt to determine whether or not a phenomenon exists. That's exactly what Bertrand Russell had in mind when he suggested that Aristotle ought to have looked in Mrs. Aristotle's mouth instead of writing a philosophical discourse on gender differences.

Appropriate Questions for Exploratory Research

Exploratory research is similar to the insistent question asked by columnist and *60 Minutes* commentator Andy Rooney: "Did you ever wonder about . . . ?" Anything is fair game when we try to discover what is out there, wherever "there" may be. Some examples of exploratory research questions include: Do people think differently about themselves than about others? What do jury members talk about during deliberations? Has anyone ever done research on this topic before? The last question you may recognize as the question we ask when conducting a literature review.

Exploratory questions tend to be rather general, but that does not mean they are necessarily frivolous or uninformative. At the very least, exploratory research satisfies personal curiosity, but good exploratory research also has heuristic value. It stimulates you and others to conduct even more research. For example, the attempt by members of the Chicago Jury Project to answer the question about what jurors discuss during deliberations has been the basis for hundreds, perhaps thousands, of other research projects about the behavior of jurors (Ellison & Buckhout, 1981). Nearly any question about the existence or nature of human behavior, or the lack thereof, is an appropriate question for exploratory research.

Appropriate Statistics for Exploratory Research

Just as the questions addressed through exploratory research are usually general, the data analyses used for exploratory research also tend to be general. Often, analyses for exploratory research are **qualitative analyses**—*nonnumerical analyses concerning quality rather than quantity.* For example, early research on conformity as a group process dealt with determining whether or not members of a group who initially disagreed with the majority changed their opinions during group discussions (Levine & Russo, 1987). The quality of the behavior—opinion change—was the focus of analysis; change was either there or it was not. Early researchers on this topic were not particularly interested in how much people's opinions changed, just whether there was a change.

Even when analyses are not qualitative, they usually include calculating descriptive statistics concerning central tendencies or averages—mean, median, and mode—or concerning dispersion of scores, such as range, interquartile range, and standard deviation. Sometimes, histograms or frequency polygons are used to graphically examine data in more detail or to more clearly present data. Travis (1985), for example, used charts of surgery rates in different areas of the United States to more clearly illustrate the discovery that elective hysterectomies were considerably more prevalent than either elective appendectomies or elective prostate surgery.

Other useful exploratory analyses include stem-and-leaf displays and scattergrams. Stem-and-leaf displays (Tukey, 1977) are an alternative to more traditional histograms or frequency polygons. A stem-and-leaf allows you to visualize the entire data set as a distribution of scores, without having to lose information about what the specific scores are. They also enable you to informally examine differences among groups. Figure 13.1 contains a stem-and-leaf display for the publication dates of the references cited in a social psychology textbook (Dane, 1988b).

```
187 | 1
188 |
189 |
190 |
191 |
192 |
193 | 57
194 | 6
195 | 89
196 | 11112788
197 | 122334444555666777778899999
198 | 001111111222333444455555555555555555566666666666666666666667
```

Figure 13.1 A stem-and-leaf display of the publication years for the citations included in Dane (1988b). The stem, three-digit numbers along the left side, is the century and decade of the publication year. The leaf, single-digit numbers extending to the right from the stem, complete the year. Note how easy it is to recognize the relative abundance of later references compared to the relatively few citations from earlier years. Stem-and-leaf displays enable you to represent the frequencies included in the entire data set without losing information about the specific scores.

The stem—the left side of the display—contains the root of the date, such as "187" for the 1870s. The leaf, on the right side of the display, contains the remainder of the number, such as "1" in 1871. By examining the stem and the leaf, one can reconstruct the original score: "187" together with "1" indicates 1871.

Traditionally, the digits in the leaf are ordered, increasing from left to right, as in the figure. Although not shown in this figure, you can use the same stem more than once if that makes the display easier to read. However, if you do so, you should use every stem the same number of times. Longer leafs indicate more data points, so you should also be certain to use the same spacing for all of the leafs. That way, the leafs represent the distribution of scores much as a histogram does but without masking the actual numeric values of the data.

Scattergrams, on the other hand, allow the reader to examine relationships between variables, or between two different groups measured on the same variable. However, they are more likely to be used for descriptive and predictive research purposes, so we'll postpone discussing them until those sections.

In general, data analyses for exploratory research fall under the category of "interocular trauma" analyses: the effects are so apparent they hit you right between the eyes, or they are not apparent at all. It's clear from Figure 13.1, for example, that there are more references from the 1980s than from any other decade; the length of the "198" leafs hits you between the eyes. Even if the effect in which you are interested is subtle, it becomes apparent because you are looking for it; it is either there or it's not.

The kinds of analyses appropriate for exploratory research are displayed in Figure 13.2. Now we're ready to turn our attention to descriptive research.

Descriptive Research

Descriptive research involves attempting to define or measure a particular phenomenon, usually by attempting to estimate the strength or intensity of a behavior or the relationship between two behaviors. Rather than assessing whether or not something is going on, descriptive strategies involve assessing exactly what is going on.

Appropriate Questions for Descriptive Research

Questions for which a descriptive strategy would be appropriate are those that explore the limitations of a behavioral phenomenon. These might include its distinctiveness from other phenomena, the extent to which it occurs in various situations, or its strength or quantity. Examples include such questions as: Under what circumstances do people think differently about themselves than about others? How much time do jurors spend talking about evidence during deliberations? How many different operational definitions of this phenomenon have been used in previous research? These are, of course, descriptive versions of the exploratory questions presented in the previous section. Descriptive research does not necessarily involve different research topics, but it does involve different questions about those topics.

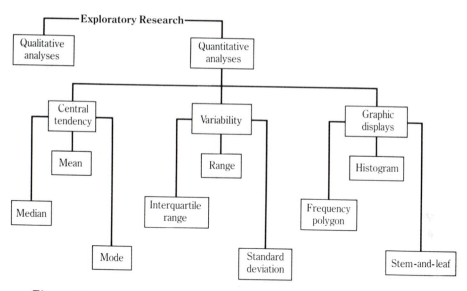

Figure 13.2   Both qualitative and quantitative analyses can be used to examine the results of exploratory research. Which quantitative statistics one should use depends on the nature of the research question; either central tendency, variability, or both may be appropriate. A variety of graphic presentations can be used to display the entire data set.

Usually, one of the purposes of descriptive research is to generalize—to relate the findings gathered from the research situation to other situations. Typically we want to generalize from the research participants to another group of people or to people in general. Obtaining an answer to the question about how much time the jurors in our study spend discussing evidence is considerably more useful if that answer can be extended to other jurors as well. Generalization requires external validity—similarity between the physical and social aspects of the research environment and the target environment (Cook & Campbell, 1979). Generalization also requires the use of inferential statistics.

Appropriate Statistics for Descriptive Research

When we attempt to generalize results, we make an inference about the relationship between the research participants and the target of our generalization. Imagine, for example, that we discovered that a particular sample of jurors spent an average of 50% of their deliberation time discussing evidence. If that research sample represents the entire population of jurors (see Chapter 16 for information about how to obtain a representative sample), then we might conclude that all jurors spend about 50% of their time in deliberations discussing evidence. That inference requires the use of inferential statistics.

Inferential statistics are *values calculated from a sample and used to estimate the same value for a population.* That is, inferential statistics are estimates, based on a given sample, of qualities or quantities existing in a larger group of individuals. The basis for all inferential statistics is a mathematical principle known as the central limit theorem. Fully explaining the central limit theorem is beyond the scope of this book and is not really necessary for our purposes. However, most statistics textbooks include an explanation of it if you are interested (see, for example, Nowaczyk, 1988; Wike, 1985; Winer, 1971).

One important aspect of the central limit theorem is that it enables us to use a sample to estimate a population if the sample has been obtained by **random selection**—*a process by which every member of the population had an equal opportunity to be included in the sample.* Random sampling, then, does not mean just any old sampling procedure, but one with a system that ensures that each person, place, or thing in the population has an equal chance of being included in the sample. Selection of a lottery winner, for example, is a random sampling procedure. The population includes everyone who entered the lottery. If all entries are placed in a large box, mixed, and then chosen one at a time, then every entry in the lottery had an equal chance of being selected.

Another important aspect of the central limit theorem is that we can use it, if we have a random sample, to estimate the amount of measurement error associated with any values obtained from the sample. Once we have determined that a sample of jurors spends 50% of their deliberations discussing evidence, we can also determine the accuracy range of that estimate. When network newspeople report that Candidate X has obtained 40% of the popular vote in an election, plus or minus 2%, they are reporting an accuracy range for the estimate obtained from their sample.

The types of inferential statistics used to analyze descriptive research data include some of the same calculations used for exploratory research, such as mean, median, mode, standard deviation, and so on. The difference is that these calculations are then used to make inferences, rather than simply describing the data collected from the sample. Other analyses include chi-square (also known as crossbreak analyses), correlations, t-tests, and analysis of variance (also known as ANOVA). Although a detailed explanation of each of these procedures is not within the scope of this text, I will provide a brief overview of their use in descriptive research.

Chi-square analyses are generally used to make inferences when the data are categorical—involve measuring participants in terms of categories such as male–female, voter–nonvoter, and so forth. Chi-square procedures can be used to determine whether a relationship exists between two or more categorical variables, or whether the categories obtained from one sample of individuals are similar to the categories obtained from another sample. That is, chi-square may be used to determine whether there is a relationship between gender and voting behavior, or it may be used to determine whether psychology majors are composed of a different ratio of men to women than are chemistry majors. Chi-square analyses are frequency analyses—they involve comparing the frequencies of various categories. Nowaczyk (1988) and Haberman's two volumes (1978, 1979) are excellent sources for more information about chi-square and other categorical analyses.

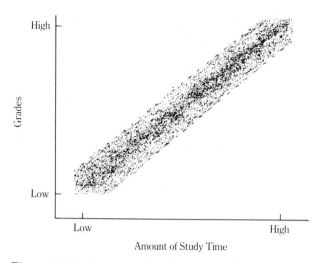

High

Grades

Low

Low   High

Amount of Study Time

Figure 13.3 A scatterplot of the relationship between amount of study time and grades. As the amount of study time increases, so do the grades. The darker areas of the plot indicate a greater number of overlapping points or higher frequency in the data set.

When research measures involve continuous variables, such as income, grade point average, age, intensity of emotion, and so on, correlational procedures are used to make inferences about relationships between variables. For example, the relationship between the size of a city and its crime rate can be described with correlational analyses. Correlations estimate the extent to which the changes in one variable are associated with changes in the other variable. Essentially, a correlation coefficient is a number summarizing what may be observed from a scatterplot.

Figure 13.3 is a scatterplot representing a positive correlation. Positive correlations reflect a direct relationship—one in which increases in one variable correspond to increases in the other variable. In Figure 13.3, the implication is that the time you spend studying is directly related to the grades you receive, and that increases in one reflect increases in the other. Notice that there are more overlapping data points in the center of the graph than at the edges of the graph, which also illustrates the general tendency for most people to study an average amount of time and receive average grades. If I could make Figure 13.3 a three-dimensional figure, you would see the data points coming out from the page toward you.

Of course, not all variables that are related exhibit a direct relationship. Figure 13.4 is the scatterplot of two variables one might expect to be indirectly or inversely related. Such a relationship would produce a negative correlation, indicating that increases in one variable are associated with decreases in the other. In Figure 13.4, it is apparent that amount of party time is inversely related to grades.

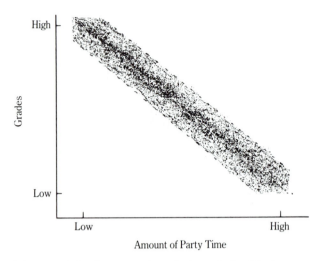

High

Grades

Low

Low   High

Amount of Party Time

Figure 13.4 A scatterplot of the relationship between
amount of party time and grades. As the amount of party
time increases, grades become lower. The darker areas in
the plot indicate a greater number of overlapping points or
higher frequency in the data set.

According to the scatterplot, the more you party, the lower your grades (or the
higher your grades, the less you party).

And finally, Figure 13.5 is the scatterplot of two variables that exhibit no relationship: shoe size and grades. Again, if I could produce the figure in three dimensions, the scatterplot in Figure 13.5 would appear to be a bell with its base on
the page and its top coming out toward you. Notice that both variables, grades and
shoe size, tend to exhibit more data points toward the center of their respective
scales, again merely indicating that more people tend to have average grades and
average shoe sizes. However, for any given shoe size, there is no particular grade
that is more prevalent, except the average grade.

More often than not, descriptive research involves trying to determine
whether two groups differ according to some quality, such as whether women or
men tend to commit more crimes, or whether psychology majors or chemistry
majors perform better on the Graduate Record Exam. Essentially, such research
involves comparing the central tendency of one group with the central tendency of
another, and t-tests (for two groups) or analysis of variance (for more than two
groups) are the appropriate statistics. Both statistics enable you to determine
whether groups have equivalent or different mean scores.

The principle underlying t-tests and analysis of variance is the assumption
that both groups, whatever they may be, represent samples from the same population. Males and females, for example, represent two different samples from the
same population—humans. If that assumption is correct, then the two samples
should have the same central tendency—the same mean. To the extent that the
two groups are different, one can include that the assumption about them being

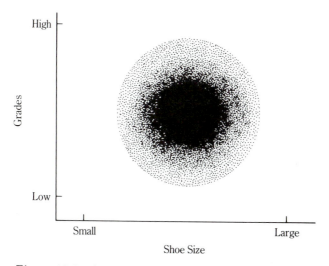

Figure 13.5 A scatterplot of the relationship between shoe size and grades. The circular pattern of the plot indicates that there is no relationship between the two variables. The denser pattern of dots in the center of the plot indicates that more people have average grades and average shoe sizes.

from the same population is wrong. Of course, that doesn't mean that in the case of males and females that one group is not human. Instead, it means that, on whatever variable is being measured, the two groups represent very different populations of humans; they are not the same on whatever the measurement dimension may be. Most any statistical text will include descriptions of t-tests and ANOVA. Nowaczyk (1988) and Wike (1985) are among the more readable; Winer (1971) is more advanced and technical.

The kinds of data and analyses for descriptive research are depicted in Figure 13.6. We next turn to a discussion of predictive research.

Predictive Research

Predictive research involves any study in which the purpose is to use one variable to predict another variable. Such research may be done in order to avoid using one of the variables because it is too expensive or time-consuming, or to avoid having to wait for an appropriate situation in which to use one of the variables. College admissions boards use the results of predictive research for accepting new students; it's too costly to wait an entire year to find out whether or not a student will do well enough to remain in school. Or one might try to predict jurors' decisions from their attitudes toward the legal system.

In any predictive research, the **response variable** is *the measure one would like to predict,* and the **predictor variable** is *the measure one hopes will predict the response variable.* Scholastic Aptitude Test scores, for example, would be the pre-

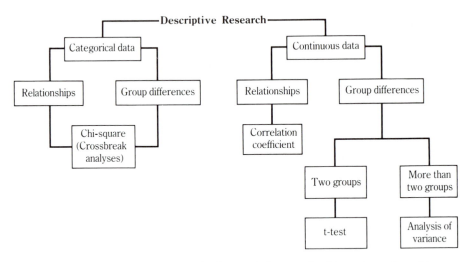

Figure 13.6 The kind of quantitative statistics one should use to analyze data from a descriptive study depends on the types of questions one is asking and the types of data one is using to attempt to answer them.

dictor variable and first-year grade point averages would be the response variable in the research admissions boards use to select students. Graduate admissions boards also make use of the Graduate Record Exam for the same purposes (Educational Testing Service, 1981).

Appropriate Questions for Predictive Research

Predictive research involves measuring relationships between two or more variables, and appropriate questions include any question that fits the general form "Is X related to Y?" Predictive versions of the questions used to illustrate exploratory and descriptive strategies would include: Does someone's self-esteem predict the impressions formed about others? Is the amount of time jurors spend talking about evidence related to their verdict? Can I predict the outcome of my research from the research of others? Box 13.1 contains a summary of the ways in which these questions have changed as a function of the research strategy. Notice that as the questions posed within any given topic change, so will the answers one can expect to obtain.

Prerequisites for Predictive Research

Because predictive research involves assessing whether or not one variable can be used to predict another, we need to be able to determine the extent to which the separate variables actually measure what they are supposed to measure; that is, both variables must be valid. Equally important, however, is that both variables must be as reliable as possible. The requirement for very high reliability results

---

BOX 13.1   Exploratory, Descriptive, and Predictive Research Questions

Exploratory:	Do people think differently about themselves than about others?
Descriptive:	Under what conditions do people think differently about themselves than about others?
Predictive:	Does someone's self-esteem predict the impressions formed about others?
Exploratory:	What do jury members talk about during deliberations?
Descriptive:	How much time do jurors spend talking about evidence during deliberations?
Predictive:	Is the amount of time jurors spend talking about evidence related to their verdict?
Exploratory:	Has anyone ever done research on this topic before?
Descriptive:	How many different operational definitions of this phenomenon have been used in previous research?
Predictive:	Can I predict the outcome of my research from the research of others?

---

from the fact that the predictive power of the predictor variable is limited to its reliability. If SAT scores, for example, are 80% reliable, then the best they can do is predict first-year college grades 80% of the time. Put another way, if the correlation between random halves of the SAT test is only 89%, then 89% is also the highest correlation we can expect to obtain between SAT scores and grades. More information about how to assess reliability and validity is incorporated into Chapter 14.

Statistics for Predictive Research

The types of statistical analyses used for predictive research are all based on correlation—the measure of the degree to which two or more variables are related. In addition to correlation coefficients themselves, the other predominant statistical procedure is regression analysis.

A correlation coefficient generally consists of both an algebraic sign and a number. The sign indicates the direction of the relationship: positive for direct, negative for inverse. In predictive research, the sign is generally not important, except perhaps as a check on calculation accuracy. When our purpose is to predict one variable from another, it makes no difference whether we predict from a direct or inverse relationship. If you look back at Figures 13.3 and 13.4, for example, you should be able to see that one can predict grades equally well from amount of time spent studying or from amount of time spent partying.

What is important in predictive research is the numeric value of the correlation coefficient. Correlation coefficients can range from -1.00 to $+1.00$; any coefficient outside this range results from calculation error. A coefficient of -1.00 represents a perfect, inverse relationship and enables prediction with 100% accuracy. Similarly, a coefficient of +1.00 indicates a perfect, direct relationship and 100% predictive power. Such coefficients, however, are extremely rare in the behavioral sciences. A coefficient close to zero indicates no relationship at all and therefore no predictive power. The scatterplots in Figures 13.3 and 13.4 reflect coefficients of about +.75 and −.75, respectively.

More often than not, however, predictive research involves trying to construct a prediction equation, not simply determining the extent to which two variables are related. We might, for example, want to construct an equation to predict the amount of time jurors spend deliberating from the length of the trial. If we could construct such an equation, judges and other court personnel could use the equation to schedule other hearings during the deliberation. If a judge knew the jury was going to deliberate for about two hours, for example, the judge could schedule several short hearings during that time and still be ready to hear the verdict when the jurors have finished deliberating.

Regression analyses are used to construct such prediction equations. A **regression equation** is *a formula for predicting a score on the response variable from the score on the predictor variable.* One example of a regression equation with which you are probably familiar is the expression used to convert Fahrenheit temperatures into Centigrade temperatures. In general, regression equations take the form:

$$Y' = mX + b$$

where Y' is the predicted score, m is a regression coefficient, X is the score on the predictor variable, and b is a constant. For Fahrenheit to Centigrade conversions, the equation is:

$$F = 1.8C + 32$$

Predictions from a regression equation are approximate and depend on the strength of the relationship between the two variables: the stronger the relationship—the closer the correlation coefficient is to either −1.00 or +1.00—the more accurate the prediction. Fahrenheit and Centigrade temperatures are highly correlated simply because they are both highly valid and highly reliable measures of the same thing. The amount of prediction error is very small; however, it is not zero. There is always some error in any measurement, and therefore there is always some error in any prediction made from a measurement.

Estimating the margin of error associated with predictions also falls under the category of regression analysis. Although the mathematics involved are beyond the scope of this text, almost any behavioral science statistics text (such as Nowaczyk, 1988) contains the information you would need. There are also times when more than one predictor variable is used in research, such as when a college admissions board uses SAT scores, high school grades, and high school ranking to predict first-year college grades. In such instances, the analysis known as multiple regression is used. Although considerably more complicated in terms of mathematics, multiple regression relies on the same basic principles as correlation and simple regression. Kerlinger (1979) contains a very readable introduction to multiple regression.

Explanatory Research

The purpose of explanatory research is to test whether or not one or more independent variables can cause one or more dependent variables. A single explanatory research project, however, will not involve all the potential causes for a given effect, but instead will concentrate on a few. As you learned in Chapter 5, the purpose of explanatory research is to demonstrate that one variable can cause the other, not to demonstrate that the independent variable is necessarily the only cause.

Appropriate Questions for Explanatory Research

Questions for which explanatory strategies are appropriate are those in which a causal relationship is being considered. Using the same topics as in previous sections, these might include: What causes people to think about the reasons for their behavior? Do different instructions about reasonable doubt affect the length of jury deliberations? Why are my results different from those obtained in previous research? You should also recall from Chapter 5 that explanatory research requires that you be able to manipulate the independent variable and randomly assign participants to the different levels created through manipulation.

Appropriate Statistics for Explanatory Research

You have probably guessed by now that explanatory research involves the use of inferential statistics. If so, you are correct. Because experimental procedures involve creating different groups representing the different levels of the independent variable, inferential statistics are used to determine the extent to which the different groups actually perform differently on the dependent variable. If you can reject the assumption that the groups represent samples from the same population, then you can conclude that the independent variable had some effect.

Any statistical analyses designed to detect differences in central tendencies, such as t-tests and analysis of variance, are appropriate for analyzing explanatory research data. If the dependent variable is a categorical variable, such as verdicts from a jury decision, then chi-square analyses can be used to detect differences between the groups. Contrary to what you might expect, the complicated part of explanatory research is ensuring the internal validity of the research design, not the statistical procedures used to analyze the data obtained from the design.

Summary

• Research design and analyses are interdependent. How you design a project determines, in part, the statistics you will use to analyze the resulting data. However, lack of familiarity with statistical procedures may limit your ability to use a particular research design.

• Designs can be categorized in terms of their purposes: exploration, description, prediction, and explanation. Different purposes involve different designs and therefore different statistical analyses.

• Analyses for exploratory research tend to be qualitative rather than quantitative. They involve determining whether or not something has happened and are rarely complex.

• Analyses for descriptive research tend to be simple, inferential statistics that enable you to summarize the data you have obtained, usually through measures of central tendency, as well as to estimate values for the population to which you wish to generalize.

• Predictive research analyses are all based on correlational techniques in which analyses are used to determine the extent to which one variable is related to another variable. When specific predictions are required, regression analyses can be used to construct prediction equations.

• Explanatory research generally involves comparing the various groups created through the manipulation of the independent variable, and appropriate analyses include any that can be used to determine whether or not the groups created can be assumed to belong to the same overall population.

Measurement

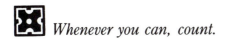 *Whenever you can, count.*

—Sir Francis Galton

Overview

The purpose of this chapter is to present an overview of measurement theory. You will learn more detail about operational definitions, reliability, validity, and techniques for determining how reliable and valid an operational definition may be. You will also learn about different levels or dimensions of measurement and the implications of these levels for statistical analyses. Finally, you will learn more about the relationship between variables and the concepts they are used to represent.

Introduction

Everybody thinks they know what measurement is. It is what you do, for example, when you use the bathroom scale to determine how much you weigh. You step onto the scale, read the number, and you have measured your weight—simple, straightforward, uncomplicated. But using that bathroom scale is only a small part of the overall measurement process, most of which occurs long before you step onto that scale. Somewhere along the line you learned about the relationship between those scale numbers and your weight; that's part of the measurement process. Also, someone designed and built the scale; that's part of the process. Someone, perhaps the same person, tested the scale for accuracy and consistency; that's part of the process as well. You may have taken the measurement process to its completion when you used the scale, but you only did the easy part.

There are a variety of different definitions of measurement, but all of them include the notion that **measurement** is *a process through which the kind or intensity of something is determined* (Adams, 1964; Allen & Yen, 1979; Anastasi, 1982). What kind or what intensity doesn't much matter; the process of measurement is the same whether you are measuring religious denomination (kind) or your weight (intensity).

The entire measurement process is a series of procedures that move us from a theoretical concept, such as weight, to a concrete representation of that concept, such as the numbers on a bathroom scale. We all think we know a great deal about measurement because we all do it every day. But we also make a great many errors in our everyday measurement. For example, I happen to own a car with a defective speedometer; it reads about 15 miles per hour faster than it should. I know about it and compensate for it. I know that a reading of 75 miles per hour is really only 60 miles per hour. Every once in a while, however, someone riding with me will look over at the speedometer and then will begin looking around for patrol cars or look at me as though I'm crazy for driving so fast. When I notice this, I try to work the speedometer's inaccuracy into the conversation. I know what the relationship between the concept of speed and my concrete representation of it is, but first-time passengers don't.

Dimensionality

Measurement is used to represent theoretical concepts, and most concepts in the behavioral sciences have more than one dimension—more than one quality that defines them. **Dimensionality** refers to *the number of different qualities inherent in a theoretical concept.* Consider, for example, the concept of social status. Some of its dimensions include occupational prestige, ethnicity (unfortunately), popularity, educational prestige, financial resources, and so on. To attempt to represent all of these dimensions in a single measurement would be impossible. Instead, those who want to measure social status select one, or a few, of the dimensions.

Regardless of which dimensions are selected, however, the researcher is measuring only a part of the overall concept. For example, you might consider financial resources to be inadequate as a sole measure of social status and decide to combine financial resources and educational prestige. Someone else may add popularity, and so on, but no one would be able to include everything. For this reason, as well as others, measurement is always incomplete. Whatever is measured is only part of the actual theoretical concept. Measurement represents concepts, but no measure can be considered to be the same thing as the concept itself.

Measurement Levels

In addition to there being any number of dimensions inherent in any theoretical concept, any dimension may be measured at one of four different levels of measurement: nominal, ordinal, interval, and ratio. Each level involves making finer distinctions within levels of the concept being measured, and each level limits the types of statistical procedures that can be used to analyze the data. The simplest level, nominal, enables one to make distinctions among categories, such as using the school one attended to measure educational prestige. The other three levels—ordinal, interval, and ratio—involve finer and finer gradations among the levels of the concept being measured.

Nominal Measurement

As you might expect from the term, **nominal measurement** involves *determining the presence or absence of a characteristic; it is naming a quality.* Because naming a quality usually involves creating categories, nominal measurement is also called categorical measurement. By naming or labeling things, we are able to distinguish among them just as your name distinguishes you from other people. Good nominal measurement, however, requires being able to categorize a person or object into mutually exclusive categories. Your name, therefore, is not a particularly good nominal measurement because other people may have the same name. Using your name does not allow one to distinguish between you and another person with the same name, although it does enable one to categorize you along with others who share your name. If we want to distinguish among individuals, a social security number is a good nominal measurement. Unless the Social Security Administration has made an error, you are the only person with your number, and one could use the number to distinguish you from everyone else.

Sometimes the label used in nominal measurement is a number, as in the example of a social security number. It distinguishes you from other people, but the number itself has no meaning beyond its use as a label. When I do research on jury decisions, for example, I usually use a "1" for a guilty verdict, a "2" for not guilty, and a "3" for not guilty by reason of insanity. The numbers only represent categories, not intensity. A verdict of "3" is no higher or lower, no more or less intense, than a verdict of "2." For this reason, nominal or categorical measurement imposes restrictions on data analyses and interpretations.

The major restriction on data analysis involves central tendency statistics or averages. The only appropriate central tendency statistic for nominal data is the **mode**—*the most frequent score in a set of scores.* Suppose, for example, that 20 people in a jury study voted guilty, 15 voted not guilty, and five voted for the insanity plea. Using the numerical assignments I described above, the modal response would be "1" (guilty).

Neither of the other two measures of central tendency—mean and median—is appropriate for nominal measures. The **mean,** *the arithmetical average of a set of scores,* is calculated by adding all the scores and dividing by the number of scores. The mean of the verdict scores described above would be $[(20 \times 1) + (15 \times 2) + (5 \times 3)] / 40 = 1.625$, a meaningless number. Because the numbers assigned to the verdict preferences are only labels, computing the mean makes no sense. The same applies to the **median,** *the 50th percentile score,* which separates the lower and upper halves of a distribution of scores. There are 40 scores in the sample verdicts, so the median would be between the 20th and 21st score—halfway between "1" and "2," or "1.5." The median, too, is meaningless for nominal measurement scales.

The above limitations do not mean that you cannot use statistical analyses on nominal data, only that you cannot use analyses that involve adding, subtracting, multiplying, or dividing the scores. You can count the number of scores, just as I did to determine the mode of the distribution. Therefore, chi-square analyses are the most appropriate statistics for such data. Essentially, chi-square analyses are used to determine whether the frequencies of scores in the categories defined by the variable match the frequencies one would expect on the basis of chance or on the basis of predictions from a theory. Nowaczyk (1988) contains a readable, more detailed description of chi-square procedures.

Ordinal Measurement

There are a variety of situations in which researchers want to do more than determine the presence or absence of a characteristic. Some assessment of intensity or degree is required; perhaps some way to order responses on a continuum is desired. **Ordinal measurement** involves *ranking or otherwise determining an order of intensity for a quality.* Letting people know you are in the top 10% of your class, for example, is making use of an ordinal measurement scale; you are reporting your rank within your graduating class.

Ordinal measurement identifies the relative intensity of a characteristic, but it does not reflect any level of absolute intensity. If you are in the top 10% of your class, for example, I know you are doing better than most of the students in your class (congratulations, by the way). But your class ranking doesn't enable me to determine how well you would do at, say, Harvard, or at Basket-Weaving State College, unless you happen to be attending one of those institutions. I also cannot determine how much better you are than the bottom 90% of your class. Ordinal measurement is like the place finishes at a horse race: the winner might be barely a nose ahead of the second-place finisher or might have won by 20 lengths. For this reason, comparisons among ordinal values are somewhat limited, but not as limited as those among nominal values.

The limitations on ordinal data result from the fact that ordinal measurement involves ranking the scores. Calculating a mean for a set of ordinal scores is about as nonsensical as it is for nominal scores. The mean for ordinal scores is the center of the ordinal scale, which doesn't change. If there are ten scores, for example, then the mean of those ranks is always going to be 5.5; if there are 20 scores, the mean is 10.5, and so on. In this case the mean is determined by the number of scores in the set, not the values of the scores that were ranked. Chi-square analyses can be applied to ordinal data, but that involves treating the ordinal ranks as though they were nominal categories. It can be done, and the results can make sense, but most computer programs limit the number of categories for this analysis to ten or less.

More generally, any statistical technique that involves comparisons on the basis of the median are appropriate for ordinal data. Witte (1980) is a good source for such analyses, as is Conover (1980). Conover's book is more comprehensive, but it is also more technical. Whether the purpose of your research is to compare groups of scores or to examine relationships through correlation, you are restricted to using statistical analyses designed for medians.

Interval Measurement

When ordinal measurement is insufficient, researchers attempt to attain an interval level of measurement. **Interval measurement** involves *a continuum composed of equally spaced intervals.* The Fahrenheit and Centigrade temperature scales are good examples of interval measurements. A change of one degree anywhere along the continuum reflects an equal amount of change in heat; the interval "degree" is equal along the entire scale. With interval data, we can compare different scores more specifically than we can with either nominal or ordinal measures. Recall that with ordinal measurement you know that a value of 5 is different from a value of 10, but you don't know how much different. With interval measurement, you know that a value of 5 is exactly five units different from a value of 10, the same difference as that between 10 and 15.

What we do not know when we use interval measurement, however, is exactly what one interval represents in terms of the quality being measured. For example, the most well-known use of interval measurement in the behavioral sciences is the IQ score or intelligence quotient, even though there is some disagreement about its status as an interval measure (Anastasi, 1982). Although it is not possible to determine exactly how much intelligence is represented by a single IQ point, it is possible to make comparisons between scores. The difference between the scores 100 and 110, for example, reflects the same amount of intelligence (whatever that is) as does the difference between 120 and 130. How much intelligence is represented by ten points is unknown, but ten points is ten points anywhere along the scale.

This limitation of interpreting interval measures—not knowing the meaning of one unit—results from the fact that interval scales involve arbitrary numbers that represent anchor points on a continuum. For the Centigrade and Fahrenheit scales, the arbitrary anchors are the temperatures at which water changes states (freezes and boils): 0 and 100 degrees Centigrade and 32 and 212 degrees Fahrenheit, respectively. Similarly, on the IQ scale the arbitrary anchor point chosen was 100, a point that purportedly reflects an intellectual capacity consistent with one's physical age.

Despite the arbitrary anchor values used for interval measurements, there are few limitations on the types of analyses that can be applied to interval data—provided, of course, that the analyses are appropriate for the questions being asked. If we wish to determine relationships between variables, correlational analyses are appropriate; if we wish to examine differences among groups, any statistic that involves comparing means, such as analysis of variance, is appropriate.

Although the arbitrary values for interval data do not restrict the statistics we may use to analyze the data, the arbitrariness of the anchors do limit the ways in which we may interpret statistical results. Suppose, for example, that you had one group with an average IQ of 150 and another with an average IQ of 75. Statistical analyses indicated that this difference was reliable, and you would like to interpret it. It is, of course, true that the mean IQ of one group is twice that of the other, but that does not mean you can claim that one group is twice as intelligent as the other. Because the numbers of an interval scale are arbitrary, it is never clear exactly how much intensity is reflected by any given number on the scale.

Ratio Measurement

In order that numbers used to measure a variable can be interpreted without restrictions, you must use a ratio level of measurement. **Ratio measurement** involves *a continuum that includes a value of zero representing the absence of a quality.* When physicists measure temperature, for example, they use the Kelvin scale, on which a value of zero represents the complete absence of heat. There are no negative values on the Kelvin scale because there cannot be less heat than no heat at all. Thus, 100 degrees on the Kelvin scale represents twice as much heat as 50 degrees. The same cannot be said for either the Fahrenheit or Centigrade scales. That the latter two scales contain a zero point does not make them ratio scales because the zero points on those two scales do not represent the absence of heat.

In the behavioral sciences, very few measurements conform to the requirements for a ratio scale, and what few there are have been constructed for the purpose of providing examples of ratio scales. Income, for example, has a zero point that represents the absence of earnings. Therefore, someone who earns $20,000 has an income twice that of someone who earns $10,000. However, income is usually used to represent some aspect of socioeconomic status, and when it does, it no longer conforms to ratio-level requirements for measurement: someone with zero income does not have zero socioeconomic status. If you are fortunate enough to have occasion to use a ratio level of measurement in your research, there will be no restrictions on your choice of data analyses or interpretations; you will also be the first person in the behavioral sciences to attain a meaningful ratio level of measurement.

Before you read on, see Box 14.1 for a summary of our discussion of measurement levels.

Reliability

Knowing what level of measurement you are using is only part of the measurement process. Another part involves determining how reliable, or consistent, the measure is. A variety of different techniques are designed for such purposes, and

BOX 14.1   Summary of Measurement Levels

Level	What's Measured	Example	Central Tendency
Nominal	Distinctions	Guilty/not guilty	Mode
Ordinal	Relative position	Socioeconomic status	Median
Interval	Arbitrary amounts	Intelligence quotient	Mean
Ratio	Actual amounts	Age	Mean

all of them rely on the extent to which one version of the measure is related to another version of the measure.

The extent to which two things are related can be measured through correlations (see Chapter 13)—statistical procedures that estimate the extent to which changes in one variable are associated with changes in another. A positive correlation coefficient means the two variables are directly related, a zero coefficient indicates no relationship, and a negative correlation indicates an inverse relationship. When assessing the reliability of a measure, correlations involve different versions of the measure instead of different variables. What follows is a brief description of the various ways in which such assessments can be accomplished.

Interrater Reliability

Whenever subjective judgments or ratings made by more than one person are part of the measurement process, the appropriate technique for determining reliability is interrater reliability. As implied in the name, **interrater reliability** is *the consistency with which raters or observers make judgments.* Using a very simple example, interrater reliability would involve the extent to which you and a friend agree about the temperature after reading the same thermometer. If you and your friend write down your daily temperature readings for a couple of weeks, the two sets of readings could be correlated. The higher the correlation coefficient (I'm assuming it would be positive), the greater the reliability of your measurements.

Another example can be drawn from studies in which physical attractiveness is measured. Such studies typically involve two or more raters making judgments about physical attractiveness on a scale from 1 to 10 (Adams, 1977). Each rater assigns a scale number to each person being rated, and interrater reliability is estimated by correlating the ratings from one judge with those from another. If the measurement process is reliable, there should be a high, positive correlation between any two judges.

Proper use of interrater reliability techniques requires observers or raters to make independent ratings. If another rater merely copies the ratings you make, for example, all that you would be testing is the other rater's ability to copy correctly; that's not reliability. Collaboration among observers or judges is not allowed. Of course, collaboration does not have to be as obvious as copying one another's ratings; even minimal discussion will destroy the independence of the ratings. Raters should make their ratings as though they were taking a final exam:

no copying, no idea sharing, no peeking. Collaborative ratings tend to appear to be more consistent, but the consistency is artificial.

Test-Retest Reliability

One of the most readily apparent ways to estimate reliability is **test-retest reliability**—*consistency estimated by comparing two or more repeated administrations of the measurement.* Despite its name, the test-retest technique does not require using a formal test as a measure; indeed, it is based on the same principle as that involved in interrater reliability. Instead of repeating measurements by using more than one rater, test-retest reliability involves repeating the measure simply by making the measurement again after some period of time has elapsed. One required assumption is that the characteristic being measured does not change over the time period; another assumption is that the time period is long enough so that you can rule out participants' memory as the basis for the second set of scores. Test-retest reliability, like interrater reliability, is estimated with correlations: the correlation between the two administrations of the measure is the estimate of reliability.

Suppose you could not get anyone to help you measure physical attractiveness; you were the only available rater. You could estimate the reliability of your ratings by making the ratings twice. You would need to ensure that you waited long enough so that you could not remember the first rating you made for any given participant, and you would have to make sure that none of the participants drastically changed their appearance, but you could use test-retest techniques.

When the measurement does involve a formal test, another prerequisite for using the test-retest technique is the absence of practice effects; that is, taking the first test should not make participants more knowledgeable or more aware of what's being measured. Because test-retest reliability involves assessing relative change between the two administrations, practice effects will undermine the basis of the reliability assessment.

Alternate Forms Reliability

When test-retest reliability is not possible, either due to practice effects, rapid changes in the characteristic being measured, or extended memory for previous responses, the appropriate technique is alternate forms reliability. **Alternate forms reliability** involves *comparing two different but equivalent versions of the same measure.* The name of this procedure is doubly descriptive, for there are two different ways to implement it. One procedure involves giving the same group of people different versions of the measure at different times; this is analogous to the test-retest procedure. The other procedure involves giving the same measure to different groups of people.

When it is possible to use different forms of a measure for the same group of people, scores from one version of the measure are correlated with scores from the other. The procedure is exactly the same as that for test-retest reliability, except that different versions of the measure are repeated. The required assumption is that the two different forms are, in fact, different but also equivalent insofar as they both measure the same concept. Different-but-equivalent forms might involve merely changing the order of items in a multiple item measure, or it may involve constructing entirely different items. Different addition items on a math test, for example, would be equivalent, but addition problems on one version and division problems on the other would not be equivalent. Similarly, differently phrased questions about attitudes toward a single topic would be equivalent, but questions about two different topics, such as sex education on one form and math education on the other, would not.

Sometimes, it is not possible to measure the same group of people more than once. In such situations, dividing a single group into two distinct subgroups may serve the same purpose. If, for example, you gave the same test to everyone in the group and then randomly divided the group into two subgroups, you could compare scores between the groups to estimate reliability. Instead of correlational analyses, however, you would have to use means, standard deviations, or some other distributional descriptors to determine the extent to which the two groups scored the same. You could, for example, use analysis of variance or chi-square for the comparison. If you divide the group randomly, there should be no difference between the two subgroups, and any difference that does emerge may reflect a lack of reliability.

Split-Half Reliability

There may be times when you cannot measure the same people more than once and cannot get enough participants to divide them into subgroups large enough to run the appropriate statistical analyses. If the measurement you are using contains more than one item, such as some sort of questionnaire, then the split-half technique can be used to assess reliability. **Split-half reliability** involves *creating two scores for each participant by dividing the measure into equivalent halves and correlating the halves.* Each half of the measure is then treated as though it were a complete version of the measure. Essentially, the split-half technique involves creating equivalent forms by dividing the measure, rather than the group of participants, in half. The scores on the two halves are then correlated, just as with the alternate forms procedure. Again, the higher the correlation, the greater the reliability.

The major prerequisite for the split-half procedure is the ability to create equivalent halves of the measure. One way to do this is to separate the odd- and even-numbered items. Note, however, that this is only one way to split the measure. Ideally you should create and correlate all possible halves of the measure, and then use the average correlation coefficient as your measure of reliability. This process can be incredibly cumbersome and tedious. A ten-item measure, for example, can be split into half 252 different ways. To create and correlate all those possible halves would take more time than it's worth. Even if you automated the procedure with a computer, you would still end up using a great deal of time and effort, not to mention paper for all the printouts.

Fortunately, Rulon (1932) developed a formula that enables researchers to split a measure only once and obtain an estimate of the average correlation that would result from the longer procedure of creating all possible halves. Rulon's formula is an inferential statistic. By calculating a correlation coefficient from a single split-half, it enables you to estimate the average correlation coefficient you would obtain from all split-halves. As with other statistical procedures we've discussed, providing details or formulas for Rulon's procedure is beyond the scope of this book. The procedure is not all that complicated, however, and Rulon's article is not difficult to read and understand. But if you cannot find a copy of the Rulon article, most measurement textbooks, such as Allen and Yen (1979), contain a description of the procedure.

Item-Total Reliability

When you use a measurement that includes more than one item, it is often necessary to determine the reliability of the individual items. If you develop a questionnaire to measure attitudes toward insanity pleas, for example, you should determine the reliability of each item. If you can be confident about the reliability of each of the items, then you can also be confident about the reliability of the entire measure.

Item-total reliability is *an estimate of the consistency of one item with respect to other items on a measure.* As you might expect, the procedure involves correlating the score on one item with the total score on the rest of the items. The total score represents "everything else" being measured, and the item-total correlation is therefore a measure of the relationship between the single item and "everything else."

If a measure contains a large number of items, calculating all of the item-total correlations can be a very time-consuming and laborious process, even if you use a computer for all of the calculations. Kuder and Richardson (1937) developed a shortcut formula that can be applied to the entire measurement, much like Rulon's (1932) shortcut for split-half reliability. It is known as the Kuder-Richardson 20 formula and can be found in their original article and in most measurement textbooks. Anastasi (1982), for example, includes the Kuder-Richardson 20 formula as well as alternative formulae for various measurement levels. Also, many software packages, such as SAS and SPSS, include the procedure.

The result of the Kuder-Richardson 20 formula is a single correlation coefficient that is an estimate of the average of all of the coefficients that would be obtained from a true item-total procedure. It is an inferential statistic. If the correlation is high—.80 or higher is usually sufficient—then all of the items are reliable and the entire instrument is reliable. If the coefficient obtained from the formula is low, then at least one of the items is unreliable, and you would have to examine each of them to discover the unreliable one(s). That examination would, of course, involve calculating separate item-total correlations for each item.

Refer to Box 14.2 for a summary of reliability procedures.

BOX 14.2 Summary of Reliability Procedures

Procedures	Conditions	Analyses
Interrater	Multiple judges	Correlation between raters
Test-retest	No practice effect	Correlation between scores
Alternate forms		
2 forms, 1 group	Equivalent forms	Correlation between scores
1 form, 2 groups	Random assignment	Between-group differences
Split-half	Equivalent items	Rulon's split-half
Item-total	Multiple items	Kuder-Richardson 20

Validity

Reliability is a necessary condition for quality measurement, but it alone is not sufficient. Reliability is only the extent to which the measure is consistent, and before accepting and using any measure, you must also make sure it is valid. Validity, you should remember, refers to the extent to which a measure actually measures what it is supposed to measure—whether, for example, a questionnaire about the insanity plea really measures people's attitudes toward the insanity plea. Just as there are different ways to estimate reliability, there are different techniques for estimating validity. Which of the following techniques you use depends on both the specific requirements of the study you are doing and the facilities you have available.

Face Validity

Suppose your instructor gave you a test in your research methods class, but the test contained only differential calculus problems. You would probably complain, claiming the test was not fair, and you might even contend that the test was invalid. You would be using face validity as the basis of your complaint. **Face validity** is *consensus that a measure represents a particular concept.* It is sometimes called expert validity or validation by consensus. When face validity involves assessing whether a measure deals with a representative sample of the various aspects of the concept, it is also called content validity. Whatever it is called, it is based on the notion that a good measure should look like a good measure to those who are in a position to know; those whose opinions matter should agree that a measure is measuring what it's supposed to measure.

Face validity is a rather limited test of validity. It is, after all, not much different from claiming "My mother said so," except that "an expert" replaces "my mother" in the claim. Although appeals to personal authority are not sufficient grounds for argument in a scientific approach, an appeal to expert authority can be used as a starting point in the process of evaluating a measure's validity. If a researcher cannot demonstrate face validity, the researcher is likely to have a difficult time convincing others that a measure is valid.

Concurrent Validity

Just as face validity relies on authoritative experts, concurrent validity relies on authoritative measurements to establish validity. **Concurrent validity** involves *comparing a new measure to an existing, valid measure.* The difference between concurrent and face validity is that you rely on an existing, valid measure instead of the consensus of experts; you rely on data instead of opinion. Concurrent validity is a specific form of criterion validity; the existing measure is the criterion against which the new measure is validated. The comparison is usually accomplished by correlating the old and new measures in much the same way that alternate form reliability is determined. Indeed, assessing concurrent validity is one of the major starting points for most predictive research projects. If you develop a new measure of intelligence, for example, concurrent validity could be assessed by correlating your new measure with either the Stanford-Binet or Wechsler Adult Intelligence Test. The higher the correlation coefficient, the more valid your new measure.

It is not too difficult to understand the major limitation of concurrent validity: the new measure you are examining cannot be any more valid than the old measure you have selected for comparison. If the validity of the existing measure was established through face validity, for example, then your use of concurrent validity is actually an approximation of face validity. It is always important, therefore, to determine how the validity of an existing measure was established before using it as a comparison in concurrent validation.

Predictive Validity

Predictive validity is another specific form of criterion validity, except that **predictive validity** *is established by comparing a measure with the future occurrence of another, highly valid measure.* The most well-known example of predictive validity is college entrance examinations and their ability to predict first-year performance in terms of college grades. For predictive validity, you simply use the new measure, wait for an opportunity to use the comparison measure, and then compare the two. The comparison measure is usually a very different form of measurement, such as grades versus a multiple choice test, or it is an unquestionable standard to which all other, similar measures are compared (such as grades for college performance again).

The same limitations for concurrent validity apply to predictive validity procedures: how the validity of the comparison measure was established limits the validity of the new measure. Usually, however, the limitation is not as important because the new measure is being developed specifically to predict the existing measure; that is, the existing measure is considered valid by definition. With college entrance examinations, for example, grades are by definition valid measures of college success. Whether or not that should be the case is an entirely different question. If another standard is chosen, then the new measure is compared to that.

Construct Validity

Construct validity involves *determining the extent to which a measure represents concepts it should represent and does not represent concepts it should not represent.* It is similar to an essay question in which you are asked to compare and contrast two different but possibly related concepts. Construct validity involves both making comparisons between a new measure and existing, valid measures of the same concept and contrasting the new measure with existing, valid measures of a different concept. It also involves testing the extent to which comparisons and contrasts are affected by the method used for the measure (Campbell & Fiske, 1959).

The first part of construct validity is called **convergent validity**—*the extent to which a measure correlates with existing measures of the same concept.* It is similar to concurrent validity but involves one important difference: convergent validity includes comparisons with more than one existing measure. A new measure of college success, for example, would be compared not only to grades but to employment after graduation, perceived success, and so on. Ideally, the existing measures should involve at least two different measurement methods, one of which is the same method as the new measure. For example, a new questionnaire on attitudes toward insanity pleas should correlate highly with both an existing, valid questionnaire about insanity pleas and participants' verdicts for a simulated trial in which insanity was a plea.

Using different measurement methods for the existing standards enables you to test the extent to which the correlations between the new and existing measures are related to the type of measurement method used. Two questionnaires about the insanity plea, for example, would be somewhat correlated by virtue of the fact that they are both questionnaires. If the new measure correlates with both another questionnaire and some different method, such as simulated verdicts, then you can be more comfortable with the new measure's validity. It's the same principle behind using multiple choice and essay questions on the same examination: some people might do well with one or the other simply because they know how to use that particular answer format, but a student who does well on both formats is more likely to know the subject matter.

The second part of construct validity is called **divergent validity**—*the extent to which a measure does not correlate with measures of a different concept.* Again using a questionnaire about the insanity plea as an example, testing divergent validity might involve contrasting the new measure with a valid questionnaire about the effectiveness of parole procedures. As a measure of attitudes toward the insanity plea, the new measure should not correlate highly with a measure of attitudes toward parole; they are two different concepts. Using different measurement methods for the contrasting measures again ensures that any lack of correlation does not result from different methods per se. If you were to include all of the above measures in the same study and were to calculate all of the correlations, you might obtain the correlation matrix presented in Table 14.1, which illustrates results indicating that the new measure is a valid measure of attitudes toward the insanity plea.

Table 14.1 Correlation coefficients for high construct validity

	New NGI	Old NGI	Verdict	Parole Q	Parole D
New NGI*	1.000	.950	.890	.216	.220
Old NGI	.950	1.000	.900	.116	.198
Verdict	.890	.900	1.000	.105	.026
Parole Questionnaire	.216	.116	.105	1.000	.960
Parole Decision	.220	.198	.026	.960	1.000

*Not guilty by reason of insanity

Epistemic Correlation

At the beginning of this chapter (and in Chapter 2 as well) we learned that a measure represents, but is not the same thing as, a theoretical concept. There may be several different dimensions of a concept, of which the measure taps only some. There are also many different ways to operationally define a theoretical concept, and no measure can tap all of them. Therefore, any measure, no matter how valid and reliable, represents only a portion of the total theoretical concept.

Any score obtained from a measure contains two components: a "true" score component and an "error" score component. The true component refers to the validity of the measure; it is the part of the measure that is doing what it is sup-posed to do. The error component reflects all of the things that can go wrong in the measurement process. The fewer things that go wrong, the smaller the error component. It is an accepted axiom of measurement theory, however, that the error component is never equal to zero; there is always, without exception, some error involved in any measure.

The theoretical relationship between the true component of a measure and the concept it represents is called an **epistemic correlation.** Despite its name, an epistemic correlation cannot be calculated; it can only be logically determined. Consider, for example, annual income as a measure of social status: even though we all know that a higher income indicates a higher social status, it includes only one dimension of the concept. Thus, within certain limitations, we know that there is a positive epistemic correlation between income and social status. We cannot calculate that coefficient, but we can be reasonably certain that it is positive.

Before we could analyze data obtained in a study using income as a measure of social status, however, we would also need to know what level of measurement—nominal, ordinal, interval, or ratio—annual income represents. Annual income obviously cannot represent a ratio level because zero income does not reflect zero social status. Once you have given the matter some thought, you will realize that income probably does not represent an interval level of measurement either. To merit interval level status, an income change of, say, $10,000 would have to represent the same amount of change in social status at any amount of income; clearly, this is not so. A change from zero income to $10,000 represents a considerably larger increase in social status than does a change from $1,000,000 to $1,010,000. The best we can do with income as a measure of social status is declare it an ordinal scale.

On the other hand, the very same measure—income—could be an interval or perhaps a ratio scale if used to represent a different theoretical concept. If, for example, we used income to represent contribution to the tax base, it may be an interval level of measurement. Although an economist might disagree about its being at the interval level of measurement, the point is that the epistemic correlation must be evaluated before we can analyze data. Even though we cannot calculate it, we must make a logical decision, based on the concept itself, about the correlation between the concept and its measure. Understanding theoretical concepts and the measures used to represent them are equally important parts of good behavioral-science research.

Summary

• Measurement is the process through which we translate the kind or intensity of a theoretical concept into a concrete variable. Most behavioral-science concepts include more than one dimension, not all of which can be easily included in a single variable.

• There are four different levels of measurement, all but one of which involve limitations on data analyses, interpretations, or both.

• The nominal level of measurement is the simplest and involves categorical distinctions of kind. Statistical analyses involving frequencies or the mode as the central tendency are the only appropriate analyses.

• The ordinal level of measurement involves degrees of intensity and reflects only relative amounts. Frequency analyses may be appropriate, but central tendency analyses based on the median are more likely to be the best analyses for such measures.

• The interval level of measurement represents intensity on an equal-interval continuum. The continuum, however, is composed of arbitrarily assigned values and does not contain an anchor for the absence of the quality being measured. Although there are no limitations on appropriate analyses, interpretations should not include multiplicative comparisons such as "twice as much."

• Ratio levels of measurement are extremely rare—perhaps nonexistent—in behavioral sciences mainly because the zero point of the measure must represent the absence of the quality being measured. If achieved, however, there are no restrictions on analyses or interpretations.

• Reliability involves the extent to which a measure is consistent, and it can be estimated through a variety of different techniques. All of these techniques, however, generally involve comparisons between different versions of the measure.

• Interrater reliability can be assessed when there is more than one person making ratings or judgments. It is accomplished by correlating one rater's scores with another rater's scores.

• Test-retest reliability involves presenting the same measure to the same people at two different times and then correlating the scores. Alternate forms reliability involves presenting the same people with two different versions of the same test and again correlating the scores. Alternatively, the same test can be given to two randomly divided subgroups and then compared with appropriate central tendency analyses.

• Split-half reliability involves comparing random halves of a multiple-item measure using a formula invented by Rulon. An alternative for multiple-item measures is item-total reliability, which involves comparing each item score with the total score using the formula invented by Kuder and Richardson.

• Validity refers to the extent to which a measure is related to its theoretical concept. Face validity refers to consensus about the relationship, whereas concurrent validity refers to the correlation between a new measure and one that has otherwise been demonstrated to be valid. Concurrent validity is one form of criterion validity. Another form of criterion validity, predictive validity, refers to the correlation between a new measure and a standard that is, by definition, valid.

• Construct validity refers to multiple comparisons with existing, valid measures of the same concept and multiple contrasts with valid measures of a different concept. The new measure should correlate highly with the former measure and not at all with the latter measure.

• An epistemic correlation is the derived relationship between a measure and its theoretical concept. It cannot be calculated but must be used to determine the level of the new measure.

CHAPTER FIFTEEN

Scaling

*The elaboration of theoretical constructs . . .
entails an obligation to measure them.*

—Scott (1968, p. 204)

Overview

The purpose of this chapter is to provide the information you need in order to use and construct measurement scales. You will learn when using scales may be appropriate, how to assess the reliability and validity of an existing scale, and information about various formats for constructing scales. You will also learn about the different types of scales commonly used in the behavioral sciences and ways to administer them. Finally, you will learn a little more about the problems inherent in doing research on multidimensional concepts, including sources to consult for existing scales.

Introduction

Because no measure is perfectly reliable or perfectly valid, we often use some sort of triangulation process to "zero in" on the concept we are trying to measure. In my high school physics class, for example, we always made three measurements and used the average of those three measurements as the recorded data value. The reason for using three measures was not apparent then, but it is now: using the same measure three times and recording the average increases the overall reliability of measurement; an average reduces random error.

In the behavioral sciences, however, we rarely have the luxury of making the same measurement more than once. Putting a ball bearing on a balance three times is very different from asking a person to answer the same question three times; the latter usually involves little more than testing someone's memory of their first answer. Similarly, measuring the crime rate in a city three times requires the assumption that the rate does not change over time, which is not a safe assumption.

Instead of making the measurement three times, we usually measure the same concept in several different ways. One way to accomplish this is to use a **scale**—*a measurement instrument that contains a number of slightly different operational definitions of the same concept.* If you have ever completed a questionnaire that seemed to contain many similar questions, you have first-hand experience with a scale. Simply generating a number of seemingly redundant questions, however, does not a scale make.

The key to the notion of a scale is the phrase "slightly different operational definitions." Each item on a scale is a different operational definition of the same concept, and combining the items into a scale allow us to "zero in" on the concept from a variety of different directions. All of the general measurement principles outlined in Chapter 14 also apply to scales. For example, scales can operate at any of the four different levels of measurement—nominal, ordinal, interval, or ratio—and all must be tested for reliability and validity. Scales, however, usually provide several advantages over single-item measures; one such advantage is a higher level of measurement than any of the individual items that together constitute the scale itself.

Common Aspects of Scales

Perhaps the best way to learn how to evaluate scales is to learn how to generate a scale yourself. For that reason, we begin with ways to generate scale items. Then, after you understand how to construct a scale, you will find it considerably easier to learn about how to evaluate someone else's scale. There are a number of different ways to generate scale items, and they differ as a function of the type of scale being constructed. Details about item generation will be covered shortly, but first we need to consider some common aspects of all forms of scales.

Face Validity of Scale Items

First among the general issues surrounding scale item generation or evaluation is the face validity of items. Although face validity is not a necessary characteristic of every item on a scale, at least some of the items must demonstrate face validity. On the other hand, there is no reason to include items that are clearly not face valid, no matter how interesting they may seem to be. The general (if ungrammatical) rule of thumb for generating scale items is the same as that for generating invitations to a family reunion: if it ain't related, it ain't included.

Instructions for Completing Scales

Face validity ensures that you and other behavioral scientists will understand the items you have included on a scale, but that doesn't mean respondents will know what they are being asked to do. The most elegant or the most face-valid scale will be useless if the people who are to complete it cannot understand the instructions or don't know what's being asked of them.

Any instruction about how to complete the scale should be worded clearly and simply. If at all possible, provide examples of anything you want the respondents to do. Similarly, items that make up the scale must be clear and understandable. Questions that require information unavailable to respondents, for example, cannot be either reliable or valid because the respondent would only be guessing. If the people who will complete your scale are not likely to know the size of the federal deficit, for example, it makes little sense to ask them whether they think it's too large. Similarly, asking for information respondents may consider to be none of your business is likely to lead to a number of missing, or intentionally inaccurate, responses. If you are trying to measure honesty, don't ask people how often they cheat on their income tax returns unless you are sure they will provide an honest response. Apply the rules of ethics discussed in Chapter 3; don't ask respondents to reveal anything you would not be willing to reveal.

Item Bias

Perhaps the most important consideration common to all scale items is **item bias**—*the extent to which the wording or placement of an item affects someone's response.* An item may be biased for a variety of reasons; some are more subtle than others. Perhaps the best (worst?) example of a biased item comes from a survey sent to me by my former congressional representative. The survey was devoted to defense spending, and the first item was "Do you favor increasing defense spending to prevent Communist aggression?" This item has just about everything wrong with it that could possibly be wrong.

First, the item is a **double-barreled item**—*a single item that contains two or more questions or statements.* The item raises two issues, one concerning increases in defense spending and another about Communist aggression. Some respondents are likely to have opposing views on the two topics and would find it difficult to respond. They might, for example, oppose Communist aggression but not wish to increase defense spending. You might also have noticed the item was emotionally worded. Communist aggression is an "emotional flag"—something few American citizens would advocate, regardless of their political views or opinions about defense spending. The item is also ambiguous; there is no indication of how much of an increase the respondent is being asked to advocate or reject. Similarly, there is no indication of the type of Communist aggression to be prevented. All of these forms of bias make it extremely difficult for someone to respond to the item in any manner other than without thinking about it.

Perhaps the most important among the item's shortcomings is the fact that few, if any, respondents would have access to the kind of information required to make a rational decision. For example, not many people have an idea about how much money is currently being expended for defense, let alone that amount of defense spending set aside specifically for preventing Communist aggression. Nor do many people have any idea how much more money might be needed to prevent Communist aggression.

Finally, the placement of the item as the first in a series about defense spending introduces bias throughout the series. The implicit link between increases in defense spending and Communist aggression make it difficult for respondents to say no to other items about increasing defense spending. Once someone has agreed with the notion that increasing defense spending is a good idea for preventing Communist aggression, for example, that person will find it difficult to disagree with other items about increasing defense spending. I was not at all surprised when the representative voted in favor of all increases in defense spending, including "Star Wars," claiming he was simply doing what his constituents had requested. Heavily biased scale items may be politically useful, but they have no place in good behavioral research.

Formats for Scale Items

Just as there are a number of different types of item bias, there are a number of different formats in which to present an item. The simplest of these is the **forced choice format**—*a response format in which respondents must choose between discrete and mutually exclusive options.* The following item is an example:

Should defense spending be increased? Yes   No

The respondent is forced to choose between increasing spending or not, hence the name "forced choice." The forced choice format is most appropriate when responses can be easily categorized.

More often than not, however, responses are not so easily categorized. One's response to changing defense spending, for example, may be more a matter of how much to change, rather than simply to change or not to change. In such cases, the graphic format is the most widely used response format. The **graphic format** involves *presenting a continuum on which respondents make a choice.* Illustrated below are a number of different ways to use a graphic format:

What is your opinion of changing the level of defense spending?

1	2	3	4	5
It should definitely be decreased		It should remain the same		It should definitely be increased

The respondent is still required to make a choice, but the choices reflect positions on a continuum. It is even possible for someone to choose a position between 3 and 4, and in such cases a graphic format can include "markers" between the points, such as:

What is your opinion of changing the level of defense spending?

1.....................2.....................3.....................4.....................5

It should	It should	It should
definitely	remain the	definitely
be decreased	same	be increased

Other versions of the graphic format include presenting only the labels for the endpoints of the continuum, presenting additional labels along the continuum, including more numbers along the continuum, and so forth. Regardless of the variations in its appearance, the graphic format reflects a continuum of responses. The respondent is presented with a graded choice rather than a forced choice. Whatever version of the graphic format you use, however, you should be sure the endpoints reflect legitimate responses. The extreme endpoints should not be so extreme that no one would consider them to be potential responses. Of course, adequate instructions are also necessary. You might ask respondents to circle the number, or draw a vertical line through the point, that best represents their opinion.

Providing response alternatives in a graphic format is not the only way to present a continuum of responses. The itemized format can be used to accomplish the same purpose. Instead of presenting a continuum of responses, the **itemized format** involves *presenting a continuum of statements representing various choice options.* Each statement is a response, and together the statements reflect a continuum of potential responses. The graphic item illustrated above could be presented through the itemized format as follows:

( ) Decreasing the level of defense spending is absolutely essential to the well-being of our country.
( ) Keeping defense spending at its current level is the best thing to do right now.
( ) Increasing the level of spending is absolutely essential to the well-being of our country.

Note that the first item represents one extreme, the second item represents a neutral point, and the third item represents an extreme that is the opposite of the first. Of course, more than three items would normally be included in an itemized format, but three are enough for illustration purposes. Instructions for the illustrated items would include asking respondents to place a mark in the parentheses corresponding to the item that best represents their opinions. The essence of a graphic format—a continuum of responses—is presented with a series of statements. Respondents must choose one of the statements—they cannot choose between two represented positions—and so the items must be very carefully chosen to represent an adequate gradation of responses.

Although the itemized format seems to be relatively straightforward, it is often very difficult to generate a series of statements that reflect a continuum without including some double-barreled items. The key is to ensure that only one aspect of the issue varies from statement to statement. You would not want to include, for example, the notion of protecting the country under the "pro-increase" items and include the notion of social welfare under the "anti-increase" items. When using the itemized format, you need to be sure that neither the opening statement nor the response items are double-barreled.

Sometimes it makes sense to ask respondents to weigh the relative importance of specific issues. The **comparative format** involves *making direct comparisons among various positions*. One example of the comparative format, again using defense spending, appears below:

Which of the following ways to increase the defense budget is most preferable?

a. increa e the size of the national debt
b. increaue income taxes
c. increase other types of taxes
d. decrease money spent on social welfare programs
e. I prefer not to increase the defense budget

In another version of this format, respondents could be asked to rank the presented alternatives from most to least preferable. Regardless of which version is used, however, the comparisons must be distinct and legitimate.

We've only briefly touched on a few of the many different types of item formats used in research. The format you choose in constructing a scale depends on the respondents to whom you intend to administer the scale and the concept you want to measure with the scale. Although there are no clear-cut rules, whichever item format is likely to be best understood is the format you should choose. Such a choice requires pretesting to determine the clarity of the items. It is also preferable to use items that reflect the highest possible level of measurement, provided that level makes sense for the item. You would not want to try to use an ordinal level of measurement and a graphic format, for example, with an item that merely asks respondents to indicate their gender.

Just as items should be chosen specifically for research purposes, the manner in which you combine those items should match your research purposes. For this reason, some of the major types of scales currently used are presented below. As you familiarize yourself with them, think about how you might use them in a research project of interest to you.

Thurstone Scales

One of the levels of measurement described in Chapter 14 is interval measurement, a level at which values on a continuum represent equal amounts of a single conceptual dimension. Although interval measurement is extremely difficult to attain with a single item—equal spacing of alternatives in a graphic format is not the same as equal intervals—it can be approximated with a scale constructed using the Thurstone technique. Invented by Thurstone and his colleagues (1929; 1931; Thurstone & Chave, 1929), its formal name is the **equal-appearing interval**

technique; *it contains a series of items, each of which represents a particular point value on the continuum being measured.* It is an itemized format scale designed so that the items reflect specific points on the response continuum.

Item Generation in Thurstone Scales

A few years ago, the president of the college at which I was teaching decided to allow the campus police to carry handguns. Because the police had never carried handguns before, the decision upset many students. My students wanted to measure attitudes toward the decision, and they did so using the equal-appearing interval technique. The first stage in creating a Thurstone scale is to generate a pool of potential scale items. Each item should be a statement reflecting a particular point of view relevant to the concept under consideration, and the pool of items should reflect the entire range of views included in the concept. The number of items required for this initial pool varies but should be somewhere between 100 and 200 items. If 200 items seems like a lot of items to generate, keep in mind you will use a team of people to generate them rather than doing it all yourself.

For example, 24 students were involved in generating the pool of 230 items for the handgun survey. After generating the items, every student independently rated all 230 items on an 11-point scale ranging from very much in favor of campus police carrying handguns (assigned a value of 1) to very much against campus police carrying handguns (assigned a value of 11). The same 24 students (four more than the recommended minimum of 20) who generated the items also judged the items. The requirement of at least 20 judges is one of the major drawbacks to the Thurstone technique, but it can usually be overcome. The important parts of the item generation process are to obtain a pool that reflects the range of the continuum and to make sure the judges are making their judgments independently.

Item Analysis and Selection in Thurstone Scales

After all of the items have been generated and judged, the scale values assigned by the judges for each item are tabulated and the median value used as the actual scale value of the item. In the handgun project, there were 24 judges, which meant that the value halfway between the 12th and 13th values was the median. The median, you recall, is the 50th percentile of a distribution of scores. You must also calculate the semi-interquartile range, a measure of variability or degree of dispersion. The semi-interquartile (S-I) range is calculated by determining the scale values at the 75th and 25th percentiles and dividing the differences between the values by two:

$$\text{S-I range} = \frac{75\% - 25\%}{2}$$

The final phase of item selection involves determining which items of the initial pool of items will appear on the final scale. The selection criteria include items with scale values closest to whole numbers, in this case 1 through 11, and items

Table 15.1 An example of a Thurstone scale

Item #	Scale Value	S-I Range	Item
1.	6.0	.000	I don't care if security officers carry guns.
2.	2.3	.087	Because security officers are carrying guns, an accident could happen and it would lead to more trouble.
3.	8.1	.359	Security officers will receive more respect if they carry guns.
4.	4.3	.469	I believe campus police are less competent than local and state police.
5.	7.0	.113	Security officers should carry guns because the crime rate in our town is rising.
6.	10.3	.333	The campus police are here for our protection and guns maximize that protection.
7.	5.4	.390	I wish no one needed a gun but, if that is what has been decided, then there is nothing I can do about it.
8.	3.0	.354	Being able to carry guns will increase the security officers' feelings of importance and go to their heads.
9.	1.5	.125	I don't trust the campus police with guns.
10.	9.2	.125	Radical students or someone from off campus may get out of control without the safeguard of guns.
11.	9.9	.131	Carrying a gun will assure the security officers of greater personal safety, especially at night.

with the smallest semi-interquartile ranges. It is in this final phase that the number of items in the initial pool plays the greatest role. The more items in the initial pool, the more likely you will have items with whole-number scale values and small semi-interquartile ranges. Finally, the items are arranged in random order on the questionnaire.

When the class followed this procedure, the students produced the scale presented in Table 15.1 above. Notice that very few of the item values are exactly whole numbers. Although preferable, whole numbers are not essential so long as the scale values reflect as much of the entire range of the continuum as possible. As you examine the items, note also that the scale values themselves do not represent equal intervals. That is, 9.9 (item 11) is 1.8 points from 8.1 (item 3) but only 0.4 points from 10.3 (item 6). The interval between any two scale values may not be equal to the interval between two others, but there exist equal intervals that underlie the values: a difference of one scale point between two items anywhere along the continuum represents the same amount of opinion. The minor differences among the actual intervals are unimportant because the scale values are themselves part of the continuum that exhibits equal intervals.

As you complete the item analysis, it is important to select items with the smallest possible semi-interquartile range because you want to avoid potential overlap between items. For example, the largest semi-interquartile range in Table 15.1 is 0.469 (item 4), which is fairly large. This means that the difference between the 25th and 75th percentiles was nearly a full scale point, which is almost large enough to make the item useless for pinpointing a respondent's attitude.

Ideally, all semi-interquartile ranges should be smaller than half of the difference between an item's scale value and the scale value of the closest item. For example, the scale value for item 4 is 4.3, and the closest scale value is 5.4 for item 7. Thus, the semi-interquartile range for item 4 should be no larger than (5.4 − 4.3) / 2 = 0.55. Clearly, 0.469 is smaller than 0.55, but not by much. Item 4 is acceptable, but just barely so. There was no item with a smaller semi-interquartile range that also had a scale value close to 4.0, so we had to decide to either use item 4 or not represent that scale value. We decided on the former, another instance in which the real world of research is not the same as the ideal world of research.

Administration of Thurstone Scales

When administering an equal-appearing interval scale, the scale values and semi-interquartile ranges are not displayed on the questionnaire. The second and third columns in Table 15.1 would not appear on the final questionnaire, only the randomly chosen item number and the item itself. The respondent is asked to check any of the items that reflect his or her opinion. Ideally, respondents should check only one item, partly because using the equal-appearing interval scale involves assuming that respondents' opinions are sufficiently defined to make it difficult for them to agree with more than one item. A respondent's score is the scale value of the item selected. Sometimes, however, respondents will choose more than one item, in which case the respondent's score is the median of the scale values for all items selected.

Pros and Cons of Thurstone Scales

As a way to construct an equivalent difference scale, the equal-appearing interval technique is one of the best. Over the years, a variety of research projects have demonstrated that, so long as one follows the rules, the beliefs of the judges do not have a major impact on the final scale (Kidder, 1981). Whether my students were in favor of handguns or not, for example, made no difference in terms of generating or rating the initial pool of items. If you follow the rules for constructing and selecting items, the technique will produce a very close approximation of an interval measurement.

There are, however, some disadvantages to the Thurstone technique. The entire procedure is relatively time-consuming and requires a team of at least 20 raters. Unless you can use a classroom full of students, you may have to run a pilot project in order to get enough generators/raters for the initial pool. Also, because the median of item values is used whenever respondents check more than one item, it is possible for two respondents to check entirely different items and receive the same score. Choosing items with whole scale numbers and minimal semi-interquartile ranges will reduce, but not necessarily eliminate, this problem. Also, preliminary reliability and validity studies that concentrate on ensuring that the scale is unidimensional (see Chapter 14) will help overcome this problem.

Likert Scales

One alternative to the time- and labor-intensive effort required to construct a Thurstone scale is the technique developed by Likert (1932). Known as a Likert scale, this technique also begins with generating a pool of initial items. The **Likert scale** *consists of items reflecting extreme positions on a continuum, items with which people are likely either to agree or disagree.* The items are typically presented in a graphic format that includes endpoints labeled "agree" and "disagree."

Item Analysis and Selection in Likert Scales

After a pool of face-valid items has been generated, the entire pool of items is administered to a sample of respondents. These pretest respondents indicate their preference for each item, just as if they were completing the final version of the scale. Then an item analysis is completed. (This phase of Likert scale construction is often skipped by those who report using a Likert-type scale, but you should not skip it.) The most common form of item analysis is the item-total correlation described in Chapter 14, but other, similar analyses are acceptable. Items with the most extreme (positive and negative) item-total correlations are selected for the final version of the scale.

    The reason for selecting items with the most extreme item-total correlations is to produce a scale that is unidimensional. The more extreme an item-total correlation, the more strongly the item is related to other items on the scale. Ideally, you should select the ten or 20 best items, place those items on yet another version of the scale, and then administer the new version to a different sample of respondents. Then, recalculate the item-total correlations and again select only those items with extremely high correlations—absolute value of .80 or higher. This last, extra phase of item analysis constitutes an added check for unidimensionality without the bias that may be produced by some of the poorer items in the initial pool. Not too many researchers actually complete the extra step, but it could prevent problems later in your study. It's best to do every step until you are sufficiently familiar with scale construction to know when you can "get away with" skipping something.

Administration of Likert Scales

Once you have chosen the final group of items, respondents should be asked to provide a response to each and every item. Scores for the scale are determined simply by adding the values of the responses, which is why the Likert scale is also called a summative scale. The summation process, however, is not always straightforward. When using a graphic format, it is desirable to alter the graphic so that "agree" is not on the same side for every item. This allows you to identify respondents who have simply checked one side of the page instead of responding to each item. For example, two items on a Likert scale might look like this:

1. I think statistics are fascinating.
   agree/ / / / / / /disagree

2. Research methods is an extremely interesting course.
disagree/ / / / / / /agree

For any one of the items, agree might be scored a "1" and disagree scored an "8." But you would have to count from the left for the first item and from the right for the second. It's not difficult, but it does require paying careful attention to what you are doing.

Philosophies of Human Nature Scale

One example of a well-constructed Likert scale is Wrightsman's (1974) philosophies of human nature (PHN) scale. Wrightsman first identified what he considered to be six major dimensions of general philosophies of human nature, dimensions on which people evaluate other people. Using the philosophical and social scientific literature, statements from mass media, and student essays, Wrightsman generated 20 items for each of the six dimensions. (Most people generate more than 20 items per dimension in the initial pool, but Wrightsman was extremely familiar with both scaling techniques and his subject matter.) He then administered the initial pool to students from three different colleges, who provided responses on a six-point graphic format. Wrightsman used six-point graphics to prevent anyone from choosing a neutral point. Maximum disagreement was scored "−3," and maximum agreement was scored "+3." Because a Likert scale is, at best, an interval-level measure, what numbers are chosen for the endpoints don't make any difference.

For his item analysis, Wrightsman first separated the items according to the dimensions they were supposed to measure and conducted separate analyses for each dimension. Even though there were six dimensions to the PHN scale, Wrightsman ensured that each part of the scale was unidimensional by conducting separate analyses for each part. Instead of using item-total correlations for his item analysis, Wrightsman elected to use analysis of variance.

After obtaining total scores, Wrightsman separated the respondents from each college into three groups—the upper and lower 25% and the middle 50% of the sample—based on their overall scores. For each of the three groups, he then calculated the mean rating for each item and compared the group means using analysis of variance. Thus, just as with an item-total correlation, he was testing whether a score on one item was related to the overall score for the rest of the items. In order to ensure generalizability, he conducted separate analyses for each of the three colleges.

Table 15.2 contains a summary of the results of the analysis for the item "Most people are basically honest," which is from the trustworthiness dimension of the scale. The trustworthiness dimension measures the extent to which an individual believes people are basically trustworthy. The item rather obviously exhibits face validity, and the results of the item analysis provide further evidence of its quality. For example, the difference between the means of the upper and lower 25% of the sample is statistically significant across all three colleges. The balance of the means is good—the mean of the upper 25% is higher than the mean of the

Table 15.2   Sample item analysis for the PHN scale

| College | Mean Response | | | Difference | | | |
	Upper 25%	Middle 50%	Lower 25%	Upper Minus Lower 25%	Stat. Signif?	Good Balance?	Right Order?
W	1.0	−0.2	−2.0	3.0	Yes	Yes	Yes
P	1.8	1.1	−0.3	2.1	Yes	Yes	Yes
B	1.9	0.9	0.4	1.5	Yes	Partly	Yes

SOURCE: Adapted from Wrightsman (1974)

middle 50%, which in turn is higher than the mean of the lower 25%—except for College B. For College B, the mean of the lower 25% was not significantly different from the mean of the middle 50%. Because the item did discriminate between those who trusted and those who did not trust other people, the item was eventually included in the final version of the scale.

From an initial pool of 120 items, Wrightsman selected 84 items for the final version of the PHN scale. The scale is too long to reprint here, but Wrightsman (1974) contains a list of the items, as well as a great deal more detail about its construction and use. Wrightsman, incidentally, is one of the relatively few researchers who completed the second analysis phase of Likert scale construction. As you will discover in the section below, the Likert scale is not without its problems and critics.

Guttman Scales

The Thurstone and Likert techniques were designed to use more than one item to measure the same concept. Thurstone's technique should produce items ordered along a unidimensional continuum. Even though Likert's technique does not produce ordered items, it too should produce a unidimensional scale. Guttman (1944), however, criticized both techniques, claiming that neither resulted in a truly unidimensional scale.

The problem, according to Guttman, is that one respondent could obtain the same score as another respondent, even though the two respondents had agreed with or checked completely different items. To Guttman, this prevented the Thurstone and the Likert scale from being truly unidimensional. On a **Guttman scale,** *it is possible to order both the items and the respondents on a single, identifiable continuum.* The Guttman scale is also called either a scalogram scale or a cumulative scale.

Ideal Response Pattern in a Guttman Scale

Perhaps the best way to describe a Guttman scale is to illustrate the response pattern of an ideal or perfect scale, presented in Table 15.3. If the items are

Table 15.3 Proportion of respondents agreeing with each item on a perfect
Guttman scale

Scale Score	Item Number									
	1	2	3	4	5	6	7	8	9	10
0	0	0	0	0	0	0	0	0	0	0
1	1	0	0	0	0	0	0	0	0	0
2	1	1	0	0	0	0	0	0	0	0
3	1	1	1	0	0	0	0	0	0	0
4	1	1	1	1	0	0	0	0	0	0
5	1	1	1	1	1	0	0	0	0	0
6	1	1	1	1	1	1	0	0	0	0
7	1	1	1	1	1	1	1	0	0	0
8	1	1	1	1	1	1	1	1	0	0
9	1	1	1	1	1	1	1	1	1	0
10	1	1	1	1	1	1	1	1	1	1

ordered on a continuum from easiest to most difficult to endorse, the pattern of responses forms two triangles. The upper right triangle consists only of zeroes, whereas the lower left consists of ones. From this pattern, it is possible to deduce exactly which items were chosen by any respondent simply by knowing the respondent's score.

Everyone who agreed with item 10, for example, also agreed with items 1 through 9. If a Guttman scale is perfect, only those who agreed with items 1 through 9 would also agree with item 10, only those who agreed with item 1 would also agree with item 2, and so on. To some extent, this is also what should occur with a Thurstone scale, but the results of a Thurstone scale rarely turn out that way. The advantage of the Guttman technique is that the item analysis is designed to ensure that a nearly perfect pattern of responses will occur.

Item Generation in Guttman Scales

Items are generated for a Guttman scale in much the same way as for the other scales; one writes an initial pool of items that exhibits face validity and covers the range of possible opinions. For a Guttman scale, however, the items will eventually be ordered on the conceptual dimension. Once written, items are administered to a sample of respondents, who are asked to check every item with which they agree. A respondent's score on a Guttman scale is simply the number of items with which the respondent agrees.

Item Analysis in Guttman Scales

The scores from the initial group of respondents are then subjected to a very different item analysis called a scalogram. A **scalogram analysis** basically is *a* *determination of the extent to which the pattern of actual responses fits the ideal pattern.* The pattern displayed in Table 15.3 is an ideal pattern against which a set of ten items would be compared.

The key to a scalogram analysis is the number of discrepancies—differences between actual and ideal responses—exhibited by the respondents. For example, a respondent who agrees with item 2 should also agree with item 1. If the same respondent did not agree with item 3, then he or she should not agree with items 4 through 10. If, however, a respondent agreed with items 1, 2, and 4 but disagreed with all other items, the pattern of responses could be represented by a series of plus and minus symbols, for which each plus represents agreement and each minus represents disagreement:

$$+ \; + \; - \; + \; - \; - \; - \; - \; - \; -$$

The above respondent would have one discrepancy: agreeing with item 4 (or failing to agree with item 3). If we add the number of discrepancies for all respondents, subtract that sum from the total number of responses, and then divide that difference by the total number of responses, the resulting proportion is the **coefficient of reproducibility (CR)**—*the proportion of fit between a perfect Guttman scale and one's data.* The exact formula for a coefficient of reproducibility can be found in most measurement textbooks (see, for example, Anastasi, 1982).

A CR greater than .90 is sufficiently high to conclude that the scale items form a reliably unidimensional scale (Edwards, 1957). During the early phases of Guttman scale construction, it is necessary to eliminate items that cause too many discrepancies. By creating a matrix similar to that displayed in Table 15.3, you can easily identify items that do not fit the pattern of zeroes and ones required for perfection.

Removing undesirable items from the item pool and administering the remaining items to another group of respondents should increase the resulting CR. The process, however, can be very slow and painstaking. Although time-consuming, it is best to remove only one item at a time because it may well be that a particular item, and its associated bias, is causing other items to exhibit less than ideal response patterns. Removing too many items at a time can result in wasting a number of good items.

Although scalogram analysis is rarely used for such purposes, it is also possible to examine the pattern of responses for each respondent instead of examining the pattern for each item. Examining the pattern for each respondent could enable you to identify those respondents with the greatest number of discrepancies. That is, you could use a scalogram analysis to identify subgroups within your respondents, subgroups for whom measurement of a particular concept may have to be accomplished through some other means.

Guttman Scaling to Study Riots and Political Participation

Wanderer (1969) used a Guttman scale to study riots during the summer of 1967, the so-called "long hot summer" of the 1960s. The purpose of the study was to develop some way to predict future occurrences of such riots, and Wanderer was particularly interested in predicting the intensity of riots. He created a scale using vandalism, interference with fire fighters, looting, sniping, calling out the state police, calling out the national guard, and the number of people killed as items on a Guttman scale. The scale exhibited a CR of .92 and enabled Wanderer to identify a number of variables that could be used to predict the severity of future riots.

Guttman scales may also be used to test theories that involve assumptions about ordered categories. For example, Milbrath's (1965) theory of political participation included a description of participation as a hierarchically ordered concept. The hierarchy ranged from the lowest level—participation in a national election—to the highest level, defined as voting in local elections. On the basis of extensive survey data, Verba and Nie (1972) attempted to test Milbrath's theory by subjecting participation levels to a scalogram analysis. Those data failed to produce a reasonably high CR, and Verba and Nie concluded that political participation did not conform to a unidimensional hierarchy.

Disadvantages of Guttman Scales

Despite its seemingly clear-cut procedures for producing unidimensional scales, the Guttman technique is not without problems. It is best used to measure concepts or dimensions that are very well-defined; otherwise, trying to write items that reflect only one dimension can be extremely difficult. Eliminating bad items one at a time can be very time-consuming and may require repeated administrations of the ever-decreasing item pool with different samples of respondents.

Satisfactory coefficients of reproducibility may also be difficult to obtain if the respondents in the sample are very heterogeneous. You may have to identify and eliminate certain subgroups in order to obtain a sufficiently homogeneous group of respondents before obtaining a CR greater than .90. Of course, restricting the sample in this manner is likely to reduce the generalizability of the final version of the scale. It is also possible to construct a Guttman scale using item formats other than forced choice, but most other formats require computer assistance for the considerably more complicated scalogram analyses.

Semantic Differential Scales

The Thurstone, Likert, and Guttman scaling techniques have three things in common: they involve the preparation of a pool of items that exhibit face validity, they require some sort of analysis in order to select a final set of items, and they are designed specifically to measure unidimensional concepts or a single dimension of multidimensional concepts. In this section, we turn to a rather different measurement scale, one that does not share any of the above commonalities. The **semantic differential scale** *is designed to measure the psychological meaning of concepts along three different dimensions: evaluation, potency, and activity.*

Developed by Osgood, Suci, and Tannenbaum (1957), the semantic differential scale is not used to measure how much of a particular quality (such as social status) someone has or how much someone believes in a particular concept (such as human trustworthiness), but rather what someone understands a particular concept to be—that is, the subjective meaning of a concept. Instead of measuring respondents' attitudes toward research methods, for example, you might use a semantic differential scale to measure what people think research methods are. The meaning of the concept being measured is defined by the general dimensions of evaluation, potency, and activity.

Evaluation refers to *the overall positive or negative meaning attached to the concept.* Such labels as "good," "bad," "attractive," and "dirty," are part of the evaluation dimension. **Potency** refers to *the overall strength or importance of the concept.* Potency includes such labels as "strong," "weak," "superior," and "useful." **Activity** refers to *the extent to which the concept is associated with action or motion.* Such labels as "fast," "slow," "active," "passive," and "deliberate" qualify for the activity dimension. Thus, an individual's subjective perception of research methods might be good (evaluation), important (potency), and exciting (activity).

Item Generation in Semantic Differential Scales

Generally, you do not have to generate a pool of items for a semantic differential scale. Instead, adjective pairs that reflect the three dimensions inherent in the scale are generated. A partial example of a semantic differential scale is presented in Table 15.4, which also includes the instructions that typically accompany the scale. The adjective pairs are not separated into the different dimensions of the scale, but rather are randomly ordered throughout the entire scale.

One of the main advantages of the semantic differential scale is that the same list of adjective pairs can be used to measure the meaning of a variety of different concepts. Those listed in Table 15.4, for example, could apply equally well to concepts such as research methods, education, social welfare, prisons, and many other concepts. An additional advantage is the existence of a variety of sources for more complete lists of adjective pairs. Osgood et al.'s (1957) book contains such lists, as does Snider and Osgood (1969), Jenkins and Russell (1958), and Kerlinger (1972). Equally important, however, is the fact that you have the ability to add or delete as many adjective pairs as may be appropriate for the concept you want to measure.

Administration of Semantic Differential Scales

To score a semantic differential scale, one simply sums the ratings given to each adjective pair within each of the three dimensions. One of the major disadvantages of the semantic differential scale is that, unless the set of adjective pairs has been used a number of times in the past, complicated analyses are required to assess the reliability of the scale. Unless prior research has already provided very definite direction, you should use factor analysis to determine the measurement dimension to which a particular adjective pair belongs. Although the actual procedure is very complicated—far too complicated to describe here—**factor analysis** is *a statistical technique used to separate continuous variables into groups that mea-*

Table 15.4 Sample semantic differential scale

Instructions: For each adjective pair listed below, place a mark at whatever point along the blank line that most accurately reflects the extent to which you believe the adjectives describe politicians.

pleasant	: : : : : : :	unpleasant
bad	: : : : : : :	good
beautiful	: : : : : : :	ugly
angular	: : : : : : :	rounded
kind	: : : : : : :	cruel
passive	: : : : : : :	active
fair	: : : : : : :	unfair
delicate	: : : : : : :	rugged
wise	: : : : : : :	foolish
fast	: : : : : : :	slow
positive	: : : : : : :	negative
weak	: : : : : : :	strong
valuable	: : : : : : :	worthless
dull	: : : : : : :	bright
clean	: : : : : : :	dirty
deep	: : : : : : :	shallow
heavy	: : : : : : :	light
honest	: : : : : : :	dishonest

sure single dimensions of a multidimensional concept. Kerlinger (1979) provides a very understandable conceptual description of the technique, and Lindeman, Merenda, and Gold (1980) provide an introduction to the mathematics of factor analysis.

Semantic Differential Scaling to Study Officers of the Court

Although factor analyzing the adjective pairs on a semantic differential scale can be problematic, it can sometimes produce added benefits. Some years ago, Saul Kassin and I used a semantic differential scale similar to the one in Table 15.4 for a pilot study dealing with the main participants in a criminal trial (judge, defendant, prosecutor, and so on). Although the complete set of results is too complicated to summarize here, we did obtain some interesting and useful results. For example, the defendant was considered to have the least active role in the trial, less active even than that of the courtroom bailiff. Of equal importance, however, were the results that led us to conclude that the kind of adjective pairs in the three dimensions differed as a function of the trial participant being rated. The adjective pair "intelligent–unintelligent," for example, contributed to the potency of the trial judge but did not contribute to the potency of the defendant. From these very tentative findings, Kassin and I were able to generate a number of different research hypotheses, many of which were subsequently put to empirical tests in other research projects (see, for example, Wrightsman, 1983, 1987).

Q-sort Scales

Just as the semantic differential scale is typically used to measure the meaning of concepts, a **Q-sort** is *a scale used to measure an individual's relative positioning or ranking on a variety of different concepts.* The Q-sort technique was adapted by Stephenson (1953) and has remained popular among researchers interested in measuring characteristics of individuals. One way to further describe the Q-sort technique is to consider it to be a combination of Thurstone and semantic differential scaling, for aspects of both techniques are involved. Various items representing different concepts are generated. The respondent then sorts these items into ranked positions on the dimensions of the concepts. The items used in Q-sort scales should be face valid, and double-barreled items should be particularly avoided because of the multidimensional nature of the technique.

Administration of Q-sort Scales

Administration of a Q-sort is almost identical to the item analysis phase of Thurstone scaling, with one very important difference: with the Q-sort technique, it is the sorters who are being measured, not the items. The sorting is nearly identical to the initial item judgment phase of the Thurstone technique. Judges are asked to categorize the items on the basis of some dimensional criterion. Unlike the Thurstone procedure, however, the sorter is also asked to make the number of items in the categories conform to a normal distribution. For example, if 100 items were to be sorted into 11 categories, the sorter would be instructed to distribute the items such that the number of items in each category would approximate the distribution below:

number of items:	3	4	7	11	15	20	15	11	7	4	3
category number:	1	2	3	4	5	6	7	8	9	10	11

Of course, the number of items to be placed in each category will depend both on the number of items in the initial pool, and the number of categories. The formula for determining the number of entries in each category is the formula for the normal distribution. Unfortunately, the formula is extremely complex, and I don't suggest using it unless you have access to a computer to do the calculations for you. Most software packages, for example, will generate values and frequencies that match the normal distribution for any number of items or categories. For the most part, however, just about any symmetrical distribution that approximates the normal distribution—small frequencies at the ends, proportionately larger frequencies toward the middle—will be good enough for most purposes. Different labels applied to the endpoints enable you to assess different concepts, such as "approve–disapprove" for attitudes, "honest–dishonest" for politicians, "like ours– not like ours" for societies, and so on.

After the initial pool of items (between 60 and 90 is the recommended number) has been sorted, the category number assigned to each item is used to calculate correlations between the various individuals who did the sorting. That is, sorters become the variables in the calculation of correlation coefficients, and the category numbers assigned to the different concepts become the scores for the variable. The results of these analyses are usually displayed in a matrix labeled by the sorters' name, or other identification along the top and side, and containing correlation coefficients as matrix entries. From this matrix it is possible to identify sorters who are similar to each other. Again, despite its similarity to the Thurstone technique, the emphasis of the Q-sort is on the sorters themselves, not on the items they are sorting.

Use of Q-sort and Postcards to Examine Self-Concept

Sometimes the items sorted in a Q-sort procedure are somewhat unusual. Stephenson (1980) provided an example of such unusual items when he asked a four-year-old girl to sort 18 postcard pictures of other little girls. He asked her to sort these cards under seven different instructions. Table 15.5 presents the results he obtained after subjecting the girl's ratings to a factor analysis, from which three factors or groupings emerged. From these we can make some inferences about her relationships with others. For example, her perceptions of herself correspond well with her perceptions of what her dog thinks of her and with her perceptions of the "very best girl." She considers her mother and teacher to have similar views of her, and she seems to consider her older brother, rather than her mother or teacher, to represent what she will be like as an adult.

Table 15.5 Factor structure from a child's Q-sort of picture postcards

Sorting Instructions	Factor 1	2	3
Most like me	X		
The very best girl	X		
Me according to my pet dog	X		
Me according to mommy		X	
Me according to my teacher		X	
Me according to my brother			X
Me as a grown-up			X

SOURCE: Adapted from Stephenson (1980)

Stephenson's results are not all that surprising. Most children probably believe their pets think as they do, and most probably consider themselves to be exemplary children. What is surprising, however, is that these very sensible results were obtained using postcards. The postcard pictures cannot readily be said to exhibit face validity; they were just pictures of young girls. Yet, a fair amount of insight into the thought processes of a young child was obtained with the combination of Q-sort and factor analysis.

Disadvantages of Q-sort Scales

Given the above example, it is fairly easy to realize that Q-sort scales can be very powerful when used to develop or to attempt to test theories in the behavioral sciences. Q-sort scales are not, however, without disadvantages. One of their major shortcomings is that they are extremely difficult to use with large samples. The size of the correlation matrix rapidly outgrows the capacity of even the most sophisticated computer software. Measurement with a Q-sort scale is frequently limited to the smallest of samples—a single person—which makes generalization rather difficult. Many replications are necessary for any reasonable level of generalization. On the other hand, if the questions asked in your research project are intended for exploratory or heuristic purposes, then Q-sort can be an extremely useful and powerful scaling technique.

Sociometric Scales

The Q-sort technique is most useful for measuring various aspects of an individual or a few individuals. The scaling technique we next consider is most prevalently used for descriptive research among groups. A **sociometric scale** is *a scale designed specifically for measuring relationships among individuals within a group* (Proctor & Loomis, 1951). Sociometric scales—sometimes called sociometry—have also been used to measure social choice (Kerlinger, 1973). Very simply, the technique involves asking members of a group to make choices among other members of the group.

Administration of Sociometric Scales

Consider, by way of example, the other members of your research methods class. Which three people do you most like? Which three do you like the least? Such questions are the basis of a sociometric scale. If every person in your class answered these two questions, you would have enough information to be able to construct a profile of your classmates—a "who's who" in terms of popularity. Of course, the questions might just as easily be worded in terms of working with, eating with, or doing anything else with others in your class. Similarly, one could inquire about the people with the most and least financial status, intelligence, or any other concept of interest. If you are wondering about popularity, ask a popularity question. If you are wondering about perceived intelligence, ask about intellectual qualities. Thus, item generation for a sociometric scale is relatively easy and is directly related to the research question.

As you have probably guessed by now, a sociometric scale involves relatively simple procedures. Item generation is straightforward, as is the presentation format. The question(s) may be asked by way of a questionnaire, an interview, or observations of behavior. For example, without asking anyone anything, you could observe the pattern of conversation within a group. Scores could be assigned on the basis of how many times each person talks to every other person, thereby measuring popularity. If written or verbal questions are posed, the response format could be forced-choice, graphic, or any other suitable format.

Reliability and validity of the items used on a sociometric scale depend, primarily, on simplicity and face validity; that is, the simpler and more specific the question(s) used, the more reliable the measure. Similarly, the more directly the questions pertain to the theoretical concept under consideration, the more valid the measure.

Scoring of Sociometric Scales

In addition to being relatively easy to administer, sociometric scales are easy to analyze. Researchers using them are typically interested in either the number of choices assigned to individuals in the group or a global measure of the cohesiveness of the group. The status of any group member can be determined simply by counting the number of "choices" received by that person and dividing that count by the number of people making those choices. The more choices received by any one group member, the more that person is perceived to have of whatever is being asked about in the question.

Assessing group cohesion is a bit more complicated than individual assessment, but it is based on the same idea. **Group cohesion** refers to *the degree of mutual attraction among members of a group*. If everyone likes everyone else, cohesion is extremely high; if everyone dislikes everyone else, cohesion is extremely low. Using a sociometric scale involves estimating cohesion by comparing the number of mutual likes to the total number of possible mutual likes. Consider, for example, a group consisting of ten people. Five of the people originally formed the group and remain best friends. Each of the other five people were brought in by one of the original group members, but are not considered friends of anyone else in the group except, of course, the member who brought that person into the group.

One way to create sociometric data from such a group (see Table 15.6) is to ask each person in the group to consider each of the other people in the group and decide whether or not that other is a friend. A "Y" in the table represents a yes response, an "N" a no response. The total number of possible mutual choices is $(10 \times 9) / 2 = 45$. This is not the total number of choices made, which is 95, but the total number of possible *mutual* choices. The number of actual mutual choices can be determined simply by counting the mutual "Y" responses, such as

Table 15.6   Sociometric analysis of a hypothetical group

	Target									
Rater	1	2	3	4	5	6	7	8	9	10
1	–	Y	Y	Y	Y	Y	N	N	N	N
2	Y	–	Y	Y	Y	N	Y	N	N	N
3	Y	Y	–	Y	Y	N	N	Y	N	N
4	Y	Y	Y	–	Y	N	N	N	Y	N
5	Y	Y	Y	Y	–	N	N	N	N	Y
6	Y	N	N	N	N	–	N	N	N	N
7	N	Y	N	N	N	N	–	N	N	N
8	N	N	Y	N	N	N	N	–	N	N
9	N	N	N	Y	N	N	N	N	–	N
10	N	N	N	N	Y	N	N	N	N	–

rater 1 likes rater 2 and rater 2 likes rater 1. The total number of actual mutual choices, then, is 15. By forming a ratio of these two values we arrive at a cohesion value:

$$\text{Cohesion} = \frac{\text{Number of mutual attractions}}{\text{Number of possible mutual attractions}}$$

In our example, the cohesion value is 15 / 45 = 0.33, which is not considered to be a great deal of cohesion.

In addition to general group cohesion, the sociometric scaling technique can be used to identify groups within groups, as is also illustrated in Table 15.6. The pattern of yes and no responses to the question about being friends clearly demonstrates the existence of a central core of mutual friends (raters 1–5). This same result can also be illustrated through a **sociogram**—*a figure depicting relationships among entities.* In the example, the entities are members of the group and the relationship is defined as "being friends." Figure 15.1 is an illustration of a sociogram, one that would result from the data contained in Table 15.6. The existence of a central core of friends is obvious from the figure, as is the notion that each member of the core has one other friend outside the core.

The sociometric technique, like the Q-sort technique, is not easily administered to a large group, particularly if one is interested in measuring group cohesion. With the aid of computer analyses, however, this shortcoming can be eliminated for the sociometric technique. Sociometric analyses have been most heavily used, as you might expect, in research concerning proximity and similarity as important factors in the development of relationships. Festinger, Schachter, and Back (1950), for example, demonstrated the influence of proximity by using a sociometric analysis of social interaction patterns in an apartment complex. Rokeach and Mezei (1966) demonstrated that similarity of opinion was a more important determinant of preference for work partners than was race. What is important to remember, however, is that conclusions are, as in all research, limited to the question asked. Simply finding that relationships tend to form according to racial,

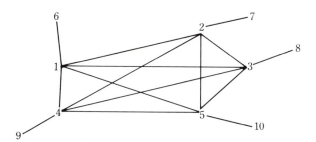

Figure 15.1 A sociogram resulting from a central core of five mutual friends, each of whom has another, exclusive friend. The source for this sociogram is the data in Table 15.6.

socioeconomic, physical, or some other category does not mean that the label applied to the category is the cause of the relationship. The category used may be a correlate of the cause, but experimental research (Chapter 5) is required to rule out alternative explanations.

Using Scales

For the most part, the use of scales in research involves attempting to measure preexisting characteristics of individuals. As mentioned at the beginning of this chapter, such measurement attempts are likely to involve the memories and self-presentation concerns of the respondents. With few exceptions, notably the semantic differential and Q-sort techniques, each of the different types of scales has been designed to measure a unidimensional concept or a single dimension of a multidimensional concept. Even though any one of the procedures, such as Wrightsman's (1974) philosophies of human nature scale, may be adapted for multidimensional measurement, special efforts must be made to ensure that measuring one of the dimensions does not introduce bias with respect to measuring other dimensions of the same concept.

Multiple Scale Administration

One way to avoid cross-dimensional bias—measurement of one dimension affecting the ability to measure another dimension—is to develop a scale for measuring each dimension separately. For each of the dimensions, separately assess the reliability and validity of the scale used to measure that dimension, just as you should do when you measure more than one unidimensional concept with several scales.

Thus you consider each dimension you will measure as a separate measurement problem to be solved. Then, after you have a collection of separate scales about which you know the reliability and validity, combine the scales into a single questionnaire. You ought also to conduct at least one pretest with the full battery of scales, again estimating reliability, to ensure that the other scales are not introducing bias.

Using Existing Scales

Most of this chapter emphasizes the development of measurement scales, mainly because understanding how to develop a scale is also the best way to learn how to select an existing scale. As you might expect, it is not always necessary to develop your own measurement scale; often an existing one will suit your purposes. You have probably come across a number of these scales while reading research literature, and you should consider using an existing scale if one exists; it is much easier, and using existing scales adds to accumulated knowledge.

Finding existing scales, however, is not limited to intentional or accidental exposure through journal articles. A number of different source volumes contain a multitude of scales, sometimes including the research conducted to determine their reliability and validity. Miller's (1977) volume, for example, contains a number of scales and includes information about modifying the scales to fit your specific research purposes. The volume edited by Robinson and Shaver (1969) is a compilation of attitude measurement scales, and Buros's (1961, 1965) collections of scales for intellectual qualities are highly useful for those interested in measuring intelligence. These are only a few of the compilations of existing measurement scales, but I would guess that many of the concepts of interest to you would be included, or at least referenced, in one or another of them. Perusing your own library's card catalog, under "measurement" or "scales," will also provide additional sources of scales.

When using an existing scale, it is usually only necessary to cite the source of the scale in your research report. For example, if your research project involved using the philosophies of human nature scale, it would be necessary to cite Wrightsman's (1974) book, but it is not necessary to review all of the developmental research that went into creating the scale. On the other hand, any modifications you make to existing scales should be accompanied in your research report by a full description of those modifications.

Similarly, if the scale you are using is an original or recently developed scale, it is best to include an explanation of the scale and its reliability and validity credentials. Of course, it is always necessary to provide some sort of description of the scale in your method section. Readers deserve to know about the properties of the measures you are using without having to consult additional material.

Summary

- Measurement scales are used whenever one item is not sufficient to represent the complexity of a concept or when it is not feasible to repeatedly use the same operational definition.
- Every item on a scale has the potential to produce a biased response. Thus, every item should be examined for bias. The format for presenting a scale should be chosen to maximize respondents' understanding of the scale.
- The Thurstone technique is used to create a scale that represents the full range of positions toward the concept being measured. It, like the Likert tech-

nique, approximates an interval level of measurement. The Likert scale involves creating a series of extreme position statements to which respondents are asked to react through a graphic format. The Guttman scalogram technique ensures a true interval level of measurement, but it is more difficult to use than either the Thurstone or Likert techniques.

• The semantic differential scale is used to measure the psychological meaning of a concept; it consists of a series of adjective pairs that can be categorized in terms of evaluation, potency, and activity. Unless a set of adjective pairs has already been demonstrated to be reliable and valid, factor analysis is required to demonstrate these qualities.

• The Q-sort technique is typically used to assess the reactions of a small group of respondents. The emphasis of measurement is on the relative meaning of items included on the scale.

• The sociometric technique is most often used to assess relationships within a defined group, including a general measure of cohesiveness. Although essentially a technique that measures choices among the group members, the wording of the criteria for the choices can include nearly any concept in the behavioral sciences.

• Even though most types of scales were originally designed to measure unidimensional concepts, all can be adapted to measure multidimensional concepts. Such adaptations, however, must guard against cross-dimensional bias.

• Regardless of the type of scale desired, you should first consider using an existing scale before creating a new one. Existing scales have the advantage of preexisting reliability and validity data, and they add to the accumulation of knowledge.

• Whenever a measurement scale is used in research, the report should contain enough information about it to enable the reader to understand the scale and its levels of reliability and validity.

CHAPTER SIXTEEN

Sampling

I don't like turnips, and I don't like liver. Call it prejudice if you wish, but I have no intention of ever trying either again just to make sure I don't like them. I am sure.

—Andy Rooney (1982, p. ix)

Overview

In this chapter you will learn how to select the people or things from which you plan to obtain data. You will learn about terminology used to describe sampling, as well as the theory and importance of sampling distributions. You will also learn about the difference between the two major types of sampling procedures: probability and nonprobability sampling. In addition to learning how to use the various procedures, you will learn about the advantages and disadvantages of each.

Introduction

Like columnist and "60 Minutes" commentator Andy Rooney, most people have an aversion to one or another type of food. They've tried it, didn't like it, and insist there is no need to try again. When I was in college, I hated coconut. I tried it several times and disliked it each time I tried it. You would have had to pay me a semester's worth of tuition to get me to eat anything with coconut in it. One night, eating at the home of a friend, I asked for a second piece of cake. My friend was very surprised. She knew I didn't like coconut, and she knew that her mother had included coconut in the cake. She thought I was eating the first piece just to be polite. When she told me, I was equally surprised, as well as curious. Had my tastes changed? What was going on?

No, my tastes had not changed. Instead, I had become a victim of sampling error. Until I ate that cake, all I had ever sampled was processed coconut, which I continue to dislike. Eventually I learned that fresh coconut had been used in the cake. I had generalized from my limited experience with processed coconut to all coconut; I had stereotyped all coconut on the basis of my experience with only processed coconut.

Generalizing from a sample is something that every one of us does every day. We may be attempting to answer a question about people without including all people in our sample. We may see one episode of a television program and decide never to watch the program again, watch one of a director's movies and decide to see more of them when we get the opportunity, and so on. Avoiding incorrect generalizations due to sampling error is what this chapter is all about. Before learning how to avoid sampling error, however, we have to learn a little of the jargon associated with sampling.

When discussing **sampling**—*the process of selecting participants for a research project*—scientists tend to use a great deal of jargon. One reason for all the jargon is that we need to be able to communicate very specific notions about sampling to those who will read our research reports, and very specific notions often involve jargon. As always, if you can avoid jargon in your own reports, so much the better, but you need to understand the jargon to be able to read others' reports.

Sampling unit and **sampling element** are both used to refer to *a single "thing" selected for inclusion in a research project.* If you sample people, a person is your unit or element. If you sample television shows, then a single program is the unit, and so on. *All possible units or elements that can be included* make up the **population.** A population is an abstract concept, something that cannot be seen or measured, even though it consists of concrete units. The population of the United States, for example, can be estimated but it cannot be accurately counted. You can never be sure you have counted everyone; someone could be hiding, for example, or a new person could be born after you have already counted "everyone" in a particular location.

Instead, we do research on a **sample**—*a portion of the elements in a population.* Any part of a population is considered a sample, and any given sample can be a part of more than one population. You and two of your classmates, for example, are simultaneously a sample of your class, a sample of university students, a sample of students in general, a sample of the people living in whatever country in which you may reside, and so on. A sample, then, is a concrete portion of a population, probably of more than one population.

Although a sample is a portion of a population, technically the sample is not selected from the population. Instead, samples are selected from a **sampling frame**—*a concrete listing of the elements in a population.* Again using you and your classmates as examples, I could select you from the registrar's list of all students at your campus, which would then be the sampling frame, but I could never be sure that the registrar's list included the entire population. Some students may be left off the list, some may be included on the list even though they are no longer students, and so forth. Essentially, the sampling frame is the largest possible sample of a population; it is everything that can be selected.

A **parameter** is *a value associated with a population.* It is an abstract value simply because we cannot calculate, for example, the mean of a population if we don't know how many units are in the population and cannot measure the entire population. Instead of calculating parameters, we have to estimate them from **statistics**—*values associated with samples.* Because a sample is always concrete, we can calculate statistics. When we use statistics to estimate parameters, the statistics are inferential statistics. However, because they are estimates, inferential statistics always contain some amount of error, usually error resulting from the sampling process.

Sampling error is *the term applied to the extent to which a sample statistic incorrectly estimates a population parameter.* Consider, for example, the taste I had associated with coconut. Because I had only sampled processed coconut, that test contained some sampling error. I used that taste, however, to make inferences about all coconut, just as a sample statistic is used to make an inference about an entire population. The more error involved in the sampling process, such as my ignoring raw coconut, the greater the sampling error of an inferential statistic.

If you had asked me how confident I was about my reaction to coconut before I ate that piece of cake, I, like Andy Rooney, would have told you I was 100% certain. That would have been a statement about a **confidence level**—*the probability associated with the accuracy of an inferential statistic.* I might have said the probability of my disliking any coconut you gave me was 1.00, a probability we now know was an overestimate. Indeed, a confidence level of 1.00 is always an overestimate, for no statistic can be 100% accurate. There is always going to be some sampling error, a confidence level less than 1.00, simply because we can never be sure exactly what is and is not included in any given population.

Enough jargon. You now know that units and elements are things and that units and elements make up populations and samples. Populations are abstract collections of everything, whereas samples are only a portion of things in the population. A sampling frame is the largest sample that can be obtained from a population; it is almost every thing in the population. Further, statistics are sample values, which are often used to estimate population parameters (values). Any statistic contains some amount of error, which can be determined by calculating the confidence level associated with the statistic. Whenever a sample is taken from a population, there is always some sampling error. Fortunately, under certain conditions we can estimate sampling error, which is what we turn our attention to next.

Sampling Distributions

In this section we will deal with the basis for estimating sampling error and confidence limits. If you have had a course in statistics, you've probably seen this material before. But if you are like most of us, you can always use a review. If you have yet to complete a statistics course, this material is necessary to understand the reasons for most of the sampling procedures discussed later in the chapter.

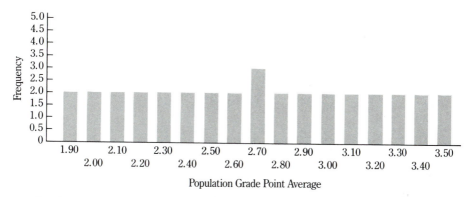

Figure 16.1 The population of 35 grade point averages obtained from a fictitious class of students. The population mean is 2.70, and the shape of the distribution, although not bell-shaped or normal, is symmetrical.

The basis for all statistics dealing with sampling distributions is sampling theory. We will use a running example in which we are interested in discovering the mean grade point average (GPA) of the students in your methods class. We will have to assume that everyone in your methods class constitutes a population, which also means we will not be able to calculate the mean GPA of the entire class. Because I don't know your grade point averages, we'll use fictitious numbers, including the fiction that there are 35 students in your class.

The simplest way for you to discover the mean GPA in your class is to ask everyone to tell you. But not everyone may be willing to tell you what their GPA is, or some may be absent on the day you decide to collect data. Suppose you ask four people in your class: the people sitting in front of you, behind you, to your left, and to your right. They report GPAs of 3.5, 2.0, 2.2, and 1.9, and you add your own GPA of 3.2. You now have a sample of five students and can calculate the sample mean:

$$(3.5 + 2.0 + 2.2 + 1.9 + 3.2) / 5 = 2.56$$

The question is whether 2.56 is a reasonable estimate of the mean for the entire class. The answer is, you have no way of knowing: you might have asked four other people and obtained a different sample mean.

The Population

Suppose that the distribution of grade point averages in your entire class is the distribution illustrated in Figure 16.1; the distribution of your sample is shown in Figure 16.2. The mean of the population is 2.70, which is not exactly the same as the sample mean of 2.56. Clearly, the sample statistic is not an accurate estimate of the population parameter, but you should already know that statistics are never perfectly accurate.

Notice how flat the population distribution is—2.70 is the only value for which there are three scores; all the rest have two scores. Of course, in a real research

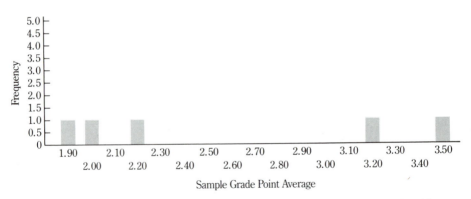

Figure 16.2 A sample of five scores obtained from the population depicted in Figure 16.1. The mean of the sample is 2.56, and the shape of the sample distribution is neither bell-shaped nor symmetrical.

project, we would only be able to guess the shape of the population distribution, although we could make that guess on the basis of the shape of the sample distribution. The point is that the population of scores is not a normal, bell-shaped distribution; nor does it have to be for sampling theory to be applicable. What is required, however, is that the sample be selected randomly from the population.

Random Selection

The key to being able to use a sample statistic to estimate a population parameter is the manner in which the sample is selected. **Random selection** includes *any technique that provides each population element an equal probability of being included in the sample.* Choosing the four people sitting closest to you in the classroom does not provide everyone in the class an equal chance of being included in the sample, and so the sample illustrated in Figure 16.1 is not a random sample. Therefore, we have no way of being able to estimate the amount of error included in that sample. If, however, you put the names of everyone in class into a hat and drew out five names, you would obtain a random sample. Later in the chapter you will learn about the variety of ways in which a random sample can be obtained, but they are all basically derivations of this "everyone's names in a hat" procedure.

Standard Error

If a sample has been randomly selected from the sampling frame, it is possible to estimate the amount of error in the sample by taking advantage of certain properties of sampling distributions. A sampling distribution is a distribution of statistics created by repeatedly selecting random samples from a population. Assume that instead of the four people around you, you randomly selected five students from your class. If you calculated the mean GPA of that sample and then repeated the same procedure another 199 times, you might obtain the sampling distribution presented in Figure 16.3.

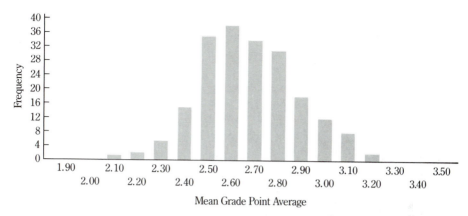

Figure 16.3 The sampling distribution of means obtained from 200 randomly selected samples of five grade point averages from the population depicted in Figure 16.1. The mean of the sampling distribution is 2.68, which is almost equal to the mean of the population: 2.7. The sampling distribution also resembles the normal distribution more than the population distribution.

Compare Figures 16.3 and 16.1. Although the two distributions have almost identical means, their shapes are very different. The population distribution in Figure 16.1 is very flat, whereas the sampling distribution in Figure 16.3 is peaked and considerably less spread out. Even though there are more scores in the sampling distribution—200 compared to 35 in the population—the variability of the sampling distribution is smaller. The standard deviation of the population is 0.48, whereas that for the sampling distribution is 0.21, less than half than that of the population. This is always the case; sampling distributions exhibit less variability than does the population distribution.

The **standard error** of a statistic is *the standard deviation of its sampling distribution.* Even though it is a standard deviation like any other standard deviation, it merits a special name because it comes from a sampling distribution. Thus, for our example, the standard error of the mean—the standard deviation of the sampling distribution illustrated in Figure 16.3—is 0.21. The standard error is what enables us to determine the amount of sampling error that exists in any random sample we select—but only when the sample is selected randomly.

Once again, however, we must come back to the real world of research. It is fine to run around generating sampling distributions, but that requires a great deal of time and effort, as well as more information about the population than is usually available. But, if a single sample has been randomly selected, we don't need to generate sampling distributions. Because the first sample we selected was not a random sample, we won't use it; let me instead demonstrate with the first sample I selected in order to create the sampling distribution in Figure 16.3. That sample consisted of GPA values of 1.9, 3.3, 2.7, 2.6, and 3.4.

The mean of this random sample is 2.78, and its standard deviation is 0.61. As sample statistics, they are supposed to be estimates of the population parameters and, forgetting about the fact that we actually know what those parameters are, we can estimate the population mean and standard deviation to also be 2.78 and 0.61, respectively. In order to calculate the standard deviation of the sampling distribution of means—the standard error of the mean—all we have to do is apply the formula below:

$$S_m = \frac{S}{\sqrt{n}} \, ,$$

where S_m is the standard error, S is the standard deviation of the sample, and n is the size of the sample.

Substituting the values of our sample yields $0.61 / \sqrt{5} = 0.27$. Recall, however, that the actual standard deviation of the sampling distribution pictured in Figure 16.3 is 0.21, which is close but not the same as our calculated value for the standard error of the mean. The difference results from the fact that the calculation formula is based on the assumption that the sampling distribution contains an infinite number of samples. A sampling distribution, then, is actually an abstract notion, something we can approximate but cannot actually produce. Because we cannot generate an infinite number of samples, no concrete sampling distribution is ever going to have exactly the same standard deviation as the value calculated from the formula, except through coincidence.

Confidence Intervals

What remains to be done is to determine the amount of sampling error in our sample, which involves calculating a **confidence interval**—*the inclusive, probabilistic range of values around any calculated statistic.* Remember that at the beginning of this exercise we wanted to estimate the mean grade point average of everyone in your methods class; that is, the population mean. Our sample mean, 2.78, is an estimate of the population mean, but we also know that it is an imperfect estimate. The population mean may or may not be 2.78, but it certainly ought to be close to 2.78. The question, then, is how close. What is the range of values around the sample mean that could reasonably include the population mean; that is, what is the confidence interval of our statistic?

We could, of course, simply say the population mean is somewhere between 0.0 and 4.0, and we would be absolutely correct. But that would be uninformative; we knew that before we collected any data from the sample. But the more restricted we make the range of values, the less sure we can be about whether that range contains the population mean. What we must decide, then, is how sure we want to be. Or put another way, what are we willing to accept as the probability that the range we select is wrong? In the behavioral sciences, the rule of thumb for being wrong is a probability of .05—five chances in 100 of being wrong.

We can take advantage of the central limit theorem in order to create our confidence interval. We know from that theorem that about 95% of all scores in a normal distribution fall within about two standard deviations of the mean. Because a sampling distribution is composed of an infinite number of randomly selected samples, any sampling distribution is normally distributed. Therefore, we can infer that 95% of our sample means should fall within plus or minus two standard errors of the mean. Our estimate of the population mean is 2.78, and our estimate of the standard error is 0.27. Thus, we can be 95% certain that the true population mean is somewhere between [2.78 − 2(0.27)] and [2.78 + 2(0.27)], or somewhere between 2.24 and 3.32. The probability that we are wrong is .05. By starting with a sample of five students, we have estimated that the mean of the population is between 2.24 and 3.32. In doing so, we made use of sampling theory and the central limit theory, and we had to calculate a sample mean, a sample standard deviation, and the standard error of the sample mean.

Sample Size

If the confidence interval we estimated above is too wide for your liking, you can achieve a smaller interval by increasing the size of the sample. Look again at the formula used to calculate the standard error of the mean:

$$S_m = \frac{S}{\sqrt{n}}$$

Notice that the square root of the sample size is in the denominator of the formula. What this means is that the larger the sample size, the smaller the standard error of the mean. And the smaller the standard error of the mean, the smaller the confidence interval about any estimate. To get a smaller confidence interval, select a larger sample.

Figure 16.4, for example, contains a sampling distribution of 200 samples, but the size of each of the samples is 10. This distribution was created from the same population as that depicted in Figure 16.3, but this distribution is considerably

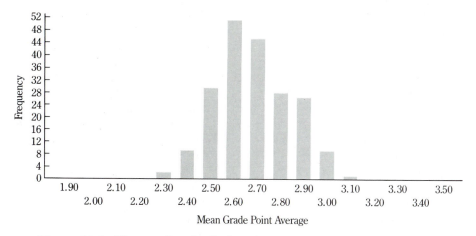

Figure 16.4   The sampling distribution of means obtained from 200 randomly selected samples of ten grade point averages from the population depicted in Figure 16.1. The mean of the sampling distribution is exactly 2.704, which is close enough to the population mean (2.70) to call them equal. The sampling distribution also resembles the normal distribution more than the population distribution.

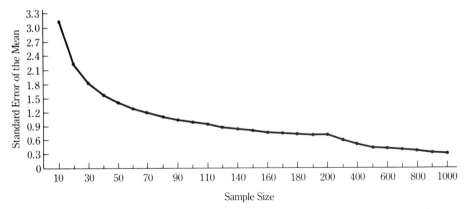

Figure 16.5 The relationship between standard error of the mean and sample size. All samples have a standard deviation of 10. As the sample size increases, the standard error decreases, but increases in sample size beyond 50 do not alter the standard error a great deal.

more narrow. The standard deviation of the sampling distribution for n = 10 is 0.16, whereas that for n = 5 is 0.21.

Although I could continue to illustrate sampling distributions with larger and larger sample sizes, you can see the relationship between sample size and standard error by examining Figure 16.5. Figure 16.5 was created by assuming, for illustration purposes, that the standard deviation of the sample was 10. The size of the sample, indicated on the ordinate, varies from ten to 1000, but the standard deviation of the sample deviation of the sample remains at 10. As the sample size increases, the size of the standard error decreases. The change, however, is not linear. When the sample size changes from 10 to 50, the change in the standard error is considerable. Beyond samples of 50, however, increasing the sample size does not dramatically affect the standard error. Thus, it is not always reasonable to attempt to obtain the largest possible sample.

Probability Sampling

The foregoing discussion of sampling distributions relied entirely on samples resulting from a random sampling procedure. To create the distributions in the various figures, I used a computer to generate 200 random samples from a population that contained 35 grade point averages. As mentioned before, whenever you can obtain a random sample, you can rely on the central limit theorem and the properties of the normal distribution to determine the amount of sampling error in your sample. In general, **probability sampling** is *any technique that ensures a random sample;* that is, a technique that ensures that every element in the sampling frame has an equal chance of being included in the sample. There are a number of variations on the "names in the hat" example discussed before, and we turn our attention now to describing those variations.

Simple Random Sampling

Names selected from a collection of name tags in a hat or a list of random numbers generated by a computer program are both examples of **simple random sampling**—*techniques that involve an unsystematic random selection process.* Basically, simple random sampling involves identifying every element in the sampling frame and choosing them on the basis of any planned process that also ensures that every element has an equal opportunity of being selected. When sampling frames are too large for slips of paper in a hat or some similar procedure, a random number table can be used.

A random number table is exactly what its name denotes: a table containing random numbers, or numbers arranged in no particular order. Random number tables usually contain thousands of random numbers, but Table 16.1 will serve as an illustration. The table contains five rows of random numbers, arranged in five columns with five numbers per column—a mere 125 random numbers. With a table similar to but larger than Table 16.1, any researcher can select any size sample from any sampling frame.

The first step in using a random number table is to determine the size of the sampling frame—the largest number that may be needed from the table. Consider, for example, the sampling frame of the fictitious population of grade point averages I created earlier. Because there are 35 students in the class, the largest possible number would be 35. Even though Table 16.1 contains five-digit numbers, we only want two-digit numbers for our sample. We must decide, then, which two of the five digits in a column we will consider to be valid. Whether we choose two digits on the left, two on the right, or some other pair doesn't matter, so long as we are consistent. For this example, we will use the two right-most digits in each column.

Suppose we want to obtain a simple random sample of five students from among the fictitious class of 35. We must next decide how we will move through the table: down the columns, up the columns, or across the rows. Any direction will suffice, but we must be consistent in our direction. We'll move down the columns simply because it seems natural to me. That means when we come to the bottom of one column, we move to the top row of the next.

We also need to choose a starting point. Any starting point is as good as any other, but the choice ought to be without bias. I always just close my eyes and put my finger on the page. For this example, I closed my eyes and put my finger on column three, row two of Table 16.1, and we will use that as our starting point for selecting a sample of five from a sampling frame containing 35 elements. In column three, row two, the two right-most digits are 8 and 9. Already we have a problem; 89 is too large. Whenever we encounter a number outside the range of our sam-

Table 16.1   An abbreviated random number table

82308	73580	84282	89252	64760
32893	42779	02789	48072	95170
59909	22076	65703	21811	50465
05551	64931	35873	68960	44968
50035	54365	62603	99069	93005

Table 16.2 A simple random sampling procedure using Table 16.1

Row	Column	Number	Comments
2	3	89	Discard, outside range
3	3	03	Selected, n = 1
4	3	73	Discard, outside range
5	3	03	Discard, already selected
1	4	52	Discard, outside range
2	4	72	Discard, outside range
3	4	11	Selected, n = 2
4	4	60	Discard, outside range
5	4	69	Discard, outside range
1	5	60	Discard, outside range
2	5	70	Discard, outside range
3	5	65	Discard, outside range
4	5	68	Discard, outside range
5	5	05	Selected, n = 3
1	1	08	Selected, n = 4
2	1	93	Discard, outside range
3	1	09	Selected, n = 5

sample complete with students 3, 11, 5, 8, 9

pling frame, we simply ignore it and move on to the next number. The same thing is done with any repeat numbers—those we have already selected. Table 16.2 contains the results of my use of the random number table.

As you read through Table 16.2, you probably noticed that many of the numbers had to be discarded. There will, of course, always be some discards, but we encountered many of them because the size of my sampling frame, 35, was considerably smaller than the maximum two-digit number, 99. With a larger sampling frame, say 60 or 70, we would have encountered fewer numbers outside the range. Usually, discards and repeats are not overly troubling. When using a random number table in a real research project, for example, you would not write all the comments included in Table 16.2. You would instead simply write down the numbers of the selected sample elements.

Systematic Random Sampling

As you may have also noticed while perusing Table 16.2, simple random sampling can be a rather inefficient way to select a sample. With a very large sampling frame and a large sample, you could spend several hours paging through a random number table. **Systematic random sampling** is accomplished by *choosing elements from a randomly arranged sampling frame according to ordered criteria.* Frequently, systematic random sampling is accomplished by choosing every tenth, 15th, or some other "nth" element in the sampling frame. Just as in simple random sampling, however, several decisions need to be made before you can begin.

First, and most obviously, you need to decide the size of the sample. If, for example, you want a sample of 50 people from a sampling frame containing 900, then you want a proportion of 50 / 900 = 0.055 of the entire sampling frame. Inverting that proportion, 1 / 0.055 = 18, provides the "nth" or multiple to use in the procedure; that is, if you want 50 people from a sampling frame of 900, choose every 18th person.

Second, you need to decide on a starting point in the sampling frame list. Again, finger pointing or some other unsystematic means is recommended. If, for example, you randomly put your finger on element #14, then your sample would include numbers 14, 32, 50, 68, and so on until you have all 50 elements.

As described above, systematic random sampling produces the same result as simple random sampling: a random sample. Both procedures require a list of the sampling frame, but sytematic random sampling requires that the list be in random order. If the elements in the sampling frame list are not randomized, problems will arise whenever there are simple or periodic trends in the sampling frame listing.

Simple trends are *systematic and consistent changes in some quality inherent in the sampling frame elements.* For example, a mailing list you obtained from someone else may be ordered in terms of postal codes. Depending on the starting point you choose and the proportion sampled, a postal code order may result in some codes, such as those for underpopulated areas, being skipped in the sampling process; thus such codes would not have an equal chance of being included. If you selected every 30th name, postal codes represented by fewer than 30 names may not be included at all.

Periodic trends are *cyclic changes that repeat throughout the sampling frame.* Babbie (1983), for example, mentioned a study in which the sampling frame consisted of soldiers arranged in squads. Each squad contained ten soldiers, and the sergeant's name was always listed first in each squad. A researcher who systematically sampled every tenth soldier obtained a sample composed entirely of sergeants, simply because his starting point happened to be a sergeant's name. The other members of the squad never had a chance to be included in the sample, and it was not, therefore, really a random sample. Similarly, a list of students arranged according to year in school and grade point averages could result in sampling only seniors. Thus, before using any sampling frame list for systematic random sampling, be sure the list is in random order. Without a randomly ordered listing, systematic random sampling is not truly random.

Stratified Random Sampling

Both simple and systematic random sampling require a list of the sampling frame and that the elements in the sampling frame are relatively homogeneous. If your sampling frame is not homogeneous but instead contains subgroups, such as seniors, juniors, and so forth in a listing of university students, then you may need to represent those subgroups in your sample. Whenever subgroups of a population are necessary for research purposes, stratified random sampling results in less sampling error than occurs in either simple or systematic random sampling.

Stratified random sampling is accomplished by *using random selection separately for each subgroup in the sampling frame.* Stratified random sampling for a sampling frame of university students would involve either simple or systematic sampling within the senior class, the same procedure within the junior class, and so on until all classes are represented in the sample. The subgroups within the sampling frame are treated as though they were separate sampling frames themselves.

By using stratified random sampling, you can be sure your sample will contain equal or some other proportionate numbers of males and females, people with ages above and below 30, or any other subgroups that are desirable. If you want to select a specific number of each subgroup members, the technique is also called probability sampling with quotas. In that case you establish a quota for each subgroup and then randomly sample members of that subgroup until the quota is met. The key, however, is that you are using a random sampling procedure within each subgroup, and so the final sample is indeed a random sample.

Cluster Sampling

Simple, systematic, and stratified random sampling are all variants of the basic name-in-a-hat process described earlier. Essentially, the entire sampling frame is listed and elements are randomly selected from it. Sometimes, however, you don't have a list of the sampling frame and cannot obtain one. You would not, for example, be likely to be able to find or generate a sampling frame list for all college students in the United States. When sampling frame lists are unavailable, researchers use **cluster sampling**—*randomly selecting hierarchical groups from the sampling frame.* The groups included in the sampling frame are called clusters, and

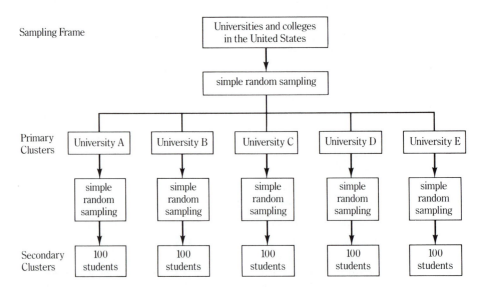

Figure 16.6 A two-stage cluster sampling procedure for obtaining a random sample of 500 college students in the United States. Five universities are randomly selected from among all those in the U.S., and then 100 students are randomly selected from each of the five universities.

you sample finer and finer gradations of clusters until you are at a level at which you can obtain a list of elements.

To select a random sample of 500 college students in the United States, for example, you could first create a sampling frame consisting of a list of colleges and universities (my encyclopedia has one, and there are other sources for such a list). Using simple random sampling, you could randomly select, say, five colleges from this list. Then, from those clusters, you could randomly select 100 students from each college to obtain a random sample of 500 college students residing in the United States. Figure 16.6 illustrates this sampling procedure.

Usually, whenever the sampling frame is so large that you need to use cluster sampling, you will very likely need to include some sort of stratification as well.

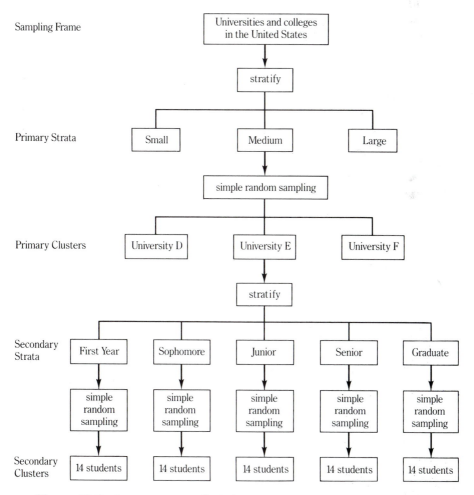

Figure 16.7 A two-stage stratified cluster sampling procedure for obtaining a random sample of 630 college students representing small, medium, and large schools as well as all four undergraduate years and a single group of graduate students.

To obtain a sample of U.S. college students, for example, you probably want to be sure to include some students from small, medium, and large institutions, or some from each of the four regions of the country. Once you have selected the strata, you might also want to select various levels of students—graduate students, seniors, and so on—within each college. Such a multistage, stratified cluster sampling process is illustrated in Figure 16.7.

Combining different probability sampling procedures is not uncommon, and it is acceptable to combine any two or more probability sampling procedures. So long as you limit yourself to random selection procedures, you are free to be as creative as is necessary to obtain the sample you want. What is not acceptable, however, is combining probability with nonprobability sampling procedures.

Nonprobability Sampling

Unlike probability sampling, **nonprobability sampling** refers to *any procedure in which elements have unequal chances for being included.* If you choose elements on the basis of how they look, where they live, or some other criteria, you limit the chances of those who do not meet the criteria. There are several different types of nonprobability sampling procedures, but they all have one thing in common: when a nonprobability sample is obtained, you cannot estimate sampling error. Because nonprobability samples are not random samples, it is usually impossible to determine the appropriate sampling distribution, which is required for estimating sampling error.

Accidental Sampling

The most common procedure for obtaining a nonprobabilty sample is **accidental sampling**—*selection based on availability or ease of inclusion.* As you might guess, the person-on-the-street interviews often shown during local newscasts are examples of accidental sampling. The interviewer selects whoever is willing to talk in front of the camera, and the sample is further made accidental by selecting the most intelligible respondents for broadcast on the air. Accidental sampling is also called availability sampling, but it is likely to be mislabeled as "random" by those who do not understand the nature of a truly random selection process.

Those who mistakenly refer to accidental sampling as random sampling tend to argue that they didn't use any selection criteria at all. Instead, they claim they interviewed the first 25 people to walk out of, say, a movie theater. But that does, in fact, involve selection criteria. Specifically, selecting the first 25 people out of the theater limits the chances of inclusion of those who sat near the front, those who stayed to watch the credits, those who were so moved by the movie they sat for a while to regain their composure, or those who for some other reason delayed their departure.

One of the best examples of the problems that may be encountered when attempting to generalize from an accidental sample is the embarrassment of the editors of *The Literary Digest* (1936) when they used an accidental sample to predict the outcome of the 1936 U.S. presidential election. Their problem was, simply, that their prediction was incredibly wrong. They initially sent out ten million ballots and obtained a sample of two million returns. Those returns indicated a 57% to 43% margin in favor of Alf Landon over Franklin Delano Roosevelt. Instead, Roosevelt obtained about 63% of the actual popular vote.

With such a large sample, even an accidental sample, someone unfamiliar with sampling theory might expect the sampling error to be very small. But that's exactly the point underlying our knowledge about sampling theory: no matter how large the sample, there is no way to estimate sampling error without a random sampling procedure. Unfortunately, the editors of *The Literary Digest* had used telephone books and automobile registration records in their sampling frame. In the mid-1930s, telephone and automobile owners tended to be among the wealthier members of the population, and wealthier voters, then as now, tended to vote Republican.

The editors' sample was composed primarily of Republicans, which explains why they predicted that the Republican candidate, Landon, would be the winner. The standard error of their sample would have been extremely small, but *only* if the editors had wanted to predict the voting patterns of Republicans. Of course, Republicans were not the only voters to vote in the 1936 election, and the editors ended up looking rather silly.

Purposive Sampling

For some research projects, particularly exploratory or pilot projects, you may want to obtain a sample of specific individuals. **Purposive sampling** refers to *procedures directed toward obtaining a certain type of element.* If you were developing a questionnaire designed to measure prejudice, for example, you might want to include in your sample both members of a known bigoted group, such as the Ku Klux Klan, and members of, say, the National Association for the Advancement of Colored People. If the questionnaire was valid, the former group ought to score considerably higher than the latter. Although the two samples would enable you to assess validity, you would still have no logical basis for attempting to generalize the results to any particular population.

Quota Sampling

One of the many ways in which those interested in such things attempt to predict the outcomes of elections is **quota sampling**—*selecting sampling elements on the basis of categories assumed to exist within the population.* At first glance, quota sampling appears to be the same as stratified random sampling, but there is an important difference. In stratified random sampling, elements are randomly selected within the stratified groups. Quota sampling, on the other hand, is more akin to stratified purposive or stratified accidental sampling. Presumed subdivisions of the population, not a concrete listing of the sampling frame, are the bases of the selection process.

For those interested in predicting the outcomes of elections, quota sampling usually involves selecting voters from what are called key precincts—those that exhibit a good track record of outcomes similar to the overall election results. There may be a historical reason to believe that the precinct results will match the overall results, but the continuation of that match cannot be guaranteed. If there has been a shift in the population in the precinct, or a shift in the thoughts or activities of the voters in the precinct, then the precinct results will no longer match the overall election results. Indeed, political scientists use changes in the predictive ability of key precincts as a measure of political shifts, such as growing conservatism, for one example.

Although quota sampling may produce a sample that appears to be a miniature version of the population, the appearance is more illusory than real. It is possible to obtain certain percentages of males and females, Blacks and Whites, wealthy and poor, and so on, but failure to randomly select within those categories makes it impossible to determine the amount of sampling error. Despite its apparent attractions, it is best to avoid quota sampling if you want to generalize your research results.

Quota sampling led to the famous 1948 photograph of Harry Truman holding a newspaper with the infamous headline DEWEY DEFEATS TRUMAN. Based on the 1940 census, the correct percentages of various types of voters had been included in a quota sample, but the percentages had changed since the census. In the intervening eight years, the need to increase production to support U.S. efforts during World War II had led to a major shift in the population from rural to urban areas. The 1940 census figures did not reflect that shift, and the quota sample used by the newspaper had underestimated urban voters (who tended to vote Democrat). The early election returns from key precincts chosen on the basis of the outdated census information, coupled with the desire to be the first on the street with the election results, produced the incorrect headline.

Representative Samples

The primary goal of any sampling procedure is to obtain a **representative sample**—*a sample that resembles the population within an acceptable margin of error.* The phrase "within an acceptable margin of error" should immediately clue you in on the fact that probability sampling procedures are required for representative samples, simply because sampling error can be estimated only for randomly selected samples.

Of equal importance, however, is the phrase "resembles the population." Random selection, simply because it is random, may result in a sample that does not resemble the population. The odds are against such an occurrence, but some likelihood exists. In a predominantly male college such as the United States Air Force Academy, for example, a simple random sample might well not include any female students. If the population evidences distinct subgroups, some stratification will be required to obtain a representative sample.

Alternatively, some types of research projects do not require that much attention be paid to sampling procedures. We already noted that exploratory projects may not require a probability sample; an accidental or purposive sample may be all you need. One of the more difficult practices for many to understand is the use of volunteer participants in experimental research. I'm often asked, for example, "How can using college students tell you anything about what real jurors will do?" (See, for example, Dane & Wrightsman, 1982.) To understand why sampling may not be important in experimental research, it is necessary to recall the purpose of explanatory research.

The purpose of explanatory research is to demonstrate that one variable causes another (for more detail, see Chapter 5). By using an accidental sample, you can do exactly that. Whatever the undefined characteristics of the population from which the sample came, you know that the population includes the independent variable as a characteristic because you manipulated it in the sample. Even though you do not know anything else about the imaginary population from which the sample was selected, you do know that the sample represents a population that has experienced the independent variable. Therefore, the inferential statistics used to examine group differences are based on a random sample, and sampling error can be estimated. Of course, you cannot generalize the experimental results to any particular population, but that is not the main purpose of experimental research.

Summary

• A unit or element is any one thing selected for inclusion in a research project. Populations are abstract collections of elements that can be defined by a sampling frame. Samples are selected from the sampling frame—the concrete representation of the population.

• Parameters are values exhibited by a population and, like the population, are abstract. Statistics—values obtained from a sample—must be used to estimate parameters. All estimates, however, contain some amount of sampling error, which must also be estimated in order to determine the accuracy of the statistic.

• A sampling distribution is a distribution of statistics that could be obtained from repeated samples drawn from the same population. Confidence intervals can be calculated by taking advantage of the nature of sampling distributions, which is defined by the central limit theorem. The standard error of a statistic is the standard deviation of its sampling distribution, and it can be estimated if the sample was selected on the basis of some random sampling procedure.

• Simple random sampling involves identifying all elements in a sampling frame and using a procedure that provides every element an equal chance of being included in the sample. Systematic random sampling also involves a listing of the sampling frame, from which elements are selected by some systematic procedure. A stratified random sample includes dividing the sampling frame into subgroups—strata—from which random samples are separately selected.

• Cluster sampling can be used whenever a listing of the entire sampling frame does not exist. Increasingly more specific elements are randomly selected until one reaches the level at which one can randomly select the elements to be included in the research project.

• Nonprobability sampling includes any sampling procedure that does not result in a random selection process. Accidental sampling involves selecting whatever elements are convenient, whereas purposive sampling involves selecting specific units of interest. Quota sampling involves an accidental or purposive sample selected from presumed subgroups in the population. Regardless of which nonprobability sampling procedure is used, sampling error cannot be estimated.

• A representative sample is any randomly selected sample that resembles the population. Most, but not necessarily all, random samples are also representative. Whether or not a sample represents a population of interest can also depend on the purposes of the research project.

Evaluation Research

 Modern nations should be ready for an experimental approach to social reforms.

—Campbell (1969, p. 409)

Overview

Although not truly a separate type of research method, program evaluation research involves sufficiently different issues to merit separate consideration. In this chapter you will learn about those issues, as well as some of the methods through which program effectiveness or planning can be evaluated. A review of operationalization will be presented, but the topics will be covered from the perspective of attempting to measure variables with minimum alteration of normal routines. You will also learn about the political ramifications of evaluation research. Finally, the ethical issues presented in Chapter 3 will be reviewed with emphasis on the ways they apply to program evaluation research specifically.

Introduction

Let me begin this chapter by pointing out that evaluation research is not a method in the same way that experimental or archival research are methods. Instead, in this context evaluation refers to the purpose for which research is completed, and it may involve any of the methods described in Chapters 5 through 9. It also involves assessing some aspect of a program designed to alter the world in which we live.

Let me also point out that you will probably not have an opportunity to conduct any evaluation research at this point in your career. As you read on you will discover that evaluation research requires considerably more expertise than anyone at the beginning of their research career could possibly have. However, you are likely to read reports of evaluation research, and therefore this chapter is oriented toward consuming rather than conducting such research. We won't completely ignore conducting evaluation research, however, and this chapter may serve as a resource later on, when you do have an opportunity to conduct evaluation research.

According to Rossi and Freeman, "**evaluation research** is *the systematic application of social science research procedures in assessing the conceptualization and design, implementation, and utility of social intervention programs*" (1982, p. 20, emphasis added). This is a rather long, involved definition, and each of its parts deserves attention. The components illustrate the variety of questions that can be asked and answered through evaluation research.

Any attempt to alter the world may be considered a social intervention. When people attempt to change a particular situation, such as hunger, they implement a social intervention; that is, they do something to try to alter the conditions under which people live, presumably for the better. When such attempts involve a specific target group and are planned, social interventions become social programs. In this context, the school you are attending can be considered a social program.

From the perspective of social intervention, education is a planned attempt to alter the immediate experience of a specific target group: students. At a different level of analysis, education is also a program designed to increase the effectiveness of any number of unspecified programs; at least we are told in commencement speeches that educating people will improve the world in general. Other examples of social programs include Aid to Families with Dependent Children, community mental health centers, and the efforts of musicians to relieve famine around the world, such as those of U.S.A. for Africa.

Whenever a social intervention is evaluated, one very reasonable, simple, and appropriate question is asked: Does it work? The utility of a social program includes, in part, the effectiveness of the program—whether you are, for example, learning anything as a result of your education. To those paying for the program, another reasonable question centers on the cost of the program: Is it worth the money we are spending? Program utility, then, refers not only to the benefits received by its participants but also to the cost of the program relative to either its absence or an alternative program.

By definition, any social program includes a set of procedures for its administration—a plan for implementation. Evaluation research often involves examining implementations, sometimes in the planning stage and sometimes after they are underway. Indeed, evaluation of programs both as they are planned and as they are implemented is what Campbell was calling for in the opening quote for this chapter. To some extent, evaluating planning involves trying to predict the future, but that is pretty much what we do any time we generalize from existing research results. Evaluation research, then, generally involves the application of a variety of research methods to decide more effectively how to design and implement a social program and how to determine its effectiveness.

Summative and Formative Evaluation

According to the above definition, evaluation research can be conducted at any phase of a program. The way in which evaluation research is practiced, however, actually falls into two major categories: summative and formative evaluations.

A **summative evaluation** is *an assessment of the outcome of a program.* Also called outcome evaluation, summative research involves determining the goals that were actually reached by a completed program. For example, outcome evaluation may be used to determine the number of tons of food delivered to Ethiopians as a result of the July 1985 "Live Aid" concert. The goals measured by a summative evaluation may or may not be those included in the original plan of the program, and the research is usually accomplished through archival, survey, experimental, or quasi-experimental methods. Because manipulations of independent variables are not always possible in evaluation research, quasi-experimental designs tend to be used more often than experimental designs.

A **formative evaluation** is *an assessment of the process of a program.* Also called process evaluation, formative evaluation involves judging the means by which a program is operating. Questions about the effects of a program can be involved, but they are addressed with respect to how the effects are produced. Rather than using methods that measure differences among groups, formative evaluation researchers are more likely to concentrate on participant observation and other field research methods. Data tend to be qualitative but can be quantitative as well.

Summative and formative evaluations differ in terms of the questions asked about a program—what it has accomplished and how it is operating, respectively. Although there are methods that tend to be used more for one than the other purpose, any method that appropriately addresses the relevant question can be used for either type of evaluation research.

Consumers of Evaluation Research

Perhaps one of the greatest differences between evaluation research and the other types of research discussed in Part II of this text concerns the consumers—the people who will use the results of the research. Thus far, most of our discussions have focused on other behavioral scientists as the major consumers of research results. Evaluation research, however, is action research conducted in order to effect a change in the way things are done, and its consumers include not only other scientists, but also program administrators and recipients, policy makers, and anyone else with a vested interest in the program being evaluated.

The fact that those with a vested interest in the program are also most likely to be the ones who commission or sponsor the evaluation research can produce some rather sticky ethical and practical problems for researchers. When someone's reputation or employment is on the line, the presumed objectivity with which the results may be considered tends to fade a bit. The "experimenting society" envisioned by Campbell and others does not yet exist. Primarily for this reason, the way in which measures and procedures are determined for evaluation research may not be as straightforward as they may seem to be for other types of research.

The Hartford Project: An Example of Evaluation Research

Operationalization

Attempting to operationalize the concepts involved in any research project is no easy task. When the major reason for making the attempt is to evaluate a social program, the task can very quickly become extremely difficult. Program goals are often defined before anyone has contemplated doing research, and they are rarely as well-defined as the theoretical concepts with which we work when conducting other types of research.

Throughout this section, we'll use a crime control intervention program designed to reduce burglaries and robberies in the Asylum Hill area of Hartford, CT (Fowler, 1981) as a continuing example. The program has been called both the Asylum Hill Project and the Hartford Project; we'll use the latter title, primarily because it's the better-known name.

Similarity to Basic Research

Like any research project, the Hartford Project was based on existing theory and research. For example, several researchers had pointed to the advantage of physical measures to control neighborhood crime. A high level of surveillance in a mixture of homes and businesses, together with a sense of cohesion or belongingness, were theorized to reduce or retard criminal activity. The Hartford Project was the first in a series of studies designed to examine these theoretical issues in an actual neighborhood setting.

Also like any other research project, evaluation research includes a great deal of decision making and planning before any data are collected. The variety of questions that can be asked about a program is as great as the variety of questions that can be asked about a theory; it is limitless. Whether about theory or programs, a single study cannot address all questions. Indeed, one of the reasons we'll study the Hartford Project as an exemplary piece of evaluation research is the combination of its similarity to the general research process and its inclusion of a wide range of evaluation-specific issues. The Hartford Project, for example, included both formative and summative purposes, but we're getting ahead of ourselves.

The Problem

In any evaluation research project, defining the problem is the first step. What is the present situation, and what about it should be the target of the evaluation, are the main questions involved in defining the research problem. If the program is ongoing, these questions can be addressed through archival research or interviews with key program personnel. In the Hartford Project, they were addressed through formative evaluations.

According to Fowler, "from the outset, [the project] was intended to be an integrated, multifaceted program which included physical design, police, and citizen components working in concert to reduce criminal opportunities" (1981, p. 167). Not only was the Hartford Project the first of its kind; it was also an effort to tackle a social problem—crime—that seems to invite more problems than solutions. Some form of preliminary assessment was necessary before the operationalization of the project could be finalized.

It was necessary to obtain descriptive data about the physical design of the neighborhood, and so a team of design experts studied Asylum Hill. For example, some of the conditions that required change included a great deal of traffic on residential streets, a high number of pedestrians who did not reside in the neighborhood, a public park that seemed "overrun" by drunks and teenagers, and the frequent use of private and semiprivate areas, such as backyards and parking lots, as alternatives to sidewalks.

Other preliminary information was obtained by surveying residents, particularly about their fear of crime and experience with victimization. Police records were examined to obtain baseline data about the frequency and patterns of criminal activity. The police officers working in the neighborhood were also surveyed, and observational research provided information about the activities of residential organizations.

The Program

As a result of the information collected during the planning stage of the program, a number of changes in the Asylum Hill neighborhood were suggested. These eventually became incorporated into a planned innovation—a social program for reducing crime. According to Fowler (1981, p. 169), the program included three components:

1) A police team was to be permanently assigned to the area in order to increase police familiarity with the local crime problem and with criminals and to strengthen ties between police and citizens.
2) The vehicular traffic through the neighborhood was to be restructured by the use of street closings and the introduction of one-way streets. Through these changes and the introduction of visual neighborhood boundaries, it was hoped that the residential nature of the area would be emphasized and that residents would be more able and willing to exert control over the activities in their neighborhood, thereby making operation of outside offenders more difficult.
3) Resident organizations were to be developed and encouraged to provide a mechanism for residents to work with police, to participate in the planning of the details for the physical design changes and, perhaps, to involve residents directly in efforts to strengthen the neighborhood and reduce crime.

Just as a single research project can rarely test an entire theory, a single innovation can rarely affect the full range of difficulties included in a social problem, or even the full range of measures in a single program. Those designing the project realized that a program may be designed to reduce all crime, but implementing and evaluating such a program would be impossible. Too many crimes are extremely difficult to detect, such as spouse and child abuse, and other crimes may be too infrequent, such as murder. Instead, the program was to focus on two crimes only: burglary and robbery. These two crimes were chosen because they were somewhat common in the area and were typically committed by perpetrators unknown to the victims, and because the program designers believed they produced fear.

In the Hartford Project, the ability to measure processes and outcomes was considered in the planning of the program. This is one advantage inherent in deciding to evaluate a program before it is fully designed and implemented. Not all programs, however, are implemented with evaluation in mind; many researchers find themselves having to deal with unmeasureable program goals.

The Questions

The most obvious question to be addressed was simply whether the project reduced crime. As a program designed specifically for that purpose, perhaps it is the only question of merit. The Hartford Project, however, was not designed only to reduce crime. Again because the project was planned with evaluation in mind, there were actually four questions:

1) In what ways was the program as implemented similar to or different from the one that was planned?
2) Did the rates of burglary and robbery, and the residents' concerns about those crimes, decrease as a result of the program?
3) If so, what features of the program produced those results? If not, for what reason did this program fail to produce those results?
4) What, if anything, does this experience teach us about how to affect crime and fear in other neighborhoods? (Fowler, 1981, p. 170)

As pointed out earlier, the Hartford Project included both formative and summative evaluations. Formative evaluation was used in the design of the program. The first question restates the general purpose of formative evaluation but does so from a summative perspective: Did we do what we planned to do? The second question is most clearly an outcome issue, a summative evaluation question: Did the program accomplish what it was designed to accomplish? The third question involves causal analysis, an attempt to determine the cause(s) of whatever effects were produced by the program. The fourth question is a crossover question; from the viewpoint of the Hartford Project it is summative, but from the viewpoint of a continuing series of crime control projects it is formative. How these questions were answered, or not answered, through the data collected is the issue to which we next turn.

The Measures

Fowler (1981) pointed out several difficulties encountered in attempting to obtain reliable and valid measures for the project. These difficulties, or at least some of them, are likely to be encountered by most evaluation researchers (see, for example, Reicken & Boruch, 1974).

The first of these difficulties stemmed from what Fowler (1981, p. 172) described as "vague, meaningless, or extremely complex" concepts. One of those concepts is fear of crime, for which reliable and valid measures were required at the outset of the project in order to obtain baseline information. Because previous research (as of 1973) was of little help in operationalizing fear of crime, the researchers relied on theory (see, for example, Parsons, 1951) to derive their measures. Eventually, fear of crime was operationalized as a combination of the likelihood of personal victimization and a subjective assessment of the general severity of victimization for a particular crime. That is, an individual's level of fear was related both to the perceived chances of becoming a victim and a belief about how dangerous and uncomfortable being a victim might be.

Another problem inherent in attempting to operationalize various concepts surfaced because the evaluation team was composed of researchers from different disciplines. No small amount of effort was devoted to becoming familiar with one another's specialized jargon and measurement processes. The social psychologists, sociologists, criminologists, and urban designers all were required to translate terms and concepts—the meanings of which they took for granted—for the benefit of the others. Such communication difficulties are more common than you might think because those conducting evaluation research are typically outsiders with respect to the program. Evaluation researchers must communicate with practitioners, administrators, clients, and others who may be unfamiliar with the jargon of research and may have their own brand of jargon. Just think back, for example, about how much jargon you have picked up reading this textbook. Did you know, for example, what "quasi-experimental," "sampling distribution," or "regression artifact" meant? How many of your friends who haven't taken this course would understand these terms? The glossary is full of jargon, and you're just beginning to deal with research.

The second problem encountered in the project was attempting to measure systematically processes that were not systematic. Describing or measuring changes in everyday human behavior is often problematic in summative evaluation research but is equally as often necessary in formative evaluations. One of the processes to be evaluated in the Hartford Project was the use of space by those residing in and outside of the neighborhood. To measure vehicular traffic, for example, mechanical counters were deployed day and night to monitor traffic at strategic locations in the neighborhood. To measure pedestrian traffic, observers counted pedestrians at certain times of the day. The observers also coded the direction of movement and estimated age, ethnic status, and other demographic characteristics. The combination of research strategies for the purpose of measurement was necessary to measure all of the components of the project.

The third problem centered on attempting to measure the impact of the program. In basic research, replications or random assignment aid in the logical process of attributing an effect to the treatment of participants; that is, in causal analysis. In evaluation research, however, replications are extremely rare. Funds were not available in the Hartford Project, for example, to redesign several neighborhoods, nor could the researchers randomly assign people to live in different neighborhoods or randomly assign some outsiders to visit or stay out of the neighborhood.

More often than not, the impact of a new program is assessed by comparing the preexisting conditions with conditions after the program. Without random assignment, however, this before–after design is highly susceptible to a variety of alternative explanations (see Chapter 5). When the research environment is a city neighborhood, history and mortality effects are of particular concern. Another approach, more often used with existing programs, is to identify a similar unit of analysis—a neighborhood, individuals, and so on—not involved in the program and use it for comparison. For the Hartford Project, the difficulty of finding another neighborhood similar to Asylum Hill precluded that approach.

A combination of approaches was used instead. Baseline data were collected in the Asylum Hill neighborhood, and the outcome measures were compared to those data. Also, two neighborhoods adjacent to Asylum Hill were selected as "control" neighborhoods. The adjacent areas were chosen, in part, because one possible outcome of the physical redesign was displacement—movement of criminal activities out of Asylum Hill and into some other neighborhood. Although displacement solves the problem of crime in one location, it does not produce any net reduction in crime.

Ecosystem Measures

Measuring victimization rates and fear of crime were attempts to measure the impact of the program from the perspective of the recipients or clients. The Hartford Project researchers had an advantage over other evaluation researchers because they had a pretty good idea of the clients' desired level of service: the residents of Asylum Hill presumably desired zero victimization and zero fear of crime. A zero-level outcome, however, cannot always be assumed to be the desired level.

Developed from the concept of stakeholder evaluations (Bryk, 1983; Gold, 1981), **ecosystem measurement** involves *the simultaneous measurement of level of service received and level of service desired by clients.* In an educational program, for example, students may be asked to describe both the depth of coverage provided for a particular topic and the depth of coverage they desired for the topic. Ecosystem measures, and stakeholder evaluation in general, are based on the assumption that those who have a stake in the program are valuable resources for determining the desired level of service.

Ecosystem measures enable you to determine whether the perceived level of service was less than, equal to, or greater than the desired level of service. Regardless of the extent to which such information is to be used to determine the level of service that should be provided, ecosystem measures provide information beyond a simple satisfactory/unsatisfactory measure of the program. The more that clients can be assumed to be competent judges of the desired level of service, the more informative and valuable ecosystem measures become.

The Results

In case you are wondering about the outcome of the Hartford Project, the program did both lower crime rates and reduce residents' fears about crime. The complete results are too lengthy to outline in this chapter, but you can read about them in Fowler's (1981) report. It is an interesting report, and it is fascinating if you are interested in program evaluation or criminal justice issues. Now, however, we must turn to the relative advantages and disadvantages of the use of experimental designs for evaluation.

The Controversy Over the Use of Experiments in Evaluation Research

Boruch (1975) provided what is perhaps the best elucidation of the controversy over the use of experiments in evaluation research. The controversy involves four major issues: difficulty, qualitative information, innovation, and ethics. No straightforward solutions appear to be forthcoming, although there are guidelines that are beneficial to both beginning and experienced scientists.

Difficulties with Experiments in Evaluation Research

The *possibility* of using experimental designs in evaluation research is not part of the controversy; it is possible (and has been for some time) to manipulate variables and randomly assign participants to different conditions within almost any program that can be evaluated. Boruch provided over 200 examples of experimentally evaluated programs, including programs in job training, criminal justice, social welfare, and many other fields. It is not, however, always *easy* to use experimental designs in evaluation research.

The difficulties inherent in the use of experimental designs are not difficulties with the designs per se. After all, random assignment is not a difficult procedure, nor is manipulating a variety of different variables likely to be included in program evaluation. Instead, the difficulties appear to revolve around the willingness of program administrators to allow the use of experimental designs, as well as the ability of other research procedures to measure up to experiments.

The key factor appears to be the type of program being evaluated. Boruch points out that the difficulty is directly related to the extent to which the effects being evaluated are dependent on program staff and personal skills. Social service programs, for example, involve greater difficulty than do programs involving technological innovations. Administrators of social service programs often resist the use of experiments for evaluation simply because an experiment is too often perceived to be a perfect test of a program. The argument is not with the use of experimental designs, but with the perceived inability of scientists to measure the effects of social service programs. A potentially good idea for social service may be deemed a bad idea not because it is ineffective, but because a supposedly perfect experiment did not include an accurate measure of the benefits of the program. That is, the problem is not with determining the cause, but with measuring the effect.

Similarly, Boruch points out that critics of experiments consider them to be too narrow in scope (to test only a few variables) or too brief in duration (only one measurement of the dependent variable(s) instead of multiple measurements over a period of time). Again, however, these criticisms are not related to design considerations, but rather to the financial and political considerations that are a part of all evaluation research. Interviews, for example, are more expensive than questionnaires, which in turn are more expensive than archival measures. It is often the case that waiting a number of years in order to longitudinally monitor the progress of a program is not politically feasible. Research takes time, and both proponents and opponents of social programs are usually anxious to learn of a program's effectiveness as quickly as possible.

The above viewpoint from the administrators' perspective is, of course, based on a lack of familiarity with experimental designs and research in general. There is, of course, no perfect experiment, nor should anyone ever consider the results of a single experiment to be the final word on any issue. What is required to overcome this problem, in addition to better measures of outcome variables, is education about the value of experimental research as well as its limitations.

Qualitative Information in Evaluation Research

The second issue in the controversy also appears to revolve around misperceptions about experimental research. Specifically, experimental research is perceived to preclude the collection of qualitative data. Clearly, researchers who use experimental designs tend to favor quantitative measures, but that preference has little to do with experimental design itself. Instead, it would seem to be more reasonable to conclude that those who prefer quantitative data also prefer experimental designs. Neither randomly assigning participants to conditions nor manipulating independent variables necessarily requires the use of quantitative dependent variables. Although design and measurement are related, the relationship between them is simply not that strong.

Innovation in Evaluation Research

The third issue connected with using experimental designs for evaluation research is that such designs, when used to test the outcome of a program, cannot provide information about what other new programs might work. An experimental test of a traffic safety program, for example, might answer whether the program produces a lower accident rate; but if the answer is no, it doesn't lower the accident rate, then the experiment does not provide information about the potential effectiveness of alternative programs.

Although this is a valid criticism, it is not new. Indeed, this same criticism can be directed at all research in which theories are tested. If only one theory is tested in a research project, the researcher is limited to information about that theory. The theory is either supported or not—a program either works or it doesn't. Regardless of the research design, one obtains information only about what is tested.

Campbell (1971) has offered one solution to the innovation problem, a solution based on what has been done in theory-testing research to overcome the same problem. The solution is, very simply, to use experimental designs to test the relative effectiveness of two or more programs, just as many experiments test the relative effectiveness of competing theories. The question then becomes whether one program is better than the other. If more than one alternative exists for a social service program, or any other program for that matter, but enough money is available to fund only one of them, Campbell suggests implementing a simultaneous test of alternatives rather than what is typically done now—a sequential test of first one, then the other, program.

Also within the context of innovation, Boruch pointed out that many opponents of experiments in evaluation claim that rigorous—that is, experimental— tests of programs will limit creativity for developing new programs. Essentially, the argument is that incentives to be creative will be reduced if those responsible for development fear that their creations will be "shot down" by an evaluator armed with an experiment. This issue is similar to one addressed earlier, that of the unwillingness of administrators to accept the results of experiments because they perceive them to be final. Drawing an analogy between theory-testing and evaluation research, however, destroys the logic of this criticism. Certainly, creativity in terms of theory development has not suffered from the use of experimental designs, and there is no reason to assume that creativity with respect to program development will also suffer.

What may be affected, however, are the careers of those who propose innovative programs. If the effectiveness of a proposed program is used to determine whether or not a program administrator or developer will be retained, for example, then not too many administrators or developers are going to be open to rigorous evaluation. Again, Campbell suggested adopting an experimentation approach to program development to solve this problem. If evaluation of administrative and development performance is based on a track record of success, as opposed to the success of a single program, then individuals may be more willing to try something new.

Ethics in Evaluation Research

Perhaps the greatest controversy over the use of experimental designs for evaluation revolves around the ethical issues of random assignment. Opponents of experiments have likened random assignment to randomly denying treatment to those who would otherwise receive a program's services. Recall from Chapter 3, however, that failing to test a program adequately before implementing it also constitutes a potential breach of ethics.

Most program evaluations involve a test of whether the program is beneficial or ineffective. More often than not, limitations on the number of participants in most programs are based on financial rather than methodological considerations. That is, with or without random assignment, monetary constraints limit the number of participants who could potentially benefit from the services being evaluated. In such cases, holding lotteries to select and assign participants may be the fairest means by which to implement an experiment (Reicken & Boruch, 1974). When the individuals involved have equivalent needs, lotteries are perceived as fair, and the procedures for a lottery are not much different from those normally involved in random assignment.

Although ethical questions rarely have easy answers, the general balancing act concerns whether random assignment places a greater burden on participants than does a nonexperimental design. If the answer is yes, then a quasi-experimental design should be used to complete the evaluation. Withholding benefits to potential program clients through random assignment is not the only ethical issue involved in evaluation research, and so we turn now to some other ethical considerations.

Ethical Considerations in Evaluation Research

Like all research, evaluation research does not occur in an ethical vacuum. Indeed, because evaluation research is often contracted for or paid for by those running the program being evaluated, evaluation research poses some ethical issues not normally considered in other types of research. Evaluation research involves trying to serve four masters: yourself, the program clients, the program staff, and the program administrator(s). In the ideal world of Campbell's (1971) experimenting society, these four masters share the common goal of obtaining sufficient information to decide the best way to implement a program to solve a social problem.

In the not-so-ideal world of practicing evaluation research, the four groups may have very different, and sometimes competing, interests. You want to complete a high-quality research project, the clients want their problem solved, the staff members want to be able to function effectively and efficiently, and the administrators want a low-cost, favorable evaluation of the program. The Evaluation Research Society (ERS Standards Committee, 1982) has published a set of standards to aid evaluation researchers in their attempts to promote the ideal while working in the not-so-ideal. The discussion below is based on those standards, and I strongly urge you to read the original document before attempting to conduct any evaluation research.

Formulation and Negotiation

Before beginning an evaluation project, all parties involved should reach a mutual understanding of the task, the methods, the rationale, and the shortcomings of the project. The rights of all individuals involved in the project should be of major importance, and one should not attempt projects beyond one's expertise and resources. Any agreements reached during the negotiation and formulation stages should be specified in writing, for the documents may clarify subsequent misunderstandings.

To the extent possible, the agreement should contain a clear statement of the purpose and description of the program to be evaluated, including identification of the expectations and needs of clients, decision makers, and other potential users of the results. The objectives of the evaluation should be clearly specified, as should any reasonable estimate of the cost of the evaluation. Within the context of outlining any possible conflicts of interests, the feasibility of the evaluation and any restrictions on dissemination of the results should also be specified.

Structure and Design

In addition to methodological interests, the design of an evaluation project is influenced by "logistical, ethical, political and fiscal concerns" (ERS Standards Committee, 1982, p. 13). Such influences are not, however, sufficient reason for failing to provide the best possible design, regardless of the type of evaluation chosen during the negotiation phase. The design should be clearly specified and should be appropriate for the purposes of the evaluation. For outcome studies, for example, the design should be adequate for identifying the relative differences between treatment and control groups. Sampling methods should be specified and justified in terms of the purposes of the evaluation.

Any measures involved in the project should be clearly described, including their levels of established reliability and validity. Finally, the cooperation of any individuals involved in implementing the actual data collection procedures should be obtained. If you plan to involve staff members in data collection, for example, the best possible design will be worthless if the staff cannot collect the data.

Data Collection and Preparation

Like any good research project, the procedures and means for data collection should be planned in advance and should include some way to determine whether the plan is being followed. Training and supervising may be required to ensure that those collecting the data are following the proper procedures. To whatever extent possible, the plan for data collection should include an effort to assess the reliability and validity of the data as they are collected. That a preexisting measure has exhibited reliability and validity in previous studies is not an absolute guarantee that the same will hold true for the way in which you use it in your research. Chances are it will, but it never hurts to check.

The actual data collection procedures should involve a minimum amount of disruption to the routine of the program. Staff members usually have enough to do without being asked to take on the extra burden of collecting data. Informed consent should be monitored, particularly if those who are clients or data collectors are to be exposed to any risks. Depending on the sensitivity of the data, safeguards should be established to protect confidentiality or anonymity. Also, safeguards must be developed to ensure against loss of the data, including documentation of the sources, collection procedures, and preparation of the data.

Data Analysis and Interpretation

The data analyses should be chosen to match the purpose and design of the project and the data collected. Rather than simply relying on what others have done or what is convenient, the chosen analyses should be clearly justified in light of the underlying assumptions and limitations inherent in them. Care must be taken to match analyses with the type of data collected. Sufficient documentation should be maintained so that others may replicate the analyses, including procedures used to clean or transform variables.

When interpreting data, care must be taken to avoid drawing conclusions beyond the limitations of the data and their analyses. Particularly if the decision makers are not well versed in the use of statistics, the difference between statistical significance and practical significance should be clearly explained. Cause–effect conclusions should be drawn only when appropriate, with clear reference to any remaining alternative explanations. The report should clearly distinguish among empirical results, opinions, judgments, and speculations.

Communication and Disclosure

In addition to care concerning the differences among results, opinions, judgments, and speculations, the final report should clearly convey the research findings. Any assumptions made during the project should be explicitly included, particularly those assumptions relevant to the final recommendations or conclusions. Any limitations of the research, within or without the researcher's control, should also be specified and related to the final recommendations.

Dissemination of the final or any preliminary reports should be completed within the guidelines specified in the initial agreement. Only those authorized to publicize the results should do so. Those who have contributed to the project should be acknowledged and should receive whatever feedback is appropriate. Finally, preparation of a data base and its documentation should be completed as outlined in the initial agreement.

Use of Results

Because evaluation research is invariably conducted to provide information to those who must make decisions about the program, it is essential that the results be made available in sufficient time to allow them to be used. And although one cannot be responsible for others' misinterpretations of results, there is an ethical requirement to attempt to prevent misinterpretations, as well as to attempt to correct them when they become known.

Because the researcher is probably the most fully informed about the results, the researcher may be called upon to make policy recommendations. Similarly, personal interests may lead a researcher to adopt an advocate role. Although policy recommendations and advocacy are not unethical themselves, care must be taken to separate them from the results. Understanding research results does not necessarily make one an expert on policies and implications. As with any research, departures from reasonable conclusions drawn from the data must be labeled as such.

Summary

• Evaluation involves the use of behavioral research methods to assess the conceptualization, design, implementation, and utility of intervention programs. In order to be effectively evaluated, a program should have specific procedures and goals, although formative evaluation can be used to develop them. Summative evaluations, on the other hand, deal with program outcomes.

• For evaluation research, administrators, clients, staff, and others with a vested interest must be included with behavioral scientists in the research audience. Operationalizing concepts in evaluation research involves translating goals and procedures into reliable and valid variables. The expanded audience for evaluation research poses an additional burden with respect to ensuring that consumers understand the variables involved in the research.

• When the desired level of some dependent variable is something other than zero, ecosystem measures can be used to compare desired outcomes to obtained outcomes. Using ecosystem measures, however, requires an assumption that those being measured are in a position to know what levels of service they desire.

• Although experimental designs provide the best way to test cause–effect relationships, some controversy exists about their use for evaluation. With the exception of the ethics of random assignment, however, most of the controversial issues result from misunderstandings about the use and utility of experimental designs. When more potential clients exist than can be served by a program, a lottery may be the solution to problems concerning random assignment and decisions about who will or will not receive services.

• There are a number of other ethical issues of significance to evaluation research. The Evaluation Research Society has published standards for ethical conduct that should be used as guidelines by those who conduct evaluation research.

REFERENCES

Adams, G. R. (1977). Physical attractiveness research: Toward a developmental social psychology of beauty. *Human Development, 20,* 217–239.

Adams, G. S. (1964). *Measurement and evaluation in education, psychology, and guidance.* New York: Holt, Rinehart & Winston.

Adorno, T. W., Frenkel-Brunswick, E., Levinson, O. J., & Sanford, R. N. (1950). *The authoritarian personality.* New York: Harper & Row.

Allen, M. J., & Yen, W. M. (1979). *Introduction to measurement theory.* Belmont, CA: Wadsworth.

American Psychological Association. (1981). Ethical principles of psychologists. *American Psychologist, 36,* 633–638.

American Psychological Association. (1983). *Publication manual of the American Psychological Association* (3rd ed.). Washington, DC: Author.

Anastasi, A. (1982). *Psychological testing.* New York: Macmillan.

Aronson, E. (1980). Persuasion via self-justification: Large commitments for small rewards. In L. Festinger (Ed.), *Retrospections on social psychology.* New York: Oxford University Press.

Babbie, E. R. (1979). *The practice of social research.* Belmont, CA: Wadsworth.

Babbie, E. R. (1983). *The practice of social research.* Belmont, CA: Wadsworth.

Bachrach, A. J. (1981). *Psychological research: An introduction.* New York: Random House.

Back, K. W. (1980). The role of social psychology in population control. In L. Festinger (Ed.), *Retrospections on social psychology.* New York: Oxford University Press.

Bales, R. F. (1950). A set of categories for the analysis of small group interaction. *American Sociological Review, 15,* 257–263.

Bales, R. F. (1970). *Personality and interpersonal behavior.* New York: Holt, Rinehart & Winston.

Baron, R. A. (1980). A note on rude awakenings: Some effects of being fleeced. *SASP Newsletter, 6*(6), 1.

Bartley, W. W. III. (1962). *The retreat to commitment.* New York: Knopf.

Baumrind, D. (1964). Some thoughts on the ethics of research: After reading Milgram's "Behavioral study of obedience." *American Psychologist, 19,* 421–423.

Baumrind, D. (1981). The costs of deception. *SASP Newsletter, 7*(4), 1.

Becker, C. J., & Seligman, C. (1978). Reducing air conditioning waste by signalling it is cooler outside. *Personality and Social Psychology Bulletin, 4,* 412–415.

Bem, D. J. (1981). Writing the research report. In L. H. Kidder (Ed.), *Research methods in social relations.* New York: Holt, Rinehart & Winston.

Bem, S. L., & Bem, D. J. (1970). Case study of a nonconscious ideology: Training the woman to know her place. In D. J. Bem (Ed.), *Beliefs, attitudes, and human affairs.* Pacific Grove, CA: Brooks/Cole.

Berkman, D. (1963). Advertising in *Ebony* and *Life:* Negro aspirations vs. reality. *Journalism Quarterly, 40,* 53–64.

Berkowitz, L., & Donnerstein, E. (1982). External validity is more than skin deep: Some answers to criticisms of laboratory experiments. *American Psychologist, 37,* 245–257.

Bingham, W. V. D., & Moore, B. V. (1924). *How to interview.* New York: Harper & Row.

Boruch, R. F. (1975). On common contentions about randomized field experiments. In R. F. Boruch & H. W. Reicken (Eds.), *Experimental tests of public policy.* Boulder, CO: Westview Press.

Bray, R. M., & Kerr, N. L. (1982). Methodological considerations in the study of the psychology of the courtroom. In N. L. Kerr & R. M. Bray (Eds.), *The psychology of the courtroom*. New York: Academic Press.

Brazzill, W. (1969). A letter from the south. *Harvard Educational Review, 39,* 348–356.

Brehm, J. W. (1966). *A theory of psychological reactance*. New York: Academic Press.

Bryk, A. S. (Ed.). (1983). Stakeholder-based evaluation. *New Directions for Program Evaluation, No. 17*. San Francisco: Jossey-Bass.

Buros, O. (1961). *Tests in print*. Highland Park, NJ: Gryphon Press.

Buros, O. (Ed.). (1965). *The sixth mental measurement yearbook*. Highland Park, NJ: Gryphon Press.

Butler, J. M., Rice, L. N., & Wagstaff, A. K. (1963). *Quantitative naturalistic research*. Englewood Cliffs, NJ: Prentice-Hall.

Campbell, D. T. (1969). Reforms as experiments. *American Psychologist, 24,* 409–429.

Campbell, D. T. (1971, September). *Methods for the experimenting society*. Presented to the American Psychological Association, Washington, DC.

Campbell, D. T., & Fiske, D. W. (1959). Convergent and divergent validation by the multitrait-multimethod matrix. *Psychological Bulletin, 56,* 81–105.

Campbell, D. T., & Stanley, J. C. (1963). *Experimental and quasi-experimental designs for research*. Chicago: Rand McNally.

Conover, W. J. (1980). *Practical nonparametric statistics*. New York: Wiley.

Cook, S. (1981). Ethical implications. In L. H. Kidder (Ed.), *Research methods in social relations*. New York: Holt, Rinehart & Winston.

Cook, T. D., & Campbell, D. T. (1979). *Quasi-experimentation: Design & analysis for field settings*. Chicago: Rand McNally.

Copenhaver, M. M., & Dane, F. C. (1987, March). *Effects of quantified instructions for reasonable doubt: Upper limits and reactance*. Presented to Southeastern Psychological Association, Atlanta, GA.

Crano, W. D., & Brewer, M. B. (1973). *Principles of research in social psychology*. New York: McGraw-Hill.

Crawford, J., & Crawford, T. E. (1978). Development and construct validation of a measure of attitudes toward public exposure to sexual stimuli. *Journal of Personality Measurement, 42,* 392–400.

Dane, F. C. (1979). *Status report: Kansas jury project*. Unpublished manuscript, University of Kansas, Lawrence.

Dane, F. C. (1985). In search of reasonable doubt: A systematic examination of selected quantification approaches. *Law and Human Behavior, 9,* 141–158.

Dane, F. C. (1988a). *Community reactions to field testing genetically altered organisms*. Grant proposal submitted to Environmental Protection Agency.

Dane, F. C. (1988b). *The common and uncommon sense of social behavior*. Pacific Grove, CA: Brooks/Cole.

Dane, F. C., & McPartland, F. (1985). *Attitudes toward public displays of intimacy: An exploratory study*. Unpublished manuscript, Clemson University, Clemson, SC.

Dane, F. C., & Thompson, J. K. (1985). Asymmetrical facial expressions: A different interpretation. *Cortex, 21,* 301–303.

Dane, F. C., & Wrightsman, L. S. (1982). Effects of defendents' and victims' characteristics upon verdicts. In N. L. Kerr & R. M. Bray (Eds.), *Psychology in the courtroom*. New York: Academic Press.

Deaux, K., & Major, B. (1987). Putting gender into context: An interactive model of gender-related behavior. *Psychological Review, 94,* 369–389.

Deutsch, M. (1950). Fifty years of conflict. In L. Festinger (Ed.), *Retrospections on social psychology*. New York: Oxford University Press.

Dickson, P. (1981). *The official rules*. New York: Dell.

Diener, E., & Crandall, R. (1979). An evaluation of the Jamaican anticrime program. *Journal of Applied Social Psychology, 9,* 135–146.

Dillman, D. A. (1978). *Mail and telephone surveys: The total design method*. New York: Wiley.

Dillman, D. A., Gallegos, J. G., & Frey, J. H. (1976). Reducing refusal rates for telephone surveys. *Public Opinion Quarterly, 40,* 360–369.

Dunnette, M. D. (1966). *Personnel selection and placement*. Belmont, CA: Wadsworth.

Durant, J. (Ed.), (1985). *Darwinism and divinity: Essays on evolution and religious beliefs*. New York: Blackwell.

Durkheim, E. (1951). *Suicide*. Glencoe, IL: Free Press.

Educational Testing Service. (1981). *Guide to the use of the graduate record examination*. Princeton, NJ: Author.

Edwards, A. (1957). *Techniques of attitude scale construction*. Englewood Cliffs, NJ: Prentice-Hall.

Ellis, L. (1988, April). *The influence of feminist values on television viewing habits.* Presented to Southeastern Psychological Association, New Orleans, LA.

Ellison, J. W. (1965). Computers and testaments. In J. W. Ellison (Ed.), *Computers for the humanities.* New Haven, CT: Yale University Press.

Ellison, K. W., & Buckhout, R. (1981). *Psychology and criminal justice.* New York: Harper & Row.

Erickson, K. T. (1967). A comment on disguised observation in sociology. *Social Problems, 14*(4), 368.

ERS Standards Committee. (1982). Evaluation research society standards for program evaluation. *New Directions for Program Evaluation, 15,* 7–19.

Fassnacht, G. (1982). *Theory and practice for observing behaviour* (C. Bryant, Trans.). London: Academic Press.

Federal Register. (1981). *46*(16), 8366–8392.

Festinger, L., Schachter, S., & Back, K. (1950). *Social pressures in informal groups: A study of human factors in housing.* New York: Harper & Row.

Flanagan, T. J., & McLeod, M. (Eds.). (1983). *Sourcebook of criminal justice statistics—1982.* Washington, DC: U.S. Government Printing Office.

Forgas, J. P. (1982). Episode recognition: Internal representation of interaction routines. In L. Berkowitz (Ed.), *Advances in experimental social psychology.* New York: Academic Press.

Fowler, F. J., Jr. (1981). Evaluating a complex crime control experiment. In L. Bickman (Ed.), *Applied social psychology annual, Vol. 2.* Newbury Park, CA: Sage.

Frank, J. (1981). Social psychology and the prevention of nuclear war: What is our responsibility? *SASP Newsletter, 7*(2), 8.

Gellert, E. (1955). Systematic observation: A method in child study. *Harvard Educational Review, 25,* 179–195.

Glass, G. V., McGraw, B., & Smith, M. L. (1981). *Meta-analysis in social research.* Newbury Park, CA: Sage.

Glazer, M. (1972). *The research adventure: Promise and problems in field work.* New York: Random House.

Gold, N. (1981). *The stakeholder process in educational program evaluation.* Washington, DC: National Institute of Education.

Gold, R. L. (1969). Roles in sociological field observation. In G. J. McCall & J. L. Simmons (Eds.), *Issues in participant observation.* Reading, MA: Addison-Wesley.

Gorden, R. L. (1969). *Interviewing: Strategy, techniques, and tactics.* Pacific Grove, CA: Brooks/Cole.

Greenberg, M. S., & Ruback, R. B. (1982). *Social psychology of the criminal justice system.* Pacific Grove, CA: Brooks/Cole.

Gross, A. E., Green, S. K., Storck, J. T., & Vanyur, J. M. (1980). Disclosure of sexual orientation and impressions of male and female homosexuals. *Personality and Social Psychology Bulletin, 6,* 307–314.

Guttman, L. L. (1944). A basis for scaling qualitative data. *American Sociological Review, 9,* 139–150.

Haberman, S. J. (1978). *Analysis of qualitative data: Volume 1. Introductory topics.* New York: Academic Press.

Haberman, S. J. (1979). *Analysis of qualitative data: Volume 2. New developments.* New York: Academic Press.

Hall, E. T. (1959). *The silent language.* New York: Doubleday.

Haney, C., Banks, C., & Zimbardo, P. (1973). Interpersonal dynamics in a simulated prison. *International Journal of Criminology and Penology, 1,* 69–97.

Hartwig, F., & Dearing, B. E. (1979). *Exploratory data analyses.* Newbury Park, CA: Sage.

Hawkins, D. F. (1977). *Nonresponse in Detroit area study surveys: A ten-year analysis.* Chapel Hill, NC: Institute for Research in Social Sciences.

Hearnshaw, C. S. (1979). *Cyril Burt: Psychologist.* Ithaca, NY: Cornell University Press.

Hill, C. T., Rubin, A., & Peplau, L. A. (1976). Breakups before marriage: The end of 103 affairs. *Journal of Social Issues, 32*(1), 147–168.

Hilton, T. F. (1981). The moral majority and social psychology: An issue for the profession. *SASP Newsletter, 7*(2), 5.

Holsti, O. R. (1968). Content analysis. In G. Lindzey & E. Aronson (Eds.), *The handbook of social psychology.* Menlo Park, CA: Addison-Wesley.

Humphreys, L. (Ed). (1975). *Tearoom trade: Impersonal sex in public places.* Chicago: Aldine.

Hunt, M. (1974). *Sexual behavior in the 1970s.* Chicago: Playboy.

Institute for Social Research. (1976). *Newsletter, 4*(Autumn), 4.

Jacobs, J. (1967). A phenomenological study of suicide notes. *Social Problems, 15,* 60–72.

Jenkins, J., & Russell, W. (1958). An atlas of semantic profiles for 360 words. *American Journal of Psychology, 71,* 688–699.

Jensen, A. (1969a). How much can we boost IQ and scholastic achievement? *Harvard Educational Review, 39,* 1–123.

Jensen, A. (1969b). Reducing the heredity-environment uncertainty: A reply. *Harvard Educational Review, 39,* 449–483.

Johnson, J. M. (1975). *Doing field research.* New York: Free Press.

Kamin, L. J. (1974). *The science and politics of IQ.* Potomac, MD: Erlbaum.

Kelley, H. H., & Thibault, J. W. (1978). *Interpersonal relations: A theory of interdependence.* New York: Wiley.

Kerlinger, F. N. (1972). The structure and content of social attitude referents: A preliminary study. *Educational and Psychological Measurement, 32,* 613–630.

Kerlinger, F. N. (1973). *Foundations of behavioral science research.* New York: Holt, Rinehart & Winston.

Kerlinger, F. N. (1979). *Behavioral research: A conceptual approach.* New York: Holt, Rinehart & Winston.

Kerr, N. L., & Bray, R. M. (Eds.). (1982). *The psychology of the courtroom.* New York: Academic Press.

Kidder, L. H. (1981). *Research methods in social relations.* New York: Holt, Rinehart & Winston.

Kilpatrick, J. J. (1984). *The writer's art.* New York: Andrews, McMeel & Parker.

Kinsey, A., Pomeroy, W. B., & Martin, C. E. (1948). *Sexual behavior in the human male.* Philadelphia: Saunders.

Kinsey, A., Pomeroy, W. B., Martin, C. E., & Gebhard, P. H. (1953). *Sexual behavior in the human female.* Philadelphia: Saunders.

Klecka, W. R., & Tuchfarber, A. J. (1978). Random digit dialing: A comparison to personal survey. *Public Opinion Quarterly, 42,* 105–114.

Kleinke, C. K. (1975). *First impressions.* Englewood Cliffs, NJ: Prentice-Hall.

Kounin, J., & Gump, P. (1961). The comparative influence of punitive and nonpunitive teachers upon children's concepts of school misconduct. *Journal of Educational Psychology, 52,* 44–49.

Kuder, G. F., & Richardson, M. W. (1937). The theory of estimation of test reliability. *Psychometrica, 2,* 151–160.

Kuhn, T. (1962). *The structure of scientific revolution.* Chicago: University of Chicago Press.

LaFrance, M. (1979). Nonverbal synchrony and rapport: Analysis by the cross-lagged panel technique. *Social Psychology Quarterly, 42,* 66–70.

Lasswell, H. D., Lerner, D., & Pool, I. de S. (1952). *The comparative study of symbols.* Stanford, CA: Stanford University Press.

Latané, B., & Darley, J. M. (1968). Group inhibition of bystander intervention in emergencies. *Journal of Personality and Social Psychology, 10,* 215–221.

Lazarsfeld, P. F., Pasanella, A., & Rosenberg, M. (Eds.). (1972). *Continuities in social research.* New York: Free Press.

Leahey, T. H. (1980). The myth of operationism. *The Journal of Mind and Behavior, 1*(2), 126–143.

Leventhal, H., & Sharp, E. (1965). Facial expressions as indicators of distress. In S. Thompkins & C. Izard (Eds.), *Affect, cognition, and personality.* New York: Springer.

Levin, J., & Spates, J. (1970). Hippie values: An analysis of the underground press. *Youth and Society, 2,* 59–72.

Levine, J. M., & Russo, E. M. (1987). Majority and minority influence. In C. Hendrick (Ed.), *Review of Personality and Social Psychology,* (Vol. 8). Newbury Park, CA: Sage.

Lewin, K. (1946). Action research and minority problems. *Journal of Social Issues, 2,* 34–64.

Liebow, E. (1967). *Tally's corner.* Boston: Little, Brown.

Likert, R. (1932). A technique for the measurement of attitudes. *Archives of Psychology,* No. 140.

Lindeman, R. H., Merenda, P. F., & Gold, R. Z. (1980). *Introduction to bivariate and multivariate analyses.* Glenview, IL: Scott, Foresman.

Linz, D., Slack, A., Kaiser, K., & Penrod, S. (1981, October). *Meta-analysis of defendant characteristic studies.* Presented at the Bicennial Convention of the American Psychology-Law Society, Cambridge, MA.

Literary Digest, The. (1936). Landon, 1,293,669: Roosevelt, 972,897. pp. 5–6.

Loftus, E. F., Loftus, G. R., & Messo, J. (1987). Some facts about "weapon focus." *Law and Human Behavior, 11,* 55–62.

Malandro, L. A., & Barker, L. (1983). *Nonverbal communication.* Reading, MA: Addison-Wesley.

Marsden, P. V., Reed, J. S., Kennedy, M. D., & Stinson, K. M. (1982). American regional cultures and differences in leisure time activities. *Social Forces, 60,* 1023–1049.

Mazis, M. B. (1975). Antipollution measures and psychological reactance theory: A field experiment. *Journal of Personality and Social Psychology, 31,* 654–660.

McCall, G. C., & Simmons, J. L. (Eds.). (1969). *Issues in participant observation*. Reading, MA: Addison-Wesley.

McDougall, W. (1908). *Introduction to social psychology*. London: Methuen.

McDowall, D., McCleary, R., Meidinger, E. E., & Hay, R. A., Jr. (1980). *Interrupted time series analysis*. Sage University Paper series on Quantitative Applications in the Social Sciences, 7–21. Newbury Park, CA: Sage.

McGrew, W. C. (1972). *An ethological study of children's behavior*. New York: Academic Press.

McHugo, G. J., Lanzetta, J. T., Sullivan, D. G., Masters, R. D., & Englis, B. G. (1985). Emotional reactivity to a political leader's expressive displays. *Journal of Personality and Social Psychology, 49*, 1513–1529.

Mead, M. (1969, Spring). Research with human beings: A model derived from anthropological field practice. *Daedalus,* 361–386.

Merton, R. K., Fiske, M., & Kendall, P. L. (1956). *The focused interview*. Glencoe, IL: Free Press.

Merton, R. K., & Lazarsfeld, P. F. (Eds.). (1950). *Continuities in social research: Studies on the scope and method of "The American soldier."* New York: Free Press.

Milbrath, L. W. (1965). *Political participation: How and why do people get involved in politics?* Skokie, IL: Rand McNally.

Milgram, S. (1963). Behavioral study of obedience. *Journal of Abnormal and Social Psychology, 67*, 371–378.

Milgram, S. (1964). Issues in the study of obedience: A reply to Baumrind. *American Psychologist, 19*, 848–852.

Milgram, S. (1965). Some conditions of obedience and disobedience to authority. *Human Relations, 18*, 57–76.

Mill, J. S. (1965). Utilitarianism. In O. A. Johnson (Ed.), *Ethics: Selections from classical and contemporary writers*. New York: Holt, Rinehart & Winston.

Miller, C., & Swift, K. (1988). *The Handbook of Nonsexist Writing*. New York: Harper & Row.

Miller, D. (1977). *Handbook of research design and social measurement*. New York: McKay.

Mindick, B. (1982). When we practice to deceive: The ethics of metascientific inquiry. *The Brain and Behavioral Sciences, 5*(2), 226–227.

Monette, D. R., Sullivan, T. S., & DeJong, C. R. (1986). *Applied social research*. New York: Holt, Rinehart & Winston.

Morton, A. Q. (1963). A computer challenges the church. *The Observer,* November 3.

Mosteller, F., & Wallace, D. L. (1964). *Inference and disputed authorship: The Federalist*. Reading, MA: Addison-Wesley.

Munsterberg, H. (1913). *On the witness stand*. New York: Doubleday, Page & Company.

Nachmias, D., & Nachmias, C. (1981). *Research methods in the social sciences*. New York: St. Martin's Press.

Nederhof, A. J. (1981). *Some sources of artifact in social science research: Nonresponse, volunteering and research experience of subjects*. Unpublished doctoral dissertation, Rijksuniversiteit te Leiden, Netherlands.

Nowaczyk, R. H. (1988). *Introductory statistics for behavioral research*. New York: Holt, Rinehart & Winston.

Osgood, C. E. (1959). The representational model and relevant research methods. In I. de S. Pool (Ed.), *Trends in content analysis*. Urbana: University of Illinois Press.

Osgood, C. E., Sporta, S., & Nunnally, J. C. (1956). Evaluative assertion analysis. *Litera, 3*, 47–52.

Osgood, C. E., Suci, G., & Tannenbaum, P. (1957). *The measurement of meaning*. Urbana: University of Illinois Press.

Ostrom, C. W., Jr. (1978). *Time series analysis: Regression techniques*. Sage University Paper series on Quantitative Applications in the Social Sciences, 07–009. Newbury Park, CA: Sage.

Parker, L. C., Jr. (1980). *Legal Psychology*. Springfield, IL: Charles C. Thomas.

Parsons, T. (1951). *The social system*. New York: Macmillan.

Parsons, T. (1969, Spring). Research with human subjects and the "professional complex." *Daedalus,* 325–360.

Patterson, M. L. (1976). An arousal model of interpersonal intimacy. *Psychological Review, 83*, 235–245.

Patterson, M. L. (1982). A sequential functioning model of nonverbal exchange. *Psychological Review, 89*, 231–249.

Peter, L. J. (1980). *Peter's quotations: Ideas for our time*. New York: Bantam Books.

Phillips, D. (1971). *Knowledge from what? Theories and methods in social research*. Chicago: Rand McNally.

Piaget, J. (1984). Piaget's theory. In P. Mussen (Ed.), *Handbook of child psychology, Vol. 1* (4th ed.). New York: Wiley.

Piliavin, I. M., Rodin, J., & Piliavin, J. A. (1969). Good samaritanism: An underground phenomenon? *Journal of Personality and Social Psychology, 13,* 289–299.

Proctor, C., & Loomis, C. (1951). Analysis of sociometric data. In M. Jahoda, M. Deutsch, & S. Cook (Eds.), *Research methods in social relations.* New York: Holt, Rinehart & Winston.

Prosser, W. L. (1964). *Handbook of the law of torts.* St. Paul, MN: West.

Reicken, H. W., & Boruch, R. F. (Eds.). (1974). *Social experimentation: A method for planning and evaluating social intervention.* New York: Academic Press.

Robinson, J., & Shaver, P. (1969). *Measures of social psychological attitudes.* Ann Arbor, MI: Institute for Social Research.

Rokeach, M., Homant, R., & Penner, L. (1970). A value analysis of the disputed federalist papers. *Journal of Personality and Social Psychology, 16,* 245–250.

Rokeach, M., & Mezei, L. (1966). Race and shared belief as factors in social choice. *Science, 151,* 167–172.

Rooney, A. (1982). *And more by Andy Rooney.* New York: Atheneum.

Rossi, P. H., & Freeman, H. E. (1982). *Evaluation: A systematic approach.* Newbury Park, CA: Sage.

Rulon, P. J. (1932). A simplified procedure for determining the reliability of a test by split-halves. *Harvard Educational Review, 9,* 99–103.

Runyan, W. M. (1982). *Life histories and psychobiography: Explorations in theory and method.* New York: Oxford University Press.

Safire, W. (1984). *I stand corrected.* New York: Times Books.

Sagan, C. (1980). *Cosmos.* New York: Random House.

Sales, S. M. (1972). Economic threat as a determinant of conversion rates in authoritarian and nonauthoritarian churches. *Journal of Personality and Social Psychology, 23,* 420–428.

Schachter, S., & Singer, J. (1962). Cognitive, social, and physiological determinants of emotional state. *Psychological Review, 69,* 379–399.

Schulz, R. (1976). Effects of control and predictability on the physical and psychological well-being of the institutionalized aged. *Journal of Personality and Social Psychology, 33,* 563–573.

Schwartz, H., & Jacobs, J. (1979). *Qualitative sociology: A method to the madness.* New York: Free Press.

Scott, W. F. (1968). Attitude measurement. In G. Lindzey & E. Aronson (Eds.), *The handbook of social psychology, Vol. 2.* Menlo Park, CA: Addison-Wesley.

Seider, M. S. (1974). American big business ideology: A content analysis of executive speeches. *American Sociological Review, 39,* 802–815.

Seiler, L. H., & Murtha, J. M. (1981). Victory at HHS: Final regulations for the protection of human subjects of research provide a balanced compromise. *SASP Newsletter, 7*(2), 6–7.

Shaver, K. G. (1981). Federal funding for social psychology: The end of an era? *SASP Newsletter, 7*(2), 1, 3–4.

Shaver, K. G. (1982). NSF and social psychology: Past trends and future prospects. *SASP Newsletter, 8*(2), 1, 3–5.

Sheehy, E. (Ed.). (1976). *A guide to reference books.* Chicago: American Library Association.

Simon, R. J. (Ed.). (1975). *The jury system in America: A critical overview.* Newbury Park, CA: Sage.

Smith, C. P. (1981). How (un)acceptable is research involving deception? *IRB: A Review of Human Subjects Research, 3*(8), 1–4.

Snider, J., & Osgood, C. (Eds.). (1969). *Semantic differential technique: A sourcebook.* Chicago: Aldine.

Snyder, M. (1987). *Public appearances and private realities.* New York: Freeman.

Solomon, P. R. (1985). *A student's guide to research report writing in psychology.* Glenview, IL: Scott, Foresman.

Solomon, R. L. (1949). An extension of control group design. *Psychological Bulletin, 46,* 137–150.

Steeh, C. G. (1981). Trends in nonresponse rates, 1952–1979. *Public Opinion Quarterly, 45,* 40–57.

Stephenson, W. (1953). *The study of behavior.* Chicago: University of Chicago Press.

Stephenson, W. (1980). Newton's fifth rule and Q methodology: Applications to educational psychology. *American Psychologist, 35,* 882–889.

Strunk, W., Jr., & White, E. B. (1979). *The elements of style* (3rd ed.). New York: Macmillan.

Sutton, F. X., Harris, S. E., Kayson, C., & Tobin, J. (1956). *The American business creed.* New York: Schocken Books.

Thurstone, L. L. (1929). Theory of attitude measurement. *Psychological Bulletin, 36,* 222–241.

Thurstone, L. L. (1931). The measurement of social attitudes. *Journal of Abnormal and Social Psychology, 26,* 249–269.

Thurstone, L. L., & Chave, E. J. (1929). *The measurement of attitudes.* Chicago: University of Chicago Press.

Travis, C. B. (1985). Medical decision making and elective surgery: The case of hysterectomy. *Risk Analysis, 5,* 241–251.

Tukey, J. W. (1977). *Exploratory data analyses.* Reading, MA: Addison-Wesley.

Tunnell, G. B. (1977). Three dimensions of naturalness: An expanded definition of field research. *Psychological Bulletin, 84,* 426–437.

United States Bureau of the Census. (1979). *Statistical abstracts of the United States.* Washington, DC: U.S. Government Printing Office.

Veatch, R. M. (1982). Limits to the right of privacy: Reason, not rhetoric. *IRB: A Review of Human Subjects Research, 4*(4), 5–7.

Verba, S., & Nie, N. H. (1972). *Participation in America: Political democracy and social equality.* New York: Harper & Row.

Wanderer, J. J. (1969). An index of riot severity and some correlates. *American Journal of Sociology, 74,* 500–505.

Wartofsky, M. W. (1968). *Conceptual foundations of scientific thought.* New York: Macmillan.

Warwick, D. P. (1975). Tearoom trade: Means and ends in social research. In L. Humphreys (Ed.), *Tearoom trade: Impersonal sex in public places.* Chicago: Aldine.

Watson, R. I. (1967). Psychology: A prescriptive science. *American Psychologist, 22,* 435–443.

Weick, K. E. (1968). Systematic observational methods. In G. Lindzey & E. Aronson (Eds.), *The handbook of social psychology, Vol. 2.* Reading, MA: Addison-Wesley.

Weimer, W. B. (1979). *Notes on the methodology of scientific research.* Hillsdale, NJ: Erlbaum.

Whitman, D., & Dane, F. C. (1980). The use of psychology in jury selection. *American Business Law Association Regional Proceedings,* 78–90.

Wike, E. L. (1985). *Numbers: A primer of data analysis.* Columbus, OH: Merrill.

Winer, B. J. (1971). *Statistical principles in experimental design.* New York: McGraw-Hill.

Witte, R. S. (1980). *Statistics.* New York: Holt, Rinehart & Winston.

Wrightsman, L. S. (1974). *Assumptions about human nature: A social psychological approach.* Pacific Grove, CA: Brooks/Cole.

Wrightsman, L. S. (1983). *The Kansas jury project: An update.* Unpublished manuscript, University of Kansas, Lawrence.

Wrightsman, L. S. (1987). *Psychology and the legal system.* Pacific Grove, CA: Brooks/Cole.

Zimbardo, P. G., & Meadow, W. (1974, April). Sexism springs eternal—in the *Reader's Digest.* Presented at Western Psychological Association, San Francisco, CA.

GLOSSARY

accidental sampling—selection based on availability or ease of inclusion

action research—research conducted to solve a social problem

activity—the extent to which the concept is associated with action or motion in a semantic differential scale

alternate forms reliability—consistency estimated by comparing two different but equivalent versions of the same measure

anomie—lack of integration into a social network; general sense of instability or disintegration

anonymity—exists when no one, including the researcher, can relate a participant's identity to any information pertaining to the project

archival research—any research in which a public record is the unit of analysis

authoritarianism—a psychological concept characterized by submission to authority figures, ethnocentrism, and preoccupation with strength or power

baseline design—design in which preindependent variable measures are compared with postindependent measures

behavior—an action completed by a respondent

behavior change—any change in participants from which one may infer some alteration of behavioral style or capability

beneficent subject effect—effect that occurs when participants are aware of the research hypothesis and attempt to respond so as to support it

blind rater—one who is unaware of either the research hypothesis or the experimental group from which the responses came

case study—an intensive study of a single participant over an extended period of time

chance response tendencies—replacing formal category definitions with idiosyncratic definitions

checklist coding schemes—coding systems for which the behaviors and their meanings are determined prior to making observations

cluster analysis—statistical technique that groups variables according to the degree of similarity exhibited among the variables

cluster sampling—randomly selecting hierarchical groups from a sampling frame

codebook—a record of the codes assigned to a project's measures; it contains information about the storage structure of the data file

coding—attaching some sort of meaning to observations

coefficient of reproducibility (CR)—the proportion of fit between a perfect Guttman scale and one's data

coercion—includes using threats or force, as well as offering more incentive than what would reasonably be considered fair compensation

comparative format—providing respondents direct comparisons among various positions

compensatory education—attempting to raise the educational level of individuals whose education has been disadvantaged for one reason or another

complete observer—one who observes an event without becoming part of it

complete participant—one who fully participates in the events but is not known to the other participants as a researcher

computer-assisted telephone interviewing (CATI)—reading questions from and recording responses directly into a computer file

computer card—thin paper card in which holes may be punched and read by machine

computer disk—thin, round piece of plastic on which magnetic impulses are stored

concepts—abstract words that represent concrete phenomena

concurrent validity—comparing a new measure to an existing, valid measure

confederate—someone who is apparently a research participant but is actually a member of the research team

confidence interval—the inclusive, probabilistic range of values around any calculated statistic

confidence level—the probability associated with the accuracy of an inferential statistic

confidentiality—exists when only the researchers are aware of the participants' identities and have promised not to reveal those identities to others

construct validity—the accuracy with which a variable represents a theoretical concept

content analysis—research method used to make objective and systematic inferences about theoretically relevant messages

contingency analyses—analyses used to determine the probability that the results for one variable are related to the results for another variable

contingency item—an item in a survey instrument that is relevant only if a certain response was provided for a previous item

continuous time sampling—observing every instance of the behavior for the entire duration of the event

convergent validity—the extent to which a measure correlates with existing measures of the same concept

criteria for growth—standards that can be used to decide that one explanation is better than another

cross-sectional design—design that involves one measurement of different groups that represent different time periods

cross-tabulation—counting the codes from one field that occur for each code in another field

data case—all the data values corresponding to a single participant

data cleaning—identifying and correcting erroneous codes

data code—the symbol or number used to represent a specific value for an operational definition

data field—an area set aside to hold data codes for a specific measurement

data file—all of the data for a single research project

data organization—a system for the accurate storage and retrieval of the information obtained during a research project

data record—a collection of data fields that is only one line long

data transformation—changing original data values through mathematical functions

debriefing—a procedure by which any relevant information about the project that has been withheld or misrepresented is made known to participants

deception—providing false information about the research project

definitional operationism—the failure to recognize the difference between a theoretical concept and its operational definition

definitive study—a research project that completely answers a question

dependent variable—the effect under investigation

descriptive research—examining a phenomenon to more fully define it or to differentiate it from other phenomena

design—the number and arrangement of independent variable levels in a research project

determinism—the assumption that every event has at least one discoverable cause

deviant case sampling—observing individuals who do not seem to fit some pattern exhibited by others you have observed

dimensionality—the number of different qualities inherent in a theoretical concept

direct entry—process whereby data are entered directly into the data file

discriminant analysis—a statistical technique designed to estimate the relationship between any number of predictor variables and one or more categorical response variables

divergent validity—the extent to which a measure does not correlate with measures of a different concept

double-barreled item—a single item that contains two or more questions or statements

dynamic hypothesis formulation—generating and revising working hypotheses

ecological fallacy—mismatch between units of analysis and the research hypothesis

ecosystem measurement—the simultaneous measurement of level of service received and level of service desired by clients

edge coding—writing the data code in the margin of the dependent variable form before entering the codes into the data file

elaboration—a process in which data analyses are used to explore and interpret relationships among variables

epistemic correlation—the theoretical relationship between the true component of a measure and the concept it represents

equal-appearing interval technique—scaling technique that produces a series of items, each of which represents a particular point value on the continuum being measured

ethical balance—the relative equality researchers must maintain between their obligation to promote intellectual freedom and contribute to knowledge and their obligation to fairly treat the very people to whom these obligations are owed and to whom the knowledge is to be distributed

ethological system—detailed and comprehensive recording of behaviors with little or no inferred meaning

evaluation—the overall positive or negative meaning attached to the concept in a semantic differential scale

evaluation research—the systematic application of social science research procedures in assessing the conceptualization and design, implementation, and utility of social intervention programs

event sampling—observing one behavior contingent upon the presence of another behavior

existing data—the archived results of research accomplished by someone else

experimental research—the general label applied to methods developed for the specific purpose of testing causal relationships

experimenter bias—the experimenter's differential treatment of experimental groups

explanatory research—examining a cause–effect relationship between two or more phenomena

exploratory research—an attempt to determine whether or not a phenomenon exists

ex post facto explanations—untested causal statements applied to observed relationships

external validity—the relationship between the research experience and everyday experience

face validity—consensus that a measure represents a particular concept

facts—phenomena or characteristics available to anyone who knows how to observe them

factor analysis—a statistical technique used to separate continuous variables into groups that measure single dimensions of a multidimensional concept

factorial design—a design that includes more than one independent variable

field journal—notebook into which you enter your observations

field research—the general label applied to a collection of research methods that include direct observation of naturally occurring events

focused interview—technique in which an interviewer poses a few predetermined questions but has considerable flexibility concerning follow-up questions

forced choice format—response format in which respondents must choose between discrete and mutually exclusive options

formative evaluation—an assessment of the process of a program

frequency distribution—a tabulation of the number of times a given observation is made; in single-field analyses, it is a tabulation of the number of times a given code is detected in the data file

goodness-of-fit test—a test in which data values obtained from one sample are compared to theoretical values to determine whether or not the two sets of values are equivalent

graphic format—a graded continuum on which respondents make a choice

group cohesion—the degree of mutual attraction among members of a group

Guttman scale—scale on which it is possible to order both the items and the respondents on a single, identifiable continuum

heritability index—an estimate of the proportion of influence that genetic factors exert upon a particular trait

heterogeneity of variance—any instance in which group variances are disparate

heuristic value—the property of stimulating additional research activity

history effect—effect produced whenever some uncontrolled event alters participants' responses

hypothesis—a statement that describes a relationship between variables

inadequate sampling—occurs when only a subset of events is recorded and the sampling process is not systematic

independent variable—the suspected cause under consideration

inductive reasoning—a process of generalization; it involves applying specific information to a general situation or future events

inferential statistics—values calculated from a sample and used to estimate the same values for a population

informant—anyone who is knowledgeable about the participants to be observed

informed consent—providing potential research participants with all of the information necessary to allow them to make a decision concerning their participation

instrumentation effects—changes in the manner in which the dependent variable is measured

intellectual honesty—individual scientist's ability to justify the use of science itself

interaction—occurs when the effect of one variable depends on which level of another variable is present

internal validity—the extent to which the independent variable is the only systematic difference among experimental groups

interpretation—process whereby recorded observations are used to describe events, generate hypotheses, or test hypotheses

interrater reliability—the consistency with which raters or observers make judgments

interval measurement—a continuum composed of equally spaced intervals

interview—a structured conversation used to complete a survey

item bias—the extent to which the wording or placement of an item affects someone's response

itemized format—a continuum of statements representing various choice options

item-total reliability—an estimate of the consistency of one item with respect to other items on a measure

latent content—inferred, underlying, or hidden meaning in material that makes up an archive

Likert scale—items reflecting extreme positions on a continuum, items with which people are likely either to agree or disagree

longitudinal designs—designs in which the same participants are repeatedly measured over time

main effect—an effect produced by a single independent variable

maleficent subject effect—effect that occurs when participants are aware of the research hypothesis and attempt to respond so as to undermine it

manifest content—the physical or noninferential material that makes up an archive

matching—assigning participants to groups in order to equalize, across groups, scores on any relevant variable

maturation—any process that involves systematic change over time, regardless of specific events

mean—the arithmetical average of a set of scores

measurement—a process through which the kind or intensity of something is determined

median—the 50th percentile score

meta-analysis—integrating research findings by statistically analyzing the results from individual studies

mode—the most frequent score in a set of scores

mortality effects—effects caused by the loss of participants during a research project

multiple regression—a statistical technique for estimating simultaneous correlations among any number of predictor variables and a single, continuous response variable

mundane realism—the extent to which the experience of the participants is similar to the experiences of everyday life

natural event—an event that is not created, sustained, or discontinued solely for research purposes

necessary cause—something that must be present in order to produce the effect

negative case analysis—searching for data that disconfirm a tentative hypothesis, revising the hypothesis to include the disconfirming data, searching for more data, and so on

nominal measurement—determining the presence or absence of a characteristic; naming a quality

nondirective interview—technique in which the interviewer encourages the respondent to discuss a topic but provides little or no guidance and very few direct questions

nonjustificationism—a philosophy whose major premise is that we cannot logically prove that the way we go about doing research is correct in any absolute sense

nonprobability sampling—any procedure in which elements have unequal chances for being included

objectivity—a property of observations in which they can be replicated—that is, observed by more than one person under a variety of different conditions

observer-as-participant—an observer who is known to the participants as a researcher but does not take an active part in the events

operational definitions—concrete representations of abstract theoretical concepts

opinion—an expression of a respondent's preference, or feeling, or behavioral intention

order effects—changes in participant responses resulting from the order in which participants experience multiple levels of an independent variable

ordinal measurement—ranking or otherwise determining an order of intensity for a quality

outlier—a data value that is widely discrepant from other values for the same variable

paradigm—a logical system that encompasses theories, concepts, models, procedures, and techniques

parameter—a value associated with a population

participant-as-observer—one who is known as a researcher but is fully participating in the ongoing activities

participant bias—any intentional effort on the part of participants to alter their responses

participant characteristics—variables that differentiate participants but cannot be manipulated and are not subject to random assignment

participant observation—observational research method in which the researcher becomes part of the events being observed

periodic trends—cyclic changes that repeat throughout a sampling frame

pilot study—an abbreviated version of a research project in which the researcher practices or tests the procedures to be used in the subsequent full-scale project

population—all possible elements that could be included in research

potency—the overall strength or importance of the concept in a semantic differential scale

pragmatic action—determining how we should go about putting a scientific approach into practice

predestination—the assumption that events are unalterable

prediction—identifying relationships that enable us to speculate about one thing by knowing about some other thing

predictive validity—comparing a measure with the future occurrence of another, highly valid measure

predictor variable—the measure one hopes will predict the response variable

pretesting—administering research measures under special conditions, usually before full-scale administration to participants

probability sampling—any technique that ensures a random sample

probe—a phrase or question used by an interviewer to prompt a respondent to elaborate on a particular response

purposive sampling—procedures directed toward obtaining a certain type of element

Q-sort—a scale used to measure an individual's relative positioning or ranking on a variety of different concepts

qualitative analyses—nonnumerical analyses concerning quality rather than quantity

quota sampling—selecting sampling elements on the basis of categories assumed to exist within the population

random assignment—procedure that provides all participants an equal opportunity to experience any given level of the independent variable

random digit dialing—a sampling procedure in which a valid telephone exchange is randomly sampled from a region and the telephone number is completed with four randomly selected digits

random selection—any technique that provides each element of the population an equal probability of being included in the sample

ratio measurement—a continuum that includes a value of zero representing the absence of a quality

rational inference—the difficulty inherent in supporting any claim about the existence of a universal truth

reactance—the proposition that whenever someone's perceived freedom is threatened, the person is motivated to reassert that freedom

recording—the manner in which a permanent copy of the observation is made

reductionism—the logical fallacy of drawing conclusions about individuals' behaviors from units of analysis that do not deal with individuals

regression equation—formula for predicting a score on the response variable from the score on the predictor variable

repeated measures design—a specific factorial design in which the same participants are exposed to more than one level of an independent variable

representative sample—a sample that resembles the population within an acceptable margin of error

research—a critical process for asking and attempting to answer questions about the world

response variable—the measure one would like to predict

sample—a portion of the elements in a population

sampling—the process of selecting participants for a research project

sampling element—a single "thing" selected for inclusion in a research project

sampling error—the extent to which a sample statistic incorrectly estimates a population parameter

sampling frame—a concrete listing of the elements in a population

sampling unit (also **sampling element**)—a single "thing" selected for inclusion in a research project

scale—a measurement instrument that contains a number of slightly different operational definitions of the same concept

scalogram analysis—a determination of the extent to which the pattern of actual responses fits the ideal pattern of a Guttman scale

scatterplot—a graph in which corresponding codes from two variables are displayed on two axes

schedules—survey instruments that are essentially orally administered questionnaires

science—systematic approach to the discovery of knowledge based on a set of rules that defines what is acceptable knowledge

selection effect—an alternative explanation of research results produced by the manner in which the participants were recruited or recruited themselves

self-administered survey—a survey in which respondents complete the instrument without intervention by the researcher

self-determination—the concept that individuals have the right, and are assumed to have the ability, to evaluate information, weigh alternatives, and make decisions for themselves

self-presentation—concern for the impression one makes on others

semantic differential scale—a scale that measures the psychological meaning of concepts along three different dimensions: evaluation, potency, and activity

simple random sampling—any technique that involves an unsystematic random selection process

simple trends—systematic and consistent changes in some quality inherent in sampling frame elements

single-participant designs—designs specifically tailored to include only one participant in the study

skewed distribution—an asymmetrical distribution

snowball sampling—sampling technique that involves obtaining suggestions for other participants from those you have already observed

split-half reliability—consistency measured by creating two scores for each participant by dividing the measure into equivalent halves and correlating the halves

social exchange—an interpersonal relationship in which an individual's willingness to enter or remain in the relationship depends on expectations of rewards and costs

sociogram—a figure depicting relationships among entities

sociometric scale—a scale designed specifically for measuring relationships among individuals within a group

standard error—the standard deviation of the sampling distribution of a statistic

statistic—a value associated with a sample

statistical regression effect—an artifact of measurement that occurs when extreme scores are obtained

stratified random sampling—using random selection separately for each subgroup in a sampling frame

sufficient cause—something that will produce the effect

summative evaluation—an assessment of the outcome of a program

survey research—obtaining information directly from a group of individuals

systematic observation—a research method in which events are selected, recorded, coded into meaningful units, and interpreted by nonparticipants

systematic random sampling—choosing elements from a randomly arranged sampling frame according to ordered criteria

temporal priority—the requirement that causes precede their effects

testing effects—changes in responses caused by measuring the dependent variable

testing–treatment interaction—a situation in which research participants experiencing one level of the independent variable may be more sensitive to testing effects than participants experiencing a different level of the independent variable

test-retest reliability—consistency estimated by comparing two or more repeated administrations of the measurement

time-interval sampling—observing whether a behavior occurs during a specified interval within the duration of the event

time-point sampling—selecting only those behaviors that occur at the end of a specific time interval within the duration of the event

transfer sheets—preprinted data sheets onto which codes are written before entry

unconscious ideology—a prejudice that has lost its label as prejudice and has become an implicit assumption that strongly affects the roles of certain members of a society

units of analysis—the objects about which you would like to answer your research question

units of observation—the specific material to be measured

unobtrusive observation—observing others without their knowledge

validity—refers to the extent to which a claim or conclusion is based on sound logic

variable—a measurable entity that exhibits more than one level or value

voluntary participation—the participants' rights to freely choose to subject themselves to the scrutiny inherent in research

withdrawal design—design in which levels of the independent variable are presented and removed several times

worldview—the basic set of untestable assumptions underlying all theory and research

AUTHOR INDEX

Adams, G. R., 253, 323
Adams, G. S., 248, 323
Adorno, T. W., 8, 323
Allen, M. J., 248, 256, 323
Anastasi, A., 39, 53, 248, 251, 256, 276, 323
Aristotle, 233, 234
Aronson, E., 75, 323, 325, 328, 329

Babbie, E. R., 47, 125, 185, 299, 323
Bachrach, A. J., 49, 201, 323
Back, K. W., 121, 284, 323, 325
Bales, R. F., 155–156, 158, 323
Banks, C., 47–49, 50, 325
Barker, L., 216, 326
Baron, R. A., 11–15, 54, 67, 323
Bartley, W. W., III, 3, 4–5, 323
Baumrind, D., 43, 44, 323, 327
Becker, C. J., 8–9, 10, 15, 323
Bem, D. J., 172, 212, 216–217, 225, 323
Bem, S. L., 172, 323
Berkman, D., 173, 323
Berkowitz, L., 148, 323, 325
Berra, Y., 30–31
Bickman, L., 325
Bingham, W. V. D., 128, 323
Boruch, R. F., 312, 315–317, 318, 323, 328
Bray, R. M., 11, 184, 323, 324, 326
Brazzill, W., 55, 324
Brehm, J. W., 33–34, 324
Brewer, M. B., 174, 324
Bryant, C., 325
Bryk, A. S., 314, 324
Buckhout, R., 11, 16, 234, 325
Buros, O., 286, 324
Burt, C., 10, 53, 325
Butler, J. M., 147, 324

Campbell, D. T., 33, 80, 88, 90–91, 105, 148, 237, 259, 307, 308, 309, 317, 318, 324
Chave, E. J., 268, 328
Conover, W. J., 251, 324
Cook, S. W., 38, 234, 328
Cook, T. D., 88, 105, 148, 237, 324
Copenhaver, M. M., 77–79, 81–91, 324

Crandall, R., 148–151, 324
Crano, W. D., 174, 324
Crawford, J., 218, 324
Crawford, T. E., 218, 324

Dane, F. C., 11, 30, 41, 45, 51, 77–79, 81–91, 96, 105–107, 124, 150, 184, 214, 215, 216–226, 235, 279–280, 305, 324, 329
Darly, J. M., 150, 326
Dearing, B. E., 138, 325
Deaux, K., 26, 324
DeJong, C. R., 51, 327
Deutsch, M., 34, 324, 328
Dewey, T. E., 304
Dickson, P., 188, 324
Diener, E., 148–151, 324
Dillman, D. A., 126, 132, 134–135, 324
Disraeli, B., 202, 205
Donnerstein, E., 148, 323
Dunnette, M. D., 157, 324
Durant, J., 16, 324
Durkheim, E., 5–6, 28, 183–184, 185–186, 324

Edwards, A., 276, 324
Ellis, L., 176, 325
Ellison, J. W., 171, 325
Ellison, K. W., 11, 16, 234, 325
Ellsberg, D., 175
Englis, B. G., 174, 327
Erickson, K. T., 38

Fassnacht, G., 148, 325
Festinger, L., 284, 324, 325
Fiske, D. W., 259, 324
Fiske, M., 129, 327
Flanagan, T. J., 217, 325
Fogarty, J. C., 3
Forgas, J. P., 162, 325
Fowler, F. J., Jr., 310–315, 325
Frank, J., 16, 325
Freeman, H. E., 308, 328
Frenkel-Brunswick, E., 8, 323
Frey, J. H., 132, 324

Galileo, 25
Gallegos, J. G., 132, 324
Galton, F., 247
Gebhard, P. H., 124, 326
Gellert, E., 156, 325
Glass, G. V., 184, 325
Glazer, M., 40, 325
Gold, N., 314, 325
Gold, R. L., 158–160, 325
Gold, R. Z., 142, 279, 326
Gonsoriek, J. C., 218
Gorden, R. L., 128, 325
Green, S. K., 222, 325
Greenberg, M. S., 6, 325
Gross, A. E., 222, 325
Gump, P., 174–175, 177, 326
Guttman, L. L., 274–277, 325, 331, 337

Haberman, S. J., 142, 238, 325
Hall, E. T., 216, 325
Hamilton, A., 171
Haney, C., 47–49, 50, 325
Harris, L., 181
Harris, S. E., 171, 328
Hartwig, F., 138, 325
Hawkins, D. F., 132, 325
Hay, R. A., Jr., 107, 327
Hearnshaw, C. S., 10, 53, 325
Hendrick, C., 326
Hill, C. T., 120–123, 140, 325
Hilton, T. F., 8, 325
Holsti, O. R., 170, 172, 174, 325
Homant, R., 171, 177, 328
Hotvedt, M. E., 218
Humphreys, L., 39–40, 42, 44–45, 49, 50, 51,
    52, 160, 325, 329
Hunt, M., 124, 217, 325
Huxley, T. H., 61, 62

Izard, C., 326

Jacobs, J., 5–6, 11, 28, 76–77, 164, 172, 325,
    328
Jahoda, M., 328
Jay, J., 171
Jenkins, J., 278, 325
Jensen, A., 53–55, 67, 326
Johnson, J. M., 165, 326
Johnson, O. A., 327

Kaiser, K., 185–186, 326
Kamin, L. J., 16, 53, 326
Kassin, S., 279–280
Kayson, C., 171, 328
Kelley, H. H., 134, 326
Kendall, P. L., 129, 327
Kennedy, M. D., 181–183, 185, 326
Kerlinger, F. N., 4, 111, 143, 245, 278, 279,
    282, 326
Kerr, N. L., 11, 184, 323, 324, 326
Kidder, L. H., 271, 326

Kilpatrick, J. J., 212
Kinsey, A., 124, 326
Klecka, W. R., 131–132, 326
Kleinke, C. K., 216, 326
Kounin, J., 174–175, 177, 326
Kuder, G. F., 256, 262, 326
Kuhn, T., 24–25, 326

LaFrance, M., 155, 326
Landon, A., 303, 326
Lanzetta, J. T., 174, 327
Lasswell, H. D., 170, 326
Latané, B., 150, 326
Lazarsfeld, P. F., 141, 326, 327
Leahey, T. H., 33, 326
Lerner, D., 170, 326
Leventhal, H., 155, 326
Levin, J., 173–174, 326
Levine, J. M., 235, 326
Levinson, O. J., 8, 323
Lewin, K., 8, 326
Liebow, E., 159–160, 326
Likert, R., 272–274, 326, 335
Lindeman, R. H., 142, 279, 326
Lindzey, G., 325, 328, 329
Linz, D., 185–186, 326
Loftus, E. F., 6, 326
Loftus, G. R., 6, 326
Loomis, C., 282, 328

Madison, J., 171
Major, B., 26, 324
Malandro, L. A., 216, 326
Marsden, P. V., 181–183, 185, 326
Martin, C. E., 124, 326
Marx, K., 7–8
Masters, R. D., 174, 327
Mazis, M. B., 34, 326
McCall, G. C., 160–161, 327
McCall, G. J., 325
McCleary, R., 107, 327
McDougall, W., 24–25, 327
McDowall, D., 107, 327
McGraw, B., 184, 325
McGrew, W. C., 156, 158, 327
McHugo, G. J., 174, 327
McLeod, M., 217, 325
McPartland, F., 45, 216–226, 324
Mead, M., 37, 38, 51, 327
Meadow, W., 172–173, 329
Meidinger, E. E., 107, 327
Merenda, P. F., 142, 279, 326
Merton, R. K., 129, 141, 327
Messo, J., 6, 326
Mezei, L., 284, 328
Milbrath, L. W., 277, 327
Milgram, S., 31, 42–45, 46, 48–49, 50, 54, 67–
    68, 327
Mill, J. S., 58, 327
Miller, C., 215, 327
Miller, D., 286, 327

Mindick, B., 38, 327
Monette, D. R., 51, 327
Moore, B. V., 128, 323
Morton, A. Q., 171, 327
Mosteller, F., 171, 177, 178, 327
Munsterberg, H., 6, 31, 327
Murtha, J. M., 55–57, 328
Mussen, P., 327

Nachmias, C., 4, 327
Nachmias, D., 4, 327
Nederhof, A. J., 129, 132, 134, 327
Newton, I., 328
Nie, N. H., 277, 329
Nixon, R. M., 37–38, 175
Nowaczyk, R. H., 112, 203, 238, 241, 244, 250, 327
Nunnally, J. C., 179, 327

Osgood, C. E., 179, 277–279, 327, 328
Ostrom, C. W., Jr., 107, 327

Parker, L. C., Jr., 6, 327
Parsons, T., 41, 173, 313, 327
Pasanella, A., 141, 326
Patterson, M. L., 216, 327
Paul, W., 218
Penner, L., 171, 177, 328
Penrod, S., 185–186, 326
Peplau, L. A., 120–123, 140, 325
Peter, L. J., 233, 327
Phillips, D., 123, 327
Piaget, J., 114, 327
Piliavin, I. M., 147, 150, 328
Piliavin, J. A., 147, 150, 328
Pomeroy, W. B., 124, 326
Pool, I. de S., 170, 326, 327
Proctor, C., 282, 328
Prosser, W. L., 168, 328
Proxmire, W., 11–15

Reagan, R., 11, 174
Reed, J. S., 181–183, 185, 326
Reicken, H. W., 312, 318, 323, 328
Rice, L. N., 147, 324
Richardson, M. W., 256, 262, 326
Robinson, J., 286, 328
Rodin, J., 147, 150, 328
Rokeach, M., 171, 177, 284, 328
Rooney, A., 234, 288, 290, 328
Roosevelt, F. D., 303, 326
Rosenberg, M., 141, 326
Rossi, P. H., 308, 328
Ruback, R. B., 6, 325
Rubin, A., 120–123, 140, 325
Rulon, P. J., 256, 262, 328
Runyan, W. M., 175, 328
Russell, B., 233, 234
Russell, W., 278, 325
Russo, E. M., 235, 326

Safire, W., 212, 328
Sagan, C., 20, 22, 27, 61, 328
Sales, S. M., 7–8, 10, 15, 33–34, 328
Sanford, R. N., 8, 323
Schachter, S., 208, 284, 325, 328
Schulz, R., 100, 328
Schwartz, H., 164, 328
Scott, W. F., 263, 328
Seider, M. S., 171, 176, 328
Seiler, L. H., 55–57, 328
Seligman, C., 8–9, 10, 15, 323
Sharp, E., 155, 326
Shaver, K. G., 11, 328
Shaver, P., 286, 328
Sheehy, E., 65, 328
Simmons, J. L., 160–161, 325, 327
Simon, R. J., 11, 16, 328
Singer, J., 208, 328
Slack, A., 185–186, 326
Smith, C. P., 43, 328
Smith, M. L., 184, 325
Snider, J., 278, 328
Snyder, M., 25, 328
Solomon, P. R., 227, 328
Solomon, R. L., 91–92, 102, 328
Spates, J., 173–174, 326
Sporta, S., 179, 327
Stanley, J. C., 80, 88, 90–91, 324
Steeh, C. G., 132, 328
Stephenson, W., 280–282, 328
Stinson, K. M., 181–183, 185, 326
Storck, J. T., 222, 325
Strunk, W., Jr., 211, 212, 215, 328
Suci, G., 277–279, 327
Sullivan, D. G., 174, 327
Sullivan, T. S., 51, 327
Sutton, F. X., 171, 328
Swift, K., 215, 327

Tannenbaum, P., 277–279, 327
Thibault, J. W., 134, 326
Thompkins, S., 326
Thompson, J. K., 96, 324
Thurstone, L. L., 268–271, 274, 280, 328
Titche, A., 226
Tobin, J., 171, 328
Travis, C. B., 184, 185, 329
Truman, H. S., 304
Tuchfarber, A. J., 131–132, 326
Tukey, J. W., 138–139, 235, 329
Tunnell, G. B., 147, 149, 329

Vanyur, J. M., 222, 325
Veatch, R. M., 42, 329
Verba, S., 277, 329

Wagstaff, A. K., 147, 324
Wallace, D. L., 171, 177, 178, 327
Wanderer, J. J., 276–277, 329
Wartofsky, M. W., 22–23, 329
Warwick, D. P., 54, 329

Watson, R. I., 26, 329
Weick, K. E., 151–152, 329
Weinrich, J. D., 218
Weimer, W. B., 22, 146, 329
White, E. B., 211, 212, 215, 328
Whitman, D., 30, 329
Wike, E. L., 202, 206–207, 238, 241, 329
Winer, B. J., 204, 238, 241, 329

Witte, R. S., 251, 329
Wrightsman, L. S., 6, 184, 190, 273–274, 280, 285, 286, 305, 324, 329

Yen, W. M., 248, 256, 323

Zimbardo, P. G., 47–49, 50, 172–173, 325, 329

SUBJECT INDEX

Abstract of research report, 226
Accidental sample, 135–136, 301–303, 331
Action research, 8–9, 331
Activity, 278, 331
Aggregate data, 183–184
Alternate forms reliability, 254–255, 331
Alternative explanations, 79–88
Analysis of variance
  and Likert scale, 273–274
  and variance heterogeneity, 203, 334
  in descriptive research, 240–241
Association statistics, 140–141
American Psychological Association
  ethical code, 58–59
  publication manual, 212–213
Anomie, 5, 184, 331
Anonymity, 51, 331
Archival research, 169, 331
Audience, 172–174
Authoritarianism, 8, 331
Authorship, 171
Awareness
  and measurement scales, 39
  and voluntary participation, 39–40

Baseline design, 114–116, 331
Behavior, 331
  in survey research, 122–123
Behavior change, 46–48
  aftereffects of, 50
  defined, 46, 331
Beneficent subject effect, 86–87, 331
Blind rater, 331
Bureau of the Census, 6–7, 139–140

Case study, 113–114, 331
Causal analysis, 76–79
  and quasi-experiments, 105–106
  necessary cause, 163, 335
  sufficient cause, 163–164, 338
Central limit theorem, 238
Chance response tendencies, 157, 331
Chi-square statistic
  as goodness-of-fit, 138–139

Chi-square statistic *(continued)*
  for nominal data, 250
  for ordinal data, 250
  hierarchical, 142
  in descriptive research, 238
Cluster analysis, 181–182, 331
Cluster sampling, 300–301, 331
Coding, 331
  codebook, 195–196, 331
  data, 189; *see also* Data coding
  defined, 154
  edge, 196, 333
  in content analysis, 177–178
  in participant observation, 163
  of observations, 154–156
  using checklists for, 156, 331
Coercion, 39, 332
Cohesion, 283–284, 334
Comparative item, 268, 332
Compensatory education, 53, 332
Complete observer, 158, 332
Complete participant, 159–160, 332
Computer
  -assisted telephone interview, 133, 332
  card, 332
  disk, 332
Concept, 22, 332; *see also* Theories
Confederate, 42, 332
Confidence interval, 294–295, 332
Confidence level, 290, 332
Confidentiality, 51–52, 332
Consumers, 309
Content analysis, 169–180, 332
Contingency analyses, 140, 332
Contingency item, 126, 332
Contract research, 17
Correlation
  as association statistic, 140–141
  in descriptive research, 239–240
  in participant observation, 164–165
  in predictive research, 243–244
Creationism, 16, 27
Cross-tabulation, 198
Credence Clearwater Revival, 3

Criteria for growth, 24–25, 332
Criticism, 13–14
Cross-sectional research, 110, 332

Data
  cleaning, 197–198, 332
  coding, 192–197, 332
  direct entry, 197
  ethical issues of analyses, 52–53
  organization (defined), 189, 332
  preying upon, 208–210
  reduction, 198–199
  storage media, 190–192
  transformations, 202–205, 332
Debriefing, 49–50, 332
Deception, 42–44, 332
Definitional operationism, 33, 333
Definitive study, 30–31, 101–102, 333
Dependent variable, 77, 333
Descriptive research, 6–7
  appropriate questions, 236–237
  defined, 6, 333
  statistics, 237–241
Determinism, 31, 333
Developmental research,
Deviant case sampling, 161, 333
Dimensionality, 248, 333
Discriminant analysis, 143, 333
Discussion section of research report, 224–225
Distributions
  heterogeneous, 203
  of proportions, 204
  skewed, 203
Double-barreled item, 265, 333

Ecological fallacy, 185–186, 333
Ecosystem measures, 314, 333
Elaboration analyses, 141–143, 333
Epistemic correlation, 260–261, 333
Equal-appearing interval scale, 268–271, 333
Ethical balance, 38, 333
  and consequences, 40
  formal guidelines, 55–58
  in evaluation research, 318–320
  in experiments, 99–101
Ethological system, 156, 333
Evaluation
  as purpose of research, 307–321, 333
  as semantic dimension, 278, 333
  of research, 9–18
Evaluative assertion analysis, 179–180
Event sampling, 154, 333
Evolution, 16
Existing data analyses, 180–186, 333
Experimental design, 88–99, 333
  basic design, 88–90
  basic pretest design, 90–91
  use in evaluation research, 315–318
Experimenter bias, 87, 333
Explanatory research, 7–8, 245
  and experimental design, 75–76

Explanatory research (continued)
  appropriate questions, 245
  defined, 7, 333
  statistics, 245
Exploratory research, 5–7
  appropriate questions, 234
  defined, 5, 334
  statistical analyses, 235–236, 237
Exploratory statistics, 138
Ex post facto explanation, 142, 334

Fact, 22, 334
  in survey research, 121–122
Factor analysis, 334
  for Q-sort, 281–282
  for semantic differential, 278–279
Factorial designs, 92–96, 334
Field journal, 161–163, 334
Field research, 147, 334
Forced choice item, 266, 334
Formative evaluation, 309, 334
Frequency distribution, 197, 334

Golden Fleece Award, 11–15, 54
Goodness-of-fit, 138–139, 334
Graphic item, 266–267, 334
Guttman scale, 274–277, 334

Heritability index, 53, 334
Heuristic value, 31, 334
History effect, 80, 334
Hypothesis, 33, 334

Independent variable, 77, 334
Inductive reasoning, 23, 334
Informant, 160, 334
Informed consent, 40–42
  and researcher's identity, 46
  defined, 40, 334
  retraction of, 48–49
  sample form, 41
Instrumentation effect, 82–83, 334
Institutional Review Board (IRB), 56–57
Intellectual honesty, 26–27, 334
Interaction, 93–95, 334
Interaction process analysis, 155–156
Interpretation, 156, 335
Interrater reliability, 253–254, 335
Interval measurement, 251–252, 335
Interviewing, 128–133
  face-to-face method, 131
  focused, 129, 334
  nondirective, 129–130, 335
  telephone, 131–133
Introduction, 62
  organization of, 70–71, 216
  relevant information, 63–65, 216–218
  sources of information, 64–69
Intrusion; see Naturalness
Item-total reliability, 256, 335

Kuder-Richardson 20 formula, 256

Latent content, 177, 335
Likert scale, 272–274, 335
Longitudinal research, 335
  and time-series, 109

Mail surveys, 133–135
Main effect, 96–97, 335
Maleficent subject effect, 87, 335
Manifest content, 177, 335
Manipulation, 77
  described in research report, 221
  ethical considerations, 100
Matching, 84, 112, 335
Maturation, 335
  as alternative explanation, 80–81
Mean, 249, 335
  standard error of, 292–294
Measurement
  defined, 248, 335
  levels of, 248–252, 253
Median, 249, 269, 335
Meta-analysis, 184–185, 335
Method section of research report, 219–221
Mode, 249, 335
Mortality effect, 85, 335
Mundane realism, 79, 335

National Research Act, 55–57
Naturalness, 147, 335
  of observation, 149–150
  of settings, 150
  of treatment, 150–151
Negative case analysis, 164, 335
Nominal measurement, 249–250, 335
  and data structure, 138
Nonjustificationism, 22–27, 336
Normal science, 24
Nuremburg Code, 55–56

Objectivity, 25, 336
Observation
  and error, 28–29
  and generalization, 29
  unobtrusive, 39, 339
Observer-as-participant, 158–159, 336;
  see also Observation, unobtrusive
Operational definition, 33, 336
Opinion, 122, 336
Order effects, 97–98, 336
Ordinal measurement, 250–251, 336
Outlier, 202, 336

Paradigm, 24, 336
Participant observation, 147, 158–160, 336
Participant-as-observer, 159, 336
Participant
  and harmful aftereffects, 50
  bias, 86–87, 336
  characteristics, 99, 113, 336

Participant (continued)
  compensation of, 52
  considerate treatment, 48–50
  section in research report, 219
Philosophy of science, 21–22;
  see also Nonjustificationism
Physical harm to participants, 43–44
Pilot study, 43, 336
Population, 289, 336
Potency, 278, 336
Pragmatic action, 25–26, 336
Predestination, 31, 336
Predictive research, 7, 241–242
  and reliability, 242–243
  appropriate questions, 242
  defined, 7, 336
  statistics, 243–245
Predictor variable, 241, 336
Pretesting, 127–128, 336
Probe, 130, 336
Psychological Abstracts, 66
Psychological harm to participants, 44–45
Purposive sampling, 303, 336

Q-sort scale, 280–282, 336
Quasi-experimental research
  and causal analysis, 105–106
  nonequivalent groups pretest design, 111–112
Quota sampling, 161, 303–304, 337

Random assignment, 78, 337
  ethical considerations, 100
  in evaluation research, 315–316
Random digit dialing, 132, 337
Random selection, 238, 337; see also Sampling
  and sampling distributions, 292
  simple, 297–298, 338
  systematic, 298–299, 338
Ratio measurement, 252, 337
Rational inference, 22–24, 337
Reactance, 33–34, 337
Recording, 154, 337
Reductionism, 186, 337
Regression
  discontinuity design, 109–111
  equation for prediction, 244–245, 337
  multiple regression analysis, 142–143, 335
  statistical artifact, 83–84, 338
Reliability, 252–257
  in predictive research, 242–243
Repeated measures design, 96–99, 337
Reports
  ethical requirements, 53–55
  for participant observation, 165–166
  fraudulent, 53
  organization, 212–213
  style, 214–216
Representative sample, 304–305, 337
Reproducibility coefficient, 276, 331
Research
  choosing a topic, 32–33

Research *(continued)*
    critical evaluation, 9–18
    definition, 4, 337
    first law of, 201
    goals, 5–9
Results section of research report, 221–224
Response bias, 126, 335
Response variable, 242, 337
Reverse psychology; *see* Reactance
Revolutionary science, 25

Sampling, 288–306
    defined, 289, 337
    described in research report, 219
    distributions, 290–296
    inadequate, 157, 334
    in content analysis, 175–177
    nonprobability, 301–304, 336
    probability, 296–301, 336
Scale
    bias, 265–266
    defined, 264, 337
    face validity, 264
    formats, 266–268
    instructions, 265
    using, 285–286
Scalogram analysis, 275–276, 337
Scatterplot/scattergram, 198, 337
    in descriptive research, 239–240
    in exploratory research, 235
Schedules, 128, 337
Science
    and nonscience, 27–28, 32
    defined, 21, 337
    public support for, 12–13
Selection
    as alternative explanation, 84–85, 337
    as independent variable, 113
Self-determination, 45–46, 338
Self-presentation, 11, 338
Semantic differential scale, 277–280, 338
Semi-interquartile range, 269
Significance, 207–208
Single-participant designs, 117, 338
Skew, 203, 338
Snowball sampling, 161, 338
Social exchange theory, 134, 338
Social Science Citation Index, 67–68
Sociometric scale, 282–285, 338
Solomon four-group design, 91–92
Split-half reliability, 255–256, 338
Standard error of mean, 292–294, 338
Statistic, 338
    inferential, 237–238, 290, 334
    qualitative analyses, 235, 336
Stem-and-leaf display, 235–236
Stereotypes, 214–215
Stratified sampling, 299–300, 338
Summative evaluation, 309, 338

Survey
    defined, 120, 338
    described in research report, 220
    format, 125–127
    instructions, 125
    purposes, 120–121
    self-administered, 133, 337
    topics, 123–124
Systematic observation, 151–158
    defined, 151, 338
    purposes, 147–148

T-test, 240–241
Temporal priority, 76–77, 338
Test-retest reliability, 254, 338
Testing effect, 81–82, 338
Textbooks, 64–65
Theory
    and inductive reasoning, 23
    evaluation of, 22–24
    in research reports, 29–30
    utility of, 63
Thurstone scale; *see* Equal-appearing interval
        scale
Time sampling
    continuous, 152, 332
    interval, 153–154, 338
    point, 153, 338
Total design method, 134–135
Time-series
    interrupted design, 106–109
    multiple design, 109
    statistics for, 107

Unconscious ideology, 172, 338
Unit of
    analysis, 176, 339
    observation, 176, 339
    sampling, 289, 337
Unpublished research, 68–69

Validity
    concurrent, 258, 332
    construct, 34, 259–260, 332
    convergent, 259, 332
    divergent, 259, 333
    external, 113, 149, 334
    face, 257, 264, 334
    general definition, 34, 339
    in field research, 148–149
    in systematic observation, 158
    internal, 88, 148–149, 335
    predictive, 258, 336
Variable, 33, 339
Voluntary participation, 39–40, 339

Withdrawal designs, 116–117, 339
Worldview, 14–16, 339

TO THE OWNER OF THIS BOOK:

I hope that you have found *Research Methods* useful. So that this book can be improved in a future edition, would you take the time to complete this sheet and return it? Thank you.

School and address: _____

Department: _____

Instructor's name: _____

1. What I like most about this book is: _____

_____

_____

2. What I like least about this book is: _____

_____

_____

3. My general reaction to this book is: _____

_____

_____

4. The name of the course in which I used this book is: _____

_____

5. Were all of the chapters of the book assigned for you to read?　Yes　No

   If not, which ones weren't? _____

_____

6. On a separate sheet of paper, please write specific suggestions for improving this book and anything else you'd care to share about your experience in using the book.

Optional:

Your name: Date:

May Brooks/Cole quote you, either in promotion for *Research Methods* or in future
publishing ventures?

    Yes: _____   No: _____

    Sincerely,

    Frank Dane